The Wrong Hands

The Wrong Hands

Popular Weapons Manuals and Their Historic Challenges to a Democratic Society

ANN LARABEE

OXFORD
UNIVERSITY PRESS

OXFORD
UNIVERSITY PRESS

Oxford University Press is a department of the University of Oxford. It furthers the University's objective of excellence in research, scholarship, and education by publishing worldwide. Oxford is a registered trade mark of Oxford University Press in the UK and in certain other countries

Published in the United States of America by Oxford University Press
198 Madison Avenue, New York, NY 10016, United States of America

Library of Congress Cataloging-in-Publication Data
Larabee, Ann, 1957–
The wrong hands : popular weapons manuals and their historic challenges
to a democratic society / Ann Larabee.
p. cm.
ISBN 978–0–19–020117–3 (hardback)
1. Radicalism—United States—History. 2. Underground literature—United States—History.
3. Explosives—Handbooks, manuals, etc.—History. 4. Weapons—Handbooks, manuals, etc.—History.
5. Political violence—United States—History. 6. Terrorism—United States—History. I. Title.
HN90.R3L37 2015
303.48′4—dc23
2015001253

1 3 5 7 9 8 6 4 2

Printed in the United States of America on acid-free paper

Books are not absolutely dead things, but do contain a potency of life in them to be as active as that soul was whose progeny they are; nay they do preserve in a vial the purest efficacies and extraction of that living thing that bred them. I know they are as lively, and as vigorously productive, as those fabulous Dragon's teeth; and being sown up and down, may chance to spring up armed men.

—*John Milton, "Areopagitica"*

CONTENTS

ACKNOWLEDGMENTS

My greatest thanks go to Randy Scott, of Michigan State University Library archives, and the staff in the Interlibrary Loan section. Many of the documents I viewed were difficult to obtain. Special thanks go to David Foreman, who allowed me special access to his papers at the Denver Public Library, and to Yvonne Creamer, who got me there. I had an invaluable discussion with Jason Scott, who has collected many of the old BBS textfiles and has great insight into those early days of the Internet. William Powell was willing to correspond with me about his sources for *The Anarchist Cookbook*. My best intellectual companion has been Arthur Versluis, editor of the *Journal for the Study of Radicalism*, who has always strived for balance and sensitive observation. David McBride, of Oxford University Press, was a thoughtful editor and gave many invaluable comments on the manuscript. The anonymous reviewers provided much helpful advice. Richard Bach Jensen shared my enthusiasm for the project and liked to talk about historical anarchism and policing. Randall Law urged me to think about terrorism and technology in a broader context. With his probing mind, Paul Sunstein helped me work out my conclusions. At the eleventh hour, Ronen Steinberg provided me with a few crucial insights. Thanks to Beverly Gage, Claudia Verhoeven, and Carola Dietz, the "terror chicks," for encouraging me from the beginning. This book is built on the work of many fine scholars, too numerous to mention, who have lately been thinking about the histories and consequences of wars on terror. I also owe special thanks to Lissa Blon-Jacot, Jay Jacot, and Maksen Kai Mecher for giving me the moral support, the meals, and the writing space to get the job done.

Introduction

Al-Qaeda's online magazine, *Inspire*, appeared on the Web in 2010. It included a section on "open source jihad," defined as "a resource manual for those who loathe the tyrants; includes bomb making techniques, security measures, guerrilla tactics, weapons training and other jihad related activities." In its first issue, it provided instructions for how to "make a bomb in the kitchen of your mom."[1] This was a step-by-step guide, illustrated with glossy photographs, for making a bomb in a pressure cooker. Responding to the news of *Inspire*, Republican congressman Peter Hoekstra called for the nation to "ratchet up our law enforcement and intelligence counterterrorism programs," warning that "we underestimate this kind of radical jihadist propaganda at our peril."[2] *Inspire*'s editor was a young US citizen, Samir Khan, who had traveled from Charlotte, North Carolina, to reside with the radical cleric and senior al-Qaeda operative Anwar al-Awlaki in Yemen. Both were killed in 2011 in a secretive drone strike: highly controversial because it involved the assassination of an American citizen without trial. While some observers wondered whether Khan had been killed for editing a magazine, the Obama administration said he was collateral damage. It was not, however, unhappy at his death.[3]

When the Tsarnaev brothers bombed the Boston Marathon in 2013, a photograph of one of the devices was released, showing what appeared to be a piece from a pressure cooker. Internet forums and news stories buzzed with the speculation that the bombers were al-Qaeda and had used *Inspire*'s bomb-making directions. Some wondered what could be done about such texts, whether censorship was in order. *Inspire*, along with other "jihadist" texts, appeared as evidence in the indictment of the surviving bomber, Dzhokhar.[4] The government was preparing a case that would feature his radicalization process, made deadly by dangerous instructional speech.

Popular weapons instructions like "Make a Bomb in the Kitchen of Your Mom" have been around for a very long time and have excited curiosity, hope, fear, and anger. Efforts to control them, suppress them, and use them against public enemies in the United States go back to the nineteenth century, when the first anarchist directions for making bombs and dynamite appeared in a Chicago courtroom, leading to the executions of four innocent men who circulated them. Unresolved questions linger over whether what we read and watch—or simply own in our computers and on our bookshelves—can reveal our states of mind, our predispositions, our beliefs, and our willingness and preparation to act. Sometimes, as in the Tsarnaev case, a direct link appears between popular technical instruction and the construction of a weapon, making works like "Make a Bomb in the Kitchen of Your Mom" acceptable evidence of a suspect's know-how to carry out a crime. But the history of popular weapons manuals in the words of their own makers, in the courts, on evidence lists, and in testimony at congressional hearings shows that their meanings go far beyond the merely technical.

This book explores why radical groups and alternative publishers have produced popular weapons manuals, how police detectives and prosecutors have used them to pursue political enemies, and how scientific and legal experts have tried to suppress them. Central to the debates over popular weapons manuals is whether they allow information to fall into the wrong hands, a shifting designation that has accommodated, for example, labor movement organizers, anti-development environmentalists, anti-nuclear activists, school shooters, white supremacists, anti-government militias, and armed jihadists. During police investigations, popular weapons manuals found on the bookshelves and the computer hard drives of those deemed the wrong hands are instantly taken as signs of their malevolent intentions. In an important sense, though, the anonymous hands shown making illegal weapons in these manuals are always the wrong hands because they challenge the right hands of law and order, which are charged with public protection.

Popular weapons manuals have been called "knowledge-based speech," "dangerous instructional speech," "terrorist speech," or, more popularly, the "bomb-making manual," "the mayhem manual," and "the anarchist cookbook." In efforts to define and regulate this form of speech, the category has been hazy. Policy-makers and legal experts have only a fuzzy definition of what may be problematic texts. In 1996, the US Congress ordered the attorney general to conduct an investigation into the public availability of bomb-making instruction. Not surprisingly, FBI investigators found many texts on explosives from both "underground" and mainstream sources, not only on the Internet, but also in the Library of Congress.[5] More recently, policy experts on terrorism have attempted to identify a subcategory of "terrorist speech" that involves online instruction in making suicide vests, ammonium nitrate fertilizer bombs, biological weapons, ballistic missiles, and other dangerous weapons. Some have concluded that the Internet is a "virtual training camp" for radicals, who circulate encyclopedias of weapons information and offer consultation in weapons making.[6] Other analysts have challenged the practical application of this online technical information, but have remained interested in the prevalence of "terrorist *techne*" on "jihadi" websites.[7] Many terrorism consultants and analysts fear that we are facing a time of escalating access to widespread dangerous information that puts us in unprecedented danger. Terror experts suggest that terrorists are "knowledge workers" who excel at digital transfers of technical and tactical knowledge.[8]

Fully understanding popular weapons manuals and their historic challenges to our tolerance for radical speech can help us develop a framework for realistically judging their dangers. Our current understanding is thin and distorted. On the ground, the police look for the same infamous titles in the possession of suspects during searches and seizures. Books and computers are confiscated as evidence of evil intent and conspiracy. In the courts, sensational texts are introduced as evidence to prove criminal intention and sometimes purely to taint the suspect's character. The same texts—like *The Anarchist Cookbook* and its online variants—tend to turn up time and time again: on evidence lists, in court cases, and in news stories. Governing bodies pass laws that enhance the ability of the police to charge suspects with the production and possession of dangerous instructional texts.

In the United States some caution has been exercised to always combine such charges with more serious charges that a suspect has intended to actually implement the technical information, but, in Britain, it is possible to be thrown in jail simply for possession of popular weapons manuals with no requirement that the suspect be proven to have used them for a terrorist purpose.[9] For example, in 2007, eighteen-year-old Abdul Patel was found guilty under the Terrorism Act for possessing *EOD: Improvised Explosives Manual,* but acquitted of the charge that he planned to use it in a terrorist attack. Published by Paladin Press in 1991 and written by a bomb squad consultant, this book contained information on how to produce a variety of improvised explosive devices, including radio-controlled detonators. Patel joined Samina Malik, known as "the Lyrical Terrorist" because of her violent poetry, who was convicted for possession of an "extremist library," including an official technical manual for a sniper rifle. Malik won her appeal against these charges.[10] The perceived danger surrounding Patel and Malik was not simply ownership of dangerous books, but the context in which they were found. Patel is the son of Mohammed Patel, a veteran of the Afghan war against the Soviets, whose charity shop was alleged to be "a meeting place for Islamist extremists."[11] Other seemingly damning evidence included a book on the Taliban and a picture of Osama bin Laden and the message "Kill Bush" on Patel's mobile phone. Malik had visited the websites of radical Islamist clerics and had worked at a bookstore at Heathrow airport where she wrote a note on the cash register roll that proclaimed her desire for martyrdom. Yet the prosecution was not able to prove terrorist conspiracy in these cases, and relied instead on the flimsier section 58 of the Terrorism Act that suggests mere interest in violent crime is criminal.[12]

As British legal scholar Ian Cram has argued, cases like Malik's "raise normative issues of principle concerning the circumstances, if any, in which the state is entitled to criminalize the mere possession of information."[13] One issue is whether speech like a bomb-making manual is a distinct form of speech and an appropriate exemption to free speech protections. Some have argued that "instructions for building a bomb are not a point of view" that deserves protection.[14] Others are skeptical, suggesting that democratic states have overstepped their bounds in legislation aimed at terrorist speech, which is often passed during times of perceived emergency.[15] Laura Donohue maintains that emergency legislation ends up enshrined in criminal law without sufficient oversight, broadening the base of potential suspects beyond what was originally intended.[16] Two key laws have been passed in the United States to regulate dangerous instructional speech: 18 U.S.C. § 842(p), which bans the teaching or demonstration of a making or use of an explosive weapon, and 18 U.S. Code § 2339, which prohibits "providing material support to terrorists." Terror suspects have recently faced charges under these statutes in highly controversial cases that have raised questions about what kinds of speech are now forbidden.

Although the problem of popular weapons manuals may seem a special challenge of our fight against terrorism and our digital environments, it is not a new one. In the United States, popular weapons manuals have provoked a series of confrontations between radicals and governing authorities over the freedom to circulate potentially dangerous, unclassified technical information. The outcomes of these confrontations have avoided the more severe repression of other Western democracies, but have represented a significant fluctuation in social tolerance of dissenting speech. With individualism, freedom of speech, and love of technology enshrined in public culture, the US federal government has generally conceded that popular weapons manuals can't be formally censored. However, some texts, like *The Anarchist Cookbook*, have become what anarchist Johann Most once called "literary Satans," used in criminal profiling and as legal evidence to demonize persons critical of the state. With the escalation of information in digital environments, both overt and covert means of censorship have intensified. Whether our time merits a special set of rules to control this form of speech is the subject of this book, which examines direct confrontations between radicals and the government over the right to technical information.

Defining the Genre

The first task is to identify what kind of technical speech has seemed dangerous enough to warrant surveillance, criminal profiling, and punishment. Print materials have most often entered the courts, but instructional speech may also be relayed through verbal instructions and audiovisual materials. Generally, the texts that have fallen under government scrutiny consist of these types:

1. Training manuals produced by military branches. These manuals are unclassified documents in the public domain. Veterans (who may become members of radical organizations) carry them into wider circulation, and public libraries sometimes collect them. They may contain information about blasting during military operations, care and handling of firearms, biological and chemical weapons, and improvised explosive devices used in irregular warfare. These are only perceived to be dangerous when alleged criminals and political radicals own them.
2. Popular weapons manuals produced by paramilitary publishers. These manuals may simply be direct reprints of official army training materials in the public domain. Often an anonymous, self-proclaimed expert has compiled the work from a variety of legitimate sources—such as military manuals and science textbooks. These manuals may contain information on biological and chemical weapons, improvised explosive devices, and firearms and missiles. The texts aim to translate technical information into the ordinary speech of do-it-yourself (DIY) popular mechanics. Hauled before congressional committees and into the courts, paramilitary publishers have often claimed a legal right to publish this kind of information.
3. Weapons manuals produced by radicals. These texts have the stated aim of providing weapons information so that their audiences may resist the state. The DIY ethos becomes a political statement that radicals have the right to the violent knowledge typically controlled by the state. These manuals strongly resemble those produced by military and paramilitary publishers with the exception that they include an introduction and commentary that is overtly political. Although they contain information found in other sources, the texts are most likely to provoke efforts at suppression.

As this book will show, fictional works containing technical description have sometimes come under surveillance, but overall they have remained in a separate category of imaginative, rather than technical, speech. The category does not include classified technical information, which falls under a different set of controls.

Authorship of popular weapons manuals is difficult to identify. The genre relies on collation and outright plagiarism as the information is copied from text to text, like culinary recipes. That is why the word "cookbook" has been applied to these manuals; they strongly resemble this more benign form of technical exchange. The "recipes" contain ingredients lists and procedural directions and often hold the promise that they can be made in an ordinary household setting, with simple, easily obtainable tools and materials. Typically, any political statements are made in introductions and conclusions, so that the stated intention is added to a technical core. These are distinct forms of speech that coexist uneasily, especially since political speech is more ephemeral than the technical information continually circulated across many texts. In recent years, technical instructions are often accompanied by weak disclaimers that the information is "for educational purposes only" or by references to the First Amendment.

Popular weapons instruction circulates in a variety of venues. This book is primarily concerned with its textual dissemination, from the rudimentary handouts in paramilitary groups to handbooks published by commercial presses to websites. Recipe books for weapons have been found in written form since at least the twelfth century. Then, handbooks combining magic and pyrotechnics appeared, including the "vagabond" Marcus Grecus's *Book of Fires for the Burning of Enemies*, which compiled formulas for incendiary weapons and secret handwriting and other illusions.[17] It wasn't until the nineteenth century—with its expanding international news media, professional consolidation of science and technology, and violent conflict between radical groups and elites—that the dirty tricks and pyrotechnics handbooks became the site of political struggle. Then, popular weapons information began circulating in radical newsletters and pamphlets and continued throughout the twentieth century to be associated with a dissident and alternative press. Paramilitary publishers catering to anti-communist, white supremacist groups appeared in the early 1960s, widely disseminating DIY explosives manuals and reprints of military training manuals that are still circulating today.

In the early 1990s, much of this information, already existing in print media, was uploaded to pyrotechnics BBS (bulletin board system) forums and eventually found its way into torrents and websites. Photographs in popular weapons instruction are relatively new because of the risks and difficulties of obtaining clear images and the cost of reproduction. Prior to the digital age, publishing outfits could afford to include a few grainy photographs, but independent creators usually relied on the written form. This has changed dramatically with the multimedia capabilities of digital technologies, so that "Make a Bomb in the Kitchen of Your Mom" features very clear color photos. Since the advent of video hosting sites, video versions of older print directions and video demonstrations of amateur experimentation have proliferated. Multimedia productions enhance instructional clarity, transfer, sharing, and access: users no longer need to understand the printed language.

The information found in popular weapons manuals can also be found in other sources and represents a state of common, widely dispersed knowledge about explosives and weapons engineering. It is not classified information. One of the most common arguments against criminalizing popular weapons manuals is that the information they convey is already in the public sphere. Even if the information were banned from the Web, an energetic would-be bomb maker can go to a research library and find information in accessible government documents and standard chemical and engineering textbooks. Indeed, authors of popular weapons manuals readily plagiarize from other sources, and this plagiarism is often seen as a political act, a theft of what Irish nationalists in the nineteenth century called "the resources of civilization." Many authors and publishers of popular weapons manuals present themselves as Prometheuses, liberating information from the hands of the powerful and placing it in the hands of the people.

For these authors, the application of knowledge is not as important as the democratizing of the knowledge that maintains governmental power. Despite their fantasies of military and scientific prowess, many authors of popular weapons manuals are not proficient as military engineers, nor are their instructions especially reliable or useful, because they exist solely in the realm of theory.[18] Rather, these authors aim to empower people with the mere idea that they can command the resources of civilization if they should so choose. The means of rebellion are always present and seemingly concretized in practical knowledge. The mode of address is both to an inside audience of rebellious readers and to an outside audience of authorities exposed as having only a fragile control of knowledge. Although the vast majority will never apply the information, readers avidly consume and circulate popular weapons manuals, participating as rebels against governmental and corporate control over information. Popular weapons manuals are a form of popular culture, and popular culture has often provided imaginative spaces for experimentation with rebellious identities. The motivations of the producers of popular weapons manuals have rarely been examined, though they provide insight into the formation of radical identities and sets of beliefs about technologies.

The Wrong Hands

The fear of weapons-making capabilities getting into the wrong hands is as old as the nation. When Thomas Morton arrived in Massachusetts Bay in 1628, he set up an outpost, Merrymount, where he and his seven companions began commerce with the southern New England Indians. Celebrated in American history and literature as the "Lord of Misrule," Morton shocked his Plymouth colony neighbors with his licentious antics. He was soon arrested and deported, ostensibly for selling guns to the Indians and instructing them in their use.[19] In his journal, William Bradford, governor of Plymouth, outlined a long list of grievances against Morton, including drunkenness and riotousness, rudeness and incivility, and "base covetousness" in trading liquor and guns. Bradford explained that Morton's gun trade included teaching Indians how to repair weapons and make bullets, and perhaps worst, "how gunpowder is made, and all ye materialls in it, and that they are to be had in their own land; and I am confidente, could they attaine to make saltpeter, they would teach them to make powder. O the horiblnes of this vilanie!" Bradford painted a grim future of the Indians becoming technologically superior combatants and the "colonies in these parts . . . over throwne by these barbarous savages, thus armed with their own weapons." So taken away is he by dark fantasies of murder and betrayal that Bradford stopped to apologize: "I have forgotten myself."[20]

Popular weapons instruction emulates and opposes the military power of governing authorities. This spread of knowledge may pose a direct threat to the legitimacy, if not the very existence, of those authorities. This is tacitly understood on both sides. That is why spokespersons for the state so often use the cliché "falling into the wrong hands," and why producers and disseminators of illicit instruction never do. "The wrong hands" are mysterious in the official discourse, shadowy actors who pose an existential threat. The "wrong hands," rather than the "wrong minds," implies a doing—a concrete action against government—though the information in a manual is still abstract. "The wrong hands" implies the "right hands," the government-supported entities that produce weapons and other dangerous technologies to be used in a theoretical just cause. Gatekeepers—like journalists and academic experts—allow themselves to read and openly discuss dangerous instructional texts, deciding which parts can be read and shown to the public. Their discussion of dangerous texts is surrounded by a discourse of fear and anxiety about the wrong hands that establishes their continuing role as the right hands.

Because the information is dangerous and fearful, most citizens are willing to go along with this arrangement, trusting experts for a sense of security, but a substantial number of citizens reject that control. The majority of these dissenters have no aim to commit real criminal or revolutionary acts. Their dissent lies in reproducing information outside sanctioned venues. They know that simply disseminating a dangerous instructional text is a thorn in the side of the government that legitimates itself by protecting the people. They don't even have to accompany instruction with dissenting political speech, though some do. When that happens, even though the information is publicly available in other venues, the government's law enforcement arm may come down with full force, especially on any designated enemy of the state—left or right—who dares toy with dangerous instructional speech. Investigators and prosecutors profile and then publicly vilify enemies of the state to gain public support for their condemnation. The courts and media organs are the theaters for this punishment of speech, although not all judges and editors are willing to play along. The spectacle creates a cycle in which dissenters know that producing such texts will gain the government's attention and provoke its displeasure. Sometimes this speech is tolerated, and sometimes not.

Popular weapons manuals test the boundaries of what Herbert Marcuse called "repressive tolerance." In his formulation, the United States as "an advanced industrial society" practices an uneven form of tolerance to suppress real dissent and truthful social analysis: all opinions are tolerated so that none can emerge. This tolerance has limits when it threatens an elite that holds a "privileged position" in public discourse and the means to suppress dissent through "legalized violence or suppression." Within the regime of tolerance, dissent has no "subversive sting," as Slavoj Žižek puts it. Žižek comments on President Bill Clinton's reaction to the antiglobalization protests in Seattle, Washington, in 1999, when he urged the WTO leaders to listen to the demonstrators while reminding them that they had to "behave properly" and purge the "violent extremists." Žižek calls this a form of containment: "The system is by definition ecumenical, open, tolerant, ready to 'listen' to all—even if you insist on your demands, they are deprived of their universal political sting by the very form of negotiation."[21] How to break through an illusionary, tightly administered tolerance to gain an effective dissent—a sting—is the question, opening the possibility of violence. Marcuse saw the intolerance of all violence as the prerequisite for a peaceful, truthful, beautiful society. Žižek has been more willing to argue for violence as a possibility. The popular weapons manual has the potential to deliver a real sting, and resides at the border between word and deed and therefore at the edge of tolerance.

Abbie Hoffmann's *Steal This Book* is the most self-reflective popular weapons manual ever written and was a Yippie performance of Marcuse's idea. *Steal This Book* was a manual of antiestablishment practices and provided advice on shoplifting, setting up pirate radio stations, creating political graffiti, using slugs in commercial washing machines, winning at hand-to-hand combat, making pipe bombs, and other acts of "creative disruption." Hoffman gave directions for the "Froines," a butyric acid stink bomb named after one of the Chicago Seven who had been charged under a provision of the Civil Obedience Act against bomb-making instruction. Parodying Paladin Press's how-to manuals and published in the same year as *The Anarchist Cookbook*, *Steal This Book* was promoted as "a handbook for survival and warfare for the citizens of the Woodstock Nation."[22] With loans from his friends, Hoffman had set up his own publishing company when the major publishers had refused to take it. Major newspapers refused to run advertisements for it.

Hoffman made free speech a central argument for his book. He listed the reluctant publishers on the back cover under the bold announcement that "This Book Will End Free Speech." From the Cook County Jail, where he was imprisoned for resisting arrest, Hoffman wrote in his introduction: "Literally anyone is free to print their own works. In even the most repressive society imaginable, you can get away with some form of private publishing."[23] Echoing the popular philosopher Herbert Marcuse, he warned, however, that a "repressive tolerance" might seemingly allow such small-scale productions, in the name of free speech, as long as the ideas gained no wider dissemination and disruptive force.

Steal This Book solicited state suppression—and overreaction—as a way of exposing the sham of tolerance. Hoffman tweaked the forces of government and the hegemonic mass media with his discourse of cons, dirty tricks, urban survivalism, improvised weapons, and strategies for avoiding the law. One of his "yippie proverbs" was, "Free speech is the right to shout 'theater' in a crowded fire." The FBI, which had Hoffman under surveillance for years, kept track of *Steal This Book*, as agents sent back reports on Hoffman's statements about free speech and his alleged efforts to establish a "Rip-off Institute" with experts in safe-cracking, drug dealings, and shoplifting.[24] Despite its depictions of illegal activities, the comic elements and tone of his work made it difficult to label it abetting or incitement, and the US assistant attorney general decided that it fell short of any criminal liability even though it "encouraged" criminal activity.[25] The book's comic status as a playfully perverse Boy Scout manual gave it immense popular appeal.

From the point of view of the state, avowed radicals circulating weapons-making information are definitely "the wrong hands," which the state believes it has the power to define. Only the "right hands," as defined by the state, should properly have access to such information. It is considered acceptable for certain groups to circulate technical information about explosives, bombs, and other weapons for purposes such as science education and military defense. The right hands include scientists and engineers in research institutions, military personnel, terror experts, police, students, librarians, and crime writers and journalists on the crime beat who condemn the activity. Impossible to really know, the audiences for these texts are imagined to be similarly benign. That is why an environmental activist is arrested for demonstrating an arson device, while a television station gets away with showing video footage of the same presentation.

For the government, the issue is not technical information itself, but rather who possesses it. As Donohue explains, dangerous instructional speech is usually rooted in other legitimate uses.[26] Historically, the problem of popular weapons information has arisen during a surge of fear over a violent group that has in some way opposed the government and its institutions. This fear arises only periodically despite a constant background of thousands of crimes involving explosives in the United States every year. Indeed, some ideologically motivated bombings—such as during the long period in the United States of bomb violence against blacks and Jews—are overlooked because the groups responsible have not directly challenged governmental power, and the victims are not considered worth defending. Given their publicly stated values, democracies find it difficult to overtly suppress mere antigovernment speech. Governments find other ways to discipline speech, and the new security measures percolate through the courts and law enforcement agencies. Technical information about explosives and other weapons is frightening and concrete enough that its subtle criminalization seems a practical measure to ensure public safety.[27]

In the United States, despite numerous congressional investigations and legal debates that will be discussed in this book, popular weapons manuals have never been overtly censored, as they have in more repressive regimes. The federal government has typically opted to control substances, like dynamite and ammonium nitrate fertilizer, rather than texts. Because popular weapons manuals are only conceived as dangerous when associated with radicals, they have been used primarily as a means of criminal profiling, when investigators make assumptions about the owner of such a manual, and as prosecutorial evidence to encourage impressions of a defendant's character and criminal intent. These uses of evidence have come under fire for their relevance and constitutional violations, and have led to some of the most egregious instances of judicial malfeasance and mistaken justice in US history. During periods of repression, like the 1919–1920 Red Scare, when political dissent was met with physical violence and exile, texts that encourage sabotage and guerrilla warfare have been swept up in police investigations and used to demonstrate that vast seditious conspiracies are underway. Politicians, journalists, prosecutors, and police wave these texts before the public and proclaim that severe action against the radicals, bent on murder and mayhem, must be taken. Legislative committees debate the problem of instructional speech and the limits of free speech, calling authors and publishers before them to testify. Laws are passed to deliberately impose a chilling effect and to provide the police with greater latitude in using these texts as evidence against presumed terrorists. None of these efforts have diminished the production of popular weapons manuals, which now proliferate on the Internet.

Bruce Hoffman has written that the accumulation of information has led, in part, to an "amateurization of terrorism."[28] However, amateurishness is fundamental to the way that official and unofficial knowledge domains have been defined. In the mid-nineteenth century, a split occurred, with the professional specialist worlds of technicians and scientists (including military weapons developers) on the one side, and amateurs encouraged by science education and popular science journals on the other.[29] Information about explosives and explosive devices circulated in pyrotechnics and military manuals, science textbooks, encyclopedias of household arts, and even children's fiction. During the Second Industrial Revolution, considerable economic power was concentrated in a new network of industrialists and research scientists and technicians, but there also arose an interest in popular science and technology among radicals opposed to the concentration of power and wealth. From a range of revolutionary philosophies and inspired by a democratic discourse on science, these radicals believed that technological power—the power of the new dynamite—had to be wrested from the hands of the capitalist owners and the imperial rulers and delivered into the hands of the people. At this time, the "underground" of popular weapons information flourished transnationally—from New York to Paris to Bengal to Tokyo—as radicals passed print and verbal instructions from hand to hand, sometimes attracting the eyes of police, judges, and politicians. Many of the most powerful, easily deployed weapons known today use the high explosives invented in the nineteenth century. Well-known devices such as the pipe bomb came from the nineteenth century and were described in radical texts of those days. Emerging from a context of an advancing technological warfare and internal conflict between capital and labor, radicals dreamed of exploiting aircraft—balloons—to drop bombs over cities, disguising bombs in parcels and other benign-looking objects, and pouring arsenic in the water mains to poison entire cities. This period coincides with creation of the first published anarchist cookbook—Johann Most's *Science of Revolutionary Warfare*—which introduced the genre we know today and its first court appearance in a political trial.

The weapons information "underground" grew through an increasingly literate population of military enthusiasts and household inventors who have greatly contributed to the popular weapons manual. *Backyard Ballistics* author William Gurstelle has termed this population the "Technological Underground," by which he means a space where "ardent technophiles" take intellectual, psychological, and physical pleasure in creating dangerous devices like rockets and flamethrowers in their garage workshops, resisting the enclosure of invention in "large, corporate, methodical and highly specialized work teams."[30] The "Technological Underground" is not really underground in the sense of existing in secret or in code. Rather, it is entirely aboveground: it publicly resists the enclosure of protected knowledge domains, educates people without access to these domains, liberates information for popular use, and flaunts its technological prowess. It is the slanted mirror of official military research and development. The amateurs love science and technology but rebel against its institutionalization. The activities of these enthusiasts, most of whom do not see themselves as part of any group, are mostly tolerated unless they violate safety and local nuisance laws. Many people who became intrigued by science as children can remember the illicit pleasures of blowing something up in a field and perhaps reading encyclopedias, almanacs, chemistry textbooks, and DIY explosive manuals with their edgy pleasures. The technophiles may experiment with very dangerous technologies, as in the case of Richard Handl, a former factory worker in Sweden with an interest in science, who blogged about his attempts to create a fission reaction in his kitchen with nuclear materials he gleaned from clocks and smoke detectors. Handle was arrested for violation of a public safety law, Sweden's Radiation Protection Act.[31] Few would argue against community controls on explosive, highly flammable, and radioactive materials, such as preventing their manufacture, use, and storage near residences.

There is a subtle transition from edgy backyard pyrotechnics to technological threat, when the acceptable hands become the wrong hands condemned by the government, the news media, and the scientific establishment. In my university library there is a copy of an old organic chemistry manual with directions for making picric acid, a volatile substance used in explosives. Next to this recipe, some reader has drawn in pen the symbol for anarchy. In my many travels through these kinds of texts, this is the most rudimentary example I have seen of altering explosives information with an antiauthoritarian statement. Even though it may end only in the defacement of a library book, this small symbol changes the meaning of the text, revealing that while chemistry students may use it for an ordinary education, other readers may steal it for rebellious purposes.

This book discusses these tipping points, when the anarchy sign[32] gives new meaning to instructional texts and provokes police investigations, arrests, and incarcerations; debates over their use as evidence in the courts; and congressional hearings. It begins in the nineteenth century, when small groups associated with a burgeoning labor movement become entranced with the ease of producing the new portable high explosives. The first "anarchist cookbooks" are introduced in this period, leading to the first court case to feature such a manual, with a shocking outcome that will change the course of free speech protections. Other historic legal cases will show how the courts have dealt with popular weapons manuals as problematic evidence, leading to legal disputes over freedom of speech, freedom of the press, and the right to read. The book ends by considering recent terror cases and instructions for weapons of mass destruction within this context. Biographies of popular weapons manuals show that they have had many purposes: sometimes to sew the dragon's teeth for an armed revolution, sometimes to provoke a low-level criminal resistance to the state, sometimes simply to test the government's commitment to freedom of speech, sometimes for sheer entertainment, sometimes as an angry emotional expression, and sometimes to explore political and technical ideas. In the end, it is easy to see that popular weapons manuals are not merely technical and instrumental, but cultural expressions.

Covering all the most important texts and cases, the book doesn't aim to defend popular weapons manuals, but to explore their legal, cultural, and social meanings and their challenge to public tolerance. That way, when the next criminal or terrorist case associated with a popular weapons manual appears, we will respond with a reasoned understanding. Perhaps as a society we will decide, in the interests of peace, that we must find ways to scour popular weapons instructions from public view. Or perhaps we will again decide that targeting and suppressing this form of speech is not worth the cost to a democratic society. The past lends us some cautionary tales to show that the problem is much more challenging and complex than it first appears.

1

The Science of Revolutionary Warfare

In a Chicago courthouse in 1886, a condemned man stood before the judge to make a final argument for his innocence in a case of murder and political conspiracy. His road to the gallows began in a violent confrontation between demonstrators and police at an evening labor rally. A fuse-lit grenade had been thrown, the police had opened fire, and bloody mayhem had ensued, leading to the deaths of eight police officers and at least three civilians, dozens of injuries on both sides, and the defendant's arrest for murder. Yet the prosecution had been unable to present any substantial evidence of his material association with the bomb. Using his printed words and his reading materials, the prosecution had constructed him as one of the masterminds behind a massive conspiracy, and the newspapers had painted him a violent, animalistic monster bent on the destruction of civilization, a symbolic enemy of order. August Spies's crime was vague encouragement; his public words had made him an accessory before the fact.

One of the texts introduced against him and his seven codefendants was a slender volume, *Revolutionäre Kriegswissenschaft—The Science of Revolutionary Warfare*. It was mostly a compendium of directions for making high explosives, bombs, and other covert weapons, written in a conversational style as if among friends. Like nineteenth-century pyrotechnics manuals, it included curiosities like blowpipes, invisible ink, and exotic poisons like curare and ptomaine taken from corpses.[1] Very occasionally the text would identify the potential targets of these homemade weapons in the tone of a mean-spirited joke. Describing a well-known inflammable compound often used for arson, the text observed: "Clothes, of course, burn well. In this regard experiments were made in France with detectives, and those experiments have warmed them up pretty lively." Of a successful experiment involving a forged iron globe filled with dynamite, it suggested: "Just think, if this bomb had been placed under the table of a gluttonous dinner party, or it had been thrown through a window on the table what a beautiful effect it would have had."[2] This sensational content fulfilled the expectations of most readers of the city's daily newspapers who had already damned the defendants as vicious enemies of their civilization.

Despite objections that the book was irrelevant and inadmissible, the prosecution spent most of an afternoon reading lengthy excerpts from *Revolutionäre Kriegswissenschaft*, keeping the court an hour longer than usual. The book had been found in the library of Spies's newspaper office, he had published excerpts in his socialist newspaper, *Arbeiter-Zeitung*, and he had corresponded with the author, Johann Most, a German anarchist famous for his black humor, hyperbole, and bitter invective against rulers and capitalists. Arriving in the United States in 1882, Most was well known in Chicago, where, in a duel of insults, the press had called him the "craziest lunatic" who had had the temerity to take advantage of the speech rights accorded to him in the United States: "He has clearly demonstrated that he is without principle, an incendiary, an inciter of lawlessness, rapine, and murder, and a person unfit to breathe the free air of heaven associated with his fellows."[3] The papers dared Most and his followers in Chicago to put rhetoric into action: "There is not a person in the United States who would care to restrain Herr Most from preaching [his] doctrines from Dan to Beersheba and from now until doomsday, but in case any effort should be made to carry them into effect he would find that the entire population, with the exception of a handful of lazy and crazy beer-drinkers, would rise in their wrath."[4] With fragile evidence the police witnesses tried to show that bombs allegedly confiscated from an anarchist's residence were based on the book's instructions, but the link could not be proven. Despite failed attempts to tie the book to murder, *Revolutionäre Kriegswissenschaft* stood as the threshold between speech and action. Whoever owned it, discussed it, or was even adjacent to it in the next room was guilty of a conspiratorial preparation. Presiding Judge Joseph Gary, now infamous for his bias, ruled that the defendants needed only have been near the book for the prosecution to use it as evidence of criminal conspiracy: "If there is evidence . . . tending to show a state of things, tending to show objects which individuals have in view and that those objects are the overturning of civil order by force, then the means by which it is proposed to be accomplished, are admissible in evidence, and if among those means are books treating of and instructing how to do it, the possession of those books is one thing that may be proved."[5] Set against the discussion of tolerance for violent anarchist speech, *Revolutionäre Kriegswissenschaft* had raised the stakes with its combination of revolutionary rhetoric, vague threats, and technical instructions that imaged the anarchist as smart, rational, adept, and armed, in command of a science usually employed by empire-builders, military officers, and learned men. The prosecution knew that its introduction would create a sensational narrative of the defendants conspiring with the demonized Most.

Refusing to bow down even in the final hours as the judge decided his fate, Spies defended his right to publish excerpts from *Revolutionäre Kriegswissenschaft*. Spies argued that the *Arbeiter-Zeitung* articles contained no more dangerous information than could be found in the city's dailies. He pointed to a profile in the *Chicago Tribune* of Philadelphia metalsmith George Holgate, who ran a business selling infernal machines—including a pressure-detonated grenade, a clockwork bomb, and a chemical weapon that killed any breathing thing within a hundred-mile radius—to anyone who would pay. These machines were described in some detail, in a tone of admiration and fear, as a testament to their inventor's "fertile ingenuity."[6] Spies said that he had casually read this article on a train, implying the everyday presence of bomb-making information in mainstream capitalist newspapers that denounced striking workmen with calls for the police to break their heads and dynamite them. "May I learn," Spies argued, "why the editors of these papers have not been indicted and convicted of murder? Is it because they have advocated the use of this destructive agent only against the common rabble?"[7]

Soon to be affianced to the daughter of a chemist, he had in his political rhetoric called dynamite a Minerva springing from Zeus's head, alluding to the dynamite manufacturers who named their products after powerful gods like Hercules, Vulcan, and Atlas. Now to the accusation that he had extolled the science of dynamite, he said, "If this declaration is synonymous with murder, why not charge those with the crime to whom we owe the invention?"[8] In the battle between capital and labor, dynamite had no politics. Courting martyrdom, Spies presented opposing sides with equal access to the new high explosives that chemists and engineers had called "the ideal of portable force."[9] If the forces of capital could promote, explain, manufacture, and use these explosives, so could labor. In Spies's optimistic view, dynamite gave workers an equal military advantage, but the contest was not only over the ability to use dynamite but the right to talk about it. One of Spies's codefendants, Albert Parsons, argued from a progressive notion that the anarchist newspaper he edited, *The Alarm*, was within its constitutional rights in publishing talk of dynamite and revolution, including technical instruction: "*The Alarm* was a labor paper, and it was specifically published for the purpose of allowing every human being who had a wrong to ventilate it; to give every human being who wore the chains of monopoly an opportunity to clank those chains in the columns of *The Alarm*. It was a free press organ. It was a free speech newspaper."[10] For that exercise of free speech, Spies, Parsons, and two of their fellows would be hanged, and another, Louis Lingg, would use a dynamite cartridge to blow off his own face as he sat on death row. From the time of the trial, many free speech activists and historians have considered the executions to be among the most egregious miscarriages of justice in American history, arguing that men had been murdered for their ideas.[11] Some called it a legal lynching, others a judicial suicide.[12] Whether any of the defendants, or a group of the defendants, actually conspired to throw the bomb at Haymarket is still a hotly debated issue, but no one denies that speech tolerance was an important dimension of the trial.

The Haymarket trial was the first public hearing in the United States on the popular weapons manual and the allowable contexts for the dissemination of bomb-making information. Imprisoned a year later in New York's Blackwell's Island Penitentiary for inciting a riot, Most argued from his jail cell that *Revolutionäre Kriegswissenschaft* had been transformed into a "literary Satan that scared juries and judges alike into the most barbaric convictions."[13] Like Spies, he again appealed to "fair play": if governments could publish and circulate weapons information, so could revolutionaries. Spies had recognized that a double standard existed between the mainstream press and the radical labor press. The mainstream press could tout powerful new weapons alongside editorial invective against public enemies, but, if the labor press did the same, its editors were damned through an insistence that speech proved criminal action. In his pardon of the three remaining anarchists, Illinois governor John Altgeld offered a forward-thinking view of free speech at a time when the "bad tendency test" from English common law was still the framework for deciding what speech was allowable. He explained that the defendants had not been proven to have participated in the bombing and that "they had generally, by speech and print, advised large classes of people, not particular individuals."[14] Further, the bomber, who was never found, may not have heard or read the defendants' statements. Altgeld argued that the anarchists' "violent talk" was made in a brief time of aggrievement and excitement and was therefore not evidence of a "gigantic anarchist conspiracy."[15]

The Haymarket trial would have an important role to play in the development of free speech jurisprudence as some judges and lawyers, shocked by the gruesome spectacle, pondered the implications of violently suppressing radical speech.[16] Later famous for his defense of John Scopes, a teacher imprisoned for teaching evolution, lawyer Clarence Darrow was deeply moved by the injustice and helped persuade his friend, Governor Altgeld, to pardon the remaining three anarchists. Others, including the anarchist Emma Goldman, eventually formed the Free Speech League that would influence more progressive speech protections.[17]

Their attention was to the condemned's inherent right to express revolutionary sentiments in the cause of labor, but the trial had also addressed a particular kind of speech, a speech associated with technical preparation and instructional conspiracy. *Revolutionäre Kriegswissenschaft* and the articles it inspired in the anarchist press challenged the domains of industrial and military research, offering that laborers could put technological developments to their own practical use, needing very little money or specialized equipment. Mainstream journalists reported on the novelty of homemade weapons, sometimes in great detail, thrilling readers with descriptions of bombs made from ordinary tomato cans and quoting from the "doctor of destruction," Johann Most, on their possible deployments.[18] Through the Haymarket trial, the prosecution argued that the defendants were "not only armed with the arms known to civilized warfare and drilled in tactics recognized as honorable among nations, but were also engaged in the manufacture of explosives of a kind known only to the revolutionists." The activities that went beyond "civilized warfare" were seen as most egregious, especially since the defendants were accused of "giving advice to correspondents upon these subjects with an openness and abandon that is astonishing."[19] Of *Revolutionäre Kriegswissenschaft*, the prosecution said, "It is a book which . . . shows the revolutionist to be utterly devoid of conscience, and which, for cold-blooded diabolism, has no counterpart in the whole range of literature."[20] The devilish image was repeated in the press: newspapers across the country carried a story about a police raid of Louis Lingg's bomb-making "lair," inhabited by anarchists who "looked not unlike wolves," one of them clad in red pajamas. "In the old days of belief in magic and witchcraft," the writer informed small-town readers, "it was said that black and crimson were the colors of the evil one." Included were illustrations of Lingg's smelting furnace, a dynamite cartridge, and a flask that might hold a "devil's broth of glycerine and nitric acid."[21] Lingg was the only Haymarket defendant known to have made bombs, although the samples allegedly found in his house were never conclusively tied to the Haymarket bomb fragments.[22] The proliferation of amateur weapons making had proliferated during and after the Civil War, and in most places, including Chicago, tinkering with bombs was a legal activity. Although experimentation with explosives was widespread across many domains of expertise—from the chemistry classroom to the government research laboratory to the amateur inventor's shed—the anarchists' revolutionary chemistry was associated with a temptation of science towards cold-blooded evil.

The People's Chemistry

Johann Most and other revolutionaries understood their bomb talk as a theft from hegemonic powers that used advanced weapons to suppress an anti-imperial, anticapitalist resistance that took many forms. Beginning in the late 1870s, various radical groups called for a democratic dispersal of scientific knowledge to peasants and poor laborers who, they thought, could be socially, economically, and politically elevated through scientific modernization and even militarization.[23] A prevailing theme was that the sciences, especially chemistry, should be accessible forms of knowledge and should be studied. Radicals embraced popular science and science education in the industrialized nations and their colonies, while rejecting the rise of the scientific professions that corralled knowledge through patents and closed networks of expertise. Some of these radical groups had serious military aspirations to obtain competitive weapons; others were more dilettantish and disorganized, more enamored with the idea of dynamite than its practical applications. As socialist writer Floyd Dell wrote of the Chicago anarchists, "Talk of dynamite was made largely in the American spirit of the bluff."[24] However technically ambitious they were, radical groups championed rhetoric on the importance of science, science education, and weapons making. They taught bomb making through articles, handbooks, private and public lectures, and formal classroom lessons. Bomb talk existed in a hazy area between propaganda of the word and propaganda of the deed. Its use of a common vernacular accompanied by antiauthoritarian political rhetoric made it distinct from classroom instruction. Depending on the aims of the interpreter, this speech could be read as instruction or incitement, knowledge or preparation, political tract or criminal conspiracy. The popular weapons manual's aura of theft and rebellion began here, in the late nineteenth century, in the great conflicts between capital and labor, between empire and resistance.

In the United States, formulating ways to encourage a revolution in their homeland, Irish radicals promoted science education to overcome the weakness and ignorance of the oppressed. Patrick Ford, editor of the *Irish World*, argued that the Irish needed to commandeer England's "resources of civilization," such as Gatling guns and rockets, used to suppress uprisings in its colonies.[25] In Ford's first planning meeting in 1876 to generate a "skirmishing fund," his brother Augustine recounted Aesop's fable of a fox's revenge on an eagle that has eaten her young. The fox steals a cinder wrapped in flesh from a sacrificial altar, and cunningly uses it to burn down the tree where the eagle has nested, eating her fledglings as they fall to the ground.[26] Echoed by Parsons in his final speech at the Haymarket trial, the story was an allegory for a theft of technology from the gods and its use in retributive justice. The *Irish World* suggested sending chemistry teachers to Ireland to emulate the American Revolution and its homemade gunpowder: "The masses of Irish must, by some means, be made familiar with the combination and formation of explosives. . . . If the Irish peasantry were as familiar with the mixing of those explosives as they are with wrestling, hurling, card-playing and the like, the light of 'how to free their country' would flash upon them quickly as a thunder clap."[27]

This plan was never carried out, but in the early 1880s, Irish radicals founded at least two bomb-making schools in the United States, attracting students from Scotland, England, and Ireland. The United Irishmen, whose principal spokesperson was Jeremiah O'Donovan Rossa, publicly advertised its "School of

Mines," an ironic reference to the technical education provided by Columbia University's School of Mines. O'Donovan Rossa kept bombs in his New York office and showed them to curious reporters when they stopped by. The professor of the dynamite school was the flamboyant Richard Rodgers, aka Professor Mezzeroff, who gave public lectures claiming that he could make dynamite out of handkerchiefs and old boots. His political exhortations were accompanied by thrilling outdoor explosive demonstrations. Much of the rhetoric was aimed at tweaking the British authorities—Mezzeroff was a terrible bomb maker who could never make a workable detonator and was eventually fired—but the enthusiastic threats were not all in the spirit of the bluff. Though never very proficient, radicals associated with the United Irishmen and its more secretive, Chicago-based rival, the Clan na Gael, constructed ambitious bombs made with complicated clockwork mechanisms and chemical detonators and set up kitchen labs for making nitroglycerine in British cities, carting the highly volatile substance around in fishing waders. They carried out several attacks on British monuments and government offices in the early 1880s that created considerable public panic, police crackdowns, and terror laws to suppress speech.[28]

In the United States, training activities, solicitations for funds, and revolutionary rhetoric were tolerated when it came to Irish Americans, who had an increasing presence in mainstream newspaper offices, police units, governing bodies, and voting booths. Two secretaries of state—James Blaine and Frederick Frelinghuysen—refused to comply with the British government's demands that papers like Rossa's *United Irishman*, Ford's *Irish World*, and Patrick Rellihan's *Ireland's Liberator and Dynamite Monthly* be shut down. The British foreign secretary, Lord Earl Granville, offered that the United States should be treating these agitators like the British had Johann Most, whom they had put to hard labor for a year simply for praising the bombing assassination of Tsar Alexander II. In his final word on the subject, Frelinghuysen declined to act on the matter of incendiary speech, maintaining that it could not be directly connected to a violent act.[29] In 1885, after an explosion at the Tower of London that injured American tourists, Congress considered emergency legislation to prohibit the manufacture of the new high explosives for international acts of terrorism, including a clause that forbade "in any manner aiding as accessories before the fact," aimed at instructional speech. Drafted as a symbolic gesture, it died in committee.[30] Despite increasing evidence that a few small, US-based groups were trying—albeit unsuccessfully—to wage scientific warfare against Britain and Spain, the federal government was reluctant to engage in expensive, organizationally complex investigations, for which it was not equipped, or to change federal law when its own interests were not at stake. The matter was left to the states to pass nuisance laws, based on older arson laws, against the manufacture of high explosives for use in a crime.[31]

The problem of instructional speech unfolded very differently for the Chicago anarchists who directly threatened the capitalist economy and were the prime enemies of the American state. They were members of the International Working People's Association formed in 1883 to achieve the "destruction of existing class rule" and generate a society based on free exchange, cooperative production, and equal education.[32] Written by Albert Parsons, August Spies, Johann Most, and two other delegates at the inaugural conference in Pittsburgh, its manifesto declared: "By force our ancestors liberated themselves from political oppression, by force their children will have to liberate themselves from economic bondage. 'It is, therefore, your right, it is your duty,' says Jefferson—'to arm.'"[33] For a poor, powerless group, high explosives seemed an answer to an unequal contest between capital and labor. In Albert Parsons's paper, *The Alarm*, contributors expressed admiration for Professor Mezzeroff, shared enthusiasm for public demonstrations of dynamite's force, and discussed its role in generating a revolution inspired by the early American colonists. Like many industrial chemists and engineers who were vocal in selling high explosives to the public, anarchists extolled dynamite as a "great force of civilization" and the "equalizing and emancipating agent of modern civilization," a development they felt Thomas Paine would have approved.[34] The anarchists believed that the democratizing benefits of modern science would deliver to tramps and paupers the power of armies. In a famous letter to the *The Alarm*, secretary of the Indianapolis IWPA Gerhard Lizius called dynamite the "sublime stuff": "In giving dynamite to the downtrodden millions of the globe, science has done its best work."[35] In his final speech to the court before he was hanged, Parsons elevated dynamite to a prayer: "It is the equilibrium. It is the annihilator. It is the disseminator of power. It is the downfall of oppression. It is the abolition of authority; it is the dawn of peace; it is the end of war."[36]

Idealistic talk was one thing, practical action another. Historian Paul Avrich, who interviewed many in the Chicago anarchist community, argued that a few men were resorting to weapons making, but that the gap between "advocacy of terrorism and its actual practice was very wide."[37] Carl Smith concludes that the anarchists' appeal to dynamite "is best understood as a kind of performance especially suited to anarchist politics and the romantic sensibility behind them, as an attempt at personal empowerment through rhetoric to which radicals resorted from a position of weakness."[38] Praying to dynamite was a different proposition, however, than instructing people in how to make dynamite bombs for abstract revolutionary purposes, a form of speech that was controversial at the Haymarket trial and continues to vex the legal system. *Revolutionäre Kriegswissenschaft* laid out a rationale for popular dissemination of weapons technologies and put its instructions in an everyday language that most readers could understand and use. It was obvious in its intentions, stating that it provided training in modern explosives to further the inevitable social revolution. It was not stamped, as many such manuals are today, with the dubious disclaimer: "For information purposes only." At the same time, as any teacher knows, just because a textbook is meant to be used, doesn't mean it is used.

Revolutionäre Kriegswissenschaft was written partly as provocation, partly to fill a perceived gap between purpose and knowledge, between idealism and practice, among the revolutionaries. Addressing science literacy, *The Alarm* explained to its readers that they must "study their schoolbooks on chemistry and read the dictionaries and encyclopedias on the composition and construction of all kinds of explosives, and make themselves too strong to be opposed by deadly weapons."[39] This knowledge, the paper advised, could be obtained in one week with books available in the average home. It was possible to absorb a great deal of information about high explosives and explosive devices circulated in mainstream print. Widely read technical magazines, such as *Scientific American* and *Chemical News*, frequently offered information about making nitroglycerine and dynamite, and standard nineteenth-century chemistry textbooks and government military publications described how to make torpedoes and mines, blasting units, dynamite, nitroglycerine, guncotton, and fulminates of mercury and silver. The bibliography included in the chemist Marcelin Berthelot's noted theoretical work, *Explosive Materials*, published in 1883, lists nearly five hundred works on explosives, including books and articles in French, German, and English on the manufacture, storage, use, and safety of dynamite, nitroglycerine, and guncotton. In his textbook, *Chemistry: Inorganic and Organic*, Charles Bloxam explained that nitroglycerine is "very easily prepared," gave directions for making dynamite, discussed the process of making guncotton, and described various detonators.[40] Bloxam explained that he wished students to "glide into Chemistry" without having to wade through difficult terminology, and pointed to practical uses: "The military student will find more than the usual space allotted to the Chemistry of the various substances employed in warlike stores."[41] The potential victims of these warlike stores did not need thought or naming.

Like many authors of popular weapons manuals after him, Most understood his aim as collating, translating, and adapting this information for the people. Unlike the writers of chemistry textbooks who neutrally avoided mentioning the objects of explosive violence, he plainly stated the enemies: the imperialists, the capitalists, and their hired guns, the detectives and the police. Like Bloxam, he offered a way for the military student to glide into chemistry: "We carefully avoid all scientific and technical terms, which are only apt to create misunderstanding among laymen, nor will we speak of apparatuses which [they] are not able to handle." Extolling the amateur as a key political agent, *Revolutionäre Kriegswissenschaft* borrowed from denser technical publications and put them into plain language and understandable procedures. It took, for example, technical information from official publications such as *Praktische Versuche mit Sprengstoffen* (*Practical Trials with Explosives*) published by the Austrian government, which had formed a commission to study explosives and done extensive tests on guncotton and dynamite. These studies, featuring information on how to blow down walls, were well known to explosive experts. In *Modern High Explosives*, industrial chemist Manuel Eissler lauded the "great foresight" of Austria in being the first nation to recognize the "immense value" of the new explosives and promote their use.[42] *Revolutionäre Kriegswissenschaft* included information measuring the power of dynamite blasts to suggest that the reader could acquire the advanced power to take down fortresses and prison walls. Anticipating criticism that he was emulating the power of the state, Most wrote of his sources, "What the banalities of law and order find expedient for the maintenance of the scoundrelly system of law and order is not to be despised by the revolutionists."

As it mashes together discrete instructions and experiments from official and unofficial sources, the popular weapons manual's technique of borrowing mystifies its authorship. Its power partly lies in anonymity, the evocation of a dangerous, hidden network of experts. Although Most was listed as the author, *Revolutionäre Kriegswissenschaft* referred to a "we," described collaborative experiments, and acknowledged other experts in the circuit who corrected errors and provided better methods: "We, and others, . . . have endeavored to popularize, through men of experience, the learned treatises contained in said works on the manufacture of explosives." Another anarchist work circulating in Europe, *l'Indicateur Anarchiste*, contained content similar to that in *Revolutionäre Kriegswissenschaft*, including a discussion of the poison curare. Both were compilations of useful, dangerous knowledge.[43] In court, Spies argued that Most had taken his more "repulsive" passages from *l'Indicateur Anarchiste* and referred to a rumor that a former Paris police detective had written it.[44] These kinds of publications first appeared in anarchist newspapers in Europe, and appear to have been designed by the police to provoke violence and generate support for draconian repression.[45] The lack of any clear authorship in popular weapons manuals makes their provenance difficult to establish. The technical information is free floating, moving across political and social groups.

Revolutionäre Kriegswissenschaft distinguished itself from an ordinary textbook by adapting technical processes to domestic spaces and cheap materials at hand. Economy, simplicity, availability, and effectiveness were its values. It offered that a household location could be transformed into a serviceable laboratory and that explosives could be made using ordinary tools, materials, and activities. Iron pots, porcelain vessels, wooden ladles, clotheslines, lemon squeezers, forks, scissors, coffeepots, and cleaning fluids were enlisted in instructions to make Greek fire, dynamite, guncotton, nitroglycerine, and mercury and silver fulminates. Advice was given on where to easily obtain various substances—from the drugstore to the neighboring weed lot. Directions for making explosives sounded like ordinary kitchen recipes: "Take a water proof vessel, such as a big bowl, kettle or tin pail, put in any quantity of the materials here named, pour on them the nitroglycerine, and knead them with a wooden ladle." The downfalls of using the household for the manufacture of explosives were examined. The process of making dynamite was difficult to hide since the smell could give away the kitchen lab with its open, ventilating windows, and the resulting product was often very weak. Thus, the text advised, it was always better to secretively acquire industrial dynamite rather than make it, and it acknowledged that its instructions were mostly in the experimental stage.

Despite its hesitant promises, *Revolutionäre Kriegswissenschaft* failed as a practical manual. Its procedures were sketchy, its directions incomplete, and its operations dangerous. As Emma Goldman remembered, she and her lover Alexander Berkman were not able to use Most's instructions: "A week's work and anxiety and forty precious dollars wasted!"[46] Later anarchists would dismiss Most as an irritant and a distraction from the real aims of anarchism; George Woodcock despised Most for writing of dynamite "with the sinister enthusiasm of a malevolent and utterly irresponsible child."[47] Yet *Revolutionäre Kriegswissenschaft* is often included in broad histories of terrorism to demonstrate Most's technological foresightedness and important place in the "evolution" of terrorism. Most has been absurdly called the "high priest of terrorism," the inventor of the letter bomb (really a less than ingenious use of the centuries-known Greek fire) and an imagineer of balloons disgorging bombs on cities (already fantasized during the Civil War).[48] The image of the terrorist bomb maker, like the mad scientist who operates on the fringe, often draws on conventions of ingenuity, novelty, complexity, and genius. Yet *Revolutionäre Kriegswissenschaft* offered nothing more horrifying than could be found in the discourses of legitimate warfare. It paled in comparison to a weapons manual, intended as a textbook at West Point, by the inventor of the land mine, Confederate general Gabriel Rains, who offered clockwork mechanisms and aerial devices to firebomb urban populations. Rains imagined a great bomb that would instantly clear a battlefield, emit a pestilence like the "destroying angel in Sanacherib's army," and crack open the earth "with the fire of death."[49] By the late nineteenth century, military tactics had so changed that remotely detonated bombs were fully acceptable, rockets were fired into civilian populations, dynamite was thrown into caves where fleeing populations attempted to resist imperial invasion, and chemical and air warfare was now considered acceptable.[50] *Revolutionäre Kriegswissenschaft*'s aims were modest in comparison, mostly referencing small groups engaged in acts of revenge, street fighting, and self-defense.

From the Chicago anarchists' point of view, what they were doing was no different than what the capitalists were doing, creating armed units and inventing and making weapons. Within the American context, like many militarized radical groups after them, they called on their constitutional rights to do so: the right to assembly, the right to free speech, and the right to bear arms. In the late 1870s, socialists in Chicago, along with several ethnic groups, formed militia units that drilled and paraded with flags and rifles. As the labor movement grew in strength, the Illinois State Legislature bolstered the state militias to contain labor strikes while banning these ethnic militias. In *Revolutionäre Kriegswissenschaft*, Most warned that leniency in gun laws was about to be overturned by the "governing bandits" and "mob of murderers in uniform."[51] Labor radicals would be disarmed and defenseless, unless they turned to covert weapons like easily concealed dynamite.

This message was enthusiastically received by audiences in Chicago who welcomed Most on his speaking engagements. Within six months of his arrival in the United States, Most had gone on two lecture tours, speaking to some two hundred audiences about the need for a social revolution with "blood and iron."[52] In 1884, as reported in *The Alarm*, Most told an audience in Philadelphia that "a little grease, a little acid, as cheap as blackberries, some other acids, also very cheap, give nitroglycerine. This, mixed with sawdust and put in a hollow vessel and thrown under a barracks explodes, and the devil receives the workmen's foes."[53] His weapons instructions became well known among anarchist groups and became the subject of a popular song:

> Dynamite today, dynamite tonight.
> Most tells how, he shows where:
> He says all in *Freiheit*
> And his good little book on warfare.[54]

Like the weapons manuals circulated at late twentieth-century survivalist conventions and fairs, *Revolutionäre Kriegswissenschaft* was given away at anarchist meetings and picnics.

The call to study dynamite was taken seriously in Chicago: repeated, circulated, and imitated. *The Alarm* taught its readers how to make detonators and dynamite with ordinary household items like powdered sugar and tin pipes. Most's instructions were reprinted with the translator, "A. A.," providing helpful technical addenda. For example, after "The Manufacture and Use of the Deadly Dynamite Bomb Made Easy," A. A. suggested another recipe for a detonator more easily made from a penholder and firecrackers known as "Ladies crackers," sold on the Fourth of July. An enterprising revolutionist could buy twenty-five of these for 20 cents, cut the tops off with scissors, and collect mercury fulminate. Discussing other versions of procedures for making explosives found in a chemistry textbook, "A. A." advised the readers that they would do well to first follow the "advice of practical men" rather than professors of theoretical chemistry, who did not agree on the best methods.[55] The revolutionary anarchists preached a collaborative people's science, drawing on chemistry and military engineering and encouraging research, testing, and development with the everyday objects at hand. Some anarchists in Chicago were carrying out tests and blowing up stumps and trees—one was alleged to have lost fingers in these pursuits—but the leap to armed insurrection was long.

Always at the front line of deciding what will be collected as evidence, the police had already begun criminalizing these texts before they arrived in court. Two months before the Haymarket incident, the Chicago police had searched the room of a "strange Bohemian" alleged to have murdered two men over the sale of a horse. On their evidence list was a "little pink-covered book," *Revolutionäre Kriegswissenschaft*.[56] Since the fugitive was accused of a shooting, the unrelated evidence suggested the black menace of anarchist revolution, and it would become routine for the police to search bookshelves for popular weapons manuals to damn defendants as members of radical conspiracies. Suggesting that "open and undisguised sale" of *Revolutionäre Kriegswissenschaft* would have brought "difficulties or dangers" to the distributors, Chicago police chief Michael Schaack asserted that hundreds of copies had been passed around surreptitiously.[57] The only difficulty and danger to distributors came from the police, who had decided, a priori, that the book was criminal, or in the legal understanding of the day, of bad tendency. The police had amassed a collection of artifacts and texts well before the clash in Haymarket Square, ready for use if the anarchists could be shown to have crossed the line. Later the former police superintendent, Frederick Ebersold, revealed that Schaack had concocted evidence and sent out provocateurs to "keep things stirring."[58]

Through a ghostwriter, as was typical for popular police accounts of crime, Schaack wrote a book about his pursuit of anarchists, *Anarchy and Anarchism*, published three years after the Haymarket affair and coinciding with his public exposure for corruption and graft.[59] Posing in a photo in his uniform, shoulders thrust back in an arrogant swagger, Schaack suggested that before Haymarket, "desperate men" had been experimenting for five years with dynamite weapons, and that some "were crippled by the rash and ineffectual experiments."[60] The figure of the limbless bomber often serves as a cautionary image in popular discourse, serving as a symbol to others of inevitable consequences. The crippled bomber is robbed of physical wholeness and power and thus no threat to the state.

Schaack specified who was allowed to circulate weapons information and included detailed diagrams and descriptions of anarchist bombs. He described the percentage of nitroglycerine to its stabilizing compound in dynamite and how it was fired. He suggested other compounds more dangerous and effective than dynamite. He told of the strategies of Narodnaya Volya (a Russian revolutionary group) to blow up the tsar's train with the use of mines on the railroad tracks, revealing how many pounds of dynamite they used. He provided illustrations of bombs, explaining how they worked, as of this bomb disguised as a law book:

> The outside was made of wood and pasteboard, so artistically that only the closest inspection would discover the fact that the machine was not really a book. In the center of the interior, in the place marked C, were a number of hollow bullets filled with strychnine, which poison was also plastered on the outside of the missiles. Above this were small compartments filled with fulminate, with a glass tube of sulphuric acid. To the tube was tied a string, which would break it when thrown, spilling it into the fulminate and thus exploding the dynamite with which the whole of the hollow parts of the interior was densely packed.[61]

Schaack suggested that bombs could be anywhere, hidden in books and buried under city sidewalks, a terrifying, mysterious latent force deployed by shadowy conspirators who might be anywhere, disguised as anyone, ingenious tramps and criminals infiltrating polite society intent on its destruction. The world of ordinary objects and persons masked terrible weapons carrying inexplicable underworld messages and a perverted science. As Henry James's anarchist bookbinder in *The Princess Casamassima* says, "In silence, in darkness, but under the feet of each one of us, the revolution lives and works. It's a wonderful, immeasurable trap, on the lid of which society performs its antics."[62] At the same time, Schaack's revelations of how these bombs were made and how they worked suggested benign, authoritative domains for this knowledge, the investigative and forensic world of the police, who would "meet force with force, and cunning with cunning."[63] *Anarchy and Anarchism* addressed an audience who would presumably ignore the contradiction in spreading bomb-making information while pillorying anarchists for doing the same. It was clear who had won. Transcending a moment of chaos, weakness, and vulnerability, the police could publish bomb-making information as a sign of order; the anarchists could not.

The Haymarket trial crushed the fantasies of balanced warring parties, as the state reasserted its shaken power by strangling the bomb talkers and cutting off any further speeches. There would be no tolerance for revolutionary war science associated with anarchists, socialists, or any other enemies of law and order. *Revolutionäre Kriegswissenschaft* would disappear for ninety years, until a small paramilitary press, Desert Publications, printed an anonymous translation. (It also published titles on survivalism and DIY weapons-making that an emerging right-wing militia movement embraced.) This press was later implicated in the trial of Oklahoma City bomber Timothy McVeigh for its sale of *Improvised*

Munitions from Ammonium Nitrate and other explosives handbooks frequently sold at gun shows. It was an odd place for *Revolutionäre Kriegswissenschaft* to find a home, and a sign of a continuing tension in American life over the free flow of weapons information.

The Right Hands

The anarchist cookbooks that circulated among radical groups in the late nineteenth century made extravagant promises that individuals and small groups could overthrow hegemonic powers with basic chemistry. Though the authors had an overly optimistic view that an ordinary person, with household materials and store-bought chemicals, could make, carry, and successfully deploy extremely dangerous substances and make advanced weapons, they were essentially right that high explosives would be used to harass the state, disrupt its operations, and cower its officials, even if they could not produce the desired revolution. The commercial and military zeal for high explosives in the late nineteenth century produced a plethora of formulas and devices that circulate through bomb-making instructions. Most basic bombs designs and explosive mixtures have their origins here. For example, government prosecutors argued that manuals owned by the 1993 World Trade Center bombers had shown them how to make a "rare" explosive of urea and nitric acid. That formula can be found in nineteenth-century scientific texts.[64] Faced with the prosecution's introduction of bomb-making manuals as evidence, defense attorneys, as at the Haymarket trial, often take the tack that the information can be found in many sources. That is a testament to the nineteenth century's plenitude, as the emerging science of explosives was explained in textbooks, circulated in scientific journals, and extolled in popular literature.

During the bombings of the late nineteenth century, chemists were often called to testify in criminal cases and became media celebrities who introduced the science of explosives to a literate public. The bond between science and the law grew closer. At the Haymarket trial, two chemists, Marc Delafontaine and Walter S. Haines, testified against the defendants. It is perhaps telling that they would become paid endorsers for the monopolistic baking powder industry, cigarettes, and Armour meats.[65] (Upton Sinclair would later expose the gruesome operations of Armour's Chicago packing plants, including their horrific treatment of labor.) Active across university, industry, and military settings, chemists served a social role of calming public fears while promoting new industrial products, including high explosives. As the dangers of explosives became evident through accidents, murders, robberies, and *attentats* in Europe, chemists and industrial engineers sought to establish themselves as the "right hands," containing and guiding a powerful force. The right hands included analytical chemists in university laboratories and medical colleges and industrial chemists who oversaw the mixing of explosives. Through their public relations as a new professional class, chemists set themselves apart from the irresponsible amateur, especially the stereotypical anarchist, whose use of chemistry was a threat to the progress of civilization.

Some became government inspectors and consultants who took on a political role of advising on new legislation aimed at bringing high explosives under state control. Their commentaries went beyond suggestions for licensing and regulation of storage and transport to stern pronouncements on incitement of political violence. The worlds of military, industry, and university research were presented as the proper domains where scientists had pure intentions, even as their research supported a massive surge in the imperial engines of war, perilous workplaces, and environmental destruction. Among these architects of violence, self-reflection was never a strong impulse. Just as later, with the rise of a nuclear priesthood, chemists involved in the explosive industry saw themselves as a special class above any abuses of technology.

In the late nineteenth century, the most high-profile explosives expert was Sir Vivian Majendie, England's chief inspector of explosives during the terrorist campaign of Irish radicals against British monuments, government offices, and railways in the 1880s and 1890s. Charged with regulating explosives manufacture, transport, and storage, and with examining crime scenes, Majendie was the principal mind behind Britain's 1875 Explosive Substances Act, which was often discussed and emulated in other nations. The law centralized regulation in a national office rather than leaving it entirely to local governments. In 1883, after a series of explosions at government offices in London and the discovery of an explosives laboratory run by Irish radicals in a phony paint shop in Birmingham, the law was amended to target bombing conspiracies, including punishment for "counseling" the commission of a bombing. With Majendie advising, the 1883 amendments were hastily passed in a perceived state of emergency and still remain in force.[66] At the time, the new law did little to deter the bombers who carried out escalating attacks on the railways, government buildings, and tourist sites in the years to follow.

Now considered the progenitor of the modern forensics laboratory and the bomb squad, Majendie, along with chemist August Dupré, made frequent court appearances in terror cases covered by the international English-language press.[67] Majendie was such a publicity seeker that Scotland Yard perceived him as a security risk in new cases that would have benefited from withholding details.[68] When camera-wielding reporters visited him, he showed them a wall of shelves stuffed with infernal machines he'd confiscated, including exploding cigars and time bombs. On one occasion, widely covered by the international press, he served as expert witness against Irish revolutionary John Daly, who was arrested holding three bombs and a stained paper with instructions on how to construct a device using a sulfuric acid detonator.[69] Majendie positioned twelve wooden dummies in a circle around an iron room—arranged as if they were on a sidewalk—and then set off one of the bombs. The newspapers carried descriptions of the dummies riddled with shrapnel, a graphic demonstration of the Irish threat to ordinary citizens going about their daily routines.[70]

The consulting experts like Majendie walked a line between terrifying and reassuring the public. On the one hand, they had a stake in presenting their profession as necessary to contain a threat to the body politic. The danger had to be real enough to justify a bureaucratic apparatus that included their well-compensated expertise and professional ascent. On the other hand, the experts needed to reassure the public that they had the situation under control, whether they did or not, and that the projects of civilization, involving the massive production of explosives, could go forward. A former officer in the Royal Artillery who had defended the empire against insurgents in India, Majendie presented a picture of Victorian manliness and professionalism as he walked through crime scenes making authoritative, sometimes alarming, pronouncements about the strength and properties of explosive devices. The newspapers described Majendie and his assistant Dupré packing buckets of homemade nitroglycerine in ice and submerging bombs in water to disarm them. At the same time, Majendie reassured the public that no bomber could carry enough explosives to level "considerable areas of the metropolis," or even a large building, without being detected. Nor could the average bomber excel at the complicated process of making powerful gelatin dynamite, but had to rely instead on the production of the inferior "lignin dynamite." Although regulation was needed against "promiscuous possession" of explosives, he said, excessive measures against legitimate manufacturing and trade were unnecessary.[71] Majendie knew that his profession and his assurance of public safety were threatened by the amateur misuse of chemistry and claims that anyone could make dynamite. Radical bomb-making information not only gave chemistry a bad name, but also suggested that the expertise of the professionals was superfluous. Frequently reiterated in the press was the unpleasant idea, as voiced by veteran of the Paris Commune Henri Rochefort, that "an individual who is willing to risk his life in order to throw a bomb . . . will surely be willing to spend half-a-crown buying a text-book on chemistry. There he will find as many formulae of the kind he is in search of as he is likely to require."[72] Even chemists were prone to such statements: Charles Doremus, who often consulted on nineteenth-century criminal cases involving explosives, declared that dynamite was "a good deal easier and quicker to make than griddle cakes."[73] To such sentiments, Majendie responded with reassurance that no amateur could achieve the proficiency of the professional chemist, who was also a vital force in public safety.

Chemists who worked in US government agencies and who were called upon to consult in criminal cases knew Majendie's work. Most chemists displayed little overt interest in politics, but presented themselves as professionals implicitly contributing to the growth of civilization through moral, technological, and economic progress.[74] Chemical progress was a nation-building enterprise. One of the leading chemists who knew Majendie and also consulted in political bombing cases, Charles Munroe, wrote in a popular essay on the development of high explosives: "Certainly there must have been an immense advance in civilization when man by a touch of the finger can put into operation forces as mighty as these."[75] As inventor of the shaped charge in his research with the US Torpedo Station, Munroe promoted the use of high explosives in warfare. He and many of his fellows were involved in the late nineteenth-century naval arms race, when competing powers built up massive arsenals of torpedoes and land and sea mines. These technologies, like chemical and pressure detonators used in mines, also found their way into radical bomb making.[76] In his textbook, *Modern High Explosives,* mining engineer and industrial chemist Martin Eissler admitted that modern explosives could "form a terribly destructive agent of war," but then assured his readers that these "marvels of chemical perfection" were "so completely under control, that they may be handled freely in any class of work with perfect safety, when in the hands of careful and experienced operators."[77] In their public pronouncements, chemists presented themselves as the right hands for the new explosives; Eissler warned that they were "dangerous in the hands of the ignorant or vicious, so a proper and wide-spread knowledge of them will do much to forefend their abuse either from ignorance or design."[78] When knowledge was contained within these professional domains, even with their own violent intentions, it was considered benign.

Looking beyond their ranks, some chemists saw the amorphous peril of potential "abuse" and made a concerted effort to encourage a federal explosives act along the lines of the British Explosive Substances Act. Charles Munroe's colleague and former assistant at the Torpedo Station, Thomas Chatard, was at the forefront of these efforts. In his presidential address to the Chemistry Society of Washington in 1893, Chatard raised the specters of an explosion at Dublin Castle on Christmas Eve and the bombing of a Paris mining company with a device called a "marmite," made from a cooking pot. He also mentioned a woman arrested in Ohio for carrying a large quantity of explosives to blow up a neighbor's house. But the anarchists made a better symbol. Chatard read a long excerpt from a popular magazine on Nikolai Kibalchich, a young chemist trained at a Russian government engineering school who built devices for Narodnaya Volya, known worldwide for its successful bombing assassination of

Tsar Alexander II. Acknowledging that chemists gone wrong could easily make a variety of explosives, Chatard wanted a federal licensing law to prevent abuses, calling on professional chemists as "public men" with specialized knowledge to join him.

Although he presented this proposed law as simple and minimal, he urged swift, warrantless searches based on hearsay. While mere unlawful possession would earn the violator a light sentence, speech would bring down the heaviest hand of the law: "Any attempts to make a criminal use of explosives—any threats, verbal or written, to do so—any incitements, verbal or written, of others to make such use against anybody in particular or society in general, or an expressed approval of such actions, should meet with speedy and severe punishment, which no legal technicalities should be permitted to delay." Chatard urged that the punishment for this dangerous speech be hard labor, so that "the Johann Mosts, O'Donovan Rossas and Louise Michels of society would speedily find their occupations and themselves gone to the penitentiary, where their usefulness to the world would be much increased."[79] Hard labor was undoubtedly better than hanging.

Chatard and Munroe continued to press for federal regulation for the next two decades, when finally a convergence of circumstances—World War I and the Red Scare—made the federal government more receptive to explosives regulation.[80] Wishing to expand its funding and influence, the ambitious US Bureau of Mines, under the Department of the Interior, pushed for emergency wartime legislation to regulate the manufacture and storage of explosives. A licensing system was put into effect, designed to shut down explosives manufacturing by perceived anarchists, Bolsheviks, and subversive foreigners. It lasted, however, only a short time. The bureaucracy of inspectors was dismantled at the end of the war, and explosive regulation was again returned to state and local governments, where public nuisance laws held sway. Such regulations, as legal historian William Novak points out, could be "a powerful and punitive technology of public action." Originally aimed at arsonists, who were despised as "the antithesis of civilized, ordered life," nuisance laws gave the police the right to enter and tear down premises and confiscate salable goods.[81] Under licensing laws for explosives, persons were often required to prove "fitness," which could be variously interpreted by fire commissioners, who might, for example, require that the candidate speak English. These subtle measures made for unfair application of the law, but regulation of substances was preferable to the more draconian measures of singling out symbolic enemies during perceived emergencies.

Appearing in science-related magazines, popular fiction punished amateur bombmakers through humorous stories about their brushes with death caused by credulity, ignorance, and incompetence. Bad instruction played a central role. Even without Most's explicit revolutionary goals, the amateur was a chaotic threat at least to himself (the popular imagination was always of a male), if not to all of civilization. In popular science writer J. West Roosevelt's story "Rather Too Much Energy," the brilliant, wealthy amateur Singer skims through a turgid German pamphlet on nitrogen tetrachloride. With only the superficial knowledge of distracted attention, he concocts the substance in his well-equipped household laboratory. His assistant, Van, warns him after the fact that the explosive is powerful enough to have killed a group of scientists who contributed to the pamphlet, as it had warned in an overlooked footnote. Singer and Van try to discard the explosive through a series of near misses, including an encounter with a large, friendly, bounding dog that nearly knocks them over as they are transporting the delicate substance outdoors. They then wrap it in a package that is accidentally sent to Singer's fiancée. Fortunately, the concoction leaks from the vial and harmlessly evaporates.[82]

The professional organ *Chemist & Druggist* ran an illustrated version of Robert Barr's story about a journalist, Marshall Semkin, who infiltrates a heavily beer-drinking anarchist organization in London but can't find a way of extracting himself. Semkin enlists his friend Sedlitz, an American chemistry student and amateur actor, to engage in a performance of dynamite instruction for the anarchists at a special meeting. Semkin introduces his friend as having studied explosives for a lifetime, and Sedlitz mounts to a platform, stumping as if on a wooden leg, with an eye patch and his arm in a sling, injuries announced as caused by his deadly experimentation. Tossing dynamite about, suggesting that it is almost on the verge of explosion, Sedlitz introduces a powerful new explosive that goes off at any vibration and produces a deadly smoke. Sedlitz asks the anarchists if they are ready for an apocalyptic destruction of all London, at which they all make their excuses and flee.[83]

Other, more famous fictional characters, like Robert Louis Stevens's Zero Pumpernickel Jones, and Joseph Conrad's detonator-obsessed The Professor, featured incompetent anarchist bombmakers. They were oddities, always with ambitions beyond their means and intelligence. Popular literature performed a social policing of the new high explosives as they traveled along the arteries of industrial and imperial expansion, carried in a stampede by public relations men and military and industrial engineers. During the 1890s and a lull in political struggles, it was mostly scientists, rather than the detectives and the police, who asserted a national, professional authority over explosives, distinguishing between the competent and incompetent, the benevolent and the vicious. As one explosive manufacturer put it: "If, in view of the increased restrictions proposed in the traffic of high explosives, these misguided persons undertake to manufacture it for themselves, there is left the grim satisfaction of knowing that they run a more than fair chance of blowing themselves to pieces with their own handiwork; their wretched compounds may be safely left to mete out deserved justice."[84]

Hearing of *attentats* in Europe, the American reading public was reassured of its safety with images of crippling failure, while amateur bomb-making discourse became a world not so enamored of the new as of repetition of the old. Then, in 1901, Leon Czolgosz shot President William McKinley at the Pan-American Exposition in Buffalo. Czolgosz expressed what appeared to the police and the public to be anarchist sentiments, and he represented a symbolic enemy upon which to vent public anger. If anticolonial bombing excursions in London had seemed remote and the Haymarket affair a local conflict met with swift justice, the assassination of a president was a different matter. The anarchist would loom as a national enemy for the next two decades, and discourses on sabotage and bomb making would appear in evidence roundups and the courts. The Haymarket trial had generated intense interest in free speech that would shape subsequent events. The courts would face the problem of a dangerous instructional speech associated with symbolic enemies again and again.

2

Sabotage

In the late nineteenth century, the chemists and engineers had presented themselves as the right hands for a new and dangerous knowledge of explosive power that had to be kept from the wrong hands of the bomb-throwing anarchists. The early twentieth century saw the coming of the official bomb squad and the celebrity detective, who were firmly on the side of capital in a battle against labor. The police created a new image of themselves not only as the right hands for knowledge of explosive devices, but also as arbiters of speech, determining what sort of speech—and what sort of speakers—had a bad tendency. It was up to the police, when they went on raids, to determine what texts threatened public order. The creator of the New York City bomb squad, Arthur Woods, warned, "We must be wary of strange doctrine, steady in judgment, instinctively repelling those who seek to poison public opinion. And our laws should be amended so that, while they give free scope to Americans for untrammeled expression of differences of opinion and theory and belief, they forbid and prevent the enemy plotter and the propagandist."[1] With their newly politicized roles in regulating society, law enforcement officials involved in federal policing would identify texts associated with groups they perceived dangerous to the state, channel these texts into the courts, and release carefully chosen information from them to the news media. Defense attorneys would challenge the admission of such texts, but the police would continue rounding them up. The forces of order made little effort to understand the texts' political arguments or to see them as anything other than transparent causes of inevitable violent effects. It was their duty to identify, arrest, and incarcerate dangerous instructional speech.

The multidimensional labor movement was divided on the question of violent revolution. A very few, like the Italian-American Galleanists, sought and disseminated secretive instructions on making explosive devices. They were mostly a danger to themselves and their immediate neighbors, but they did successfully pull off a major terrorist attack that alarmed the nation. The nonterroristic anarcho-syndicalists, however, gained the most attention from the police with mere talk of sabotage. As a movement to suppress anarchists swept across Europe and the United States, the state treated sabotage as an existential threat to the state that necessitated a harsh legal response.[2]

Health Is in You!

In 1906, an Italian anarchist newspaper, *Cronaca Sovversiva* (*Subversion Chronicle*), began running advertisements on its back pages for a book called *La Salute è in voi!* (*Health Is Within You!* or *Salvation Is Within You!*). This innocuous-sounding title was not a handbook of toasts, a moral essay, or a treatise on physical culture, but a bomb-making manual that gave plain directions for making powerful nitro explosives. With about five thousand subscribers,[3] *Cronaca Sovversiva* was the organ of the Galleanisti, a small group of Italian radicals inspired by Luigi Galleani, trained as a lawyer and a leading figure in the Italian anarchist movement in the United States. Hardened by his violent confrontation with the police during the Paterson silk strike in 1902, Galleani moved from advocating a general strike to urging heroic individual acts of revenge against capitalist oppressors. Like many advocates of terrorist acts before and after him, Galleani hoped that spectacular violence would inspire a popular revolution against the ruling class. His followers, the Galleanists, were the chief suspects in a wave of bombings between 1914 and 1920, including a series of mail bomb attacks on business tycoons and government officials and a car bombing on Wall Street that killed thirty-eight people in 1920.[4] *La Salute è in voi* was first used by the police to profile suspected anarchist bombers and then by historians as evidence of the Galleanists' violence and their likely culpability for long-unsolved crimes.

The dissembling title of the manual may have been an ironic reference to Leo Tolstoy's *Tsarstvo bozhie vnutri vas* (*The Kingdom of God Is Within You*), published in 1894 and translated in Italian as *La Salute è in voi*. In this now classic text of Christian anarchism, Tolstoy proposed nonviolent resistance to the inherent violence of the state. Criticizing bombs and riots as ineffective and a violation of Christian morality, Tolstoy advocated strategies of passive resistance, such as refusing to pay taxes, take oaths of allegiance, serve on juries, or take part in military service. Tolstoy believed that if a few people refused to cooperate with the state and lived a peaceful natural existence, other people would join them, creating an idyllic social life of freedom and love under divine law. It would be a slow process, he acknowledged, and unpopular with revolutionaries who desired more rapid change.

The anonymous authors of the violent *La Salute è in voi* were not so patient, urging oppressed workers to give up lamenting their tragic state and take revolutionary action. Lamention was an ineffective response that had only earned them further poverty and imprisonment. Rather, they should arm themselves with science. It was an error, the authors wrote, to promote revolution without giving workers the technical means for its implementation. That was an error they would remedy through a how-to handbook, their own practical version of the anarchist manifesto. Like its predecessor, *Revolutionäre Kriegswissenschaft*, *La Salute è in voi!* promised to deliver military technology into the hands of the people. The book was aimed at readers who lacked the practical expertise of engineers, chemists, and laborers in mining, construction, and agriculture. These industry workers did not need manuals to learn how to obtain dynamite or put together an effective bomb. *La Salute è in voi* was highly optimistic in its belief that untrained novices could create powerful explosions through reading simple directions.

The successful political bombings carried out in this period were by people who had hands-on training as laborers in industries where high explosives were regularly used. That was the case with the Bridge and Structural Ironworkers' Union, which orchestrated 110 bombings between 1905 and 1911 to extort employers in the building trade into granting union demands. The bombers sometimes used highly dangerous, volatile nitroglycerine, but could also readily acquire dynamite and circumvent local licensing regulations. As labor journalist Louis Adamic put it, "The iron-workers could easily get hold of 'the stuff'; there was always some around every big construction job."[5] Notorious criminal Albert Horsley, known as Harry Orchard, carried out a number of bombings in the western mining region, including the murder of Idaho's governor, using devices with dynamite, blasting caps, and acid and pressure detonators. His sensational account of his life, including narrative descriptions and photographs of his bombs, appeared in the popular *McClure's Magazine* in 1907, making it all seem frighteningly easy.[6] For workers in the textile industries and anarchist journalists, especially those in the eastern cities where the Galleanists' activities began, dynamite was not so readily available, and constructing strong effective bombs was not so well understood. The book's idea that an amateur could mix high explosives at home was, as it had always been, an impractical intellectual exercise.

Beyond the boundaries of the city, knowledge of using dynamite was widely disseminated through the sales efforts of companies like DuPont, which was busily diversifying its products and would get a huge boost in profit from wartime sales. Although their competitors often vilified the Du Ponts for holding a monopoly on gunpowder production, they were also upheld as cultural heroes. In a children's book on thrilling careers, detective writer and journalist Cleveland Moffett placed the DuPont dynamite worker alongside deep-sea divers, balloonists, and lion tamers: "I thought of the power for good and evil that is in this wonderful agent: dynamite piercing mountains; dynamite threatening armies and blowing up great ships; a teacupful of dynamite shattering a fortress, a teaspoonful of the essence of dynamite—that is, nitroglycerin—tearing a man to atoms. What kind of fellows must they be who spend their lives making dynamite!"[7] In the mythology of dynamite, one who had the bravery to make and handle it commanded the resources of the empire and fueled its spectacles of power over life and death. On the ground, the DuPont sales team had begun educational campaigns, including printed instructional booklets, to train rural consumers to use their explosives for grading roads, blowing up stumps and boulders, digging ditches, opening wells, and tunneling. Dynamite had also been used out in the countryside for slaughtering cattle, blowing fish out of the water, and bombing crow's nests. Testimonials in DuPont's manuals were included to encourage farmers to adopt dynamite for field clearing: "I am using a ton of dynamite a week in this work and with the capable force that I now have the results are marvelous. Great chestnut and oak stumps succumb to the dynamite as easily as lifting a match."[8] Dynamite could be purchased cheaply in the village grocery store. In the late nineteenth century, criminal uses for dynamite, like safecracking, extortion, and murder, had followed the path of its industrial dissemination. As it traveled to the western mining regions, dynamite was associated with the daring outlaw heroes of the James Gang. Use of dynamite was courage; knowledge of dynamite was power.

La Salute used dynamite's reputation to lift cowed, emotionally weak laborers to positions of physical and psychological strength. In an introductory verse, it invoked a town in northern Italy where, in 1890, women laboring in the rice fields went on strike for higher wages and marched to the town hall shouting, "We are starving!" When a striker threw a stone and struck a guard in the head, the waiting police fired on the crowd, killing three women and wounding nineteen others. Despite the eruption of violence, the action had been successful: the workers received the raise they demanded and produced exemplary martyrs. In the following years, peasants and laborers would organize rebellions across Italy to resist expropriation of their land and the repression of the state.[9] Rejecting peaceful responses to oppression, *La Salute* urged its readers to take vengeance for the deaths of their rebellious ancestors at Conselice: "Redemption springs from audacious revolt!"

The authors of the forty-eight-page manual called themselves the *compilatori*, the compilers, and the technical information in the book could be found in ordinary treatises on practical, applied chemistry. There was nothing new or rare in *La Salute è in voi*, no complex formulas or descriptions of elaborate time detonators. The handbook's formulas could be found in a variety of widely available industrial sources, including the standard manual: Martin Eissler's *A Handbook on Modern Explosives*, published in 1897. Ordinary encyclopedias carried the formula for nitroglycerine and the composition of dynamite alongside recipes for making cordials and bronzing metal.[10] *La Salute è in voi!*

demonstrated a workable knowledge of basic chemistry, and imparted a few chemical lessons, such as how to determine the density of a liquid using Beaumé's hydrometer, a somewhat inexact instrument employed in industry settings. This technique was important because commercial grades of various substances had to be tested for purity or they would not work well in the recipes. This kind of detail lifted the anarchist manual into the realm of a more serious technical understanding. As in a textbook, the compilers provided a list of technical terms and definitions.

The references to industrial techniques and instruments suggest that *La Salute*'s original authors knew something about chemistry. That connection most likely came through a prominent chemist and avowed anarchist, Ettore Molinari, who taught at the Polytechnic Institute of Milan. Molinari authored several well-known textbooks on applied chemistry and had befriended Luigi Galleani when he was exiled from Italy and living in Paris. Molinari is said to have written the prototype for *La Salute è in voi!*, if not the book itself. *La Salute* provides the prices for different chemical substances in lire, rather than dollars, so certainly Italy was its point of origin. The emphasis on scientific procedure separated *La Salute è in voi!* from its predecessors. It gave faith that, like students in a polytechnic institute, workers could grasp the textbook-like directions and set up their own domestic laboratories.

There was one printer's error in *La Salute* that would not have escaped a professional chemist. By substituting an "i" for a "1," the text greatly reduced the quantity of sulfuric acid to less than the quantity of nitric acid in the directions for making nitroglycerine. Sulfuric acid made nitric acid more reactive with glycerin and was therefore essential in precipitating nitroglycerine. To do this, the sulfuric acid had to exceed the quantity of nitric acid. *Cronaca Sovversiva* later ran a correction with the proper measurements. In my copy of *La Salute*, from the International Institute of Social History in Amsterdam, someone has marked the correction in a very neat hand, presumably to prevent any calamities. Several historians of the Galleanists have thought that the mistake made the mixture much more dangerous, and speculated that bomb makers might have blown themselves up because of it. In reality the mixture would have simply failed to produce nitroglycerine and ended up a smelly mess of corrosive acids. The correct mixture is much more dangerous than the mistaken one. Bomb-making manuals are often surrounded by urban legends that they will destroy their users because of deadly errors. Such rumors serve as a method of social prevention to ward off amateur experimentation. However, a very foolish person who attempts to make high explosives in the kitchen does not need an error to arrive at a fatal conclusion. Even if successful in making nitroglycerine, the chemist would be susceptible to violent headaches. *La Salute*'s authors were cognizant of the dangers, and like good science teachers, provided safety measures. For example, if some hapless bomber should accidently drink his nitric acid, he could take the helpfully provided antidote of magnesia and bicarbonate of soda.

La Salute combined its chemical techniques with domestic detail, similar to a farmer's almanac or household encyclopedia. In its list of chemical ingredients, it not only gave the density and degrees Beaumé for a substance but also discussed its household applications. Nitric acid could not only be used to make nitroglycerine but also to clean metal objects; glycerine was good for soothing a worker's chapped hands; phosphorus could be mixed in dough to kill mice. These references to ordinary uses for potentially dangerous chemicals could provide cover stories for possessing or purchasing them. If a zealous detective should wonder why a suspect had sulfuric acid in his possession, his answer might be that he was cleaning copper pots. An amateur chemist might also ascertain where to buy or steal these substances: nitric acid, for example, could be found at the goldsmiths and dry cleaners. These very innocuous details were partly what made *La Salute* seem so dangerous and subversive: Domestic spaces could transform into research-and-development laboratories.

For nearly a decade, *La Salute* circulated only among anarchists who were aware of its meaning, but in 1915 it surfaced dramatically in the public sphere when two young anarchists, Frank Abarno and Carmine Carbone, were arrested for attempting to bomb St. Patrick's Cathedral in New York City. This arrest was a setup by the newly formed New York City bomb squad, whose ambitious chief, Thomas Tunney, had sent an inexperienced detective, Amedeo Polignani, to infiltrate the anarchist Bresci Circle.[11] One of many small Italian anarchist groups, the Bresci Circle was named after Gaetano Bresci, an Italian American weaver from Paterson, New Jersey, who had assassinated Italy's King Umberto I. The police already suspected the Bresci group of a plot to blow up the home of John D. Rockefeller Jr., owner of the Ludlow coal mines in Colorado. There, the state militia had set fire to a camp of striking workers and their families, killing approximately twenty, including eleven children. It was precisely the kind of incident, as at Conselice, that would provoke the violent revenge urged by *La Salute*. A few months later, on July 14, 1914, three anarchists blew themselves up in a tenement near the Bresci group's headquarters in the Italian section of East Harlem. The anarchists had first walked with their bomb to Rockefeller's home in Tarrytown. They failed to deploy the device, but even if they had, they would not have killed Rockefeller since he was on vacation. They then traveled with the bomb back to East Harlem, where the fatal accident occurred, blowing up half the building where they kept their laboratory.[12] That autumn, four bombings occurred: at St. Patrick's Cathedral, St. Alphonsus's Church, the Bronx County Court House, and the Tombs police court.

While no one took responsibility for these bombings, the city police saw them as evidence of an anarchist conspiracy and deployed Polignani as a spy in the Bresci group. In the typical fashion of the agent provocateur who trades in knowledge and power to gain acceptance, Polignani offered technical expertise as his way into the group. Disguised as "Frank Baldo," he befriended Frank Abarno, a twenty-five-year-old electrotyper, and Carmine Carbone, an eighteen-year-old shoemaker. By Abarno's and Carbone's accounts, Polignani approached them after a meeting, advocated dynamite as a political weapon, and convinced them that they should set off a bomb in St. Patrick's Cathedral. By Polignani's account, it was Carbone who had drawn him out of the meeting and suggested that they blow up the church. Later, Abarno gave Polignani a booklet that Carbone had bought for 15 cents at the Bresci Circle: *La Salute è in voi*. Polignani turned it over to the bomb squad for copying. With some of the ingredients purchased by Polignani himself and in a room Polignani had hired, the three men constructed two bombs with an explosive made of sulfur, brown sugar, black antimony, and chlorate of potash. This recipe was not based on information from *La Salute*, but was rather a well-known kind of explosive mixture used in fireworks. The bombers packed the explosive into soap tins and bound iron rods to the outside with coat hanger wire to act as shrapnel.

On March 2, 1915, Polignani and Abarno walked to St. Patrick's Cathedral with the bombs concealed under their coats, with a plan to set them off during a mass attended by hundreds of people. Carbone had declined to go, saying that he had worked late and needed his sleep. All along their journey, Abarno and Polignani were shadowed by the police, including Thomas Tunney in a limousine; fifty officers in disguise were deployed at the church. The two men entered the church and sat in the tenth pew. Then, after resting a moment as if in prayer, Abarno rose and placed his bomb near the north altar. He was immediately arrested by a police lieutenant disguised as a scrubwoman, while another officer disguised as an usher inspected the bomb, supposedly pinching out the fuse with his fingers. (Abarno claimed that he had never lit the fuse.) Afterwards, the bomb squad proudly stood for news photographs.

Newspapers across the country carried the story that the arrests of Abarno and Carbone were evidence of a powerful conspiracy, the first sally in a terrorist plot to bomb New York City. Tunney and the bomb squad fully participated in sensationalizing the events. They told reporters that Abarno and Carbone wanted to blow up the churches, the crypts, and the homes of the Rockefellers, the Carnegies, and the Vanderbilts, and allow the army of the poor to pillage the hoards of the rich. Against this threat to civilization, the bomb squad stood ready. Newspapers across the country carried photographs of the police officers dressed as smiling scrubwomen and of Owen Egan, chief inspector with the Bureau of Combustibles, who held up the bombs with their tangled wires. He was visible proof of the potential power of such bombs since he had recently had his face badly burned and his right hand mangled from defusing a package bomb sent to a judge.[13] He held a certain authority when he spoke of the bombers wrenching the iron parts from mansion fences to use as shrapnel. The story had its hero, Amedeo Polignani, who was featured in many newspapers as the young officer who had lived in the anarchist underworld and learned its secrets, including the mysteries of an anarchist bomb book.

While never mentioned by title, *La Salute è in voi* figured prominently in these stories as having taught Abarno and Carbone how to make bombs. Polignani had borrowed the book and had it photocopied by the bomb squad. This was an important component of the police's version, since other anarchists and labor activists had cast their suspicions that Polignani was a provocateur and had provided the expertise.[14] He had bought the ingredients for the bombs and had participated very actively in the plot. The police insinuated that the bombs were based on the directions in *La Salute* when this was not the case—the book did not contain instructions for the explosive mixture. Reference to the bomb manual helped sensationalize the case and rest the blame on Adorno and Carbone for having the technical knowledge to initiate the scheme. In his recounting of the case, Tunney later wrote that "mere possession of this wicked treatise would suggest that the owner was up to no good, especially if the owner, in this case, was known to be a volatile member of an anarchist circle who had already declared his intentions of wrecking something."[15] Before they obtained a lawyer, as they were on their way to their cells in the Tombs, Abarno and Carbone made rash statements to the press, including Abarno's admission that he had learned to make bombs from Carbone's copy of *La Salute*. With little command of English, Carbone told reporters that he didn't know what was in the book when he bought it and "thought it was something else—what you call it—spice." A reporter asked, "Then, why did you keep it?" Carbone answered, "I'd bought it. What would I do with it?"[16] Both Abarno and Carbone asserted that they'd been framed.

During the arraignment, hoping for clemency, Abarno unwisely told the judge that reading had deranged him, thus opening up that discussion for the court. During the trial, the prosecutor introduced a variety of anarchist books and pamphlets to prove the defendants' violent, seditious intentions. The right to read thus became central to defense attorney Simon Pollock's case. In his closing statement at the trial, Pollock argued that Abarno and Carbone "had a right to discuss matters of any kind, that they had a right to read books of any kind."[17] Furthermore, he said, "it is not for the District Attorney to denounce these boys because they availed themselves of the rights and liberties acquired by our forefathers in their historic struggles for American citizenship."[18] Since *La Salute* was the most sensational reading material introduced into evidence, Pollock argued for his clients' constitutional right to possess even bomb-making manuals. Asserting that it was Polignani who had urged the purchase of "a certain book containing descriptions of explosives," Pollock refuted Polignani's statement in court that the explosive had been made after a formula found in it: "I examined that book and did not find a formula of this kind in the book, and I challenge him or the District Attorney to find that formula in that book!"[19] When Pollock demanded that the explosive be produced, the police said that they had disposed of it, but a chemist testified that it was nothing more dangerous than could be found in an ordinary firework. There was no proof that *La Salute è in voi* had anything to do with the crime; it had been introduced to further demonize the defendants. Nevertheless, the prosecution won its case, and the judge sentenced Abarno and Carbone to six to twelve years in prison, less than the maximum sentence of twelve to twenty-five years.[20]

The Abarno/Carbone case revived the fear of the dynamite book and the sensationalism of anarchist mysteries. The fledgling NYPD bomb squad had been formed to fight the anarchist menace, taking over from the Fire Department's Bureau of Combustibles. The Bureau of Combustibles had defused hundreds of bombs over the years—bombs used mostly in extortion rackets and for revenge against employers, competitors, law officers, and estranged lovers.[21] It was readily apparent that the expertise for making primitive, low-energy bombs was widespread, yet most bombings were confined to neighborhood crime. The Galleanists espoused war against the ruling elites—a symbolic war on a grand scale that accommodated heroes and martyrs on both sides. A mysterious technical book promised extravagant power to anarchists but also provided concrete evidence to detectives. During the Red Scare, the offices of *Cronaca Sovversiva* were raided, and Luigi Galleani deported, but his adherents continued to plan terrorist attacks that caused widespread outrage.

A more sober view of the sporadic bomb attempts associated with the Galleanists suggests delusions of grandeur and general incompetence among the bombers, although it takes only one successful bombing covered by the national media to provoke fears of imminent menace and waves of repression. Three bombers were killed in the tenement explosion after the attempt on Rockefeller's life. Similarly, as part of a strike action in Franklin, Massachusetts, in 1919, four young Italian anarchists blew themselves up trying to plant a bomb at the American Woolen Company. Another Galleanist, Carlo Valdinoci, blew himself up when, in that same year, he gave himself no time to escape a bomb he planted on the doorstep of Attorney General Palmer. In the mode of the nineteenth-century press's moralizing sensationalism, the gruesome consequences for the bomber were noted in the *New York Times*: his leg was found on the doorstep across the street, a section of his spinal cord flew through a bedroom of a minister's home, and an incriminating portion of his head was found a block away on a mansion roof.[22] On several other occasions, the police confiscated bombs before they exploded or the bombs failed, as was the case with most of the thirty-six package bombs mailed to government officials and industry magnates in 1919. One postal worker was alerted to the danger when he noticed several packages that had been held because of insufficient postage. None of the Galleanists' bombs ever reached their intended targets, the robber barons, overzealous detectives, and conservative judges who courted their vengeance. They injured only bystanders or themselves.

If any of the bombers used *La Salute* as their textbook (and there is no evidence that they did), it proved inadequate for constructing fail-safe devices and anticipating difficulties in their deployment. Skirting the familiar thin line between political violence and ordinary criminality, the tactics they often used for deploying bombs were taken from the playbook of extortion rackets: the bombers would distribute a written threat of further violent attack ("pay or die") and place the device in a doorway to terrorize the victim. However, the extortionists—many of them Italian immigrants associated with the "Black Hand" gangs—usually used proven bombs based on popular fireworks that they had learned to make in Italy, where pyrotechnics was a thriving industry. These fireworks consisted of a chemical mix placed in a paper tube, artfully wrapped in twine and heavily coated with shellac to increase the force of the blast. The extortionists adapted these fireworks by packing them with shrapnel of nails, slugs, and scrap iron. They also sometimes used dynamite, stolen from construction sites, encasing the sticks in cement for greater resistance and force. The Black Hand bombs did considerable damage to buildings and were effective at terrorizing business owners and government officials.

Amateur bomb-making enterprises usually reveal the expertise available in the surrounding community, and types of bombs are chosen either because they have symbolic significance in a group's history or because they have proven effectiveness within that group's knowledge and experience. High explosives like nitroglycerine and dynamite were novel to anarchists, who had no hands-on experience of them. Without practical experience or community know-how, the anarchists and other political bombers routinely overrated their ability to handle high explosives and create workable time bombs. The anarchists' faith in their own engineering was well beyond their means. Their bombs were too ambitious, using time devices and sensitive chemical detonators that promised anonymity and quick getaways but which carried a significantly greater risk than they had assumed. Along with novelty and technical complexity came much greater danger of accidental explosions and component failure through jarring, friction, and faulty construction.

Nevertheless, the Galleanists' proficiency increased enough by 1920 for one of their members to successfully plant a car bomb on Wall Street, killing thirty-eight people. Police investigators—and later historians—believed this to be an act of revenge for the criminal indictment of two of the most famous anarchists in US history, Ferdinando Nicola Sacco and Bartolomeo Vanzetti, who were accused of murdering two payroll guards during a holdup. Many historians strongly suspect that Mario Buda, a Galleanist and close friend of the accused, carried out the Wall Street attack.[23] Initially trained in the textile and cleaning industries, Buda had spent time in an iron-mining district of Michigan in 1917 as the Galleanists prepared revenge attacks on public officials who had offended them.[24] He could very well have become more experienced with dynamite there. With its timed detonator and gelatin dynamite, the bomb was far more sophisticated than anything found in *La Salute*. Giving himself only minutes to spare, the bomber—perhaps Buda—took his horse and wagon, loaded with the bomb, to the corner of Wall and Broad Streets and parked across from J. P. Morgan and Company. He had timed the explosion to go off at noon, when the streets were crowded with office workers. Five copies of a leaflet were discovered in a nearby mailbox, printed with the extortionist demand to "free the political prisoners or it will be sure death for all of you."[25]

The authorities did not comply, and when Sacco and Vanzetti were denied their appeal and realized that they were on their way to the electric chair, they issued a final missive to their supporters, ending with the call, "*La Salute è in voi*." Both the anarchists and their pursuers would have understood the meaning of Sacco and Vanzetti's implied threat. The book had not been mentioned in the trial: it had little relevance to the case since the men were not accused of a bombing. In the background, however, the anarchist detectives saw *La Salute è in voi* as critical evidence for a Galleanist conspiracy. J. Edgar Hoover, youthful head of the Department of Justice's Central Intelligence Division (formerly the Radical Division), launched an intense search for the original pamphlet during his investigation of the package bombs and Wall Street attack when he couldn't find it in any of the disorganized federal files. Later, like the detectives, historians would use the book in their verdicts on the revolutionary violence of Sacco and Vanzetti, though no direct evidence exists that the two men ever owned, much less used, the book.[26] The importance of *La Salute è in voi* was its iconic presence, its aura of violent technical capabilities stolen from the state, rather than in any practical information or concrete evidence contained therein. Because it was in Italian, accessible to a small number of people, and read only by a small group of anarchists and detectives, *La Salute è in voi!* had limited resonance and faded quickly from view after the trial of Sacco and Vanzetti. It had proved, once again, that just the existence of such a book could challenge the authority of the state. Much of its meaning existed in the "danse macabre" between the police and the Galleanists, who both used it to generate support, rationalize violence, and inflate organizational power.

Anarchist Bombs in Popular Culture

A few years after the Wall Street attack, *Scientific American* ran a picture of a mock-up of the bomb: gelatin dynamite attached to two dry cell batteries and a clock, surrounded by iron shrapnel, positioned neatly in a wooden wagon. This reconstruction was the work of journalist Roy Giles with the help of Charles Robb from the Burns Detective Agency and NYPD bomb squad commander James Gegan, who was known for his aggressive pursuit of anyone he thought was a Bolshevik. Robb and Gegan were worried that if they showed every detail of the bomb, they'd attract a copycat killer. They would only offer their expertise if Giles left out the connections linking the explosive to the timer. The managing editor of *Scientific American*, Austin Lescarboura, concurred that he had "no desire to conduct a course in the technical details of bomb-making for the benefit of everybody who may have access to this issue of our journal."[27] For the first time in the media's coverage of bombs, a journal had publicly discussed the ethics of disseminating information about explosive devices through the visual image.

Before this moment, books, journals, and newspapers had published unexpurgated descriptions of bombs with enthusiasm, in an appeal to public curiosity. In the late nineteenth century, technical illustrations of bombs used in political assassinations and other crimes accompanied accounts of sensational bombing cases, usually associated with groups that seemed to threaten civilization. Bombs became aesthetic objects as technological fascination trumped fear. With the widespread use of photography in early twentieth-century print media, photographs of explosive devices accompanied detailed articles on bomb squad detectives and anarchist hunters.[28] Narrative descriptions of bombs were sometimes elaborate, as in this popular account of a highly unstable clockwork bomb found in a railroad yard in East Peoria:

> They had sawed out a piece of board about the width of a barrel-stave and, say, nine inches long, and they had fastened a small dry battery to it with wires that held the battery lying on its side. In front of the battery they had fastened a little alarm-clock. There was the usual thumb-key on the back of the clock to wind the alarm, and they had soldered to the flap of this thumb-key a thin strip of metal bent down in such a way that if the key were turned the strip would make a contact with another strip that had been attached to one of the poles of the battery. A telephone wire led from the clock to a ten-quart can of nitroglycerin; and there was a fulminating-cap on the end of it in the glycerin. Another wire completed the circuit from the battery into the cap.[29]

This account was given to *McClure's* by William J. Burns, head of the Burns Detective Agency, who had served in the US Secret Service. He had no reservations in 1911 about giving this narrative description of a bomb—one that could be emulated by a technically adept amateur.

A friend of Arthur Conan Doyle and a true-crime writer himself,[30] Burns enjoyed telling stories of his pursuit of the bombers with detailed descriptions of the devices he and his men had found. Like his rival, Allan Pinkerton, Burns had a detective agency and provided popular accounts of his spying activities to promote both his profession and, more importantly, himself. Burns especially courted popularity after his successful pursuit of bombers Ortie McManigal and James and John McNamara, members of the International Association of Bridge and Structural Ironworkers, who were responsible for a string of bombings (Burns counted eighty-three) against business owners who ran closed shops. In 1911 they had bombed the *Los Angeles Times* building with a clockwork device, leaving twenty people dead. Burns wrote a book about his detective work on the case: *The Masked War: The Story of a Peril that Threatened the United States, by the Man Who Uncovered the Dynamite Conspirators and Sent Them to Jail.* While these bombings of company property were more accurately described as extortion aimed at the labor union's local enemies, Burns conjured the state's imminent extinction: "The war with dynamite was a war of Anarchy against the established form of government of this country. It was masked under the cause of Labor. This is not figurative at all. It is fact."[31] *The Masked War* contained descriptions of bombs so detailed that they advised on the manufacturers of potential bomb parts: "The battery was a Columbia dry battery, No. 5, and the clock was an intermittent alarm clock, made by the New Haven Clock Company."[32] Burns provided these details to give readers, whom he addressed as "the great majority of American citizens who take life complacently," a vicarious experience of Holmesian-style detection.[33] The enemy had to be constructed as diabolically clever: Burns claimed that the clockwork bomb described above was James McNamara's own design.[34] The detective had the social and scientific authority to decipher the meaning of these details, with the reader standing as a version of Watson. Within this knowledge regime, bombs could be contained within tacit assumptions about benign detectives and their readers who would never use such details for evildoing. The satisfying ending was the capture of frighteningly adept enemies—the "fiends"—and their just punishments for using technology to destroy the civilization that produced it.

Other publicity-seeking detectives followed Burns in his pursuit of fame through anarchist chasing and bomb detection. Head of the Secret Service William J. Flynn became famous for his successful capture of German saboteurs operating in and around New York harbor during World War I and would later edit his own crime-writing magazine. In *The Eagle's Eye*, originally a silent educational film transformed by a ghostwriter into a nonfiction book, Flynn told his readers how to use dry phosphorus to burn wheat fields—more detailed than any advice found in the sabotage pamphlets—while railing against the Industrial Workers of the World (IWW) as tools of the German kaiser.[35] A fictionalized account of the pursuit of the German saboteurs—representing Flynn as "Bill Quinn"—featured a red-headed Irish librarian, Mary, at the New York Public Library who notices a strange man with pointed, lobeless ears reading from "Shelf Forty-five." The ears were important because Mary had been reading the criminologist Cesare Lombroso and knew that pointed ears meant the atavistic tendencies of the fox. Thus follows a conversation between Mary and her dashing Treasury agent, Dick: "'And—do you know what books are kept on Shelf Forty-five?' 'No, what?' 'The latest works on the chemistry of explosives!'"[36] Thus readers discovered where they might go for information on how to make a bomb, and librarians would later feature heavily in controversies over the availability of bomb-making information. With his attractive public media presence, Flynn would go on to become head of the FBI, preceding William Burns and J. Edgar Hoover.

Thomas Tunney, head of the NYPD bomb squad, wrote *Throttled!* about his pursuit of anarchists, Bolsheviks, and German spies, promoting his work as consultant to police departments across the country who were forming their own bomb squads.[37] Tunney included a few pages from *La Salute è in voi!*, in an English translation, but left out the chemical compositions.[38] It is unlikely that the general public would have had any knowledge of this book's contents without Tunney's revelation, since previously the police had only alluded to it and never mentioned it by name. Tunney's point was that the police were the proper holders of dangerous knowledge, and he dispensed just enough information to show how necessary the bomb detectors were for public safety. He warned that the bomb squad had only a photocopy of the original *La Salute è in voi*, which was still out there in circulation: "There are probably other copies from the same press in the hands of accredited bomb-throwers. If not, they may apply to the New York police department."[39] Tunney was a Bolshevik hunter: He testified before Senate hearings on "Bolshevik propaganda," reporting on a public appearance by Leon Trotsky.[40]

At a time when more sophisticated police agencies were drawn to scientific methods of detection and classification of criminals, Tunney described his own acquisition of bomb-making expertise as he became "something of a student of chemistry." He went to the DuPont office in New York and consulted Charles Munroe, expert for the US Bureau of Mines, a federal agency charged with explosives safety and research. Both DuPont and the Bureau of Mines dispensed information about explosives for free. These publications contained much more detailed information about obtaining, handling, and using high explosives than anything found in *La Salute è in voi!*. The technical language and specifications from the Bureau of Mines would be daunting without professional training or guidance, but the publications from DuPont were aimed at consumers with little knowledge of the new explosives' technologies. Tunney admitted that he had only a theoretical knowledge of explosive devices and had never made one himself: "The laboratory chemist mixes ingredients and counts his work done at the moment of explosion; the detective begins at that moment a stern chase, and a long one, back to the ingredients and the man who mixed them."[41] Yet even as Tunney read about explosive compositions in these seemingly benign government and corporate texts, the same information in *La Salute è in voi* had for him a completely different tenor. Of *La Salute*'s "exposition of making nitroglycerine," he wrote, "the mere reading . . . would make your hair bristle."[42] He pointed to *La Salute*'s warning that dynamite manufacturers should make their products more resistant to shock under freezing temperatures—familiar advice in official treatises on the same subject—as evidence of the book's diabolical nature. In their narratives, even as they dispensed details about bomb making, the celebrity detectives returned these technologies to the safe fold of modern police investigation, establishing order over the errant information and its deviant users.[43]

Facing great physical risk and trauma during their encounters with explosive devices, these detectives had a special interest in texts that talked of political violence while promising the practical means. Burns expressed his fears that his enemies in the ironworkers union were planting suitcases filled with nitroglycerine in hotel rooms next to his. Writing of *La Salute è in voi!*, Tunney remembered that as soon as he saw the book, he felt an immense protective fear for his protégé, Amedeo Polignani, who had infiltrated the Bresci Circle. Detectives who encountered bombs told the news media of the perilous risk they had faced. The persons most likely to be targeted and injured by bombers were business tycoons, government officials, and detectives and police officers, a rather small class among the general population. The celebrity detectives saw themselves as agents of the state and representatives of the body politic. If they were in danger, the very existence of the nation was in danger.

Sabotage

La Salute è in voi represented a potential for terrorism, but during the Red Scare, another much milder form of instructional publication provoked the state more than any bomb-making manual. Just before Christmas in 1917, energized by their purpose of defending the wartime nation against dangerous subversives, agents from the Department of Justice pulled up to the headquarters of the Industrial Workers of the World in Chicago and ransacked it for evidence, carrying away truckloads of print material, and even the typewriters. In a wartime nation in no mood for tolerance of criticism and dissent, the IWW's free speech agit-prop in town centers, its questioning of the reasons for war, and its calls for disruptions of wartime manufacturing had brought down the heavy hand of the law. Growing in influence among the wheat harvesters, loggers, and copper miners of the Northwest, the IWW had been under federal and local surveillance for some time, and law enforcement collected any text with the word "sabotage" as evidence of nefarious doings. Songbooks with lyrics that used the image of a black cat or a wooden shoe—the IWW's icons for rebellion—were flagged as evidence: "A sab-cat and a wobbly band, / a rebel song or two, / And then we'll show the parasites / Just what the cat can do."[44] One could not even sing about sabotage without accusations of treasonous associations with the kaiser, much less have in one's possession a sabotage pamphlet. In September 1917, federal raids were carried out on IWW offices and 166 persons arrested for violating the new sedition and espionage statutes. One hundred were eventually tried, the prosecution waving sabotage pamphlets as evidence of treason and conspiracy.

In his opening argument at the trial, defense attorney George Vanderveer declared, "You will find here in the Chicago Library five times as much literature on sabotage as we ever saw, all open for reading. Courses of instruction on sabotage and direct action and everything else are taught at Harvard, Princeton, Stanford and in universities everywhere. The I. W. W. has sold these books, partly for revenue, partly because we believe that education about anything, right or wrong, is a good thing."[45] Vanderveer evoked the time-honored argument that violent word and deed was more prevalent on the side of capital than labor and justified an open flow of knowledge, but what he meant by "sabotage" was an open question. Though the word was never well defined by the IWW, the federal agents and most mainstream newspapers were sure that labor agitators were destroying property through convenient accidents, purposeful neglect, and outright destruction of equipment. Theoretical discussions took place in the Federal Building courtroom over what action would constitute sabotage. Prosecutors explored the limits of a definition: Taking the drive wheel off a steam engine? Breaking the wheels? Leaving a nut loose on a machine?[46] No evidence could be found that any of the men had participated in such actions; all of them were found guilty. The stiffest sentences went to fifteen of the IWW's organizers: twenty years in prison.

At the height of the Red Scare, culminating from a long conflict between capital and labor, dangerous instructional speech was again at issue. Heavy with theory exploring the relationship between boss and worker in newly technologized workplaces, the IWW sabotage pamphlets were mild in comparison to Johann Most's revolutionary dynamite talk—milder than any other text included in this book—but they helped justify the government's severe repression of radical organizations. Teaching IWW doctrines was tantamount to incitement and sabotage. The perceived threat shifted from violence against persons to violence against capitalist property. Talk of destroying industrial products and equipment to gain labor demands was considered by federal agents and prosecutors to be the most heinous, unpatriotic assault on the nation. The court fights over sabotage influenced a progressive evolution in free speech jurisprudence and greater tolerance for political speech. Yet, the federal surveillance of radicals built a framework for law officers to criminalize speech they personally found threatening to their values and their persons. The legal contradiction between tolerance and criminalization exists to this day.

The sabotage pamphlets of the IWW in some ways prefigured the later handbooks of practical tips on how to destroy a political enemy's property, as circulated by groups like the Animal Liberation Front and the Army of God. They turned rebellious attention to property, rather than persons—a focus that would carry an arguable ethical distinction in works of this kind. The IWW pamphlets, however, were devoted almost entirely to educating the worker on the theory of why, rather than how. Based on the sabotage pamphlets' somewhat vague threat to workplace operations, federal and state authorities interpreted them as practical manuals that radicals would inevitably use against the industrial system. These texts developed such an aura of menace that many persons went to jail or were deported simply for owning them. Confiscated under dubious circumstances, they were often used to prove a suspect's membership in organizations alleged to "teach" sabotage and terrorism. For example, California's criminal syndicalism law, passed in April 1919, applied to anyone who "willfully and deliberately by spoken and deliberate words justifies or attempts to justify criminal syndicalism or the commission or attempt to commit crime, sabotage, violence or unlawful methods of terrorism with intent to approve, advocate or further the doctrine of criminal syndicalism." It also forbade anyone from organizing or assembling to "teach" criminal syndicalism.[47] As the prosecutions unfolded, it was clear that mere possession of sabotage pamphlets meant advocacy and teaching of sabotage.

Enacted by many states during the Red Scare, the criminal syndicalism laws specifically targeted the IWW, which advocated an economic and political system of "one big union" controlled by workers. Four pamphlets, all with the word "sabotage" in the title, became red flags to the police detectives and prosecuting attorneys bent on persecuting the Wobblies. They were Emile Pouget's *Sabotage* (1910), William Trautman's *Direct Action and Sabotage* (1912), Walker C. Smith's *Sabotage: Its History, Philosophy and Purpose* (1913), and Elizabeth Gurley Flynn's *Sabotage: The Conscious Withdrawal of the Worker's Industrial Efficiency* (1916).

Anarcho-syndicalist Emile Pouget theorized sabotage for a generation of labor radicals. After spending three years in prison for his participation in a riotous demonstration on unemployment in Paris, he gained international popularity through his writings on revolutionary syndicalism, a theory that rejected political reform in favor of a mass uprising of workers who would overthrow the capitalist elites.[48] In 1896, partly inspired by an 1895 English labor pamphlet entitled *Ca Cannie* (meaning to work inefficiently in protest of unfair labor conditions), Pouget began promoting sabotage—"bad work for bad pay"—as a way of incrementally motivating workers to the higher goal of revolution. One of France's largest confederation of trade unions officially adopted his approach, and the French police—traditionally less restrained in their persecution of radical speech than in the United States—hounded and finally chased Pouget into exile in London under charges for incitement.

Pouget's *Sabotage*, first published in France in 1910, laid out the rationale for such tactics, and while not really a how-to book, contained inventive examples to inspire a worker's rebellious creativity. "Accidentally" dropping a trowel down a smoke shaft. Sprinkling water on a cement wagon. Adulterating varnishes to turn them black. Damaging silk with oily fingers. Boiling stones in soup. Putting sand in machine gears. Cutting telegraph wires before a strike. Pouget's examples of sabotage needed no specialized knowledge—the knowledge of scientific elites—but rather depended on opportunity, deviousness, and the available tools at hand. But beyond a few inventive suggestions, Pouget was far more interested in ethical justifications for sabotage. French workers, he explained, had transformed the meaning of the word "sabotage" into "a new form of social warfare."[49] Sabotage literally meant to make wooden shoes (*sabots*), but was also a slang expression for working clumsily. (A more romantic version of the word's origin came from a popular labor legend of striking French weavers who threw their shoes into the looms before walking out of a mill.) For Pouget, sabotage represented the natural, ancient conflict between capital and labor, and ill-treated workers often used the tactic "unconsciously and instinctively."[50] His goal was to organize this activity into a formal revolutionary method, on par with boycotting and striking. Comparing sabotage to guerrilla warfare, Pouget promoted ceaseless class warfare that would keep workers in fighting trim and encourage individual initiative and psychological toughness.

Pouget argued that workers must seize the tools controlled by elites, echoing the Marxist argument that elites controlled the resources of civilization that workers must reclaim. Anarchist bomb-making manuals focused on a Promethean theft of explosive energies, while Pouget maintained that workers already had tools in their possession that they could use to their own ends, if they only realized their strength. It was within their power to use these tools slowly and inefficiently, or even alter or destroy them outright. For example, some disgruntled workers had filed their spades down to a smaller size to reduce the dirt they shoveled. This was a concrete sign to the boss that their wages were too low and that they would work accordingly. As would become a familiar cautionary in sabotage manuals, Pouget laid out certain prohibitions against harming people: bakers could not wage a class war by poisoning the bread. Rather, bakers could more effectively refuse the boss's orders to adulterate the bread with cheap ingredients and run up his costs by using the finest ones. It was the boss who was the real saboteur, sabotaging the baker's skill by forcing him to poison the consumer with adulterants. If workers fully used their skill and expertise, they could sabotage the boss's sabotage. Pouget also had distaste for the secrecy that helped keep the boss in power. He advocated an "open-mouthed sabotage": whistle blowing on unethical business practices and revealing industrial secrets to damage the boss's profits. Vacillating between the call to damage equipment or merely slow down work production, Pouget's *Sabotage* never advocated murder. The actions described were aimed at technical systems rather than persons.

Nevertheless, a portion of the labor movement considered *Sabotage* a troubling development. The book's English translation was published first by a New York City commercial publisher and then by Charles H. Kerr, Chicago editor of the *International Socialist Review*. In the first decade of the twentieth century, Kerr's publishing house introduced readers to European scientific socialism and worked to advance the socialist program in the United States.[51] One of the founders of the IWW, William "Big Bill" Haywood, became associate editor of the *International Socialist Review* in 1911 and worked closely with Kerr. Influenced by European anarcho-syndicalists whom he had met on his travels, Haywood advocated direct action and sabotage, a position highly controversial among trade unionists and socialists, many of whom preferred strategies of peaceful negotiation and political action.[52] Hardened by his brutal encounters with strikebreaking state militias and local police, Haywood gave an instantly famous speech at Cooper Union to contentious members of the Socialist Party of America, urging them to throw off their "law abiding" identities and bring "anguish to the boss" with "a little sabotage in the right place at the proper time."[53] However, confusion existed as to the meaning of sabotage, since it could mean a work slowdown or more physical damage to equipment. The open provocation drew strong criticism from socialist leaders like Eugene Debs, later imprisoned for speaking against the war, who rightly worried that such speech "played into the hand of the enemy" by opening the doors to madmen, spies, and agent provocateurs.[54] The Socialist Party passed a resolution against sabotage, and Haywood was expelled from its executive committee as a signal to socialists to proceed with caution. With its educational missions and reasoned ethical arguments, Pouget's *Sabotage* entered this controversy.

IWW leaders pursued the concept of sabotage as a means of direct action, psychological empowerment, and symbolism that dramatized the struggle. To unify workers as political agitators and to create a sense of common struggle, they cultivated youthful, militant, heroic identities—the Rebel Boy and the Rebel Girl—in a protest culture of song and poetry, cartoons, pageantry, parades, and public performance.[55] The federal government was suspicious of their disobedient public personas, vocal disruptions of quiet communities, resistance to patriotism and war, and purposeful confrontations with law and order. Historians of the Wobblies have concluded that their expressions of violence were mostly talk; Melvyn Dubofsky called their rhetoric a "vocabulary of violence" that served their image, whereas their tactical strategies were mostly civil disobedience and passive resistance.[56] Talk of sabotage could steel workers for the cause and frame their identities as strong and confrontational rather than weak and slavish. One of the IWW's familiar, knowing icons, a black sabotage cat with its arched back and exposed claws, was meant to give an aura of witchy menace and a superstitious chill to the bosses in the spirit of the bluff.[57] The sabotage advocated, however, was the slowdown and subtle manipulation of the workplace rather than the "terrorism," "vicious sabotage," and "intentional injury to or destruction of property" imagined by the Minnesota Supreme Court when it upheld the conviction under a new criminal syndicalism law of IWW member Matt Moilen, who had put up a few 1½″-square "posters" of the black cat and the wooden shoe around the small mining village of Biwabik.[58] In the run-up to the first Red Scare, the court feared terrorism by sticker.

Soon held up by Attorney General A. Mitchell Palmer as evidence of the vast Red conspiracy,[59] the IWW's own sabotage pamphlets echoed Pouget's, arguing that workers had the power to use the industrial system for their own ends, disrupting the new efficiencies, speed-ups, and cost-cutting strategies of scientific management.[60] Referring to worker resistance to the employer's unrelenting pressure for speed, Walker Smith wrote, "The time clock has come in as the sign that the boss recognizes the instinctive sabotage that is universal."[61] In the spirit of much Marxist literature that set out to expose the inner workings of the industrial system, the pamphlets emulated Pouget: the capitalists were the real saboteurs. In the wake of Upton Sinclair's *The Jungle*—a blend of fiction and muckraking journalism that exposed the grotesque production of meat in Chicago's packing houses—the sabotage pamphlets used the example of adulteration of consumer products to make the point. The pamphlets explained rather than advised a protest method. The authors asserted that they weren't advocating sabotage, but simply revealing the dynamics of the workplace already in play.

Defending journalist Frederick Sumner Boyd, who had been arrested and imprisoned for advocating destruction of property during the Paterson silk strike, Elizabeth Gurley Flynn used her *Sabotage* to expose hidden, unethical business practices that harmed both worker and consumer. In the exploitative silk industry, she explained, silk garments contained much more than silk. Metals like tin and lead were added in the manufacturing to reduce cost, producing a much less durable garment. The process was called "dynamiting," a metaphor that Flynn knowingly used to accuse the silk manufacturers of anarchistic sabotage and to suggest that workers might steal this technique and use it to their own advantage. What was the line, she asked, between manufacturers "dynamiting" their own garments and workers doing the same to show consumers "how absolutely unusable the silk actually is that they are passing off on the public at two and three dollars a yard"?[62] Flynn's emphasis on this metaphor resonated with the anarchist weapons manuals that argued for workers secretively taking dynamite and turning it against those in power. However, Flynn saw interfering with the quality of consumer products as a nonviolent act: "Sabotage is not physical violence; sabotage is an internal, industrial process."[63] Flynn argued that workers naturally found means of resistance using (or not using) the tools at hand within an exploitative system. Flynn's discourse was replete with military metaphors. Popularly known as the new Joan of Arc because of her gender, youth, and fiery oratory, Flynn positioned worker sabotage as the natural outgrowth of imagination, inventiveness, and political passion, and her pamphlet encouraged the worker to "don his shining armor of industrial power" and to raise the "shining sword" of sabotage.[64] Flynn wrote *Sabotage*, in part, as a defense of free speech, but she would later regret it, as the book began to appear as evidence in the repressive political trials of IWW members. *Sabotage*, she later wrote, "was a form of infantile Leftism in a big way, consisting largely of 'sound and fury, signifying nothing.'"[65] (Flynn herself infamously bargained her way out of a conviction, leading historian Melvyn Dubofsky to later call her a deserter and a "headline hog.")[66]

Between 1909 and 1913, the IWW, including Flynn, had been engaged in fights over free speech as communities attempted to suppress soapbox speeches and distribution of radical labor literature during organizing efforts and strikes. Because the membership of the IWW was comprised of many migrant laborers, they could move from town to town organizing other workers and engaging in civil disobedience. They would often encounter local hostility and were frequently thrown in jail for seditious, incendiary, and unpatriotic speech, actions that also generated publicity for the organization and encouraged it to seek out further conflicts over speech. The IWW was distrustful of a legal and political system that served only the elites but supported the basic notion of free speech for airing grievances and testing ideas. When local ordinances were passed against public speech in response to labor organizing, the IWW would send in workers to give public readings of the First Amendment.[67] Before the first Red Scare, legal theorists in the judicial system had not thought free speech a particularly important matter.[68] These fights began on the ground in pitched local battles over the right to speech and assembly.

Emerging at the end of these conflicts, the sabotage pamphlets tested the limits of speech tolerance. Sabotage meant one thing to the thoughtful IWW spokespersons and another to many citizens who thought the group was foreign, trampy, unpatriotic, and seditious, with loose moral values, living on the fringes of society. To even own a book that spoke of "dynamiting" led to severe repercussions, especially during World War I, when fears of German infiltrators sabotaging wartime industries swept across an industrial landscape, already locked in fierce labor struggles. In a time of bellicose rhetoric and a strike threat to wartime industries, the government and its enforcers sought to suppress threatening speech even among the mildest dissidents who spoke against the war. For many legislators, zealous war supporters, and detectives on the hunt for spies, any talk of sabotage was immediately assumed to be treasonous and evoked visions of foreign invasion, crumbling infrastructure, and national collapse. The Bolshevik revolution in Russia heightened these fears. Intense scrutiny fell on the Wobblies, who proclaimed an antiwar, prolabor stance and right to free speech and assembly, sometimes in violent conflict with local police and strikebreakers. In the climate of war, even mild pacifist oratory could get the speaker a beating from local self-styled vigilante patriots. Mere reference to sabotage could bring down the heavy hand of the police, who raided the offices of labor organizers, confiscating texts they deemed dangerous. Many states hastily passed criminal syndicalism laws directly aimed at crushing the IWW. Motivated by old grudges, economic self-interest, and patriotic fervor, round-ups of hundreds of IWW members were carried out over dubious reports that, for example, they had burned a few haystacks and dumped trays of agricultural produce on the ground.[69] Believing that the only good war was the class war, and having the temerity to say so, the Wobblies were placed under surveillance, raided, beaten, rounded up, tried, and jailed.

Although they comprised only a small number of allegedly treasonous texts, the sabotage pamphlets were often confiscated as evidence of sedition, enough to justify imprisonment or deportation of the owner. The Espionage Act of 1917 and the Sedition Act of 1918 made it possible to prosecute those who circulated antiwar and antidraft literature or who used "disloyal, profane, scurrilous, or abusive language." Charged with controlling speech disseminated through the mails and given unprecedented power to censor, Postmaster General Albert Burleson held a broad interpretation of the Espionage Act as forbidding even a tone of disloyalty or a "disloyalty unexpressed." He banned woodcuts of the sabo cat and any speech that included the word "sabotage" or advocated the theory of industrial unionism, effectively shutting out any cultural and political expression from the Wobblies.[70] The offices of anarchist, socialist, and communist newspapers were raided, editors were arrested on specious grounds, and radical newspapers were banned from the mails.

Despite their emphasis on theory and only explanatory references to attacks on property, the sabotage tracts by Pouget, Flynn, Smith, and Trautman were collected as evidence against IWW members and other anticapitalist radicals. During the war, a probusiness volunteer spy and enforcement organization called the American Protective League, the Army's Military Intelligence Division, the Pinkertons (hired by corporations and business groups), and the Bureau of Investigation all placed the IWW under surveillance, especially in the West, where labor conflict had grown heated in the copper and lumber industries.[71] The sabotage manuals became a concrete demonstration—that an agent could thump on the table and attach to reports—of the IWW's intention to destroy American wartime production. Elected mayor of Seattle in 1918 and known for crushing the Seattle General Strike the following year, Ole Hanson bragged of closing down the city's IWW halls after a police spy campaign to collect names and to "ascertain where they secreted their literature." The police raided the halls, confiscated literature, and, Hanson said, "burned up what we did not turn over to the Government." In his tract, *Americanism vs. Bolshevism*, Hanson extensively quoted from the sabotage manuals, including Flynn's, and concluded, "All through their pamphlets and song books tales are told of sabotage being committed, and suggestions are made as to new methods of destruction."[72] All the rich cultural expression of the Wobblies—their songs, their graphic design, their political speeches, their presence in public space—was seen as a serious threat to the nation.

As the federal government decided to identify and eject undesirables, immigrants found with IWW literature were held for deportation under the Deportation Act of 1918. Simply possessing literature could bring down severe repercussions and dislocation. Typical was the case of Charles Jackson, a Danish sailor, arrested in Chicago on January 26, 1918, for vagrancy and for "advocating or teaching the unlawful destruction of property." He possessed pamphlets of Pouget and Smith, as well as IWW songs by Joe Hill, although no evidence was presented that he had ever used them to teach anything. In many such cases, simple possession of texts was associated with the active roles of dispensing information and inflaming sedition. Based on his "affiliation" with the IWW, the case was so flimsy that the Bureau of Labor had to support it by accusing Jackson of having "a loathsome contagious disease," gonorrhea, thus cementing the image of the immoral, subversive alien. The detainee was not only physically, but morally and ideologically, contagious. After months of detainment in Seattle and on Ellis Island, Jackson applied for a writ of habeas corpus and was initially denied by a US district court. He finally won his case and was released after a year of detainment.[73]

Also detained on Ellis Island were Samuel Dixon and Charles Bernat, of the local IWW branch in Seattle, charged with "advocating and teaching the unlawful destruction of property" and slated for deportation to England and Russia, respectively. The sabotage manuals had been confiscated from the Seattle office and used as key evidence against them. Federal judge Jeremiah Neterer delivered this rationale for deportation by explaining the meaning of "teaching": "There are several ways a person may teach or advocate. It need not be from the public platform or through personal utterances to individuals or groups, but may be done as well through written communications, personal direction, through the public press, or through any means by which information may be disseminated, or it may be done by the adoption of sentiment expressed, or argument made by others which are distributed to others for their adoption and guidance."[74] Sandwiched in this explanation is that the mere "adoption" of a political opinion was "teaching," apparently by contagion, and enough to justify a deportation. Bernat spent a year in detention before his release on bond. (He was reported to be suffering from severe eczema.) He remained of interest to the xenophobic commissioner general of immigration, Anthony Caminetti, who continued to seek his deportation. Dixon was deported to England, one in the first wave of hundreds of Red Scare exiles.

The sabotage pamphlets found their way through police raids and into the courts, including the Chicago trial of 1918, where the newspapers covered them with active hostility and disparagement. Typical of the sensationalism was a *New York Times* article explaining the motivations of the IWW, which it called the "American Bolsheviki." Surely alarming its high-society readers who could afford cooks and housemaids, the *Times* quoted from an alleged IWW sabotage pamphlet: "No longer does the family eat in peace. Soup is served, the family chokes. The soup has been sabotaged by emptying the contents of the red pepper shaker into it. The new cook declared her innocence. Woe again: a steak is served—the family loses its teeth. Cook had been ordered to buy the best—the butcher's bill shows that it cost $2, and it is more like leather than steak."[75] Despite its eye on Chicago, the *New York Times*, as well as the rest of the mainstream news media, ignored the escalating racial bombings, organized by real estate agents, of the homes of Chicago's black workers. Between July 1917 and March 1921, fifty-eight bombings were carried out in the city, destroying homes and leading to the deaths of two. During the IWW trial, a bomb exploded on Chicago's South Side, blowing up a porch and breaking windows down the street.[76] A bit of red pepper in the soup and leathery meat hardly compared to the violent terror campaign against blacks to whose homes the government offered no protection at all while it zealously pursued antiwar radicals. The IWW were the ideological enemies of the state.

In Oakland, California, in early November 1917, American Legionnaires raided the office of the newly formed Communist Labor Party (CLP), hurled its contents into the street, and set fire to the room. Within two weeks, twenty members of the CLP's Oakland branch were arrested under the state's new criminal syndicalism law, including its secretary, John C. Taylor. Introduced at his trial were the sabotage pamphlets of Flynn, Smith, and Pouget, allegedly found in the CLP headquarters. Convicted on two counts of the criminal syndicalism law, including advocacy of terrorism, Taylor was sentenced to one to fourteen years. Upon appeal to the California Supreme Court, Taylor argued that the pamphlets were inadmissible because he was not, in fact, a member of the IWW and no basis existed for the accusations that he had belonged to that organization or had advocated or participated in destroying factory machinery, burning haystacks, derailing trains, and wrecking streetcars. The court agreed that Taylor's alleged participation in "unlawful acts of terrorism" had not been proven, but offered that the pamphlets were admissible "as tending to show the character of the organization."[77] The court upheld Taylor's conviction on the basis that his participation in a seditious organization had been sufficiently proven. He served a year in San Quentin.[78]

A similar case involving another Oakland CLP member, Charlotte Anita Whitney, made it to the US Supreme Court, where it generated one of the most significant interpretations of the First Amendment in legal history. A vocal advocate of progressive causes from women's suffrage to the minimum wage law, and pledged to communism as a way of ending poverty, Whitney was arrested outside of a hotel after giving a talk to a women's club on slavery, racism, and economic injustice. Whitney was charged with five counts under California's criminal syndicalism act. Once again, the prosecution aimed to associate Whitney with the IWW through dubious witnesses, confiscated literature, and a "nebulous chain of associations."[79] These strategies would work well in other successful convictions under the syndicalism act. Passages from the sabotage pamphlets by Pouget, Smith, and Flynn, as well as IWW song lyrics, were read aloud for hours by the prosecuting attorneys, John Calkins and Myron Harris, to the point that the audience grew bored listening to them.[80] In his closing remarks, Harris called for the jury members to condemn terrorist doctrines and to "uphold the sacred tenets of Americanism and place with their verdict the seal of disapproval on the activities of the Communist Labor Party and its blood brother, the I.W.W."[81] Despite the thorough absence of evidence that she had advocated sabotage and terrorism or engaged in any conspiracy, Whitney was convicted on the first count of belonging to an organization advocating criminal syndicalism and sentenced to one to fourteen years in prison. She was released on bail, only to begin a labyrinthine journey through the justice system. As a woman from a wealthy family enjoying the benefits of a powerful support network, Whitney was able to sustain a difficult seven-year fight, with many setbacks, leading to the US Supreme Court.[82]

On December 14, 1925, the Court agreed to hear Whitney's case. Sitting on the bench was Justice Louis Brandeis, one of the architects, with Justice Oliver Wendell Holmes Jr., of an expansionary interpretation of the First Amendment. In a prior decision, in *Schenck v. United States,* Holmes, in a dissenting opinion, had established a "clear and present danger" test for deciding whether speech fell outside First Amendment protections, using the classic example of a person "falsely shouting fire in a theatre and causing a panic." Schenck was the secretary of the Socialist Party of America who had distributed leaflets urging men eligible for the draft to refuse enlistment because the war served only the interests of the capitalists on Wall Street. During a time of war, such utterances were considered false and treasonous. The Supreme Court upheld Schenck's conviction under the Espionage Act, determining that his speech intended to influence others to break the law and damage the successful prosecution of the war. Although the Court consistently refused to overturn convictions of political prisoners in the lower courts, the "clear and present danger" test began to replace the long-standing, highly subjective, and restrictive "bad tendency" test for which a court only had to assume that speech was likely to cause social harm and lawbreaking, even in the distant future, to convict the speaker.

When Whitney's case arrived at the Court, Brandeis and Holmes had been thinking through First Amendment issues as they overthrew the "bad tendency test" with assertions that "civic courage"[83] and a free marketplace of ideas were necessary to democracy. Whitney and her lawyers had made due process, rather than free speech, the basis of their appeal, but Brandeis saw the case as an opportunity to set forth a civil libertarian interpretation of the First Amendment. The justices had decided against Whitney, and Brandeis concurred for jurisdictional reasons, but he delivered an eloquent opinion that refuted accepted wisdom on the state's power to regulate speech. Brandeis criticized California's criminal syndicalism law as giving "the dynamic quality of crime" to "the mere act of assisting in forming a society for teaching syndicalism, of becoming a member of it, or assembling with others for that purpose." Brandeis included "the right to teach" as a fundamental right related to free speech and assembly. These fundamental rights were only subject to restriction, he wrote, if they imminently threatened the state's existence. Holmes had famously written in a prior case that even persuasive speech that overturned the democratic state deserved protection in the marketplace of ideas: "If in the long run the beliefs expressed in proletarian dictatorship are destined to be accepted by the dominant forces of the community, the only meaning of free speech is that they should be given their chance and have their way."[84] Brandeis argued that speech threatening the state's existence was not protected; however, the Court had not yet determined what kind of speech would constitute such injury. He alluded to the sabotage manuals: "The fact that speech is likely to result in some violence or in destruction of property is not enough to justify its suppression. There must be the probability of serious injury to the State." Even speech that most citizens believed "to be false and fraught with evil consequence" was constitutionally protected. Brandeis spoke idealistically against the fear that led to witch hunting, evoking a society of "courageous, self-reliant men, with confidence in the power of free and fearless reasoning."[85] Brandeis's opinion would reverberate through many discussions of First Amendment rights, although it would take forty years for the Court to rule criminal syndicalism laws unconstitutional. Whitney's conviction was upheld, but with substantial support from powerful friends, she was pardoned by the California governor.

The journey of the IWW sabotage pamphlets through the legal system accompanied the development of modern understandings of speech rights. Today, the IWW's sabotage pamphlets have lost the aura of menace—created by social conflict and war—that had provoked such excessive anger, hostility, violence, and repression. Although many at the time perceived them as a threat to the state's existence, no proof was ever presented that they had caused any destruction of property, and indeed the IWW's alleged acts of sabotage remain apocryphal. The sabotage manuals were important not for their content but because they were associated with a demonized group whose powers had been wildly inflated by the public. At the same time, truly violent radicals, like the racist real estate agents of Chicago and a revived Ku Klux Klan, used dynamite to bomb black homes and institutions with impunity. Also operating were small extremist organizations—some political, some purely criminal—that carried out bombings to extort local business owners and government officials, to vex government officials, and to enact revenge. The expanding First Amendment doctrine seems even more remarkable given the context of fear the bombings of the 1910s helped generate. Outside the courts, the newly developing police agencies charged with solving these crimes collected information about political suspects. They had few qualms about using dangerous instructional texts to heighten public fears and profile and ensnare public enemies.

During the first decades of the twentieth century, federal policing had grown dramatically and had turned from pursuit of wealthy and powerful criminals charged with corruption to the pursuit of vocal dissenters in what Richard Gid Powers, in his history of the FBI, calls the "pernicious pageantry of symbolic politics."[86] Growing in power and often in rivalry with each other, the Bureau of Investigation, the Secret Service under the Treasury Department, and other agencies gained public support for federal policing by chasing symbolic enemies. Associated with little-understood groups considered deviant and treasonous, bomb-making and sabotage manuals would continue to figure into these pursuits, representing the perilous violence of technologically adept enemies. After Director William Burns was ousted from his position for corruption, J. Edgar Hoover became head of the Bureau of Investigation in 1924. Under his leadership, one of the chief purposes of the agency was to amass dossiers on political enemies. The FBI could use bomb-making and sabotage manuals in these extensive dossiers to demonstrate the danger of whatever political enemy was in its path.

3

The Anarchist Cookbook

Published in 1971, *The Anarchist Cookbook* is an infamous compendium of information—from the useful to the ridiculous—for handling firearms and making eavesdropping and phone-hacking devices, drugs, and explosive weapons. The first truly popular dangerous technical manual, it has become the literary equivalent of a folk devil: a textual deviant, a threat to society, and the stuff of urban legends. Widely imitated and plagiarized, it has achieved the status of a popular culture icon and become a cult classic among the curious, the rebellious, and the disaffected. It is also a red flag to the police and has appeared in US courts many times as evidence of conspiracy and malevolent motive. In some countries, including Great Britain, a person can be thrown in jail for simply owning *The Anarchist Cookbook* or one of its many spin-offs. In murder cases involving teens, it is often mentioned as a defining factor in their anomic development. In one murder case, it was mentioned in the court record as *The Antichrist Cookbook*.[1]

What has made *The Anarchist Cookbook* so resonant over time is its bald assertion of the people's right to stigmatized technical information. Stewart Brand's popular *Whole Earth Catalogue* had been published only two years before, in 1969, promoting human-scale technologies and a do-it-yourself ethos that spanned back-to-the-land communal and nomadic living, psychonautics, and tool-making. *The Anarchist Cookbook* echoed this countercultural interest in DIY tools and techniques, but replaced utopian community and whole systems with theft, rebellion, and creative destruction. Its author, William Powell, adopted the anarchist stereotype of the bomb thrower and reformulated an anarchism of information: information that by its very existence within a radical context resists the control of the state. Practicing anarchists would like to disavow the book for perpetuating a "dated comic book caricature" of them, but have missed its importance as an unsettling argument about danger, freedom, and knowledge that has given it an astonishing longevity.[2]

The Anarchist Cookbook emerged out of panic over a brief, dramatic surge in bombings of corporate offices, public utilities, military recruitment offices and installations, court buildings, police stations, and monuments. Bombings were by no means new in American life: bomb attacks motivated by greed, revenge, and racism were common. The bombings associated with the New Left, however, were of highly visible centers of state power. These bombings were intended to demonstrate that the empire was in crisis.[3] Although law enforcement agencies were only sporadically concerned with the white supremacist violence that had turned Birmingham into Bombingham, they mobilized against antiwar and black liberation groups. Their spies reported on organization meetings that featured training in explosives and weaponry, and, during searches and seizures, the police collected pamphlets for making bombs and explosives that seemed to support the theory of an impending guerrilla war. This evidence made its way to the highest echelons of government, where grandstanding politicians urged censorship of popular weapons manuals.

Under cover of night on March 1, 1971, members of the Weather Underground snuck into the US Capitol and placed a time bomb in a men's bathroom in a remote corridor. Their motive was to protest the US invasion of Laos. The explosion blasted the building's doors, windows, and walls, but the bombers had taken measures to avoid any casualties. The Capitol bombing was the most sensational display of what Bill Ayers would later call an "illicit craft,"[4] the bomb-making techniques shared across small groups of radicals disenchanted with peaceful demonstration. Although the Weather bombers insisted that they were performing only symbolic acts of violence in pale comparison to state violence, they provoked moral outrage across the political spectrum. A widely syndicated columnist, John Chamberlain, warned that the Capitol bombing was only the beginning of an exponential violence that was spreading by contagion. He pointed to a newly published popular weapons manual, *The Anarchist Cookbook*. Its destructive philosophy, he explained, was propelling the violence. He also pointed to the hundreds of technical books on explosives and bomb making available in the Library of Congress. He asked: "Does any Senator know how many Xerox copies have gone out of his own Congressional Library?"[5]

By the time the *Anarchist Cookbook* was published and Chamberlain had understood his duty as warning the public about dangerous information, an image had already been constructed of an anarchist guerrilla warrior adept in underground technologies and bent on destroying civilization. As an official of the US Treasury Department, charged with oversight over bombings, told a congressional hearing on explosives control, "I think it is fair to say . . . that anyone who can synthesize LSD . . . would have no difficulty at all in formulating explosive materials or constructing an explosive device."[6] With many pages devoted to manufacture of both drugs and weapons, *The Anarchist Cookbook* seemed to confirm that image, although the book mostly repackaged information from police and military manuals distributed by right-wing paramilitary publishers.

The book had no real political philosophy that tied it to the Left—no protests against racism or the war. Rather, it was as if the elusive "professional anarchist" once conjured by Vice President Spiro Agnew had written a book.[7]

In reality, its author was simply William Powell, a young student who was involved in the antiwar movement but considered himself an individualist. He would later disavow his book as "a misguided product of my adolescent anger at the prospect of being drafted and sent to Vietnam to fight in a war that I did not believe in."[8] Powell has continued to fight publishers who have bought the rights to the book, demanding they stop publishing it. When Powell wrote his famous book, he was a nineteen-year-old English major at Windham College in Vermont. A photograph in the local newspaper shows him bushy-haired and short-bearded, smoking a cigarette and wearing combat boots, as if in emulation of the young Che Guevara. When the reporter asked him about the attention his book had received, he said, "The rightists call it Communist. The leftists call it profiteering. The liberals call it neo-Nazi. That about puts it in the perspective I wanted."[9] The elusive intentions of the book have made it a political shapeshifter, but it was published at a specific moment that intersected with the state's attempt to repress radical speech.

The Senate Discussions of Popular Weapons Manuals

The historical contexts of the book reveal its sharp interventions in a conflict over radical speech. It rebuked discussions in the federal government that recommended restrictions on popular weapons manuals and their publishers and distributors. *The Anarchist Cookbook* was published by Lyle Stuart, an entrepreneur who advocated free speech and thrived on printing controversial titles. As treasurer of the Fair Play for Cuba Committee and, by his own account, a friend of Fidel Castro, Stuart had unhappily encountered the repressive excesses of the federal government when, in the wake of the Kennedy assassination in 1963, the Senate Internal Security Subcommittee had interrogated him about his Cuban involvements and the pro-Communist books he published, including Castro's *History Will Absolve Me* and Dalton Trumbo's *Johnny Got His Gun*. Asserting a connection between distribution of pornography and "Communist propaganda," the counsel, Julien Sourwine, questioned Stuart on whether he was "peddling pornography" through *Diary of a Nymph* (the case history of a nymphomaniac), *Pleasure Was My Business* (the autobiography of a madam), *Creative Marriage*, and *The Art of Marriage*. When a senator loudly accused him of being "insolent," the uncooperative Stuart replied: "Don't make loud voices at me; you don't frighten me."[10] Stuart was very well aware of the government's interest in his publishing line when he took on *The Anarchist Cookbook*. Recent

Senate hearings on popular weapons instruction had included some of the same politicians he had encountered in 1963.

Between 1967 and 1970, the US Senate Permanent Subcommittee on Investigations held hearings on "riots, civil and criminal disorders," focusing mainly on campus unrest. In 1969, four "extremist" organizations came under special investigation: Students for a Democratic Society, the Black Panther Party, the Student Non-Violent Coordinating Committee, and the Republic of New Africa. Exhibits of guerrilla warfare and bomb-making literature were introduced to demonstrate the potential violence of these groups. This was an eclectic mix of documents, ranging from nineteenth-century Russian nihilist Sergei Nechaev's *Catechism of the Revolutionist* to the *Guidebook for Marines*' chapter on "Demolitions and Mine Warfare." In 1970, the subcommittee held sessions to specifically address the problem of weapons manuals. The head of the subcommittee, John McClellan (D-AK), introduced the issue: "In my view, the circulation of printed instructions on bomb making and tactics on guerrilla warfare constitute a serious and challenging threat to our society."[11] The purpose of the hearings' final days was to identify causes and remedies for the perceived problem of violent protest, especially the increase in bombings across the country. In its focus on literature deemed seditious, Senate investigators sought to trace the connections among groups sharing guerrilla warfare and bomb-making literature, provide causal explanations for bomb violence, and explore whether the federal government could impose controls on speech. These efforts had a whiff of the House Un-American Activities Committee (HUAC) investigations, where some of the anti-communist subcommittee members, like John McClellan, had forged their careers. McClellan had also been involved in the congressional hearing on the Fair Play for Cuba Committee that had interrogated Lyle Stuart for the kinds of books he published.

Despite the decades-long bomb violence of the racist Right that had finally received some attention from the FBI, the primary focus of the hearings was on black liberation and antiwar movements. Rejecting any need to examine the social causes of urban riots and antiwar protests, McClellan worked closely with J. Edgar Hoover to establish that stricter law enforcement was the solution to the nation's problems.[12] Riots were the result of permissiveness, not poverty. An emphasis on bombings and bomb-making information, rather than political speech, furthered an agenda of gaining public support for crackdowns on radical groups. The subcommittee members heard testimony on the number of bombings that had taken place between January 1, 1969, and April 15, 1970. According to the US Department of the Treasury, there had been 4,330 bombings, 808 of which had taken place on college campuses. A further 19% were attributed to "black extremists," 14% to "white extremists," 2% to labor disputes, 1% to attacks on religious institutions, and 8% in aid of criminal activity. Sixty-four percent—2,772 bombings—were unsolved cases, creating a large gray area in the federal government's understanding of bomb violence.[13] Nevertheless, members of the subcommittee proposed that a vast left-wing revolution was taking place with an unprecedented level of bomb violence. As McClellan put it, "Bombing, terrorism and sabotage are not subjects which have been historically and traditionally familiar to the American people."[14] Ignoring the blatant history of white supremacist terrorism, Senator Charles Percy suggested: "If the extremism of the left is permitted to continue, there will be extremism of the right"[15]—this despite the recent HUAC hearings on the Ku Klux Klan, exposing bomb-making schools that trained participants to destroy power lines, radio stations, and integrated restaurants.[16] In its construction of a newly violent America, the subcommittee suggested that the New Left's revolutionary agents of anarchy and chaos were waging an unprecedented guerrilla war that could overturn the government and destroy the fabric of society. New measures had to be taken to vigorously punish and suppress these elements, including terrorist speech. When it looked at the evidence, however, the subcommittee couldn't ignore that most bomb-making literature was coming from other violent sources.

One of these sources was anti-communist, white supremacist paramilitary organizations that were already training for guerrilla warfare well before the New Left arrived on the scene. Some small groups associated with the Ku Klux Klan and the National States Rights Party had decided to wage a more organized terrorist war against Jews and blacks gaining ground through the civil rights movement. Others, like the Minutemen, imagined that communists had invaded the government or that a communist takeover was imminent and that the Soviet Union, via Cuba, was poised at the doorstep. As they saw it, their duty was to defend the homeland against these perceived invaders, tapping a deep root of racism and antigovernment sentiment. As the true patriots in their own imagination, they considered themselves citizen-soldiers with a moral duty to form resistant militias. A version of the Minuteman manual, entitled "The Terrorist's Handbook of Explosives, Primers and Booby Traps," was introduced as an exhibit in the subcommittee hearings to show the kinds of weapons information available to radical groups for paramilitary training.

There was reason to fear them. In 1965, Minuteman Keith Gilbert was convicted for possession of 1,400 pounds of TNT that he planned to detonate under the stage during Martin Luther King Jr.'s speech at the Hollywood Palladium. He expected the event to be attended by thousands of Jews.[17] In New York, Minutemen were indicted for planning to firebomb three summer camps they thought to be "communist" and bombing the campaign headquarters of historian and outspoken Communist Party member Herbert Aptheker with a timed device. Discovered in the raids were incendiary devices with delays constructed of wristwatches, flashlight batteries, and detonating caps.[18] In 1968, seven Minutemen were convicted of conspiracy to rob three banks, destroy City Hall with a pipe bomb, and blow up power transmission lines in Redmond, Washington, a suburb of Seattle. They claimed to be planning a training exercise for resistance warfare against the communists, an excuse dismissed by the jury.[19] The FBI had the Minutemen under surveillance, but New York governor Nelson Rockefeller expressed a forgiving sentiment: "These people are misguided in their patriotism."[20]

With military veterans in their membership providing expertise, the Minutemen studied army field manuals, cobbling together the information in their own technical literature and disseminating it through the mimeograph, the Xerox, and cheap offset printing. Not much of this literature survives, but the Minuteman handbook and a training handout arrived in the hands of California attorney general Thomas C. Lynch, who included parts of them in a 1965 report on politically violent groups in his state, warning that they were just short of sedition and dangerously armed.[21] The materials expressed enthusiasm about mortars and rocket launchers and included instructions for making Molotov cocktails, fuses made from sawdust and kitchen matches, cigarettes booby-trapped with nerve gas, and explosives concocted with iodine. Lynch prepared his report as an argument for the California legislation to ban private armies, using the Minutemen literature to demonstrate that the members were receiving terrorist training. Because of the gun lobby, he failed in that effort, but gained instead a law against large-bore weapons like bazookas and antitank guns.[22] Only much later, during the surge of extremist antigovernment militias in the 1990s, would many states ban paramilitary organizing and training. Then the implications of prohibiting paramilitary training—which can be considered a form of politically expressive conduct—would be debated in the courts and among constitutional lawyers.

The subcommittee also examined materials from a new kind of mail-order publisher devoted to selling popular weapons manuals to a consumer base of white supremacists and anti-communist zealots. When pushed, these publishers often espoused a libertarian view that they had the right to publish weapons information. If anything, government attention encouraged them. The subcommittee called neo-Nazi Odinist James K. Warner, who ran Sons of Liberty Press, and Donald Sisco, a former Minuteman who ran another self-publishing operation, Atlan Formularies. Warner pled the Fifth Amendment, but Sisco was more than willing to give his opinion on bomb-making manuals. Missing fingers from his left hand because of his own experimentation, Sisco was the author of the *The Militant's Formulary* and *Explosives Just Like Granddad Used to Make*, which he had compiled from late nineteenth-century texts on household chemistry. (These were later reprinted in his *Poor Man's James Bond.*) *The Militant's Formulary* was initially published by the white supremacist Sturmstrup Press, though Sisco denied any political affiliation. Soliciting laughter from the gallery, he suggested that his readers could use his book to defend against hippie "scum" and declared that the National Guard at Kent State "should all be given medals and a lot more target practice."[23] His primary defense was that the information he provided was already widely available in public libraries: "I maintain that these bomb books and the information on making bombs are so prevalent that you can't stop it. You can't even begin to stop it."[24] After his appearance, Sisco changed his name to Kurt Saxon and became a well-known figure in the survivalist movement. He was a prolific writer, producing many compiled Grandad's Formulary books and a series entitled *The Poor Man's James Bond*, which included murder methods and a recipe for the lethal toxin ricin.

The subcommittee also called Robert Brown, owner of Panther Publications. Panther Publications was one of several small mail-order publishers that reprinted US Army manuals and other military books, mostly by US intelligence veterans who hated communism. US Army manuals were in the public domain, and it was a low-cost effort for paramilitary publishers to reproduce them. Books that supported irregular operations like *Special Forces Handbook* (ST131-80) were favorites. The *Handbook* includes a section on improvised devices such as soap and gasoline napalm, a Molotov cocktail, thermite in a can, a time bomb made with peas or beans, a pipe bomb, and a pocket watch detonator. The paramilitary publishers also published elaborate weapons specifications and histories enjoyed by military buffs. Founded in 1961, Panther Publications' first book was Brown's own edited and translated version of Alberto Bayo's *150 Questions for the Guerrilla*. Brown had spent time in Cuba as a journalist and student, researching the influence of communist politics on organized labor for his master's degree from the University of Colorado. There, Brown encountered Bayo, a former Spanish anti-Franco fighter who offered his military expertise to rebel bands throughout Central America. Fidel Castro had chosen Bayo to train his guerrillas, including Che Guevara. Brown interviewed Bayo and offered to publish a translated version of his manual, which gave advice on forming guerrilla groups. It also included instructions on making various incendiary and explosive devices, such as Molotov cocktails and hand grenades from milk cans. Brown knew that Bayo's own writing had been suppressed when he was put under eight days of detention in Spain for publishing a tactical work, *La Guerra Será de los Guerrilleros*.[25] But things changed for Brown in the midst of his project when he became angry that Castro had shown himself to be a communist and an "oppressive demagogue."[26] He added to Bayo's text a description of his "Operation Counterthrust," a training program for anti-Castro Cubans and other sympathizers, and one of the hundreds of counterrevolutionary groups tolerated and encouraged by the United States during this period.[27] Brown formed Panther Publications to self-publish Bayo's book and others like it.[28] Panther's catalog promoted a counterrevolutionary guerrilla war to be waged against Castro and the communists. It went on to produce lasting classics like S. J. Cuthbert's *"We Shall Fight in the Streets": A Guide to Street Fighting,* collated from information in official British government publications and *Infantry Magazine*; and Hans von Dach Bern's *Total Resistance,* a handbook, including bomb-making instructions, for civilians resisting occupation.[29]

It was an irony that Brown's translation of *150 Questions for the Guerrilla* would become popular among radical groups of quite a different political persuasion who learned Bayo's advice to Castro: "Begin with your active groups to terrorize the population, using bombs, petards, Molotov cocktails, lighted matches in public vehicles, etc. If this fails, or if you see that the people don't respond, begin a wave of sabotage aimed in particular against the sugar centers of the interior. If this also fails, then start with personal attempts on the lives of individuals, belonging to the armed forces and the police."[30] Bayo's simple illustrations for a Molotov cocktail and other incendiaries were circulated on handouts as antiwar groups escalated their oppositional political rhetoric. Through this channel, the book found its way into evidence at the subcommittee, where the counsel, Philip Manuel, featured it as prime evidence of a possibly Cuban-sponsored violent leftist network.

Called to account for his publication of the book, Brown nervously chain-smoked and tapped his foot throughout the proceedings. The subcommittee didn't quite know what to do with him. It had suspected that his publishing firm was a front for Cuban infiltration and associated with the Black Panthers, but Brown was a Vietnam veteran with experience in US counterintelligence. Though his interrogators attempted to tie him to the Minutemen, his presence disrupted the narrative they were developing of the anarchist guerrilla warrior. Brown hid his politics, claiming that he had no association with any radical groups, and deployed the dual-use argument that his books catered to military buffs with an intellectual curiosity in weapons and guerrilla warfare. He facetiously claimed that Panther Publications would only sell the most dangerous information to police officers who wrote in on letterhead, but that he had no way of knowing whether these letters were real. McClellan pressed him on whether he was advocating violence by distributing weapons manuals. Brown responded: "Simply because we describe guerrilla warfare does not mean that we are promoting guerrilla warfare within the United States, sir. . . . Simply mailing out circulars of this nature does not mean you are promoting it."[31] He compared criminal use of one of his manuals to the Black Panthers using a General Motors car to drive to a bombing site: General Motors would not be held liable for the act, nor should Panther Publications for providing a book. Similarly, selling such a book was not much different from selling a Winchester rifle.

In its search for a witness who would support its narrative of dangerous left-wing instruction, the subcommittee called Thomas Sanders, the San Francisco

Bay organizer for the Fair Play for Cuba Committee and white business manager of the newsletter *Black Politics*. A member of the multiracial editorial board called him "the John Brown of the 1960s liberation struggles."[32] Already under investigation by the FBI, *Black Politics* was the subcommittee investigators' smoking gun for connecting leftist seditious advocacy and tactical instruction. Contributor "George Prosser," who was most likely Sanders himself, advocated a violent revolution of the oppressed masses of the world and reviled "the enervating impotence of the prolonged debating society."[33] Evoking the battle of Algiers, Prosser wrote a series of articles on preparation for the revolution, including the acquisition, stockpiling, and use of weapons. These articles proposed an anti-imperial uprising of the global masses who had been given the practical street training of the sharpshooter and the guerrilla fighter. Prosser advocated sabotage of the ammunitions supply line that passed through the San Francisco Bay Area, suggesting that a mortar could be used to blow up a munitions depot or that bombs could be deployed to disrupt shipping. He supplied Xeroxed army demolition cards that showed the force of various explosive charges and illustrated directions on how to launch a mortar and light a safety fuse. He reproduced Bayo's Molotov cocktail. *Black Politics* had begun with a mission of discussing self-defense, and not all of its readers agreed with these proposed tactics. They wrote in their letters to the editor that the Black Panther Party's position of armed self-defense was much wiser than sporadic attacks upon the police and the military, which would undoubtedly bring violent repercussion.

In his first tactical article, Prosser pointed his readers to a list of books from Panther Publications, including Cuthbert's *"We Shall Fight in the Streets"* and Bayo's *150 Questions for the Guerrilla*. In the next issue, Prosser laid out more concrete plans for sabotage. Accompanying his article was a Xeroxed ad for Panther Publications, originally appearing in *Shotgun News*, for "fantastic new manuals," some of them "never before available to the public!" These included *Land Mine Warfare*, *Special Forces Demolition Techniques*, *Notes on Guerrilla Warfare*, and the increasingly popular *Explosives and Demolitions* (FM 5-25), which also appeared in *The Anarchist Cookbook*'s bibliography.[34] Prosser wrote: "Although this publishing house [Panther Publications] is distinctly right-wing in its orientation, and definitely not sympathetic to the aspiration of the oppressed, it nevertheless constitutes a very important source of study material, of which we should avail ourselves."[35] Prosser borrowed from and emulated the form of these manuals, collating and repackaging previously published material. He also understood the possibility of his arrest for incitement and included disclaimers that he was not "advocating" guerrilla warfare and that "we do not advise action now."[36]

The subcommittee subpoenaed Thomas Sanders and ordered him to turn over his records, charging that *Black Politics* "details how to accomplish sabotage and terrorism, suggests various targets, and explains how to manufacture explosives."[37] Sanders was asked to produce copies of the newsletter, its correspondence and business records, and all back issues that contained advertisements of Panther Publications and Normount Armament Company. But Sanders refused to comply. With the help of the American Civil Liberties Union, he demanded an injunction, alleging violation of his right to free speech and due process. He lost the case because the court ruled that the Congress's "responsibility in aid of lawmaking" outweighed these protections.[38] By then, the hearings were over and *Black Politics* had been successfully repressed.

The subcommittee faced a larger challenge. Under the new Supreme Court ruling in *Brandenburg v. Ohio*, violent political speech was protected unless it provoked imminent lawless action. Clarence Brandenburg was a KKK leader in Ohio who had been captured on film at an armed rally, saying, "We're not a revenant organization, but if our President, our Congress, our Supreme Court, continues to suppress the white, Caucasian race, it's possible that there might have to be some revengeance taken."[39] He also made derogatory remarks about Jews and blacks. Brandenburg was convicted of violating the Ohio Syndicalism Act, which prohibited persons from advocating violence, in oral or written speech, as a "means of accomplishing industrial or political reform."[40] Known for its important reinterpretations of First Amendment jurisprudence, the Warren Court struck down the Ohio law, deciding that it was too broad and setting up the classic test: that speech can only be prohibited if it is "directed at inciting or producing imminent lawless action" and "is likely to incite or produce such an action." *Brandenburg* was later upheld in *Hess v. Indiana* when the Supreme Court struck down a disorderly conduct conviction. In that case, a demonstrator at an antiwar protest at Indiana University had said loudly in a sheriff's presence, "We'll take the fucking street later." The Supreme Court ruled that the test of imminent lawless action had not been met and that "the constitutional guarantees of freedom of speech forbid the States to punish the use of words or language not within 'narrowly limited classes of speech.'"[41] The Brandenburg case is upheld as one of the most shining examples of US jurisprudence. That this decision was made during a time of severe stress over dissenting groups and an increase in antigovernment violence is a testament to the strength of US speech protections.

The light of the recent *Brandenburg* decision fell over the subcommittee's attempts to suppress political speech. Chief investigator Manuel had warned at the beginning of the proceedings, "Unless it can be proved that the paper or document advocated that the reader actually blow up a target and that in turn it can be proved that the reader acted upon this prompting, existing law evidently has no effect."[42] Some subcommittee members pressed for the view that popular weapons manuals had only one targeted purpose: a guerrilla warfare manual was for the purpose of waging a guerrilla war. An alternate use, at least in their minds, was outside the range of probability. They also sought to make distributors liable by suggesting that they knew their consumers were revolutionaries who would make use of these manuals and were intentionally directing violence. However, proving this intention was difficult, especially since the distributors could always point to the military buffs and the hobbyists. Even with overtly revolutionary literature like *Black Politics*, proving "imminent lawless action" was a thorny barrier to censorship.

The possibility of censoring the mails was also explored. David A. Nelson, general counsel for the Post Office, testified on the control over materials that incited riot, treason, insurrection, or armed resistance. He pointed to the Civil Obedience Act of 1968, enacted in response to fears of guerrilla warfare, that, in part, punishes any person who teaches how to make or use weapons (including guns and bombs) knowing "or having reason to know" that the information will be used in a "civil disorder."[43] (As an example of the excessive persecution of antiwar activists, the FBI used this act's antiriot provisions to justify compiling a huge dossier on Beatle John Lennon.) However, Nelson pointed out the limitations of any efforts to control the mails. The Post Office had neither the authority to decide what to censor nor the personnel to examine every piece of mail. First class mail was sealed anyway in the absence of a search warrant.

The subcommittee wanted to know whether the mailing of a bulletin called "D.C. Piggeries" could be forbidden. This bulletin contained a map of Washington police stations, statements advocating guerrilla warfare, and diagrams of bombs. Even this literature, Nelson argued, was protected under *Brandenburg* unless it was sent solely to a group likely to carry out that action. If it were mailed to members of the subcommittee, for example, it would not produce such an action. McClellan held up Brazilian revolutionary Carlos Marighella's *Minimanual of the Guerrilla*, a tactical manual popular among leftist groups. "Certainly anyone knows," he said, "that the whole purpose of mailing it along with instructions on how to make bombs, and instructing firing groups of five or less to actually commit the act . . . is an act of subversion that should be punished."[44] Nelson answered that prosecuting the distributors would be stronger if the mailing were a "rifle shot" to a specific group and not widely broadcast. The subcommittee was making little progress in finding a solution to the problem of popular weapons instruction.

In the midst of these proceedings, in the summer of 1970, a controversial story was unfolding in the national news media: incensed librarians were reporting that agents for the Alcohol, Tobacco and Firearms Division of the Internal Revenue Service, under the Treasury Department, were requesting their patron records for evidence of seditious activity. Specifically, twenty-seven libraries were asked to produce the borrowing records for books on explosives and guerrilla warfare. The requests were traced back to the Subcommittee on

Investigations, which had asked the Treasury Department, recently given the power to regulate explosives, to look into the increase in bombings and to explore methods of detection and prevention. The most extensive sweeps were conducted in Milwaukee and Atlanta, where agents were ostensibly testing surveillance of library records as a possible investigative technique.[45] In Milwaukee, an agent asked librarians to produce the call slips for books on explosives, tried to manipulate them by suggesting that libraries had a special responsibility in a unique time of unrest, and threatened them with a subpoena when they refused. In Atlanta, librarians at the De Kalb County Library were asked about readers of Che Guevara's *Guerrilla Warfare* and *Newsweek* reporter Francois Scully's *Age of the Guerrilla*. Astonishingly, none of the paramilitary publishers who had caught the attention of McClellan's subcommittee were asked to produce their sales records or mailing lists.[46] The sole focus was on libraries.

The news spread quickly among librarians at major institutions, and the American Library Association's conference in Detroit that summer had a special session on the issue, featuring Milwaukee Library's Vivian Maddox, who had become a heroine for refusing to cooperate with the Treasury agent. The agent had been unable to surreptitiously look at call slips because the books on explosives were in closed stacks. When he approached Maddox, she had resisted giving him further access. As longtime defenders of free speech, members of the ALA were vociferously opposed to this surveillance and defended the right of their patrons to read without threat of government intervention. They didn't attempt to sort out whether certain types of books were particularly dangerous, but rather kept to a principle of the right to read any books in the library, which was conceived as a sanctuary of ideas.

Though not explicitly stated in the First Amendment, reading had recently been deemed a protected activity by the courts: a matter of privacy and personal liberty. In 1969, in *Stanley v. Georgia*, the US Supreme Court ruled that the Constitution "protects the right to receive information and ideas, regardless of their social worth, and to be generally free from governmental intrusions into one's privacy and control of one's thoughts."[47] In delivering the opinion of the Court, Justice Thurgood Marshall stated: "If the First Amendment means anything, it means that a State has no business telling a man, sitting alone in his own house, what books he may read or what films he may watch. Our whole constitutional heritage rebels at the thought of giving government the power to control men's minds."[48] Justice Marshall appealed to common sense, further arguing that censoring obscene materials because they might cause antisocial conduct was like banning chemistry books because they might lead to moonshining. Marshall's analogy is interesting here, since it implies that receiving information about chemistry, even chemistry for illegal purposes, is understood to be the right of the individual.

The ALA upheld this right to read as well as the privacy of library records. Judith Krug and James Harvey, of the ALA's Committee on Intellectual Freedom, went so far as to suggest that librarians refuse subpoenas delivered without good cause, calling the Treasury Department's tactics "witch-hunting."[49] Thirty librarians marched in front of the IRS building in protest, while the outspoken director of the Atlanta Public Library, Carlton Rochell, went on the major news networks to voice his anger at the surveillance. The librarians were joined by two senators—Samuel Ervin Jr. (D-NC) and Charles Goodell (R-NY)—who charged the Nixon government with tyranny. They demanded a thorough investigation, including the Treasury Department's criteria for the books selected. Nationally syndicated columnists Richard Spong and Art Buchwald joined the fray, both evoking Big Brother. Spong suggested, "Books are the enemies of despots."[50] With characteristic style, humorist Buchwald imagined a conversation over the information desk between librarian Philpott and treasury agent Spangle about potentially subversive books for nine-year-olds and unkempt college students, including *The Three Little Pigs*, *Chitty Chitty Bang Bang*, and *Gone with the Wind*. The witless Spangle ends with a final warning to Miss Philpott: "Unbelievable as it may sound to you, Trotsky learned everything he knew from the Odessa Public Library Branch No. 2."[51]

Subcommittee chair McClellan was unmoved by the public criticism. While he claimed that the subcommittee had never given a direct recommendation to the Treasury Department to investigate libraries, he approved of the tactic. Library records, he argued, were public records, and suggested that the country needed these surveillance tactics to defend itself.[52] Avoiding blame, the Nixon White House denied all knowledge of the library investigation, while the Treasury Department put responsibility on the individual agents for acting independently. At congressional hearings on explosives control, also taking place that summer, the assistant secretary of the Treasury, Eugene Rossides, was asked to explain these reports. He blamed "overzealous" agents and declared that the Treasury Department was strongly opposed to invading the privacy of citizens, including what they read and what they viewed.[53] After meeting with representatives from the ALA, Treasury secretary David Kennedy came forward with an official statement that his department would forbid browsing expeditions into library records, while allowing specific searches into a criminal suspect's library habits.[54] In the ALA headquarters, some librarians were further incensed by what they believed was their organization's acquiescence in allowing for selective, rather than strict, confidentiality.[55] They had won in preventing a full-scale investigation of library records by the Treasury Department, though the FBI launched its "Library Awareness Program" soon afterwards, directing its agents to enlist librarians as informants, reporting on foreign-looking or foreign-sounding patrons who were requesting scientific and technical reports.[56]

In the end, under strong public critique, the Subcommittee on Investigations had very little influence on the production and distribution of popular weapons manuals. The only malleable respondent was the US Army, which, in an attempt to stop the paramilitary publishers, reclassified some of its manuals and directed libraries to send back *Boobytraps* (FM-531) in a helpfully provided postage-paid envelope.[57] (Librarians debated whether this, too, was censorship, comparing the recall to Stalin's rewriting of history in Soviet encyclopedias.) The new protections of *Brandenburg,* the complexities of proving the intentions of readers or distributors, the difficulties in categorizing which texts were punishable, and the outspoken public defense of the right to read created a climate of resistance to the strong arm that McClellan and others had advocated. Congress's attention turned to controlling the possession and transport of explosives between states, rather than controlling reading materials. The subcommittee hearings on riots and civil and criminal disorders ended soon after, with passionate language on the destructive powers of anarchy. Senator Edward Gurney (R-FL) declared that the "fanatical plans" of the Weather Underground and other revolutionary groups "must be thwarted. It is not and can never be 'repression' to furnish law enforcement with the legal weapons with which to stop them."[58] However, there were clearly limits to the measures the government could take, limits understood and defended by many educated citizens, even in a time of panic.

In an era of deep division punctuated by bombings, not everyone shared this sentiment. Other means were always available to harass an alternative press. In October 1970, lithographers across the country refused to print an issue of the muckraking *Scanlan's Monthly* devoted to what it considered a new guerrilla warfare being waged in the United States. Catering to the sensationalism already created by the McClellan subcommittee, *Scanlan's* pointed to widespread information on bomb making as aiding the violence. It singled out paramilitary publishers like Panther Publications and suggested, "The domestic flow of blueprints for homemade weaponry has become stupendous."[59] Although the editors, William Hinkle III and Sidney Zion, were obviously critical of violent tactics and wrote not a single word of advocacy, their exposé included reproductions of political pamphlets with diagrams for bombs and incendiary weapons. The Amalgamated Lithographers of America objected, sending the Local 1 shop steward to complain that the contents of the magazine were extremely radical and un-American.

Aided by the flamboyant lawyer William Kunstler and the ACLU, Zion and Hinkle tried and failed to get lithographers in New York, California, and Denver to print the issue, but all refused.[60] They then found a receptive printer in Canada, but US Customs seized six thousand copies, citing a federal law that prohibited import of treasonous materials. The Canadian Mounties also seized copies, citing the repressive Quebec Newspaper Registration Act that had initially targeted the publications of a radical French-speaking separatist group in that province.[61] Zion and Hinkle believed that Nixon was targeting them because of their critiques of his relationship to union "thugs," a conspiracy theory somewhat borne out by John Dean III admission that Nixon had asked for an IRS investigation of *Scanlan's*.[62] *Scanlan's* finally hit the stands in January 1971, but not without resistance from Simon & Schuster, which was reproducing the issue in booklet form. The publisher excised the bomb-making diagrams, telling the press, "We would not print a Boy Scout handbook on how to blow things up."[63] Then came *The Anarchist Cookbook*.

The Anarchist Cookbook and Its Audiences

Traveling around to hippie communes, writer Elia Katz described a discussion among anarchists who were proposing to contribute to *Scanlan's* guerrilla warfare issue. They imagined their potential readers as a Midwestern boy inspired to an anarchist revolution by the colorful bomb diagrams, and a senator "with his issue of *Scanlan's* in his hand, enraged and thrilled, and calling for activation of the concentration camps."[64] These were chief impulses for *The Anarchist Cookbook*, which still inspires rebellious adolescents and attracts the repressive attentions of the law. Published in a flurry of publicity by a New York publisher rather than some small provincial press, *The Anarchist Cookbook* was one answer to the controversies, a demonstration of the right to read about the most dangerous of subjects in a time of perceived emergency.

What *The Anarchist Cookbook* demonstrated more than anything was what William Powell had read. And what he had read were publicly available sources. He found some of the information in the New York Public Library; the rest he obtained mostly from Brown's Panther Press and another paramilitary press, Combat Bookshelf. His specifications for pistols, revolvers, and semiautomatic and automatic weapons came from Panther Publications' *Foreign Weapons Handbook*, compiled from US army manuals by Sergeant Major Frank Moyer, whose intention was to fulfill "the needs of the average, non-professional individual interested in firearms."[65] Powell's crude drawings of clock and battery bombs came from *Explosives and Homemade Bombs*, by Joseph Stoffel, a retired explosive disposal officer and training instructor for the US Army who had testified to the McClellan subcommittee.[66] His diagrams for a "Bangalore torpedo" and a Molotov cocktail came from Bayo's *150 Questions for the Guerrilla*.[67] His lists of household substitutions for chemical compounds used in explosives came from US Army manual FM 5-25, *Explosives and Demolitions*, sold by Panther Publications. His bibliography includes the Minuteman manual. These texts were the items of interest to the McClellan subcommittee that had concluded its hearings the summer before *The Anarchist Cookbook*'s publication. Surely thumbing his nose at the very people who had once investigated him, Lyle Stuart launched *The Anarchist Cookbook* with a sensational publicity campaign, taking advantage of a critical moment in public debate over dangerous information. Stuart called a press conference with Powell where they spoke against surveillance by the federal government. The event created a scene: a heckler set off a stink bomb and a cherry bomb to punctuate his point that the book was crass commercialism and Powell no anarchist.[68]

Chastising author and publisher, reviewers of the book expressed dismay at its cynical commercialism and social irresponsibility. The *Christian Science Monitor* denounced the book as immoral for endangering children, while *Publisher's Weekly* argued that publishers were simply conduits for information, not judges of its morality.[69] The "anarchy" of *The Anarchist Cookbook* was roundly condemned. Max Geltman, in the conservative *National Review*, argued that the book's teachings exemplified the inevitable trajectory of "extreme libertarianism" to the "absolute excesses" of violence and revolution.[70] From the other side of the political spectrum, the literary editor of *The Nation*, Emile Capouya, wrote a scathing review that accused Powell of technical incompetence and skewed politics. The book, he said, was a reflection of the "amiable folkways" of violence that permeated American society and the moral superiority that justified its wars. As for Powell's "anarchy," Capouya wrote that he knew "some of the words and none of the music" and had failed to grasp anarchists' rejection of violence because a terrorist organization might well become the instrument of future oppression.[71] Moral condemnation did nothing to deter the book's success; if anything, it added to the book's attraction for seekers of forbidden knowledge.

Under requests from Congressman George Mahon (D-TX) and from the counsel to the president, John Dean III, the FBI investigated the book. Its Laboratory Division found nothing new in the contents and advised that its bomb-making instructions were largely accurate, but simplistic, incomplete, and hazardous. Nevertheless, the FBI investigated Stuart, Powell, and Peter Bergman, who wrote *The Anarchist Cookbook*'s introduction. It sent agents to various bookstores and attempted to ascertain whether Stuart was using the US Post Office to mail the book. After the months-long investigation, the Justice Department's Internal Security Division informed Hoover that the book violated no laws. Neither Powell nor his book could be linked to any incitement of imminent lawless action. However, the FBI did send information about the book in its training literature to warn police that the book might encourage attacks on them.[72] This was a critical shift in focus from federal prohibition to on-the-ground policing that would ensure the book's association with certain groups deemed dangerous by law enforcement. Although the book could not be proved to incite violence under federal law, the police could seize it as evidence of criminal intent.

While efforts at censorship and moral suasion had no effect, another kind of repression emerged: the confiscation of the now infamous *Anarchist Cookbook* in search and seizures and its deployment as evidence of criminal intent and conspiracy. For decades, *The Anarchist Cookbook* has been confiscated as a sign of criminal activity within a nexus of evidence associated with particular groups. This association was established early on: when the Canadian police came to arrest Karleton Armstrong, an antiwar radical on the run after bombing the Army Math Research Center at the University of Wisconsin, an officer noticed *The Anarchist Cookbook* on Armstrong's dresser and confiscated it. Investigators used the book during Armstrong's interrogation when he declared it full of errors, thus admitting his knowledge of explosives.[73] The Wisconsin bombers obtained more information from the Wisconsin Fish and Game Department's *Pothole Blasting for Wildlife*.[74] *The Anarchist Cookbook* became evidence in the 1971 trial of two Puerto Rican students, Eduardo Cruz and Wilfredo Melendez, suspected of one hundred bombings in and around New York City on behalf of a Puerto Rican independence movement. They were convicted for possession of explosives: potassium chlorate and sugar stuffed in cigarette packs, and flashbulbs, batteries, and watch mechanisms. Eduardo Cruz appealed his conviction, charging the government with illegal electronic eavesdropping because the prosecutor, during the cross-examination of a defense witness, had referred to an "underground publication": *The Anarchist Cookbook*.[75] When Patty Hearst was arrested, the FBI released to the press the evidence list from their raids of the New World Liberation Front to suggest global conspiracy. Included was *The Anarchist Cookbook* along with Marxist-Leninist literature and textbooks on explosives checked out from the University of California library.[76]

The Anarchist Cookbook, however, was not the text cited by members of the Weather Underground as their handbook of choice. It was not an especially helpful book for bomb making since it had only crudely copied diagrams and rough schematics that left much necessary information out. *The Blaster's Handbook*, produced by the DuPont Company, commonly appears as the key source of information.[77] Susan Stern described experimenting with explosives out in a remote field, aided by a chemist and *The Bombers Handbook*, a misremembering of the title. She wrote, "I read government manuals on bombing; I learned everything there was to know on the subject."[78] Bill Ayers remembers that Terry Robbins, who later died in an explosion during a bomb-making operation, studied *The Blaster's Handbook*.[79] Thai Jones writes in a memoir about his father, Jeff Jones, that the Weather Underground members "became expert at demolitions, and precious copies of *The Blaster's Handbook* were passed around and hidden beneath closet floorboards."[80] Appearing in a number of editions since 1918, *The Blaster's Handbook* was a common text kept in many workplaces, attesting to the easy availability of explosives information from official sources.

As explosives manufacturers, the Du Ponts had supplied the government with munitions since the beginning of the nation and were highly visible representatives of the military-industrial complex. Evocation of *The Blaster's Handbook* suggested that the bombers were stealing from the master's toolbox. As Stern wrote, "To go up against serpents, you have to have the knowledge of serpents. You must be a serpent yourself."[81] Cathy Wilkerson has explained her fascination with bombs and explosives: "It seemed like those with the scientific and technical knowledge were calling the shots. If we had to take up arms, I wanted to learn about them. Men should not have exclusive possession of this knowledge."[82] Although they were never very proficient bombers and indeed more of a danger to themselves because they lacked practical expertise, members of the Weather Underground attempted to imitate the state with its power over life and death. *The Blaster's Handbook* functioned as an internal symbol of a rebel generation's Promethean theft of that power. The police sometimes collected the *The Blaster's Handbook* as evidence, but it never became a literary Satan as did *The Anarchist Cookbook*, nor did it provoke any moral outrage.

Because of its broadly rebellious aura, *The Anarchist Cookbook* shifted its guilty associations readily from leftist revolutionary groups to survivalists, white supremacists, lone wolves, skinheads, and gifted psychotic teenagers in the 1980s and 1990s. Sold in militarist and survivalist bookstores, *The Anarchist Cookbook* found its way back to its right-wing paramilitary origins, but also spread throughout the culture with hundreds of thousands of copies sold and recirculated. The news media often reported its association with high-profile cases involving hate crimes, such as an Aryan Nation's plot to pipe bomb a gay disco in Boise, Idaho, and former Klansman Walter Moody Jr.'s mail bomb spree that targeted NAACP offices throughout the South and killed civil rights lawyer Robert Robinson and US district judge Robert Vance.[83] *The Anarchist Cookbook* was found in a cache of explosives owned by members of the Army of God, a violent group that targeted abortion clinics.[84] In the affidavit used to obtain a search warrant to raid the David Koresh compound in Waco, Texas, federal investigators pointed to the Branch Davidians' "extensive talk" of *The Anarchist Cookbook* as evidence, helping to create what Stuart Wright has called a "grossly exaggerated perception of the Branch Davidians as an ominous threat to society and to themselves."[85]

In the 1990s, the mass media often used the book in portraits of troubled teenagers. The police confiscated the book as evidence in arson and bombing cases involving teens. They then made this detail known to reporters, who frequently expressed alarm at the widespread availability of *The Anarchist Cookbook*: a convenient symbol of the most recent moral panic over deviant youth.[86] Reporters used it as a sociological device to account for the anomie of teens, police put teens who owned the book on their suspects lists, and school officials debated what to do about teens' access to information. In a typical case,

Atlanta police looking for suspects after the Centennial Olympic Park bombing in 1996 arrested an innocent teenage fry cook who was selling a copy of his own pamphlet, "Rise Above," most of which was lifted verbatim from *The Anarchist Cookbook*.[87] In Salt Lake City, a librarian called the local police when a teenage patron Xeroxed pages of *The Anarchist Cookbook*, an act of surveillance that raised the eyebrows of other local librarians concerned about professional ethics.[88] In his documentary *Bowling for Columbine*, Michael Moore traveled to Oscoda, Michigan, where school shooter Eric Harris once lived. There he interviewed "DJ," who told Moore that after the Columbine shooting the police put him as number two on their suspects list. The reason? It was popularly known in Oscoda that DJ owned and used *The Anarchist Cookbook*.[89] *The Anarchist Cookbook* thus achieved infamy through cultural narratives of deviant reading perpetuated by police, librarians, teachers, and reporters.

After Karl Pierson opened fire on his classmates at a Colorado high school in 2013, a co-member of his debate team mentioned to the news media that Pierson owned *The Anarchist Cookbook*, which had no demonstrable connection to the crime. William Powell again made a plea for Billie Blann, owner of Desert Publications who now owns the rights to the book, to take it out of print. NBC reported that *The Anarchist Cookbook* had been associated with a number of criminal acts, implying that somehow the book had helped cause them.[90] The real reason for these associations is that *The Anarchist Cookbook*, which has sold two million copies, is cemented in the public mind, aided by the police's pursuit of the book as evidence, as the most deviant of books.

The continuing panic over *The Anarchist Cookbook* demonstrates the social uncertainties around popular weapons manuals as they moved out of small paramilitary circles to a wider readership. The difficulty was not with the information itself since that was already available in other forms such as professional blaster's handbooks, chemistry and engineering textbooks, and army manuals. The difficulty was with the aura of deviance that surrounded the book, the deviance of the wrong hands. The right hands for this information were deemed to be the foot soldiers of the state: its military personnel and law enforcement officials. Usually, these persons were not seen as having the same potential of criminal violence, and the paramilitary publishers would often legitimate their enterprises by claiming that they were marketing to the police audience that allegedly needed the information for criminal investigations. This same audience could give demonstrations of bomb making under the guise of informing the public, as when, shortly after the publication of *The Anarchist Cookbook*, a police detective shocked the West Palm Beach Kiwanis Club luncheon by holding up the book and demonstrating how to make a car bomb, a spectacle that ended with him producing a gut-wrenchingly loud buzz as a sound effect.[91] Yet these boundaries between the right hands and the wrong hands were based on a false assumption of purity. Police officers have also been known to carry out violent crimes with *The Anarchist Cookbook* in their possession. For example, a probationary police officer in Indiana, Jerry Williams, engaged a friend in reading *The Anarchist Cookbook* while planning to deploy pipe bombs in burglaries. Their field tests of the devices led to the death of an elderly bystander.[92] Ohio state trooper Jimmy R. Jones attempted to murder his wife by placing a model rocket engine bomb in the fuel tank of her Ford Thunderbird. At his trial, his ownership of *The Anarchist Cookbook* was used as evidence that he had obtained expertise in demolitions.[93]

That the police had confiscated *The Anarchist Cookbook* in cases involving their own shows that by the mid-1990s they had been trained to see it as an instant sign of criminality. Here is a typical search and seizure that occurred when the police went to investigate a report of a break-in and discovered these indications of criminal activity in the house:

> The officers saw 1) a fluorescent lighting fixture and a soil-filled pot containing a device for measuring humidity and portions of marijuana leaves in a work room closet; 2) a book titled "The Anarchist's Cookbook" in a hall closet; 3) electronic parts and devices in the work room; 4) an assault rifle in the bedroom closet; and 5) a bag of marijuana in plain view [according to the officers] on top of a cushion on the couch. One of the officers . . . promptly executed an affidavit and a request for a search warrant for the entire premises.[94]

The Anarchist Cookbook stands out as an oddity in this list. It is a perfectly legal book, not an illegal substance, weapon, or apparatus, yet it helped trigger a search warrant. Possessing and growing marijuana are illegal activities, but reading *The Anarchist Cookbook*, even if it contains information about growing marijuana, is not. It is not clear why *The Anarchist Cookbook* was included as evidence since it demonstrated nothing at all except that the police—like the firemen of *Fahrenheit 451*—saw it as a malevolent book.

The Anarchist Cookbook in the Courts

One of the first high-profile cases challenging this subtle criminalization of *The Anarchist Cookbook* and similar books was the trial of Frank Stearns Giese, a professor who ran the Radical Education Project Collective Bookcenter in Portland, Oregon, and who was accused of conspiring to bomb two US Army and Navy recruiting centers there in 1973. In a climate of intense suspicion and surveillance by the local police and the FBI, who monitored thousands of people in Portland during this period, Giese was one of the leaders of a small radical antiwar group that decided to engage in armed struggle against industrialists and military recruiters to disrupt military operations.[95] As a navy lieutenant during World War II, Giese had become radicalized by his observation of the effects of colonialism and imperialism in North Africa, where he served.[96] The other conspirators included three former inmates from the Oregon State Correctional Institution, where Giese led book discussions on radical politics, and four owners of a painting company that hired released prisoners. At least some members of the group planned bombings and robberies of local sites like the sheriff's office, National Guard depot, and army recruiting centers, and carried out several of these crimes. Five members, including Giese, were tried and convicted for various offenses, including possession of an explosive device. Giese was acquitted of all charges but one. He was sentenced to a maximum of five years for conspiracy in connection with the bombings of the recruiting centers. Giese appealed his conviction, partly on the basis that the court had allowed inadmissible evidence: his reading material.

That evidence consisted of many books and pamphlets owned by the defendants. These included *The Anarchist's Cookbook*; *Ants in the Home and Garden*; *Special Forces Handbook*; *The Paper Trip* (about hiding one's identity); *Protect Yourself from Investigation*; *Humanity, Freedom, Peace* (containing a chapter on urban guerrilla warfare); *Road to Revolution* (on guerrilla warfare); *Socialism and Man*; *Socialist Revolution*; and *From the Movement toward Revolution*. The prosecutors featured *The Blaster's Handbook* and other books marked with the defendants' fingerprints to prove conspiracy. However, they included many of the books simply to inflame the jury's prejudices at a time when the anti-war movement had become broadly associated with anarchism and social chaos.

On appeal, Giese and his attorney, Doron Weinberg, argued that the court had erred in admitting the books as evidence, partly because Giese's First Amendment right to read had been violated. They focused on the introduction of H. Bruce Franklin's *From the Movement Toward Revolution*, an educational compilation of documents from black liberation and antiwar groups. On the witness stand, Giese had been asked by a prosecuting attorney to read a portion of a page that held his fingerprint. This quotation came from the New York Panther 21's open letter to the Weather Underground:

> We are sorry to hear that the townhouse [bomb-making accident] "forever destroyed" your "belief that armed struggle is the only real struggle." That places us in a unique position because, as Che stated—"Armed struggle is the only solution for people who fight to free themselves" and we have lost dearly loved comrades. Also—probably every experienced revolutionary has—but we realize that risks must be taken—some will

> die—others will replace them (or us)—like people rapping about ending racism, colonialism, sexism and all of the other pig "isms," exploitation and all that—but these things can only be ended by revolution—and revolution is—in the final analysis—ARMED STRUGGLE—revolution is VIOLENCE—revolution is WAR—revolution is BLOODSHED! How long have different successful national liberation fronts fought before they have won large popular support?[97]

There is nothing in the passage having to do with targeting army and navy recruitment centers or the criminal aims of Portland revolutionaries or anything revealing of the mind of Frank Stearns Giese, who was not a member of the New York Panther 21 or the Weather Underground. The discussion of revolution is sensational, but vague and indirect, commonplace and definitional.

Giese had been asked to read the passages, in his own voice, to associate him not just with his own group, but with a national underground, an allegedly vast, violent conspiracy. In his closing argument, the prosecutor again brought up the subject of books, mentioning *The Blaster's Handbook, Special Forces Handbook, The Firearm and Defense Manual, The Anarchist Cookbook*, and, again, *From the Movement Toward Revolution*, which he described as "an architectural manual, basically, of urban warfare."[98] At this point, he quoted a more specific revolutionary recommendation from this book: "Let's ALL try to pick targets with more care and planning—The object is to 1) destroy the economy—like bombing sites which will affect the economy the most; 2) ripoff money, weapons, and etc.; 3) sniping attacks."[99] Of the books together he said, "From this book to this book, you have the makings of any sort of urban warfare you'd like to participate in." He then urged the jury to "leaf through" the rest of *From the Movement Toward Revolution*, "because, as I indicated, this tells you this is another how to do it for urban warfare."[100] *From the Movement Toward Revolution* is by no means a how-to, but rather a collection of historical documents, like the well-known Port Huron Statement and the sheet music for *We Shall Overcome*, with only the occasional reference to violent revolution in some of the pieces. It was published not by a small, oppositional press like Panther/Paladin, but by the mainstream Van Nostrand Reinhold. Still, the title and a few highly selective passages gave the appearance of a violent book, leaving much to the jury's imagination, drawn from sensational media coverage of student radicals.

In his defense, Giese introduced eighteen books from his bookstore and home library to show that he sold and distributed nonviolent books and was a believer in peace and nonviolence. Like other defendants testifying in highly politicized cases, Giese used the courtroom as a forum for educating the jury about the broad goals of the Left, taking time, for example, to discuss the existentialist Albert Camus. He modeled his role as a leader of book discussions, choosing works that would have appeared in many personal libraries of readers interested in left-wing politics and culture at this time, such as John G. Neihardt's *Black Elk Speaks* and Eldridge Cleaver's *Soul on Ice*. The defense hoped that this evidence would help defeat the accusation that Giese was a bomb thrower, an accusation that his attorney argued was "as illogical, if you will, as saying that Reverend Martin Luther King was a member of the Black Panther Party." But the plan backfired because Geise's discussion of his literary habits, as evidence of good character, opened the door for a cross-examination using books like *From the Movement Toward Revolution* and *The Anarchist Cookbook* to impeach his character by associating him with well-known symbols of violent dissent.

The US Ninth Circuit Court of Appeals upheld Giese's conviction, although it was careful to disassociate its opinion from constitutional implications: "We are not establishing a general rule that the government may use a person's reading habits, literary tastes or political views as evidence against him in a criminal prosecution. In many cases such evidence would be clearly inadmissible."[101] The majority opinion, delivered by Judge Ozell Trask, instead emphasized the fingerprint evidence and the prosecutor's use of some of the books' contents to prove the association of the conspirators. Judge Trask also allowed that Giese had opened up the subject of books as character evidence, and therefore was subject to cross-examination. Judge Shirley Hufstedler, who went on to become secretary of education under President Jimmy Carter, delivered a dissenting opinion, arguing that Giese had been "convicted of conspiracy by book association in egregious violation of the guarantees of the First Amendment."[102] Judge Hufstedler challenged both the fingerprint and character evidence, stating that "no inference of any kind can be drawn about a person's character from the kinds of books that he reads. We have no basis in human experience to assume that persons of 'good' character confine their reading matter to 'good' books, or that persons who read peaceful books are peaceful people, or that persons who read books involving violence are violent people."[103]

While *The Anarchist Cookbook* has been introduced in dozens of trials, the courts—when in a more sober frame of mind—have cautioned that introduction of the book is often inflammatory and not of probative value. In a landmark case, the Ninth Circuit Court of Appeals reversed the conviction of Randy Ellis, accused of receiving and concealing explosives stolen from a mining company. *The Anarchist Cookbook*, which Ellis had borrowed from a friend, was introduced at the original trial to prove his intent to build a bomb. Ellis complained that introduction of the book was prejudicial since it "contains a lot of irrelevant and inflammatory material about such things as drugs, revolutionary politics, sabotage and inflammatory material that just don't go to any issues in the case."[104] The judge agreed and overturned Ellis's conviction. This decision was later used as precedent in the case of Briana Waters, accused of setting fire to the office of a horticulture professor at the University of Washington in 2001. Waters was believed to be a member of the Earth Liberation Front (ELF), which carried out the attack to protest genetic engineering. At Waters's trial in 2004, a file of anarchist articles was introduced that she had allegedly compiled for an ELF friend, Jennifer Kolar, who later admitted her participation in the arson. Some of these articles advocated revolution and attacks on the icons of US capitalism, such as Wall Street and Disneyland, a familiar hyperbole in some anarchist writing. Waters was convicted, but the Ninth Circuit overturned the conviction six years later, citing *U.S. v. Ellis* as disallowing admission of texts advocating political violence because they are "highly prejudicial." The appeals court further argued that the district court had "admitted the articles without ever reviewing them."[105]

The Anarchist Cookbook was again introduced in a case against Illinois resident John Rogers for possession of a homemade silencer for a semiautomatic pistol. The silencer fell under the definition of an unregistered firearm, and for that crime, Rogers received a sentence of seventy months in prison. *The Anarchist Cookbook* was admitted into evidence because a federal agent saw similarities between the book's instructions and the silencer and because Rogers admitted that he had used the book to construct it. At the trial, the prosecutor read passages of *The Anarchist Cookbook,* including passages that had nothing to do with silencers. Upon appeal, the Seventh Circuit judge, Frank Easterbrook, upheld the conviction, but acknowledged that the prosecutor should have been prevented from reading irrelevant passages, thereby "suggesting that Rogers should be convicted because he owned seditious literature, that anyone who would read a book called *The Anarchist's Cookbook* must hold his legal obligations in contempt, or that possession of the book implied that Rogers wanted to become a sniper."[106] Like many of his predecessors, Judge Easterbrook upheld the right to read and affirmed that sensational books could not be introduced in court merely to inflame opinion.

The Rogers appeal was argued on September 11, 2001, the day that a chillier climate began to descend upon citizens' rights, including their constitutional right to read. In 2008, *The Anarchist Cookbook* was introduced as evidence in the trial of Steven Parr. As a prison inmate in Wisconsin, Parr had relayed to a cellmate a detailed plan to blow up the Reuss Federal Building in Milwaukee, declaring that he was "the next McVeigh." Parr was charged with "threatening to use a weapon of mass destruction against a federal government building." At his trial, prosecutors introduced *The Anarchist Cookbook,* found in Parr's possession during his previous arrest for drug trafficking. Parr was sentenced to ten years. During his appeal, the judge ruled that the introduction of *The Anarchist Cookbook* had been a "mistake," but a harmless one, and not enough to overturn Parr's conviction.[107]

The frequent seizing of *The Anarchist Cookbook* and its introduction in the courts have transformed it into a literary Satan and its readers into deviants and criminals. No sound rationale exists for this. For one thing, the technical information is commonplace, and the book is not demonstrably any more harmful than an official military manual or science textbook. What distinguishes the book is the black cover with the word "anarchist," the use of everyday language to convey technical information, and the general aura of rebellion against government. There are many possible reasons for owning *The Anarchist Cookbook*, and certainly one of them has been created by government enforcers. Like many others of its kind, *The Anarchist Cookbook* would probably have faded into oblivion if it had not emerged during a moral panic and evoked even more surges of moral panic. Now, an interpretive circle has developed. The government's surveillance apparatus interprets ownership of *The Anarchist Circle* as deviant; some people own *The Anarchist Cookbook* to embrace what is considered deviant. Rebelling against institutional authority, adolescents, especially, are drawn to *The Anarchist Cookbook* and may keep it in their hall closets, out of nostalgia, long after they are grown. The rebellious aura of owning *The Anarchist Cookbook* has nothing to do with actually reading it, much less using it, a point missed by the police who confiscate it. Perhaps fingerprint evidence might suggest the reading of a page, but investigators can't peer into a person's mind to ascertain whether or how the book was read. The book might not have been read at all, or read carelessly and sporadically, or resisted, or transformed in the mind in myriad and unexpected ways, or been completely misinterpreted.[108]

Under the Warren Court, the right of the autonomous individual to pursue knowledge through reading was protected. In this interpretive tradition, the First Amendment ensures that individuals can seek self-fulfillment and discover truth through freedom of expression.[109] More recently, some legal scholars have argued that assumptions of an Enlightenment individual in a private home misses our embeddedness in societies to which we are indebted and that make us secure. For example, hate speech, it is argued, threatens community and should not be seen as an individual right.[110] Child pornography has presented the key test for debating whether the state can intervene in private reading. The strongest arguments in these cases are that the state must protect children from assault and violations of privacy when they are used as visual pornographic objects; the weakest and most controversial are that the material (including digitally manipulated images) encourages pedophiles to act. The question is whether, and to what extent, the state should intervene in the agency of reading subjects by seizing their books and criminalizing their acts of reading.[111] With its grim vision of firemen dismantling houses in their quest for books—now all condemned by the state as "sheer perversity" and "antisocial"—François Truffaut's film adaptation of *Fahrenheit 451* came out only five years before *The Anarchist*

Cookbook's publication. The history of *The Anarchist Cookbook* in the police stations and in the courts reveals that the activity of book seizing—without any real justification—goes on and is not merely a futuristic warning.

The Anarchist Cookbook is surrounded not only by controversies over deviant reading but on the deviant misuse of information. Its own creator, William Powell, tried to impose self-censorship by retracting the book. However, he had given his rights away to his publisher, and the book has been reprinted and imitated so many times that the gesture was inconsequential. Powell made no lasting contribution to bomb-making expertise or to formal anarchist philosophy, but he introduced a theory of technical information: technical information is fundamentally anarchistic, honoring no political boundaries, as compilers steal it for their own purposes. Despite efforts to criminalize *The Anarchist Cookbook*, the information disappears and reappears, circulating through readers and creators. Digital texts called *The Anarchist Cookbook* are not usually the authentic work, a distinction that matters little to its plagiarizers or to the police who now confiscate computers with downloaded "anarchist cookbooks." Because of its easily cut-up, mashed-up recipe form and its rebellious aura, *The Anarchist Cookbook* was one of the first books uploaded and circulated among the early adopters of the Internet, where free access is highly valued and borrowing, collating, plagiarizing, and imitating have become the primary modes of communication. In the latter phase of its nomadic career, *The Anarchist Cookbook* became a symbol of the mysterious, technologically adept terrorist of the Internet. Predictably, an increasingly sophisticate government surveillance apparatus has tried to contain its new form.

4

Hitmen

Uncle Fester's *Silent Death* offers instruction in kitchen-made poisons: phosgene, nerve gas, botulism, ricin, and "CIA shellfish toxin." Written by a professional chemist, it emulates the language of a science textbook, but offers "a celebration of that ancient and fine art, the art of poisoning."[1] For a few dollars, the curious and malevolent can now download it from the digital library, Scribd. The book was an answer to Maxwell Hutchkinson's *The Poisoner's Handbook*, which provided a rough account of making various organic poisons from plants. Uncle Fester's aim was to update such manuals by adding real science: "Prior to my typewriter driven blitzkrieg, underground books were generally entertaining, but sorely lacking in technical prowess and veracity."[2] Published by the now defunct Loompanics, *Silent Death* has featured in cases involving the production of ricin, a poison made famous by a KGB assassination of a Soviet defector and featured as a key plot point in the television series, *Breaking Bad*. Ricin is difficult to produce with any purity or in large quantity, but even without advanced technical equipment, the instructions in *Silent Death* produce a serviceable product that will kill if ingested or injected. For instance, two members of a Minnesota antigovernment group were convicted of making a strong enough quantity of ricin to murder 129 people.[3] They had received a ricin-making kit from a well-known figure in patriot groups, Maynard Campbell, who had reprinted portions of *Silent Death* in his own book, urging readers to "quietly eliminate the corrupt and unjust individuals within our 'system's' structure."[4] The prosecutor held up the cover of *Silent Death* with its menacing skull and crossbones to show how serious the defendants were.[5]

Books like *Silent Death* represent a maturation of the popular weapons manual over a few decades after the Vietnam War as paramilitary publishers expanded their scope and audience. In the 1960s, publishers like Paladin Press had begun to create an alternative network for military information with an eye to veracity and professionalism. The largest producers of weapons information are government military institutions, and the second largest are the paramilitary publishers who provide a conduit for that information into the public sphere. Located outside the publishing mainstream, these operations have popularized DIY military technologies, initially reprinting them straight from the source: official army manuals. In the courts, in news accounts, in evidence lists, in congressional hearings, in the work of terror experts and legal scholars, the titles of military manuals appear without any indication of their provenance. During the Vietnam War, army manuals entered popular circulation either by soldiers carrying them into civilian life or by one of these publishers reprinting them. As unclassified government documents, they were in the public domain and could be ordered, copied, and sold. Paramilitary publishers could reprint them without paying an author, making them a cheap source of profits. It's an open secret that a great deal of information about improvised explosive devices and other weaponry comes from Vietnam-era US Army manuals via the paramilitary publishers. The paramilitary publishers were the war state's disowned offspring, developing catalogs that glorified violent craft by inglorious shadow warriors. As delegitimized products of the state, the collation of military information gained new cultural meanings and purposes that were not subject to military control and discipline.

The paramilitary publishers like Paladin Press sold army manuals on guns and explosives that gave an edge to their fascination with the CIA's covert operations, mercenary work, and anti-communist guerrilla warfare. Army manuals on improvised explosive devices and booby traps that could be used in the field were great favorites among these publishers, especially if they could be linked to the CIA and Special Forces. Other books were alleged to be directly from the CIA, giving them an aura of special insider tradecraft. An homage to the CIA dirty war—slinking along without an official public sanction and eschewing moral approval—marked the entire line and shaped the future of the popular weapons manual.

A new model of book production appeared: setting up an alternative outfit to churn out reprinted, collated, and original books that contained illegal or at least illicit technical instruction and then claim First Amendment protections. The paramilitary publishers were associated with anti-communist sentiments, but their books did not often openly declare them. Because the technical directions were easy to follow, they transferred easily from group to group, espousing whatever political cause. Producing hundreds of popular weapons manuals, these publishers solidified the genre, forming a stable of respected writers who lent expertise and larger-than-life narrative personas. Experimenting outside the secretive, well-equipped, and highly technical spheres of military research and development, these writers foraged through available military documents and old science and technical books, developing an extensive lore of weapons handicrafts. Kurt Saxon, the author of the encyclopedic *The Poor Man's James Bond*, wrote, "As world civilizations decline and the presently powerful and affluent are reduced to beggary and helplessness, the owners of these volumes holding a veritable storehouse of both industrial and military power will survive to form dynasties."[6] Saxon wrote that he took his information from old sources that were aimed at the uneducated, so no formal education from the eggheads was needed to understand the postapocalypse archive. These recycled works entered the folkways of American culture, where they added to the informal stories, projects, and practices of would-be rebels and amateur experimenters.

The First Amendment saved these publishers from overt censorship, but as with *The Anarchist Cookbook*, their books have often appeared on evidence lists in police investigations. In the courts, prosecutors have introduced selections from the bookshelves of defendants to prove their propensity for criminality. Paladin and Loompanics titles—like *Improvised Explosive Devices, Explosives and Demolitions, Silent Death, How to Kill,* and *The Poisoner's Handbook*—are intended to shock the jury by exposing the defendant's malevolence, especially if the defendant is deemed a political enemy of the state. It goes much worse if the defendant is designated an ecoterrorist, an anarchist, a lone wolf terrorist, an Islamic extremist, or an antigovernment militia member. Some (but not all) judges admit the books as evidence, preferring evidence of a direct connection between the technical directions—like making bombs, poisons, silencers, and methamphetamines—and the criminal act. For example, if a defendant has built a silencer, it is acceptable to produce the book used to build the silencer. There are many cases, however, in which thousands of (often unread) pages of text have been dumped into evidence.

Paladin Press

By 1970, Paladin Press had established itself as the go-to publisher for DIY weapons manuals, constituting a separate source of professional-level weapons information traded in the alternative military worlds of the gun show and army surplus stores. As an FBI investigator wrote, "For the most part, cover letter or original binders on military publications are removed leading the buyer to believe that the product is a Paladin Press publication."[7] With its stolen aura of authenticity and authoritative insider knowledge, Paladin quickly pushed out the competition from other small paramilitary publishers.

Paladin's catalog encompassed dark crafts representing the underside of national power, and over the decades, the nation has had to confront its own shadow. One of the first confrontations was over Paladin's reprinting of what are now infamous manuals—*Unconventional Warfare Devices and Techniques* (TM 31-201-1), *Boobytraps* (FM 5-31), and *Improvised Munitions Handbook*. During the McClellan subcommittee hearings in 1970, these books—along with all books on explosives, bombs, sabotage, and unconventional warfare—were dangerous enough for the army to briefly reclassify them as confidential.[8] It was too late, since the reprinted manuals had found a lasting global circulation as a source for bomb-making information that makes their offshoot, *The Anarchist Cookbook*, look like child's play. Claiming that "terrorists" had obtained TM31-201 and FM 5-31 through the Freedom of Information Act, a Los Angeles Bomb Squad detective told a 1983 congressional hearing on domestic security that "the declassification of these manuals has, in my experience as a bomb technician, been tragic to this country . . . the Freedom of Information Act has killed quite a number of people." Senator Jeremiah Denton exclaimed, "It strikes me as remarkable that . . . the things you have just mentioned, which are so directed against our security and well-being, would be protected by the first amendment."[9] The Freedom of Information Act, however, was not needed to obtain official military manuals on booby-traps and explosives devices; Paladin had already provided them. Discouraged by military censors but encouraged by the interest in such offerings, Paladin began publishing original books on these topics: collated, shaped, and authored by intelligence veterans who claimed insider knowledge and found new employment as civilian instructors in the violent arts. Paladin's encounter with the government became an integral part of its dubious identity as the last frontier of free speech, although it provides legal disclaimers and has cooperated with police searching for suspects' purchase records.[10] Taking its stable of expertise from irregular wars and military intelligence operations, Paladin is no opposition to the nation. It is its byproduct.

Over the two decades following the Vietnam War, Paladin vigorously expanded its line to include US military manuals and treatises on guerrilla warfare, which were aimed at military buffs and aspiring soldiers of fortune looking for private wars against the falling dominos of communism. Under the ownership of Peder Lund, who claimed a background in the Special Forces, Paladin developed interests in survivalism, bombs and explosives, theft, dirty tricks, ninja fighting, home security, smuggling and other illicit gain, identity protection and disguise, and murder techniques. Books by Paladin Press are on the police watch and have regularly appeared in domestic murder cases. Paladin's subversive how-to manuals have found their way into domestic radical groups looking for new means of direct action. Citizen militias and paranoid loners collect them alongside their massive home arsenals in preparation for the coming collapse. Paladin's titles on improvised explosives, poisons, and booby-traps are infamous around the world for their associations with violent groups. In 1978, an article in *New Statesman* provided images from the US Army manual *Boobytraps* (FM 5-31) showing bombs made from teakettles and irons. Under a government much more given to censorship, the outraged journalist wondered why Scotland Yard couldn't find a way of removing Paladin titles from London bookstores.[11] Paladin books have traveled with the arms trade and found their way into IRA and Sinn Fein circles and al-Qaeda training camps.[12] In a Kurdish community in northern Iraq, soldiers found a trove of al-Qaeda training documents; a Special Forces officer at the scene flipped through them, observing, "This one is from our improvised munitions manual . . . That's from the booby trap manual. This is almost photocopied from our books."[13] Despite being outside the hubs of mainstream publishing, Paladin has had a global appeal, transcending the folkways of American violence that have formed and sustained it.

Unlike the satirical Situationist texts of the Yippies, such as Abbie Hoffman's *Steal This Book*, the Paladin catalog developed a repertoire for cardboard action heroes with a mordant gallows humor. Paladin texts have a bleak view of human relations and idealize a callous individual driven by profit and revenge, acting out of a stigmatized professionalism. This character has a flip side as a timid victim driven by compulsive needs for security, like the ninety-pound-weakling in old comics back-page advertisements who gets sand kicked in his face and is urged to take up bodybuilding. Paladin's inspirational persona is often an anomic individual who is doing dirty work for the state, harkening back to the press's original mission to provide information about dirty wars for privatized warriors. For example, in the mid-1970s, Paladin developed a line for debt collectors, such as *Involuntary Repossession; or In the Steal of the Night* by John Russell III, who claimed to be a trained criminologist, a private investigator, and a black belt in "go-Ju-Ruy Okinawan karate."[14] This book taught the reader to lock-pick cars, ostensibly as a guide to professional repossessors: the reviled figures who uphold the consumer debt system by collecting cars from people who haven't made their payments. Many of Paladin's books published in the 1970s and 1980s are for people in economic trouble and always anticipating personal and national catastrophe. Written under pseudonyms, the books offer fantasies of creating powerful new coping identities that use cloaking and disguise and enact rage and vengeance through practical know-how. Paladin's many books and a video—*Whispering Death*—on making silencers have been frequently used to gain convictions in murder cases.[15]

Paladin developed a stable of prolific popular writers who have provided a reliable audience for these fantasies. These usually pseudonymous authors have their own extravagant identities and distinct narrative voices. Paladin has been especially fond of authors who have held stigmatized masculine roles, such as claiming that they were involved in sordid intelligence operations like the Phoenix Program in Vietnam, operated as consultants to Latin American dictatorships, or worked as private detectives. The pseudonymous figures are larger than life, and, in certain circles, fulfill a masculine ideal of maverick violence with an undercurrent of authoritarianism. For example, one of Paladin's featured authors for many years was Rex Applegate (his real name), a former intelligence officer in World War II who wrote *Kill or Get Killed* (distributed by Paladin). It advised,

"Do unto others as they would do unto you, but do it first." Incidentally, Applegate was the inventor of a riot baton.[16]

Paladin favorite George Hayduke has published over twenty books of dirty tricks, told as folksy stories about mayhem, often with Hayduke reporting an incident from some admirably malicious third party. He took his pseudonym from a character in Edward Abbey's novel, *The Monkey Wrench Gang*, and made his name into a verb: Hayduking, meaning to perform vile tricks on others to get revenge. As devised by Abbey, monkeywrenching is a form of direct action using sabotage to stop land development, in contrast to Hayduking, which is retaliation for slights, frustrations, and disappointments. Hayduke's enemies are an uneven assortment of "pencil necks, jerks, geeks, institutions, corporations, bureaucrats, and other assorted assholes with black hearts or Styrofoam pellets for brains."[17] In his revenge stories, told in the tone of *Mad Magazine*,[18] more specific targets are mentioned: landlords, the Ku Klux Klan, antiabortion groups, and Mothers Against Drunk Driving. The mean-spirited pranks included filling a "mark's" shampoo bottle with hair remover, flinging a dirty diaper into the mark's face, and spiking food with laxatives. These pranks could escalate into running amok with "glue, wire cutters, paint, potatoes, M80s, etc." Hayduke has mentioned one inspiration: the CIA's *Freedom Fighters Manual*, a short comic book distributed to the Contra guerrillas in Nicaragua. It suggested a low-level harassment of the government through economic disruption: calling in sick to work, leaving tap water running, making fake hotel reservations, spilling liquids on important documents, putting a coin in a light socket, cutting telephone wires, dropping tacks in the road, vandalizing schools, damaging vehicle tires and batteries, and finally making Molotov cocktails.[19] Paladin's fondness for the CIA can be found across its catalog.

Some political groups have adapted this form of harassment as a method of direct action. The Animal Liberation Front (ALF) recommends Haywood's book *Get Even* for "economic sabotage."[20] A friend of ALF, the Stop Huntingdon Animal Cruelty (SHAC), used harassment techniques straight from the Hayduking playbook. Labeled by the government as an ecoterrorist organization, SHAC is an obsessive, long-term campaign to shut down Huntingdon Life Sciences (HLS), which it accuses of animal cruelty. Opponents of the company have flung red paint on buildings and private houses, inundated answering machines and email with obscene and threatening messages, thrown butyric acid into offices, put paint stripper on cars, and effaced houses with graffiti like "Puppy killer." One stock trader who had worked with HLS told a congressional hearing that SHAC had targeted his mother on its website: "Send her sex toys, have an undertaker arrive to pick up her dead body and call her collect in the middle of the night."[21] Although they argued that their speech was protected by the First Amendment, six SHAC members were convicted for inciting violence on their website under the Animal Enterprise Protection Act of 1992.[22] Similar techniques can be found in *The Army of God Manual*, which appeared in the early 1990s. Antiabortion groups used the manual for harassing and intimidating clinics with such tactics as gluing locks and flinging butyric acid—smelling of rotten milk and vomit—into entranceways. Since Hayduke is openly opposed to the antiabortion activists, their adaptation of his techniques shows the unintended consequences of writing such a book, whose readers may not share the same idea of the enemy.

Another of Paladin's prolific authors is Ragnar Benson, who specializes in survivalism and appears to have taken his pseudonym from a Chicago construction company. Suspiciously like other Paladin authors, including owner Lund and former owner Brown, he alleges to have worked in military intelligence and as a mercenary, witnessing the fight against the Batista forces in Cuba and "tracking and then trapping men on the east coast of Africa."[23] Benson often describes himself as an adventurer, like James Bond, who has been on mysterious special assignments. One of his aims is to record his alleged experiences with improvised field weapons for "historians, anthropologists, and tacticians."[24] Most of Benson's books, however, have been aimed at a more lucrative audience of antigovernment survivalists and weapons enthusiasts tinkering in home workshops and blowing things up in open fields. Speaking of a collaborator, he writes, "Perhaps uniquely, we found our greatest enjoyment—read self-fulfillment and creativity—making and using high explosives and manufacturing heavy ordnance."[25] Benson's many books provide instructions on how to make grenade launchers, flamethrowers, napalm, mortars, human traps, claymore mines, and a host of other weapons for "desperate circumstances."[26] In between technical directions, Benson tells adventure stories of his involvement with Somalian trackers, Burmese jade smugglers, Thai drug lords, Ecuadorian soldiers, Cuban revolutionaries, and possum hunters. Paladin's authors have an ambiguous relationship to the government, glorifying its intelligence and spy work while railing against it for taking away their pleasure in heavy artillery, a pastime they enjoyed in a golden age of fewer restrictions.

The first introduction of Benson's work in a high-profile case was the trial of Ahmad Ajaj, convicted of conspiracy in the 1993 World Trade Center bombing. Ajaj had been arrested when he arrived from Pakistan with a fake Swedish passport and suitcases holding two videotapes and twelve bomb-making manuals. Defense attorneys attempted to argue that Ajaj would not have had to obtain the materials in Pakistan because they were easily available in the United States. As a demonstration, defense attorneys played the Paladin video *Homemade C-4: A Recipe for Survival* before the jury. The prosecution rebutted that it was irrelevant because it contained no political message, bombing of a building, or musical chanting (nasheed), as could be found on Ajaj's videos.[27] In any event, the World

Trade Center bomb was made from urea nitrate, a very different explosive than "homemade C-4."

Benson's work rose to infamy with the trial of Timothy McVeigh for the bombing of the Oklahoma City Federal Building in 1995. Two books weighed heavily in the prosecutors' case: white supremacist William Pierce's *The Turner Diaries* (written under the pseudonym Andrew McDonald) and Benson's *Homemade C-4*. Both books were already well known in federal law enforcement circles. Already on the FBI's monitor of literary Satans, the Bureau had used *The Turner Diaries* to pursue convictions of violent Aryan Nation and Christian Identity groups. Some members of a murderous cell called The Order acknowledged that the book had served as a guide for them for setting up a terrorist organization and assassinating public figures.[28] In 1988, a civil rights activist, testifying at a congressional hearing on racially motivated violence, called the book "a blueprint and manual for the Klan's race war."[29] After the McVeigh trial, it would live in infamy as an "explicit terrorism manual."[30] However one may despise *The Turner Diaries* and its fomenting of hate, it is a work of science fiction. It imagines a future guerrilla war waged by the revolutionary Order against the governmental System that has been corrupted by blacks and Jews who are robbing citizens of their guns. In the story, the guerrillas drive a truck bomb, armed with an ammonium nitrate and fertilizer explosive, to blow up FBI headquarters, killing seven hundred people. The introduction of *The Turner Diaries* in the McVeigh case was a highly unusual inclusion of fiction as evidence against a defendant. When he was arrested, McVeigh had an envelope with photocopies and notes, including a highlighted quotation from the book: "The real value of our attacks today lies in the psychological impact, not in the immediate casualties." Citing this evidence in his opening statement at McVeigh's trial, prosecutor Joe Hartzler argued that *The Turner Diaries* was "a book [McVeigh] had read and believed in like the Bible."[31] With its sensationally violent racist content, *The Turner Diaries* was presented as both a technical blueprint for the attack and an ideological motivator. The problem was that McVeigh was not a white supremacist. He was angry at what he perceived as the government's tyrannical assault on gun rights and its disastrous standoff with the Branch Davidians at Waco. McVeigh's defense attorney rebutted that *The Turner Diaries* "is no more a blueprint, much less a reason, to blow up a federal building than Frederick Forsyth's novel *The Day of the Jackal* is a blueprint to assassinate the president of France."[32]

Hartzler used Benson's *Homemade C-4* to show that McVeigh had the technological know-how to build the truck bomb: "How do you know that Tim McVeigh knew what to do with those ingredients [he'd acquired]? In this free society, any of us can write away for a book on how to build a bomb."[33] A representative from Paladin Press testified that McVeigh had twice ordered books on bomb making, including *Homemade C-4*. Benson's book contains a rough process for making a fertilizer and nitromethane explosive, more appropriately called ANNM (ammonium nitrate / nitromethane). Benson writes that he got the idea reading about the arrest of a "despicable, bloodthirsty, Middle Eastern terrorist" who carried nitromethane in a wine bottle. (Even writers of popular books on DIY military-grade explosives have a view of the wrong hands, not seeing themselves as terrorists.) *Homemade C-4* supplies now outdated advice, illustrated with grainy black-and-white photographs, on how to purchase supplies like ammonium nitrate fertilizer and racing fuel, and cook the explosive using a coffee can, an ovenproof glass dish, plastic bags, and other household artifacts. Far beyond *Homemade C-4* in complexity and scale, McVeigh's truck bomb involved a Tovex dynamite primary detonation and barrels of explosives wired together. The Paladin video on *Homemade C-4* is on YouTube, showing some pyros blowing up a car, but nothing on the scale of a multilevel building.[34] (It also contains a stern warning about laws against home manufacturers of explosives.) Hartzler argued that the book "describes how to build a powerful bomb, and it does so in simple, understandable terms. In fact, it shows how unbelievably simple it is to make a hugely, hugely, powerful bomb."[35] Although McVeigh was clearly guilty, the use of how-to books was sensationalized, and through the rest of the decade, the federal government discussed laws designed to eliminate them.

Two years after the McVeigh trial, Paladin Press faced direct legal action in a civil suit over one of its titles. In *Rice v. Paladin*, the relatives of Mildred Horn, who was murdered along with her disabled son and his homecare nurse, sued the publisher for its title *Hitman: A Technical Manual for Independent Contractors*. Mildred Horn's husband had hired a real hitman and navy veteran, James Perry, to carry out the murders. He used specific elements from *Hitman*. All on recommendations from the book, he had bought a particular gun, used a file to erase its bore markings, drilled out its serial numbers, built a silencer, and shot two of the victims in the eyes from a distance of six to eight feet. Paladin acknowledged that Perry had ordered the book and was even willing to admit that it published it to attract potential criminals, but claimed its First Amendment right to do so under *Brandenburg v. Ohio*, which protects abstract violent speech. The victims argued that *Hitman* aided and abetted murder and was a reckless disregard for human life. Battling the case for six years, Paladin settled out of court after an appeals judge ruled that the First Amendment did not protect *Hitman* because it was an "integral part" of the murder and a vehicle for criminal conduct.[36]

Reactions to this case were deeply divided on whether works like *Hitman* should make a publisher liable or be protected by the *Brandenburg* standard. Defenders of literature, broadly defined, argued that the decision in the case was an ominous precedent leading to censorship of film and fiction that detailed crime methods.[37] Fifteen years later, with no significant effort to sue filmmakers and novelists, this appears to have been an overreaction. Others maintained that *Hitman* is a special form of speech: "highly clinical and technical [with] little if any expressive value"[38] and therefore unworthy of protection. It was compared to a manufacturer's product assembly instructions, aeronautical charts, and science textbooks that provided faulty information and were thus liable in successful injury suits.[39] These critics were in favor of a chilling effect on Paladin because they wanted to eliminate such books from society.

One of the overlooked problems with *Hitman* is that it is so obviously fictional. Lawyers discussing the case have roundly ignored the imaginative dimensions of the work. The victims' legal team discovered that the writer was not a hitman at all, but a mysterious woman living in a trailer in Florida who wrote the book because she thought she'd make enough money to alleviate a debt. These are the few details leaked about "Rex Feral's" real identity. Paladin company documents revealed that she intended to write a novel, but the publisher convinced her to turn it into a how-to manual more appropriate to its catalog.[40] The allegedly inspiring elements of the book could be extrapolated from detective stories: for example, ballistic fingerprinting was a well-known crime-solving technique and no great imagination is needed to see that filing the rifle bore would eliminate tell-tale traces.[41] *Hitman* is a strange book that extracts the murderer's method from the detective novel. One of the pleasures of reading a classic detective story is following the detective as he studies and reveals the crime method. *Hitman* strips away this plot apparatus to the method, but has a strong sense of character in the instructor/narrator, Rex Feral (King Wild in Latin), who describes himself as a tough guy, eschewing drugs and women—someone who can take a punch and has to guard against looking at ordinary people as an "irritating herd of pathetic sheep."[42] While *Hitman* doesn't rise to the level of Raymond Chandler, it carries conventions of hard-boiled detective and gangster fiction. It has imaginary scenes with characters engaged in dialogue. Eerily prophetic, tongue-in-cheek advice is given to the acolyte to read detective novels: "Sometimes the warped imagination of a fiction writer will point out an obvious but somehow never before realized method of pacification or body disposal. So don't bypass these fictional characters."[43] It contains an authorial inner dialogue: "A woman recently asked me how I could, in good conscience, write an instruction book on murder.... It is my opinion that the professional hit man fills a need in society." Rex Feral even claims that he was once "disguised as a writer."[44] *Hitman* can also be read as a postmodern parody of conventional DIY instructional speech.

Although Paladin owner Peter Lund has said that his books are above morality because they are "pure information," they have strong imaginative elements appropriate to fiction.[45] *Hitman* and other works in the Paladin line are not so easy to pigeonhole with a narrow, highly selective interpretation that they are purely technical information. It is a question whether stripping away the conventions of fiction makes a book like *Hitman* even more immersive, not for pleasure, but for a programmatic imitation of an authoritative instructor-character who has enough verisimilitude to fool a reader. The problem with using books from publishers like Paladin Press as courtroom evidence is that their form is chameleon-like. Although they contain technical directions, they resist reduction to pure information and elicit readers through fantasy.

Paladin agreed to stop selling the book in 1999, but the Utopian Anarchist Party website immediately copied it online in a text document as a gesture against "stifling the book."[46] Paladin's involvement in Timothy McVeigh's and Terry Nichols's court trials for the Oklahoma City bombing also led to its removing its titles on bombs and explosives: not for any high-minded reason, but because a new law, 18 U.S.C. § 842(p), was passed forbidding the circulation of bomb instructions for use in a federal crime. The press removed eighty-seven titles, which made up about 10% of its business.[47] This may have seemed a victory for the bill, which was designed to have a chilling effect on dangerous instructional speech, but in the long run, the books prevailed.

For a few years after Paladin bowed to censorship, I had difficulties obtaining many of its titles as part of my research for this book. Libraries have stood at the forefront of defending the right to read, but they are also selective about their collections, asserting their own control over access to texts based on tastes, patron requests, and the exigencies of space. Only a few law enforcement libraries had *Homemade C-4*, and wouldn't lend it. The online *Hitman* is easy to obtain, but the original title has all but disappeared. When I attempted to obtain Paladin's *EOD: Improvised Explosives Manual*, my request was mysteriously held up, and when it finally arrived, I was allowed to look at it only within the library confines. I had never had this happen with any other request. I had asked for *EOD* because it had shown up in the terrorism case of a London teenager, Abdul Patel, who was convicted for merely owning the book, but acquitted of the charge that he planned to use it in a terror attack. The judge found that he was not even a "radicalized or politicized Islamist."[48] Such a case represented the intensity with which the British government was cracking down on books it deemed terroristic. When I read *EOD*, I admit I was frightened by the contents, as I realized why liquids are not allowed on planes. The book also contained directions on how to make remote-controlled bombs using phones and garage door openers. At this time, cell phone bombs were being used in terrorist attacks in Europe. I had mixed feelings about the unusual controls on the book, which frustrated my access. At the same time, I found the book so irresponsible and dangerous that I was glad it was in the process of disappearing with only a few copies publicly available. I had begun my research with an absolutist view of free speech protections, but this book gave me pause. It is still difficult to obtain, and sold as a rare book worth well over $100.

In the wake of the *Rice v. Paladin* decision and the passing of 18 U.S.C. § 842(p), the Department of Justice had started exerting pressure on Internet service providers to close websites that offered weapons-making information.[49] Then suppressed Paladin books began to appear on the torrents—the peer-to-peer file-sharing sites. Some time and expertise was needed to access them, and the files carried the threat of viruses. Scribd came along, and hundreds of copies of Paladin books on explosives and every other topic suddenly became available to anyone at any time. Unlike other responsible sites, Scribd was not filtering the content except for copyright violations. Some of Paladin's discarded backlist is now on the site, including books on improvised bombs. The mere suggestion that such titles were being suppressed rallied Internet users to take a stand by scanning or retyping and uploading these texts under the banner of free speech. For example, a reproduction of the US Army's *Improvised Munitions Handbook* carries a note: "1969—original publication; 2007—Thanks to Feinstein's Electronic Edition (v. 3.0)." The reference is to Senator Dianne Feinstein, who has led a campaign against online bomb-making information since the 1990s. One problem with government crackdowns on literary Satans is that they tend then to attract celebrity status that results in proliferation, when they normally would have faded into oblivion. Culture has been very good at taking care of bad texts by eventually ignoring them, rendering them obsolete, and relegating them to irrelevance. It is, however, difficult to see the long view when your loved ones have been murdered, and you are pleading your case in court. At the time of the *Hitman* case, only 13,000 books had been sold. That's a decent figure for a midlist book, but far from best-selling. With its absurdly outdated hypermasculine narrator, *Hitman* would have gone gracefully into the dustbin of secondhand booksellers if it had not been for the attention paid to it. The same is undoubtedly true of *Homemade C-4*, available on Scribd. *The Turner Diaries*, once difficult to find, is now a cult classic still collected as evidence against white supremacists.[50] *The Turner Diaries* is still in print: the neo-Nazi National Alliance sold its copyright to Lyle Stuart, publisher of *The Anarchist Cookbook*.

Loompanics

Founded in 1975 by Michael Hoy, who was once called "an amoral egoist anarcho-capitalist," [51] Loompanics was the publisher for the lifestyle anarchist and the lumpenproletariat. An admirer saw Loompanics as representing a deep grain of democratic American life: "the America of get-rich-quick schemes, militias, tax evasion, gangland slayings, the Whiskey Rebellion, failed S & L's, life on the lamb, deadbeat dads and the electric chair."[52] Loompanics provided do-it-yourself guides for crimes like hacking, identity theft, home burglary, fraud, murder, pickpocketing, and drug manufacture, along with self-help books to live on the streets, go underground, survive encounters with the police, understand undercover operations, and stand up to surveillance, interrogation, and imprisonment. Never achieving the stature of Paladin Press, Loompanics still did a robust business of about $1.8 million a year at its peak.[53] While Paladin offered information to stateless shadow warriors camped on heavily armed homesteads, Loompanics encouraged low-level harassment of the police, the government, and other institutional authorities. Although Loompanics occasionally offered murder, it was mostly concerned with rejecting private property in a battle of wits against law enforcement. Loompanics' most infamous author, Stephen Preisler (Uncle Fester) gained the most attention because his works of clandestine chemistry were routinely collected as evidence in drug raids.

Preisler's books notoriously give directions on how to make methamphetamines, MDA, Ecstasy, and LSD. As with weapons manuals, these books contain technical instructions for illegal activities and translate pharmaceutical chemistry into easily understandable processes using household materials like plastic buckets, coffee pots, lithium batteries, and garden hoses and substances like ephedrine pills, camper fuel, pumice stones, and Vicks vapor inhalers. Preisler's chemistry, according to his citations, has been derived from old organic chemistry books and journals, some dating back to the nineteenth century. He is also the author of *Silent Death* and *Home Workshop Explosives*, which include directions on how to make high-power explosives like PETN and RDX. As a libertarian disgruntled with the "police state goon squads," their "tiny, frustrated" chemists, and their "pandering-politician masters" for "destroying our freedoms," Preisler argues that publishing drug-making instructions is the best refutation of government control and surveillance, especially in the War on Drugs. Pointing to the USA PATRIOT Act, Preisler writes in the seventh edition of *Secrets of Methamphetamine*, "The freedom to read whatever one chooses and to be unencumbered in the access to those books has been central to the Western concept of freedom for the past several hundred years. This cornerstone of our liberty is now under heavy assault."[54] His complaint is not only directed at federal drug agents but also mainstream booksellers like Amazon, which he says has refused to market his book, as if these stores had any obligation to him. He sees his work as a form of political speech against a tyrannical government. A fan of Preisler's writes that authorities "fail to see his work as being simply in the tradition of all anarchic and subversive agitprop" instead of "supplying drug dealers and terrorists with crucial information."[55] It is, however, both.

Preisler's books are routinely collected in searches and seizures as evidence of methamphetamine manufacturing. Here is a typical list of books seized in a drug raid: *The Secret Garden, Marijuana, Manufacturing Methamphetamine, Marijuana Grower's Guide, Psychedelic Chemistry, Construction and Operation for Clandestine*

Drug Laboratories, Techniques of Burglar Alarm Bypassing, How to Make Your Own Professional Lock Tools, and Eddie the Wire's *Complete Guide to Lockpicking.* The titles are not accurately transcribed in the original list, showing the sloppiness that usually attends book seizures, but *Secrets of Methamphetamine Manufacturing* and *Construction and Operation of Clandestine Drug Laboratories* are Preisler's. The judge in this case ruled that even if the defendant hadn't read the books, "his mere possession of them is clearly probative of his criminal intent."[56] The courts have often allowed Preisler's books to be used as evidence in trials of suspected drug dealers. In one notable case, a Massachusetts doctor, Jeffrey Ford, was arrested after a postal worker had observed him receiving suspicious packages, one of which held over twenty-five grams of cocaine. Police searched his house and found a package of cocaine on his bed, noting that it was alongside a *Penthouse* magazine. They also found a pistol, marijuana plants, and another bad text, *Secrets of Methamphetamine Manufacture,* which the prosecutor entered into evidence. On appeal, Ford argued that the book had nothing to do with his arrest for intent to distribute cocaine and marijuana, and its use against him was prejudicial because it "suggested a larger and more sinister involvement with narcotics." The court found that the book was admissible because of its probative value in showing Ford's intent and because it "was a tool of the drug trafficking trade."[57] The book was now defined as an apparatus that would often be mentioned in evidence lists alongside chemical laboratory equipment.[58] Subsequent attempts by defendants to argue for the prejudicial nature of the book have fallen on deaf ears in the courts, where it is unquestioningly viewed as substantiating criminal intent.[59]

The *Ford* case has also been used to justify using other books as evidence, as in *U. S. v. Brown.* After a nine-month armed standoff, US marshals took tax protesters Edward and Elaine Brown into custody for evading federal income tax—a crime for which they had already been sentenced in absentia to five years in prison. The marshals found a large arsenal of guns, ammunition, and pipe bombs and several books from a hallway shelf: *The Anarchist Cookbook, Guerrilla Warfare and Special Forces Operations, Booby Traps, Unconventional Warfare Devices and Techniques,* and *Modern Chemical Magic.* Most absurdly, this last book is simply an old pyrotechnics guide for performing stage tricks, magic demonstrations, and practical jokes. Three others are reprinted US Army manuals from the 1950s and 1960s. Yet the court claimed that these books were like *Secrets of Methamphetamine Manufacture,* extrapolating that they were tools for armed resistance. In a trial to prove that the Browns had engaged in a conspiracy to obstruct the US marshals, these titles were mentioned in the closing argument to reflect not only "the Browns' belief system," but also their knowledge of "the factual implementation of [armed] resistance." The district court used its prior *Ford* ruling to refuse Elaine Brown's appeal that the evidence was prejudicial. It refuted the argument that there was no direct forensic evidence or testimony linking Elaine to any of the books. The ruling proved once again that if a citizen resists the power of the federal government—in this case as part of the sovereign citizens movement—her bookshelf will be searched and her proximate reading materials confiscated and selectively distorted in court. The courts' willingness to tolerate the use of books as prosecutorial evidence has correlated with the strength of the defendant's antigovernment sentiments since the days of the Haymarket anarchists. Elaine Brown was sentenced to thirty-five years in prison, Edward to thirty-seven.

The most famous case involving Preisler's methamphetamine books was a confrontation with police over access to readers' records at libraries and bookstores. In 2000, Denver's North Metro Task Force, an arm of the federal Drug Enforcement Agency, approached the Tattered Cover bookstore, founded by former librarian Joyce Meskis, with a search warrant for the sales records of anyone who had purchased *Advanced Techniques of Clandestine Psychedelic and Amphetamine Manufacture* and *The Construction & Operation of Clandestine Drug Laboratories*. They had been watching a trailer home that they thought housed a meth lab and had found a Tattered Cover invoice in the garbage and other alleged evidence of a drug operation. A search of the lab turned up lab equipment and the two books, and the DEA issued a subpoena to the Tattered Cover demanding it turn over information related to the invoice and all books ordered by the prime suspect. In other cases, this tactic had worked, but Meskis refused. The DEA then issued a warrant to search the Tattered Cover, but when six officers arrived, Meskis contacted her attorney, gained a temporary injunction, and took the case to court. The trial was covered in the media, and the bookstore received local newspaper editorials and over one hundred letters in support of Meskis's position that cooperation would have a chilling effect on readers who consumed controversial books.

Tattered Cover v. City of Thornton became a cause célèbre, with Meskis receiving support from the American Booksellers Foundation for Free Expression and the Association of American Publishers, who stood up for bookstores. Under the slogan, "Support shameless purchasing of questionable books!" Daniel Handler (aka Lemony Snicket) organized a benefit that included such literary stars as Michael Chabon, Dave Eggars, Susie Bright, and Dorothy Allison.[60] In no other case had mainstream literary authors defended the right to produce and read how-to crime manuals, though their motivation was more loyalty to the Tattered Cover bookstore than a defense of meth lab handbooks. It has often been claimed in legal argument that literary writers—especially those who write crime fiction—must be able to access works like *Secrets of Methamphetamine Manufacture* to create realistic fictional worlds. The television series *Breaking Bad* relied on the believability of its meth lab operations, run by a high school chemistry teacher driven by his love for the craft. That is one of the justifications—the dual-use argument—for protecting how-to crime manuals.[61] But literary writers themselves have not had much to say in efforts to suppress them.

The Supreme Court of Colorado used constitutional balancing to decide in favor of Tattered Cover. In this case, First Amendment protections outweighed the police's need to connect the suspect to the meth-making books, though the court would have allowed it for a "sufficiently compelling reason." Revealing the discordancy of the law, the court obliquely suggested that meth-making handbooks are "expressive materials" rather than criminal tools, as in the Ford case. It argued that the public has the constitutional right to receive information and ideas, as expressed in these handbooks, as well as the right to privacy in reading. It made no distinction between the handbooks and other forms of speech: "Everyone must be permitted to discover and consider the full range of expression of ideas available in our 'marketplace of ideas.'" Quoting the Supreme Court decision in *U. S. v. Rumely*, it forecast the results if the government was allowed to demand booksellers' records: "Some will fear to read what is unpopular, what the powers-that-be dislike.... Fear will take the place of freedom in the libraries, book stores, and homes of the land."[62] *Publishers Weekly* reported that "the entire publishing industry applauded ... the decision."[63] It was an important ruling for privacy after the September 11 attacks, when the USA PATRIOT Act had expanded the police capacity to search bookstore records. A citizen could sell the books and purchase them anonymously without interference, but not own them on a home bookshelf, at least not without the risk of attracting the attention of the police.

Loompanics was not immune to social pressure to curtail its more violent offerings and dropped some of its books after the Columbine High School shootings. Feeling economic and technological pressures from online sellers, Michael Hoy closed down Loompanics in 2006. Paladin acquired the rights to forty of its titles: "We at Paladin Press have always admired the fearless Loompanics. After all, there just weren't that many publishers in the country who produced books that even we wouldn't touch!"[64] Libertarians in the blogosphere eulogized Loompanics as the loss of an important site of anarchist expression. Mark Frauenfelder, founder of Boing Boing, wrote that he was misty-eyed: "Hats off to publisher Mike Hoy for 30 years of all-American, 100% patriotic free speech!"[65] Sean Gabb, of the Libertarian Alliance think tank, remembered that when he first opened a Loompanics catalog, he "could see a world of unlimited possibilities—many of them wicked, but always presented with a scathing contempt for those who tax and rule us."[66] Some speculated that the USA PATRIOT Act had chilled Americans' willingness to buy controversial books.[67]

During their heyday in the three decades after the Vietnam War, publishers like Paladin and Loompanics thrived in the United States, taking advantage of the fascination with military hardware, antigovernment and antiauthoritarian sensibilities, do-it-yourself independence, criminality, alternative political ideas, and millenarian expectations of a social collapse demanding survival skills during tough times. The news media usually expressed curiosity, interviewing Peder Lund or Michael Hoy who defended their right to sell their books. Lund asserted that his publishing line was for "modern day Walter Mittys" and that "every man has his own line beyond which he will not go."[68] In the 1990s, with increased governmental attention to gun violence and domestic terrorism, these publishers began to encounter public hostility. In his expose of what he called "the violence industry," journalist Erik Larson condemned Paladin and Loompanics as a "distillation of the attitude of nonresponsibility that prevails in America's gun culture."[69] The McVeigh trial and the debates over the *Hitman* case brought these publishers to international attention, which included both praise and condemnation. By the end of the 1990s, interest had faded and the business of popular weapons manuals was in decline. Yet it made its mark as a cultural expression with serious repercussions.

Imitators of the manuals have appeared on the fringe of the alternative publishing spheres. For example, Timothy Tobiason, described by the *New York Times* as an "agricultural-chemicals entrepreneur from Nebraska with a bitter hatred for the government,"[70] set up a publishing outfit, Scientific and Technical Intelligence Press, to produce a series of books on "Scientific Principles of Improvised Warfare and Home Defense." This is a huge, multivolume compendium of weaponry with many manic digressions about Tobiason's fight against the federal government. Among the discussions of chemical and biological weapons is an explanation of how to collect and deliver anthrax, which brought Tobiason, who was selling his books at gun shows, into national public view after the anthrax scare in 2001. Tobiason's anthrax is an unrefined form, but the text uses the scientific and technical language once eschewed by such authors, like Johann Most and Kurt Saxon, as unnecessarily mystifying and above the common reader. Tobiason writes, "The way to fight back against lies and crooked government is with the solid application and use of science in all its forms, including the application of military sciences."[71] The apparatus of passive language, scientific formulas, and textbook design is intended to frighten the audience with its verisimilitude to official chemical and biological weapons information. As with the Uncle Fester books, the trajectory is toward greater parascientific professionalism. That said, for a serious inquiry into botulism and phosgene, a reader would have to consult a more authoritative official source.

The advent of the alternative publishers like Paladin and Loompanics produced a voluminous lore of amateur weapons making. Sourced in the production of US military manuals for covert and field operations, the mass production and increased professionalism of popular weapons manuals introduced new ways of discussing and planning violence and criminality. They found their way into the hands of murderers and thieves, diverse groups considering violence as a political tactic, terrorists aspiring to military power, survivalists preparing for the apocalypse, pyrotechnics enthusiasts, and armchair readers who only fantasized about paramilitary adventures. Increasingly on the radar of law enforcement, they found their way into many evidence lists and court cases. Offering low-tech weapons to ordinary people, they posed new challenges to governments faced with domestic and international terrorism and stimulated efforts at suppression of dangerous instructional speech. The right to own and read these manuals would continue to be challenged in the courts.

The courts have comprised the only domain in which popular weapons manuals have been seriously discussed for their psychological, political, and social meanings. Although many judges have written nuanced opinions on the introduction of reading materials against defendants, the legal questions regarding admissibility and the rules of evidence are too narrow. The police and the courts are not really interested in books. They have a highly reductive view of books in their search for causality, alleging that all reading must have a single, transparent purpose. After claiming that a suspect has planned and committed a violent act, the book's culpability as an abettor is a foregone conclusion. Only in very rare instances, however, is it possible to prove that a single book provided a specific blueprint and technical directions for an action. Far too often, popular weapons manuals are used symbolically, often by title alone, to condemn a broader, abstract enemy of the state.

5

Monkeywrenching

In the late 1990s, the Vail Ski Resort expanded into a remote bowl filled with coniferous trees that had historically protected the endangered Canada lynx, a cat that ranged widely in pursuit of the snowshoe hare in an ancient relationship of hunter and prey. Biologists were reintroducing the shy lynx into the area after it had apparently disappeared in the 1970s, the victim of traps, roads, and destruction of its high-country habitat. Environmental activists around Vail cared for the lynx and its wild, roadless habitat and had battled the proposed expansion through legal means and direct action protests, such as blocking roads to the site. Tensions between environmentalists and developers were high in 1998 when a small group affiliated with the Earth Liberation Front set fire to three chair lifts, a restaurant, and the ski patrol headquarters, culminating in what the press reported as an "ecoterrorist" attack, resulting in $12 million in damage to property. This act was widely perceived on both sides as an ineffective means of protest with damaging consequences all around.

As the hunt was on for the arsonists, in the nearby Breckenridge ski resort, the local police were attempting to link some instances of vandalism to the attack in Vail. The director of the Summit County Library, Joyce Dierauer, was surprised to receive a court order from the Breckenridge police, demanding that she turn over a list of anyone who had checked out Edward Abbey's *The Monkey Wrench Gang*, a comic novel published more than twenty years earlier about four antidevelopment radicals who camp, get high, raft, and vandalize around the Glen Canyon region, enthusiastically pulling up surveying stakes, damaging construction equipment, and eventually blowing up a bridge. The police could only ask for patrons who currently had the book because the library kept no back history of checkouts. A complete list of all patrons who had ever borrowed the book, Dierauer remembers, "was probably half the County."[1] Dierauer never found out why the book was of such interest to the police or whether it provided them any useful evidence. It was not clear why curling up with a popular novel would have transformed many patrons of the Summit County Library into ecoterror suspects, yet *The Monkey Wrench Gang*, more than twenty years a midlist bestseller, had achieved a certain status on the terrorist book watch list. It had introduced "monkeywrench" as a synonym for ecosabotage and celebrated lawless resistance without the forces of law and order prevailing in the end. Therefore, it stood out from countless crime narratives in film and fiction that provided at least as much detail on how to carry out even more violent crimes for which the guilty were punished by the swift hand of the law. *The Monkey Wrench Gang* dared to present protagonists, armed with ordinary hand tools and rudimentary technical know-how, who attack the large-scale expansion projects of loggers and developers in the West and get away with it.

The Monkey Wrench Gang is a telling case of a fictional work battered about by the shifting tides of terrorism rhetoric and paranoia. Originally received as a raucous comedy, a polemical satire, and a worthy contribution to southwestern and environmental literature, it has more recently been reduced to an "operational model," a "blueprint," and a "bible" for "ecoterrorists," as described by the terror experts who emerged as government consultants in the 1990s.[2] *The Monkey Wrench Gang* is frequently mentioned in histories, handbooks, textbooks, and encyclopedias of terrorism, where it is presented as the original "inspiration" for "ecoterrorist" sabotage.[3] Relying on a highly debatable application of the word "terrorism,"[4] these overviews typically profile a variety of groups across space and time with dubious arguments for their similarities, so that Greenpeace and the Sea Shepherd appear on a par with al-Qaeda. *The Monkey Wrench Gang* is listed among the key terms and concepts in a post-9/11 police investigator's guide to terrorism, written by a former FBI agent.[5] An article in *Studies in Conflict and Terrorism* oddly compares the book to the white supremacist *The Turner Diaries* because both allegedly portray "the most adept practitioners of leaderless resistance."[6] In 1982, in response to a critique of the book in *Environmental Ethics*, Abbey himself reacted to the terrorist label as a reductionist misinterpretation: "It would be naïve to read it as a tract, a program for action, or a manifesto. The book is a comedy, with a happy ending. It was written to entertain, to inspire tears and laughter, to amuse my friends and to aggravate our enemies. (Aggravate their ulcers.) So far about a million readers seem to have found that approach appealing. The book does not condone terrorism in any form."[7] Abbey went on to define terrorism as "deadly violence" often carried out by governments against their own people and by developers—"industrial terrorists" in his words—destroying the land and its nonhuman inhabitants. Despite authorial intention, the book found a lasting place in both criminal justice's typology of ecoterrorist groups and the lore of a social movement.

Well before *The Monkey Wrench Gang* was published, Edward Abbey had been under FBI surveillance for his pacifist statements, and he assumed that the FBI was tapping his phone after the book was published.[8] He would not have been surprised that an FBI informant was present at his funeral in 1989. She was there to spy on members of the radical environmental group Earth First!, especially Abbey's good friend David Foreman, whose own book, *Ecodefense: A Field Guide to Monkeywrenching*, had brought the FBI down on his head in a two-year, $2 million operation, involving two paid informants, an FBI infiltrator, and dozens of supporting agents. Inspired by Paladin Press's dirty tricks and weapons manuals, *Ecodefense* provided instruction in direct action methods such as tree spiking and damaging heavy equipment. Literary depictions and discussions of sabotage, rather than any tangible acts, initially mobilized these efforts at suppression. The FBI, local law enforcement agencies, politicians, industry advocates, and terror experts used *The Monkey Wrench Gang* and *Ecodefense* to profile and harass vocal enemies of logging and development. Although this kind of radical speech—including *Ecodefense*'s explicit technical instructions for sabotage—required public tolerance under the Constitution, behind the scenes the law was busy concocting ways to bring the writers and their readers under its hand and to appease the industrialists and land developers who had the most political influence.

The Monkey Wrench Gang is a work of fiction in the tradition of the mock-heroic folk tale; *Ecodefense* is a collaborative technical handbook in a folksy vernacular that crosses *The Anarchist Cookbook* with back-to-the-land handbooks. Both use detailed depictions of sabotage to deliberately test the boundaries of acceptable speech. As expressions of a more radical environmental consciousness, both navigate between parody and incitement, storytelling and instruction, entertainment and political manifesto. As a work of fiction, *The Monkey Wrench Gang* is somewhat more protected from suppression. A history of legal clashes over obscenity in literature—with literature ultimately winning out for its cultural merit—has undermined the argument that susceptible novel readers should be protected from moral corruption and contagious deviancy.[9] The literary form provides an implicit disclaimer: this is only a work of fiction. As an appellate court judge in a child pornography case wrote,

> Can the government introduce a defendant's copy of *The Monkey Wrench Gang, Lolita* or *Junky*, to prove intent? DVDs of *The Thomas Crown Affair* to prove intent to rob a bank, or *Dirty Harry* to prove intent to deprive someone of civil rights? *Huckleberry Finn* (with quotes out of context) to prove hate crime motivation? In the 1950s, people with leftist books sometimes shelved them spine to wall, out of fear that visitors would see and report them. Perhaps these days they would shelve *Huckleberry Finn* or *The Monkey Wrench Gang* spine to the wall. Readers should not have to hide what they read to be safe from the government.[10]

Nevertheless, the argument has resurfaced more acutely over another alleged literary blueprint for violent radicalism—William Pierce's white supremacist sedition fantasy, *The Turner Diaries*—featured in the trial of Timothy McVeigh. Despite its literary form, *The Monkey Wrench Gang* provoked the angry attention of the environmental enemies Abbey identified, while the nonfiction handbook *Ecodefense* brought an overbearing governmental response that added up to quasi censorship. This involved FBI agents identifying Foreman as an enemy of the state, sending in an informant who offered technical expertise for another edition of *Ecodefense*, and then hauling Foreman into court on conspiracy charges. Foreman and his fellow Earth Firsters were vocal in their resistance to the federal government, especially the US Forest Service. *Ecodefense*—a manual that helped transform vandalism into a direct action technique against government agencies and corporate developers—provided a reason for law enforcement to come down on their symbolic enemies with full force. There is no doubt that speech—especially instructional speech—was the provocation in the arrest of Foreman. In the aftermath, the third edition of the book was defiantly published with a new introduction that asserted the "patriotic duty to defend the First Amendment."[11]

Both *The Monkey Wrench Gang* and *Ecodefense* are much more complex works than blueprints for terrorism, an anemic interpretation that belies their historical, social, and political merits. Both posed important questions about technologies: technologies of environmental destruction and technologies of political action. Both took as their muse Ned Ludd, an eponym for an early nineteenth-century movement of British craftworkers who smashed the new textile machines they feared would displace them. The mythical figure of Ludd—swinging a mighty hammer at a stocking frame—came down through the decades as an icon of resistance to the capitalist machine. The simple hammer against the complex machine informed the way Abbey and Foreman (who often wrote under the pseudonym of Ned Ludd) thought of direct action. Unlike other radical groups that dreamed of military prowess through the acquisition of the advanced weaponry of the war-ready nation, Earth First! promoted the use of tools that might be found in the household shed. These environmental radicals were not aspiring to military domination but to dissuasion through harassment. They also put techniques of direct action to the fore for open discussion. This sets *Ecodefense* apart from *The Anarchist Cookbook*, with its anomic justifications and willingness for mayhem, and the early dynamite manuals with their Promethean fantasies of stealing the ideal revolutionary weapon.

Both works self-consciously explore the difficult question of dissent through illegal direct action. Edward Abbey originally called his fictional ecosaboteurs "the wooden shoe gang" in homage to early twentieth-century anarcho-syndicalists, and Earth First! pointed to the IWW as its logical ancestor, the "finest bunch of radicals ever to bless America with their presence."[12] The Wobblies not only discussed sabotage as a direct action technique, but also were strong advocates for free speech that would protect perceived enemies of the state. Focusing much of their energy in the Pacific Northwest—where Earth First! also had a locus of practice—the Wobblies presented a historic success at creating a radical brand identity through shockingly militant speech, distribution of print material, performative events, and "silent agitation" through stickers and buttons. Earth First! extended the IWW's foray into sabotage by deliberately giving elaborate instructions for it. However, having gotten its big boost from the First Red Scare seventy years earlier, federal policing was no more tolerant of sabotage talk from public enemies.

The popular *The Anarchist Cookbook* and the paramilitary publishers like Paladin Press had created a popular audience for these kinds of instructional works. Across the political spectrum, radical groups were forging identities founded in alternative technical practices, sometimes including sabotage and guerrilla warfare. They also had developed new strategies of persuasion in a television age that promoted spectacle. By the time *The Monkey Wrench Gang* appeared in 1975, political activists had learned to manipulate the mass media—to "storm the Reality Studio,"[13] as William Burroughs put it—through parody and farce. The Yippies had famously satirized the political process by nominating a pig for president. Charged under the Civil Obedience Act of 1968 with instructing demonstrators in the art of rioting, the Chicago Seven made a mockery of legal proceedings by wearing patriotic costumes and refusing any serious engagement with official efforts to suppress them. Abbie Hoffman had written his manual of antiestablishment (and often dangerous and illegal) practices, *Steal This Book.*

The Yippie strategy of combining political dissent, instruction in illegal or at least illicit activities, textual parody, and theatrical farce was adopted by the growing environmental and animal rights movements. In 1972, mainstream publisher Simon & Schuster issued Sam Love and David Obst's *Ecotage,* a collection of suggestions for harassing polluters gathered through a national contest sponsored by the small advocacy group Environmental Action, of which Love was the coordinator. Like Hoffman, who parodied the paramilitary publishers and compiled his book from expert informants' tips, Love and Obst devised their project as collaboration. These kinds of how-to manuals are usually collaborative, with a central figure coordinating information from various sources under a political thesis. Most suggestions compiled in *Ecotage* fit easily into the category of nonviolent direct action. For example, contributors suggested sending junk mail back to its originators in their post-paid envelopes or projecting a hologram of a giant death's head over New York's Central Park. Other ideas crossed into illegality, such as vandalizing construction sites, destroying billboards either by paint or saw, and drilling holes into polluters' houses to inject odiferous chemicals.

To ward off any charges of incitement, abetting, or advocacy in a litigious age, *Ecotage* gave disclaimers. This strategy was growing in popularity among citizens now used to reading warranties. Whatever the reasons for disseminating ideas for illegal activities, the authors and their publishers denied responsibility through the disclaimer. The back cover of *Ecotage* carried the proviso, "Neither Environmental Action nor the publisher suggest you go out and do any of the things described in this book. But if you're fed up with the continuing pollution of the American environment, it could give you some laughs." The book pointed to its own theatricality, quoting from the satiric opera *The Mikado,* in which the Emperor of Japan devises specialized punishments to make the guilty "a source of innocent merriment."[14] Given the book's collection of practical tactics and only sporadic humor, it is hard to believe that *Ecotage* existed simply for laughs. Some entries had a hard edge of principled maliciousness, but the disclaimer reveals how difficult it is to absolutely identify the complex intentions or culpabilities of writers and readers. The militant message, disguised in the Trojan horse of humor, gives a knowing wink through the disclaimer. In *The Monkey Wrench Gang,* Edward Abbey would raise that knowing wink to literary art.

A way to disguise risky content is to call it fiction; another is to call it "for informational purposes only." The authors of *Ecotage* suggested that they were describing environmental action that was already taking place, rather than advocating it: "It is important for readers to become aware that such ideas do exist and that there are already groups actively involved in implementing some of them."[15] The entries contain many references to antipollution vigilante James Phillips, "the Fox," who had plugged drainpipes, capped smokestacks, poured sludge in a corporate office, and delivered well-seasoned dead fish and skunks to the polluters of his beloved Fox River in Illinois. The Fox's exploits made national news when he contacted the popular columnist Mark Royko of the *Chicago Daily News,* who transformed him briefly into a national folk hero in a "nondestructive guerrilla war."[16] Part of the Fox's media appeal lay in his ingenuity, anonymity, elusiveness, and technical know-how turned against a dirty technological system. (He was eventually revealed as a high school science teacher.) *Ecotage* praised his destruction of an asphalt factory by "turning exactly the right combination of valves," and Phillips would later write an autobiography with explicit details of his exploits down to the "fourteen-inch, square-shanked screwdriver" he carried.[17] That one quixotic individual was using popular mechanics—the hobby of the alienated worker—to stop corporate pollution grounded the Fox's moral message in the appealing tangible, autonomous practices of the garage workshop and the backyard. In his epilogue to *Ecotage,* Sam Love explained that the goal was not to "destroy all technology," but to put pressure on "critical points in the technological complexes which are abusing their niches in the social/biological system."[18] These environmental activists took quite literally Mario Savio's famous metaphor (after Thoreau) that "you've got to put your bodies upon the wheels, upon the levers, upon all the apparatus, and you've got to make it stop."[19]

While the Fox was the most celebrated of the ecosaboteurs, other small groups across the country were trespassing and tampering with equipment in sewage treatment and manufacturing facilities, pulling up survey stakes for logging operations, and cutting down billboards. Sympathetic local journalists would sometimes travel out with these groups and give detailed reports on their techniques. For example, in Abbey's Southwest, five teenage "Eco Raiders" who opposed Tucson's urban sprawl into the Sonoran desert cut down hundreds of billboards in the area from 1971 to 1973. Their exploits were detailed in the *Tucson Daily Citizen*, which explained how the Eco Raiders traveled stealthily to the sites, chose their targets, notched the billboards to make sure they fell in the right direction, sawed 4/5 of the way through the posts, and used a rope to pull the boards down.[20] Two farmers threatened to blow the heads off two student journalists caught with the Billboard Bandits—six Ann Arbor, Michigan, high school students who were sawing down illegally placed billboards.[21] The saga of the Billboard Bandits, eventually arrested for vandalism, made national news, where they were treated sympathetically. At a time when highway beautification and billboard pollution were topics of national debate, the *New York Times* suggested that while these "Robin Hoods" had infuriated billboard advertisers, land-renting farmers, and local police, they had "amused and inspired most of the public."[22] Remembering a coast-to-coast movement of billboard destruction, southwest journalist Tom Miller, who had once gone out on a foray with the Eco Raiders, quipped, "Never underestimate the power of the Associated Press to spread seditious activity."[23]

In this brief period in the early 1970s, as Edward Abbey was writing *The Monkey Wrench Gang*, the national media treated ecotage as a curiosity, a sensation, and an understandable if not laudable form of direct action. The ecosaboteurs were never caught, given very light punishments, or exonerated. Their actions were often referred to as pranks and capers. The police and the courts treated their crimes as trespassing and vandalism, rather than terrorism. Ecosaboteurs could expect to face light punishment for political action that crossed into illegality. This would all change rapidly, however, as environmental activists formed larger radical organizations with greater capacity for confronting powerful industries like logging and real estate development. Instructions for illegal direct action crossed into an impassioned, high-stakes fight over land use. Knowledgeable of radical history, detailed with illegal methods, and popular enough to serve as public tests of tolerance, *The Monkey Wrench Gang* and *Ecodefense* were self-conscious exercises in dangerous instructional speech.

The Monkey Wrench Gang

In tune with the news of its day, *The Monkey Wrench Gang* portrays a small gang of ecosaboteurs escalating in tactics from blowtorching billboard frames to planting explosives, all with the final goal of destroying the Glen Canyon Dam. *The Monkey Wrench Gang*'s protagonists—surgeon Doc Sarvis, river guide Seldom Seen Smith, Special Forces veteran George Washington Hayduke, and Sarvis's medical assistant, Bonnie Abbzug—are especially opposed to the dam: a symbol of destructive development for many environmentalists. When it was built, creating Lake Powell, the dam destroyed almost two hundred miles of fertile canyon land, flooding small rivers and side canyons, driving out wildlife, drowning vegetation, and eradicating archeological history. For those, like Abbey, who had traveled this wilderness, it was a terrible loss. In 1964, a year after the dam began operations, the Pulitzer Prize–winning author Wallace Stegner wrote, "People who, as we do, remember this country before the canyons were flooded, are driven to dream of ways by which some parts of it may still be saved, or half saved."[24] Chronicling the loss of the canyon in his earlier travelogue, *Desert Solitaire*, Abbey put that dream into fictional form in *The Monkey Wrench Gang* as his ecosaboteurs set off a bomb on a new bridge near the Glen Canyon Dam, sending steel and concrete crashing into the river far below. Assembled for the bridge's ribbon-cutting ceremony, a large crowd witnesses the scene, and Abbey imagines Crumbo, the police officer pursuing the gang, explaining to the angry Utah governor: "That is their last stunt, Governor, I promise you." Crumbo then points to the huge dam: "I know it sounds crazy, but that's what they're after."[25] The dam is never destroyed in the novel, but it was a compelling vision for canyon lovers, satisfying in fantasy.

Whether Abbey was engaging in mere braggadocio when he claimed to have taken down a few billboards himself, *The Monkey Wrench Gang* was in tune with a growing national anger at unchecked pollution, rampant land development, and wilderness destruction.[26] There were some hints of its reputational future as an ecoterrorist bible in the first reviews of the book. Abbey's fellow environmental writer Jim Harrison sensed that some might see the book as dangerous, declaring that only a writer in the United States could dare such a "revolutionary novel."[27] Within a year, a few suspicious readers had decided that *The Monkey Wrench Gang* could and would provide tactics for antidevelopment saboteurs. A book reviewer in Albuquerque pointed to the detailed "tools of warfare" in the book and expressed the belief that "when this already best-selling book makes its way into paperback editions, so that the potential eco-raiders of the thin-pocketbook variety can afford it, we may be in for full-fledged guerrilla warfare against highway projects, dam-building, strip-mining, power-planting and like grand restructurings of the land and atmosphere."[28] *New York Times* correspondent Grace Lichtenstein began a profile of Abbey: "If the Glen Canyon Dam here on the Colorado River were suddenly blown up by saboteurs, Edward Abbey, the novelist, might have to take a bit of the blame—or the credit."[29] By 1979, four years after the book appeared, the *Washington Post* was offering testimony from Utah's inhabitants that the book was allegedly causing "uncanny happenings"—the theft of construction signs and destruction of bulldozers and drilling rigs. A county commissioner who may have been the model for the monkey wrench gang's nemesis, Bishop Love, pointed his finger, declaring: "Abbey had a lawyer look at [it] so that it could not be used as evidence."[30] Especially in the West with its expanses of undeveloped land, the contest over land use between wilderness proponents and industrialists, loggers, real estate developers, and federal agents had grown heated enough to generate both symbolic heroes and symbolic enemies, and *The Monkey Wrench Gang* came along at the right time to provide them.

Abbey courted his growing reputation as a dangerous writer, warning in *Playboy*, "Glen Canyon is going to go—5,000,000 cubic yards of concrete—down the river. All is ready but the printed announcements." Abbey's fantasy included a houseboat turned into a fertilizer and kerosene bomb. All of this was good publicity as Abbey solidified his reputation as a regional celebrity, and fans sent him detailed plans for blowing up the Glen Canyon Dam, obviously feeling that he hadn't displayed enough credible know-how.[31] Abbey confronted power through speech that was difficult to distinguish between mockery and advocacy. As one critic put it: "Are we to take this buffoonery seriously? Does he mean what he says, or is dam-busting, like littering, the rhetorical gesture of a notoriety seeking clown?"[32] Not a particularly new development in radical speech, the ambiguously humorous exaggerated threat was Abbey's signature.

A dimension of Abbey's novel lent itself to interpretation as a blueprint for violent action: his extensive inclusion of technical detail that comes close to directions for cutting down billboards, making explosives, exploiting vulnerabilities in construction equipment, and carrying out other acts of sabotage. For example, the novel describes the protagonists preparing to sabotage a bridge using thermite, an incendiary composition that generates high heat: "She [Bonnie Abbzug] found Hayduke and Smith mixing their powders, rolling them back and forth in a big closed container: three parts iron oxide to two parts pulverized aluminum equals thermite. Then the igniting mixture: four parts barium peroxide to one part magnesium powder." The Vietnam veteran, Hayduke, applies his military knowledge: "I'm going to blast a couple of holes in the roadway above the main arch of the bridge, one on each side. The idea is, we expose the arches, set up the thermite crucibles over the holes, ignite the thermite and let it flow down on the steel. Should burn right through it—if we've got enough mix."[33] Although this sounds alarming, the protagonists discover their preparation doesn't work. It doesn't cut through the bridge, leaving Hayduke to speculate: "What we got is just two big motherfucking spot welds on the beams. I think maybe I made the sombitch stronger than it was before."[34] Even as they embark on the slippery slope of escalating tactics, the saboteurs frequently run up against their own technological ignorance.

Like the crime writer, Abbey included instructional detail to give the novel authenticity, to pin it to the practical realism of technical processes that might be mimicked in the world outside the novel. Abbey alleged that he had done "field work" for *The Monkey Wrench Gang*; he certainly had done the kind of research the crime novelist does to render the gang's deeds believable. At least that is what provoked the law and encouraged terrorism experts to read the book as a blueprint. Abbey was greatly concerned with authenticity, writing of the western sculptor Frederic Remington, "Like most conscientious craftsman, he did not rely solely on memory or imagination but reinforced both with the reality of tangible, material *things*."[35] The novel is full of useful, nameable things: catalogs of plants and animals, gear checklists, descriptions of topographical features. It also incorporates much discussion of how-to, from cutting through metal billboard frames with a blowtorch to winching a jeep down a cliff. In this context, small-scale technical projects give the male protagonists the characteristics of knowledge, mastery, and volition, the ability to act deliberately and authentically on moral impulse.

Armed with shopping lists of necessary things for their adventures, the protagonists of *The Monkey Wrench Gang* are often engaged in technological schemes, but because these are portrayed as sensual, gratifying, small-scale, focal interactions, they stand opposed to the developers' "megalomaniacal megamachine," as Hayduke puts it, referencing Lewis Mumford's multivolume critique of modern technological systems. Mumford's life's work was demonstrating the evolution of large-scale systems into inherently totalitarian, destructive, homogenizing, warring monstrosities, overpowering organic, diverse, small-scale, ecological, and more psychically fulfilling patterns of life. In *The Monkey Wrench Gang*, the developers' bulldozers loom like alienating "dinosaurs," "dragons," or "gods" over the scraped earth and seem to move of their own volition, dwarfing their anonymous operators: "In forested areas the clearing job would require a crew of loggers with chainsaws, but here in southeast Utah, on the plateau, the little pinyon pines and junipers offered no resistance to the bulldozers. The crawler-tractors pushed them all over with nonchalant ease and shoved them aside, smashed and bleeding, into heaps of brush, where they would be left to die and decompose."[36] While the gang exploits the vulnerabilities of these giants with sand, Karo syrup, hammers, wire cutters, chisels, and screwdrivers, they don't especially understand them and can only touch their surfaces, leading Hayduke to exclaim, "All this wirecutting is only going to slow them down, not stop them.

Godfuckingdammit . . . we're wasting our time."[37] This sense of helplessness in the face of the opaque giant contrasts with the narrator's sensual description of Doc Sarvis's car engine: "the pistons, bathed in oil, slipping up and down in the firm but gentle grasp of the cylinders, connecting rods to crankshaft, crankshaft to drive shaft through differential's scrotal housing via axle, all power to the wheels." The machines whose insides the user intimately understands—even a polluting Lincoln Continental—are allowable in the logic of the novel, while the opaque devices like the giant Cat represent an alienating power that robs life and freedom, the "whole conglomerated cartel spread out upon half the planet earth like a global kraken." A saw, a blowtorch, a monkey wrench, or even thermite—the comprehensible tools available to people subject to the megamachine and its systemic violence—have limited power against it.

The most violent, knowledgeable, and adept ecosaboteur is Hayduke, who has been traumatized in the Vietnam War but has walked away with military and survivalist knowledge that he uses in a private war against the megamachine. Like *Soldier of Fortune*'s expert survivalists in the field, he is able to cobble homemade thermite, survive in the desert with portable equipment and comestibles from strategic stash points, and survive a shootout with an army of police. He slips between his concentration on cutting down high-voltage power lines to flashbacks of strafing from a "bubble-nosed dragon" on a "dusty road in Cambodia." Abbey points to his sources as the early anarchists, calling his protagonists, at times, the "wooden shoe conspiracy" and including an epigraph that gives the etymology of sabotage. His Doc Sarvis calls himself "el Mano Negro," in a reference to early anarchist saboteurs. Abbey had written his master's thesis on anarchist philosophy, mentioning Johann Most's *Science of Revolutionary Warfare* and the Chicago anarchists' bomb-making writings in *Alarm!* Specifically, he quoted the directions on how to make a pipe bomb for a "cheerful and gratifying response."[38] But the figure of Hayduke resonates more fully with another creation of the Southwest, the mercenary "knights" of Paladin Press, sharing hostility to the modern state and a fascination with guerrilla warfare and wilderness survival.

As the United States struggled to come to terms with the Vietnam War, the embittered paramilitary identities of the anti-communist Right tangled with an anxious survivalism in uncertain times, driven by visions of nuclear holocaust, communist takeover, and race war. As ethnographer Robert G. Mitchell Jr. has written, survival enthusiasts responded to an alienating rationalization of society—as represented in near comic-book form in *The Monkey Wrench Gang*—with imaginative rehearsals of collapse accompanied by evocations of "meaning-filled, concrete work that matters, honest tests of character in contests with the fateful forces of a new age."[39] In the same year *The Monkey Wrench Gang* appeared, Robert K. Brown, living in Denver, would leave his Paladin Press to found *Soldier of Fortune*, presenting the veteran and the mercenary soldier as idealized figures of masculinity, outlaw independence, and guerrilla knowledge. This magazine catered to veterans as readers and contributors within an emerging survivalist ethos. The traumatized Vietnam veteran who radically restored his autonomy by becoming a self-sufficient hermit in the wilderness became a popular legend, eventually put on the screen as Rambo who carries the war back home. Hayduke is constructed from the semiotic codes of the traumatized Vietnam veteran, radically autonomous, always on the edge of violence for which he was trained, and angry at a monstrous system that has robbed him of his place by dislodging all that he remembers, including the wilderness he loved as a child.

However, Hayduke is a comic hero. Although the character is marked by the codes of violence and anomie, the narrator humanizes Hayduke by gently mocking his preparations, inventories, procedural rules, and moral and intellectual dilemmas in his quixotic attacks on the megamachine. The relationship between his inflexible purpose and the seeming impossibility of his achieving it creates the comic situation. In the climax, Hayduke is shown as deeply vulnerable for all his acquired skills and techniques. As the police chase him into a narrow canyon where he hides wedged in a crevice, he is literally scared shitless. He puts down his rifle to take off his stinking pants and clean them: "He believes he is willing to die today but he is not willing to die sitting in his own shit."[40] Hayduke pollutes himself with his own very animal fear in a bawdy low humor that refutes his identity as an archetypal outlaw, a role that can only exist in his relationship to the law. The members of the gang comically inhabit these roles but never really fit them. One of the gang sets out to blow up a bridge disguised as a construction worker in "a yellow hard hat decorated with emblematic decals of his class—American flag, skull and crossbones, the Iron Cross" with "AMERICA—LOVE IT OR LEAVE IT ALONE" stitched on his jacket. The gang takes on these roles always in a parody of power, and in turn the narrator makes parodies of the characters through exaggeration and exposure of human contradictions and foibles. Modernization is a state of absurdity that lends itself to absurd actions and identities for everyone.

Only a very limited reading or complete misreading of *The Monkey Wrench Gang* could see it as advocacy of violence. The fictional acts of sabotage have the dimension of absurdity, as the heroes tilt against the comic book monster of the megamachine. (The satiric cartoonist R. Crumb contributed illustrations to the tenth-anniversary edition of the novel.) It is possible to imagine revolutionary readers who might study the novel for strategies, tactics, and technical directions as topographical features of the text. Abbey courted these readers when he wrote in a semiserious epigraph to the book: "This book, though fictional in form, is based strictly on historical fact. Everything in it is real or actually happened. And it all began just one year from today."[41] A weaver of tall tales, Abbey was known for this kind of utterance, a mocking warning to the state, the seriousness of which depended on the credulity of the listener. It is also possible to imagine a suspicious reader of *The Monkey Wrench Gang* who is uninterested in Abbey's form of comedy, the moral dimensions of character, and the way literature has the power to unsettle assumptions. Such a reader might believe that the author has a purpose of camouflaging a blueprint for violence underneath the bad jokes, exaggerated Manichaean characters, and absurd comic plot. A suspicious reading is a symptom of the hunt for symbolic enemies who seem to be always conspiring under the surfaces of everyday life, even a novel. The novel's plot fit well with the slippery-slope hypotheses of terror experts who assume any targeted group that speaks of violence, even in highly abstract or joking terms, is on its way to wholesale destruction, not only of dams but even of all humanity. An especially odd argument on *The Monkey Wrench Gang*'s dangers came from the founding director of the Department of Defense's Defense Threat Assessment Agency, Jay Davis, in the aftermath of the September 11 attacks. In a DOD publication directed at national defense policymakers, Davis expressed his lingering fear that a "terrorist with a sense of humor" could appear: "A terrorist with a sense of humor can probably achieve the end of destabilizing or discrediting a government without killing many or even any people, if he/she is very, very clever."[42] He then suggested that his readers read *The Monkey Wrench Gang* for insight into what he meant. It is not clear at all what distinction Davis was making between terrorism and satirical agitprop that might indeed be very unsettling to a government. Art, theater, and fiction that discredit government are protected in robust democracies, but in the post-9/11 world of the terror experts, humor was not a joking matter.

In 1981, six years after the publication of the novel, a small group of people, including Edward Abbey, splintered from an Earth First! demonstration on the Grand Canyon Bridge and headed onto the dam, accompanied by three young filmmakers from UC-Berkeley whom Abbey had invited. There, Abbey gave a speech envisioning "a civilization fit for free men and free women" and suggesting that his audience "oppose the destruction of our homeland by these alien forces from Houston, Tokyo, Manhattan, Washington, DC, and the Pentagon." He urged the crowd to "oppose, resist, subvert, delay" this destruction by "any means necessary." He never spelled out those means.[43] Then, five people, including Earth First! founders David Foreman and Howie Wolke, unfurled a long black plastic banner that slid down the front of the dam, looking very much like a crack. It was a classic piece of agitprop, given greater meaning by the fictional threat in *The Monkey Wrench Gang*. Earth Firsters had not damaged the bridge—they had *pretended* to damage the bridge—but the use of metaphor was lost on the FBI, who were brought in to pursue them as if they represented a national threat. Thus began the FBI's war on Earth First!, in which speech and image—even in fiction—were taken as terrorist deeds, a situation in which technology, rhetoric, and sabotage would take on a new dynamic.[44]

Ecodefense

The Monkey Wrench Gang's place in the ecoterrorist watch list was generated by its association with Earth First!. A small group of environmental radicals—some of whom had previously worked for mainstream environmental organizations—decided to wage a fight against escalating wilderness destruction. As the oft-told story goes, after a week of hiking around Arizona's Pinacate Desert, five friends—four of them disgruntled former environmental lobbyists who were tired of the gradualist legislative approach—struck upon the idea of forming a more radical group for defining, defending, and linking wilderness through a no-compromise environmental platform. Some of these friends evoked *The Monkey Wrench Gang* as an inspiration for an emergent ecoradical identity: antiauthoritarian, hard drinking, masculine, dramatic, irreverent, funny, in tune with the wild land, with its own developed moral code and ability to act according to natural feeling. *The Monkey Wrench Gang* didn't provide a technical blueprint for direct action so much as a satiric way of addressing power, instantly recognizable to Abbey's fans. Hayduke Lives! was one of Earth First!'s popular slogans, printed on T-shirts and bumper stickers.[45] Nevertheless, from early on, Earth First! deliberated the use of illegal direct action techniques. The Earth First! newsletter collected "ecotricks," along the lines of *Ecotage*, that evolved into a more focused strategy for damaging the profits of land developers.

Earth First's monkeywrenching rhetoric took its spirit from Abbey's Doc Sarvis: "I'm tired of people who don't do any harm. I'm tired of soft weak passive people who can't *do* anything or *make* anything. Except babies."[46] Earth First! eschewed the glossy nature shots and comparatively benign political rhetoric of mainstream environmental organizations like the Wilderness Society and the Sierra Club. Taking cues from the IWW, Earth Firsters turned to more collaborative, confrontational forms of direct action. Some traveled from town to town in a road show; wore face paint, animal costumes and radiation suits at protests; and developed a repertoire of songs that would be collected in *The Earth First! Li'l Green Songbook*, a reference to the IWW's *Little Red Songbook*. These theatrical forms of protest were turned outward to gain media attention and turned inward to give a sense of community through performance.[47] The introduction of monkeywrenching was an even more hands-on activity that pitted a hard masculinist, western, libertarian radical against the feminized, intellectualized, passive East Coast environmental lobbyist. As one environmental journalist put it, "Monkeywrenchers: what ever happened to nice little old ladies in tennis shoes?"[48] Even though many women were involved in Earth First! (including the "Hayduchess"), its early codes were masculine: men who knew how to make things; tinkerers who knew enough about technological systems to tamper with them. Monkeywrenching attempted to introduce a new semiotic code to the image of the environmental activist.

Monkeywrenchers, at one time, were laboring men who used wrenches in factories and auto repair shops. The wrench was a symbol of working-class mechanical power, and Abbey had transformed it into a symbol of muscled resistance. Bill Koehler's (aka Johnny Sagebrush's) ode to monkeywrenching, sung at Earth First! gatherings, was set to the tune of a traditional American laboring song, "I've Been Working on the Railroad."[49] Unlike a complex bomb, the simple wrench was powerfully useful, yet easy to understand and draw in a graphic design. In an age of thermonuclear weapons, the wrench was also limited in its destructive ability. This was the weapon of the resistor, rather than the world destroyer. Although Earth Firsters may have spoken theoretically about nuclear weapons or AIDS wiping out populations, they never aspired to use even limited explosive devices, much less weapons of mass destruction. Monkeywrenching was a decidedly low-tech set of practices that drew on the practical knowledge of people who rejected complex technological systems in favor of a preindustrial society. When they entertain violence, radical groups choose the weapons that most reflect their political ideals, background technical knowledge, semiotic messages they wish to convey, and tolerance for destruction and lethality.

In the 1982 spring equinox issue of the Earth First! newsletter, Foreman announced his plan to publish a collection of monkeywrenching techniques, *Ecodefense*: "a cookbook of tactics and tools beyond the traditional avenues of environmental advocacy." Foreman pointed to models—*The Anarchist Cookbook, The Poor Man's James Bond, Techniques of Harassment, Get Even,* and others from the paramilitary publishing outfits—suggesting that Earth First! would create an environmentalist version of them.[50] Like these alternative publishers, Foreman launched a small venture, Ned Ludd Books, to produce and distribute *Ecodefense* and *The Li'l Green Songbook* so that any profits would support the organization.[51] An independent operation avoided the difficulty of finding a mainstream publisher for an ecosabotage manual. Now in operation for over twenty years, Paladin Press had proven that such a venture could successfully operate and make a small profit from controversial instructional manuals. There was an audience niche, and Foreman rightly predicted that *Ecodefense* would be "the most requested and the most controversial" book he published, raising "important legal, ethical, and tactical questions."[52]

Foreman invited readers to provide technical expertise for *Ecodefense,* which was to be a collation of reader-contributed tactics. A regular "Ned Ludd" feature in the newsletter provided monkeywrenching advice sent in by readers like "Mr.

Goodwrench" (after an affable, knowledgeable GM advertising mascot), "Vincent Van Goodwrench," "Robin Hood," and "Hayduke Lives!" *Ecodefense* was to bring together the technical knowledge of the community, though Foreman accompanied his announcement with various disclaimers, saying that his intention was not to advocate monkeywrenching but to report on it to save the earth. He claimed that the book would be "for the vicarious pleasure of the armchair adventurer and we take no responsibility if some nut actually tries anything."[53] Familiar to readers of Paladin Press books, this now popular disclaimer was dubious at best and distant from the forthright earlier radical claims that the people had a right to know and, under the right circumstances, to make and use dangerous technologies as a counterbalance to governmental military power. Tailoring the typical survivalist Paladin book to the specific milieu of the environmental monkeywrencher, the book would provide information about making explosives, destroying oilrigs, harassing enemies through dirty tricks and personal attacks, and evading the law. And like the Paladin books, *Ecodefense* would test the waters of tolerance with a stubborn defiance of social mores and governmental suppression—manifested here as the FBI and the "Freddies" from the US Forest Service. Both Paladin's imaginary knights and ecodefenders claimed power through the dissemination of illicit knowledge, a threatening undercurrent of technical know-how that might be used for vicious vengeance or the righteous cause. *Ecodefense,* however, had a clear rationale and gave a set of ethical guidelines that included a statement on nonviolence: "Monkeywrenching . . . is never directed against human beings or other forms of life."[54]

Published with a foreword by Edward Abbey and coedited by "Big Bill Haywood" (a reference to the tough, one-eyed IWW founder), *Ecodefense* summarized the collective knowledge of Earth First! through advice on how to spike trees, stop off-the-road vehicles, destroy roads, pull survey stakes, destroy billboards, damage construction and logging equipment, and deter ranching operations. As Foreman wrote in his introduction, "Monkeywrenching is simple. The simplest possible tool is used. The safest tactic is employed."[55] Over three editions of *Ecodefense,* monkeywrenching evolved into an elaborate lore of tactics and techniques despite the simplicity of its tools. For example, the book offers instructions in how to make small three- or four-pointed spikes called caltrops that can pierce tires and human and animal feet. Caltrops are a simple, age-old weapon used to deter armies from advancing. The monkeywrencher could use them to blow out the tires of off-the-road vehicles or prevent logging vehicles from entering wilderness lands. As the book advised, caltrops could be purchased from mail-order outfits advertising in *Soldier of Fortune* and *Shotgun News,* but with a bit of welding expertise, the monkeywrencher could make them cheaply from common nails. Therefore, contributor "Barstow Bob" advised, the aspiring monkeywrencher would benefit from taking a welding class: "Learn to cut and weld using an Oxy-acetylene outfit. You'll be amazed at how much this will expand your horizons as a monkeywrencher."[56] Subsequent "field notes" advised other ways to make caltrops, including studding a golf ball with nails. There were unexpected dimensions to making the simple caltrop, including security considerations such as disposing of identifiable nail heads and covering the bench vise with cardboard to avoid distinctive tool markings. It's impossible to know just how many people read *Ecodefense* and tried to make caltrops, or anything else in the book, but with its "field notes" following every section, it gave the appearance that Earth First! members were extensively involved in a community project of monkeywrenching.

A large chapter was devoted to tree spiking, which became the book's most sensational, and likely most used, ecotage technique. Tree spiking was designed to prevent loggers from cutting old-growth forests in the wake of US Forest Service decisions to allow development in once-protected lands. Foreman said that tree spiking came from the tales of Northwest loggers, many of whom belonged to the IWW.[57] Not much evidence exists that the Wobblies spiked trees, although, in 1920, a Seattle journalist wrote, "Stealthy shapes gliding through an orchard on a moonless night; and a fruit tree sickened and died; a copper nail piercing its heart. Insinuation and suggestion in the logging camp; and a whirring saw in some busy mill shattered as it struck the hidden spike, maiming and injuring the workers all about it. In a word, sabotage!"[58] So tree spiking, at least as a suspected form of sabotage, had been handed down by word-of-mouth from an older conflict. Tree spiking had been sporadically practiced since it was used in the Northwest forest preservation campaign in the mid-1980s, when Earth First! was associated with three major instances.[59] Now it made a fulsome debut in *Ecodefense*, where many pages were devoted to explaining and refining the technique: what kind of nails to use, where to place them, what to wear, how to avoid detection and how to handle warning the logging companies. Three years after *Ecodefense*'s publication, tree spiking and road spiking were outlawed under the Anti–Drug Abuse Act of 1988.[60]

Although Foreman had originally suggested that the book would carry information about explosives, he now cautioned that explosives and guns were to be avoided. They were not only unpopular with most people but would attract police surveillance and repression. Once they speak of violence, radical groups are often portrayed as on a slippery slope to terrorism, but, in this case, plans were tempered as Earth First! collectively mulled over tactics. In its destructiveness, *Ecodefense* paled in comparison to the anomic survivalist books flowing out of Paladin Press. While Earth First! members debated sabotage, Paladin Press was escalating the content of its weapons manuals for a growing audience of hardcore survivalists, weapons enthusiasts, and aspiring mercenaries. *Ecodefense* focused on nonlethal direct actions—with localized targets—using low-tech tools.

Even so, *Ecodefense* was a risky enterprise that publicized secretive activities and opened them to scrutiny. The book suggested that the information should be shared in an open forum, accessible to Earth First!'s growing membership, but monkeywrenchers operated individually or in small groups suspicious of outsiders. Contributors used pseudonyms to avoid police surveillance and social condemnation, and this anonymity carried the freedom and power of a radical identity tied to technical knowledge. Secrecy also had serious risks. As philosopher Sissela Bok has written, secrecy is both a protective and dangerous strategy. It protects threatened and vulnerable identities, guards plans in their early formation, adds suspense and action, and secures property. Conversely, it can stifle creativity and judgment, create situations in which bad traits and actions go unchallenged, spread uncontrollably, and "lower resistance to the irrational and the pathological."[61] *Ecodefense* both disclosed secrets and offered ways of keeping them. This valence between secrecy and openness—a feature of many works of this kind—created vulnerabilities that would severely damage Earth First! as a social movement. Ecotage, as promulgated by Earth First!, inspired a small cell of people to secretive self-destructive plotting with an inflated sense of outcomes. In their closed world, helped along by the FBI, they moved toward grandiose schemes to disrupt the industrial grid. *Ecodefense*, as an open statement of illicit aims and techniques, drew attention from the law and became a visible symbol of "ecoterrorism," stripped of any of its original nuances in method and intention.

Ecodefense in Court

The FBI had been watching Earth First! from almost the start. Its surveillance had intensified when Earth First! focused criticism on US Secretary of the Interior James Watt. It intensified again in 1986 when anonymous saboteurs disrupted power from a nuclear power plant near Phoenix by trying to pull transmission towers together with cable slings. The FBI was suspicious of Earth First! because at least one of the members had been involved in the Minnesota Bolt Weevils, a group of farmers that sabotaged electrical transmission lines in the 1970s. Further, *Ecodefense* contained a section on sabotaging power lines, although there was no mention of the method used by the Phoenix saboteurs.[62] All of this was unfolding within a public discourse that was increasingly willing to label environmental activists as "American terrorists" even for the mildest of actions, such as unrolling a banner on a dam.[63] At a congressional hearing on wilderness preservation in Nevada, Von Sorensen, representing the state's ranchers, recounted two incidents of alleged ecotage: the destruction of eggs on a pheasant farm and damage to some tractors near a proposed wilderness site. He told the committee that Edward Abbey and Dave Foreman were the "main sabotage leaders" and that a vote for wilderness was a "vote for sabotage and terrorism."[64]

By 1988, under director William Sessions, the FBI was eager to prosecute Earth First! and escalated its label from "vandalism" to "terrorism," although the latter more often applied to bombings.[65] Through a willing informant, it learned of a handful of people in Prescott, Arizona, who had twice taken a cutting torch up the mountains and sabotaged the ski lifts at the Fairfield Snowball resort. The group called itself the "Evan Mecham Eco-Terrorist International Conspiracy" (EMETIC). The FBI recruited a voluntary informant, Ronald Frazier, who was already part of the group and used the pseudonym "Stilson," a type of wrench. Frazier was a proficient mechanic who had worked with heavy equipment. The FBI also sent in its own agent, Michael Fain, to infiltrate the group. That meant that of the six people involved, two were working for the FBI on operation "Thermcon," a reference to the incendiary thermite mentioned in *The Monkey Wrench Gang*. From 1987 to 1989, the FBI put dozens of agents to the investigation and collected 849 hours of audio surveillance. It is clear, from the transcribed portions of the surveillance, that Frazier and Fain manipulated the group by offering technical expertise and encouraging further operations. The main suspect, Mark Davis, was attracted to *The Anarchist Cookbook* and Paladin manuals, but he was reluctant to use explosives. Susceptible to grandiosity, Frazier urged that Davis try an obscure type of dynamite, "amogel," claiming that he had used it on roadwork.[66] It was Frazier who taught Davis to use a cutting torch. Posing as an oil field worker and Vietnam veteran with military expertise and access to explosives, agent Michael Fain discussed the use of thermite and was heavily involved in encouraging, planning, and acquiring materials for Davis's proposed attack on nuclear power plant lines.[67] During this period, under FBI eyes, the group shifted targets, cutting electrical poles leading to a uranium mine near the Grand Canyon. The primary aim of the FBI's costly investigation, as Fain accidentally revealed on one of the tapes, was to get to David Foreman, the compiler of *Ecodefense*. Fain infamously said, "This is the guy we need to pop to send a message."[68] Foreman's book was a red flag; the spies duly recorded any mention of it to implicate him.

Largely because of the book, FBI believed Foreman to be the mastermind of an ecoterrorist conspiracy. Frazier and Fain were sent to cajole him into participation in EMETIC's plans and to elicit any admission of guilt. Frazier used *Ecodefense* as a wedge to get access to Foreman, offering to provide content on the sabotage of heavy equipment. In an elaborate setup, Frazier gave a talk at the annual Earth First! rendezvous on sabotaging diesel engines. There he approached Foreman, who gave him two copies of *Ecodefense*, which Foreman signed with his usual, "Happy monkeywrenching!" Foreman also invited Frazier to contribute to the revised edition of *Ecodefense*. Later, after a persistent series of phone calls, Frazier went to Foreman's home with two diagrams of diesel engines, and the two talked over the relative merits of titanium dioxide and sand as abrasive agents for destroying heavy equipment. Frazier pitched the inclusion of his technical ideas in the next edition of *Ecodefense*, and suggested that more diagrams for the destruction of Caterpillar and Cummins engines could be made into marketable posters. All the while, he was taping Foreman, who expressed interest in using the posters to "freak out" the Forest Service. Foreman also told Frazier that he was not mechanical himself and could not even change the oil in his truck.[69] At no point did Foreman advocate or admit to any actual monkeywrenching—his concern was for the book.

Next in line was Fain, who asked Foreman for money, but the tape of this conversation was inaudible. Fain returned in a failed attempt to get Foreman to say that he would provide money for damaging power lines. Foreman agreed to give Fain some money out of Earth First!'s discretionary fund for "whatever work you want to do," but since the members of EMETIC were involved in other legal activities, this statement didn't directly implicate him in monkeywrenching. Furthermore, Foreman, who had never expressed interest in nuclear power plants as targets, told Fain that his proposed monkeywrenching actions were pointless. Foreman pointed to low-tech methods for damaging power lines in *Ecodefense* as an attempt to dissuade the group from using thermite.[70] Foreman was also believed to have given Mark Davis $580, but that exchange was not witnessed.

The FBI sting operation ended on the desert when twenty agents, armed with automatic weapons and night-vision field glasses, arrested two of the group—Mark Davis and Marc Baker—who did minor damage to a transmission tower feeding the Central Arizona Project, which supplies water from the Colorado River. Margaret Millet fled the scene but was arrested the next day. The three were charged with conspiracy and the destruction of an electrical transmission tower used in interstate commerce. In Tucson, the FBI arrested Foreman, who was charged with conspiracy. Charges were also eventually extended to a fifth defendant, Ilse Asplund, as the FBI made the case for a sweeping conspiracy that extended to future plans to attack power lines at the Palo Alto, Rocky Mountain, and Diablo Canyon nuclear facilities. To make their case to the press, the prosecutors engaged in hyperbole to paint the defendants as highly dangerous terrorists who might have caused a nuclear meltdown. Although the FBI dubiously claimed it wasn't investigating Earth First! as a group, the assistant US attorney, Roger Dokken, said of Foreman at a press conference: "He sneaks around in the background. He was the financier, the leader, sort of the guru to get all of this going. I don't like to use the analogy of a Mafia boss, but they never do anything either. They just send their munchkins out to do it."[71] As their trial began, a sympathetic journalist wrote that the defendants were treated with exaggerated security: "They were escorted to the defense table with the same caution that might have been directed to a quartet of Iranian hijackers."[72]

US attorney Roslyn Moore-Silver pointed to the book as both sufficient evidence of conspiracy and "advocacy of terrorist acts."[73] The prosecution held that when Foreman handed copies of *Ecodefense* to Ronald Frazier, he was advising Frazier as part of a conspiracy. In her opening remarks to the court, Moore-Silver painted *Ecodefense* as advocacy of terrorism, anarchy, and revolution, placing these words in large letters on a flip chart. Arguing bluntly that monkeywrenching was terrorism, she pointed to Foreman as its preacher. In other words, the prosecution's case against Foreman rested almost entirely on his dangerous instructional speech in a printed book—a book he had briefly discussed with the FBI spies.

Foreman and his defense team—especially his lawyer, Gerry Spence—forcefully claimed that the FBI and the US attorneys were violating the First Amendment by hinging their conspiracy case against Foreman on *Ecodefense*.[74] Foreman publicly accused the FBI of acting like the Thought Police and told readers of the Earth First! newsletter, "I will not be intimidated by this brutal attempt to silence me."[75] Unable to extract Foreman to be tried separately from the other defendants, Foreman's legal team believed that he was being targeted solely for his speech. Fully protected under the First Amendment, *Ecodefense* was a thoughtful defense of nature, Foreman's attorneys claimed. It simply provided information for people to decide for themselves. Because it reported what others had said, it was not even Foreman's own speech but hearsay. Further, the defense team was dubious as to the introduction of the book in the first place, believing it unfairly prejudicial under the Federal Rules of Evidence. In a motion to dismiss on the basis of prosecutorial misconduct, Spence argued: "The allegation is that he [Foreman] delivered the book. If this creates criminal complicity, Foreman, as well as any other citizen, would become, ipso facto, a member of every conspiracy, budding or fully bloomed, known or unknown, when he delivers a copy of *Ecodefense* to anyone belonging to such a conspiracy."[76] To the press he warned that the trial "places in jeopardy every writer and editor in America."[77] Foreman's lawyers avoided Foreman's discussions of the book with Frazier, Fain, and possibly Davis, a gray area that bordered on incitement of imminent lawlessness. Was Foreman speaking in abstract terms or was he giving specific advice in planning imminent illegal actions?

In an attempt to bolster a weak case, the prosecution went on a fishing expedition and subpoenaed Ed Caldwell, a printer in Chico, California, and his typesetter. Caldwell's tiny operation had produced two editions of *Ecodefense*. The prosecution was mostly interested in having Caldwell turn over any related files, but he refused, partly because he didn't have what they wanted, and partly because he thought they were violating the First Amendment that protected his press freedoms. When the typesetter turned over her floppy disk with the camera-ready copy of the book, Caldwell was disappointed because he thought it set a precedent. As in the old days of the IWW trial or the McCarthy hearings, the prosecution asked Caldwell if he was "a member of Earth First!." Caldwell said no, because Earth First! never had any formal, dues-paying members. He was asked whether he had ever attended an Earth First! rendezvous or had ever heard Foreman speak. (He had.) The prosecution then wanted to know why he hadn't produced the manuscript, and he pointed to the First Amendment. At this point, the questioning was abruptly terminated. The next day, during the cross-examination, Spence asked Caldwell if he would like to address the jury. Caldwell, who was shy about public speaking, launched into a defense of freedom of speech and the press that lasted several minutes.[78]

Shortly after, embarrassed by its own witnesses, including the unbalanced Ronald Frazier and the manipulative Michael Fain, the prosecution realized that its show trial on ecoterrorism was not as spectacular as it had intended, but some of the defendants knew they were headed for prison. The prosecutors and defense attorneys negotiated a plea bargain, to which Foreman and the rest of the defendants agreed. The counts were more narrowly focused on the damage to the ski lifts and the disruption of electricity at the uranium mine. The harshest sentence was given to Mark Davis: six years in prison and a fine of nearly $20,000. Foreman pled guilty to one count of conspiracy for distributing and discussing *Ecodefense*. He was given five years of probation and a $250 fine, and was forbidden to advocate monkeywrenching, a sanction he would ignore.

The completed third edition of *Ecodefense* was turned over to Ed Caldwell. Caldwell continued to sell it under his own imprint: Abbzug Press, a reference to *The Monkey Wrench Gang*'s Bonnie Abbzug. Published in 1993, the new, greatly expanded edition included an introduction, written by Matthew Lyons, that defended freedom of speech and the political importance of making *Ecodefense* available.[79] Caldwell did not sell many copies over the years, but twenty years later the entire text was anonymously scanned and made available through torrent sites, where it found a new audience. By 2009, the Ned Ludd column of the Earth First! newsletter would opine, "The art of spiking and its many technical variations has become somewhat of a lost art."[80]

Ecodefense and *The Monkey Wrench Gang* demonstrate that books accused of being terrorist blueprints have important functions as cultural expression. Through these books, a radical group took the paramilitary publishing ethos of Paladin Press and combined it with the rich history of the Wobblies to create a thoughtful, nuanced discussion of the efficacy and limitations of violence. Dissenting groups often use cultural forms—like graphic art, song, film, and theater—to create community solidary and effective messaging.[81] Earth First! used multiple cultural forms, including illegal direct action, to try to morally shock a nation that favored the powerful forces supporting land development and wilderness destruction. While Paladin Press and Loompanics were churning out socially unconscious books on imaginary guerrilla wars, apocalyptic aftermaths, bleak urban survival, and egoist gratification through the indulgence of every violent impulse, Earth First! resurrected a notion of sabotage that was mild by comparison. Earth First! talked its way out of terrorism through discussion of it. Yet it was Earth First! that drew the FBI's attention in a pursuit of barely-understood books that, in the end, looks like vendetta. The government's role to protect its citizens' lives and property was used to justify surveillance and exploitation of popular weapons manuals. The law had discovered that these manuals were convenient tools to manipulate political suspects during investigations and raise public opinion against them. However, once popular weapons manuals reached national publicity through more high-profile arrests and prosecutions that argued for their dangers, considerable pressure came to bear once again on legislators to suppress them. The initially lawless Internet would provide a new terrain for the struggle between tolerance and regulation.

6

Ka Fucking Boom

Before the 9/11 terror attacks, the state's concern over popular weapons manuals on the Internet was largely directed at children. Over the course of the twentieth century, the popular image of the young pyrotechnic experimenter would undergo a dramatic change from playful scientific genius to grim technological terrorist. Children's interest in explosive devices—like rockets and fireworks—was culturally accepted for much of the twentieth century as a sign of national glory and progress, but this would begin to change with political agitation in the 1960s and the emergence of dissident youth as a political category. Encouraged and altered by Paladin and Loompanics, the folkways of American violence crept into this new medium. The threatened and threatening precocious child became the locus of a concerted federal effort to eradicate dangerous instructional speech from the Internet. By the end of the century, a few exemplary texts—the online *Anarchist Cookbook, The Jolly Roger Cookbook, The Terrorist's Handbook*—came to symbolize a mortal danger and the corruption of innocence with dangerous technologies. Measures taken to ostensibly protect the children set the stage for the post-9/11 response to terrorist instructional speech on the Web.

Childhood is an abstract concept that has lent itself to sermonizing and political moralizing about evil and the loss of innocence.[1] Boundaries are maintained around certain forms of speech that reflect cultural ideas about children and their vulnerabilities. At the same time, children, especially teenagers, have often represented chaotic, destructive forces against social order. Progressive reformers and regulators have long asserted that parents and the state must have the ability to control unruly children. From the mid-nineteenth century, the social construction of juvenile delinquency has fluctuated with nationwide moral crusades, including ones against corrupting cultural forms like jazz, rock music, and Hollywood nudity. Public discussions of juvenile delinquency, with subsequent calls to protect the children, confirm reassuring social and legal boundaries. When a social problem is attached to malleable and controllable children, the state can assert guardianship over the vulnerable. Prevention measures aimed at children may serve as precedent for broader social control over cultural threats.

The moral panic over sharing bomb-making information on the Internet in the 1990s inflated the danger and led to a bad law, 18 U.S.C. § 842(p), which forbids a citizen from giving instructions in bomb-making if it is to be used in a federal crime. As will be discussed in the next chapter, this law is now used as a bludgeon against those alleged to have a predisposition toward terrorism, broadly defined. Section 842(p) was a response to technological change and to fears of dangerous technology falling into the hands of new sets of actors. Surrounded by rhetoric reminiscent of historian Richard Hofstadter's "paranoid style,"[2] the law was passed to prove that the government had some control over the Web's anarchic spaces. In the aftermath of the Columbine High School shooting, the 842(p) statute was pushed through with rallying cries to protect the children, wildly inflating the dangers of rough online pyrotechnic and bomb-making information, as if these were new on the American scene. The relationship between explosives and unruly children, especially boys, has a long history and for a long time was tacitly accepted as potentially dangerous, but normal. A change in tolerance came with an increasing perception that bombs, which could rend apart everyday life in a single moment, had made the world significantly more dangerous. An earlier image of the bright, misguided pyrotechnic genius was replaced by visions of terroristic youth. The juvenile bomb maker and the international terrorist would become confused in governmental efforts to suppress the folklore of bomb making.

From Genius to Terrorist

In 1851, an archetypal bad-boy character in juvenile fiction would say, "My heart and brain were so full of fire-crackers, Roman candles, rockets, pin-wheels, squibs, and gunpowder in various seductive forms, that I wonder I didn't explode."[3] Fascination with pyrotechnics is hardly surprising given that national holidays are celebrated with vigorous fireworks spectacles associated with military prowess, and popular film and fiction for adolescent audiences are filled with fire and fury culminating in big explosions. Explosives are a national pastime, enshrined in the national anthem. Children's fiction, like the Tom Swift series, has encouraged scientific curiosity about explosive devices. Amateur rocketry has been a popular backyard pursuit, and chemistry teachers have excited young imaginations through the explosive power made possible through combinations of seemingly innocuous substances.

With their beauty, danger, loud noise, and surprise, pyrotechnics have attracted a passionate fandom of amateur experimenters. Still a celebrity among pyrotechnics fans, MIT chemist Tenney Davis, who had a lifelong fascination with "amusing explosives," wrote, "No man can be so old that he fails to recall the thrills of the pyrotechnic exhibitions which he witnessed as a boy nor so old that he will not experience them again and yearn for the fun of shooting off Roman candles and firecrackers."[4] Encompassing both explosive weapons and fireworks, pyrotechnics have traditionally combined military violence and public amusement. Their danger of loud, uncontrolled violence is strongly alluring, energizing, and frightening. In the lore of American boyhood, the fascination with fireworks can be found alongside the perverse delights of the practical joke that pokes fun at a sedate social order. In a pyrotechnics pamphlet published in New York in 1821, "real engineer" Christopher Grotz not only gave directions for making the traditional fireworks displays of sparkly mermaids and dragons, but also included ways to use the highly explosive silver fulminate in dirty tricks. Placing silver fulminate in dresser drawers, on the heels of boots, in candle snuffers, and in trick spiders made of cork could create a loud report that satisfyingly terrorized the victims, especially women. Astonishingly, Grotz suggested putting silver fulminate, now considered a hazardous substance, into a victim's pipe tobacco to "cause some sport."[5] The lore of pyrotechnics was largely circulated through word of mouth, but occasionally could be found in chemistry textbooks and compilations of amusements.

From the colonial period, unruly youths shooting off pistols and powerful firecrackers on public holidays generated fear and alarm, especially since death and mayhem went along with the sport. In 1876, the *New York Times* complained of a rash of deaths and maiming among the Fourth of July's "juvenile patriots" who had been playing with silver fulminate, nitroglycerine, and other powerful explosives because they were irresistibly drawn to the noise.[6] Across the country, calls for reform have come every Fourth of July as local communities pass ordinances to bring fireworks under control, a process that is ongoing in many places. Stories of children losing eyes and fingers—a very real and frequent occurrence—have often accompanied demands for regulation. The fireworks displays of our time are much tamer in their explosive power than in an earlier unregulated period when powerful cherry bombs and dynamite bombs named after World War II ordnance were popular.

Juvenile thrill bombings and bomb hoaxes have also been around for generations, surging after World War II when a "bomb scare craze"[7] swept across the nation and provoked new ordinances against false reports. Some of the bomb making was real enough, with teenagers stealing dynamite and blasting caps, throwing them into school trashcans, blasting out windows, and occasionally killing bystanders.[8] Before the popularity of paramilitary publishers, police officers often attributed amateur bomb making to the natural intelligence or even genius of white, middle-class teens. In the 1950s, these teens were perceived as misguided boy scientists in the age of the space race with its glorification of rocket science.[9] Federal money and military expertise poured into schools to train future scientists and engineers for the Cold War. Creating an explosion or blasting a rocket was a sure way to get attention in a science class or at a science fair, and biographies of scientists recounted their experiments with explosives. In one of many examples, Bernhard Schmidt, inventor of the Schmidt telescope, lost his hand making a pipe bomb when he was fifteen years old. When his fourteen-year-old son injured his hand with glass shards from a bomb-making experiment, Thomas Edison told the press of his own boyhood mishaps, which were portrayed as the amusing price of genius.[10] Edison had destroyed his own lab in a borrowed railroad car when he was a teen. The chemistry sets widely introduced in the 1950s allowed children to experiment with what Oliver Sacks, recalling his own boyhood experimentation, called "stinks and bangs," singeing off their hair and eyebrows.[11] On black-and-white television sets, kids watched an affable former air force pilot, Mr. Wizard (Don Herbert), make oilcan rockets and create explosions using sugar, flour, and other household substances. In their later years, scientists would recall with nostalgic amusement the dangerous chemical experiments that launched their career paths.[12] Most recently, the *Myth Busters* television show on the Discovery Channel features Adam Savage and Jamie Hyneman enthusiastically creating explosions—like making an incendiary bomb from a million match heads—to encourage interest in science while advising, "Don't try this at home."

If this experimentation took a vicious turn, then such was the price of national power and progress. After all, the United States had launched the most massive bomb in history and was heavily invested in building more, to uncertain ends. Against the background of racially motivated bombings and the explosive rhetoric of the Cold War, teens were bombing mailboxes, schools, libraries, their neighbors' Volvos, and old buildings on the fringes of the suburbs.[13] Former member of the Weather Underground Bill Ayers remembers that as a child he had been set ablaze by his friend "Ken" as they were experimenting with match bombs in the Chicago suburbs.[14] Although Ayers describes "Ken" as a "D student," teen experimenters of the period were often treated as geniuses. In 1951, a Chicago teenager—arrested for setting off one hundred homemade bombs in his neighborhood—was described as "brilliant" in his psychiatric report and given ninety days probation.[15] In 1954, when three juveniles from an upper-class community in Bethesda were arrested for bombing their teachers' homes and their local public library, the *Washington Post* described their "thrill bombings" as an "incredible tale of 'brilliance' and 'mechanical genius' perverted from normal pursuits."[16] In 1956, a teenager set off a bomb in Washington Cathedral, sending flames thirty feet over the heads of a concert audience. In juvenile court, his caseworker described him as a "bright boy" and a perfectionist with an interest in science.[17] The judge dismissed the complaint. The authorities criminalized teen bomb violence, but also tolerated it as an unfortunate side effect of scientific progress. During the Cold War, authorities reflected on the risks of science and its sometimes dangerous pursuits. Still, the potentially wrong hands of young scientists could be reformed into the right hands for the government's sanctioned violence.

By the 1960s, an era wrought by public displays of social division, journalists, social scientists, and lawmakers were more likely to associate juvenile bomb makers with urban riots, racial violence, and anarchist rebellion. The introduction of crime as a national election issue, beginning with Barry Goldwater's challenge to Lyndon Johnson in 1964, raised the political stakes for the image of the juvenile offender, especially the gang member and the rioter. As the federal war on crime geared up, teenage bomb makers were key figures in contestations over social order and crime control, representing a decline of moral order, a breakdown of authority, and the possibility of social reform.[18] Bombs were very real murderous threats, but also symbols of social disorder so pervasive that they were seen as destroying the hope of the nation, the young. Although no systematic collection of bomb data yet existed, it appeared that juvenile bombings were increasing. Federal hearings on crime, riot control, explosives, and school safety often featured expert witnesses who listed incidents of juvenile bomb violence and provided evidence in the form of weapons instructions allegedly handed out to children. For example, a New Jersey police lieutenant testifying at the congressional riot hearings in 1969 produced a pamphlet for making Molotov cocktails, which he averred the Black Panthers gave to thirteen-year-olds "to make war on white people."[19] In the long wave of savage violence against African Americans in the 1950s and 1960s, reports appeared of white segregationists using cherry bombs, firebombs, and pipe bombs to intimidate the civil rights movement and drive African American students out of schools. For example, in 1957, a bomb destroyed an entire wing of Hattie Cotton School in Nashville, Tennessee. In 1958, three bombs went off at a black grade school in Chattanooga, Tennessee, and another bomb wrecked most of a high school in Clinton, Tennessee. Bombers attacked schools in Champaign, Illinois, and the school board and a warehouse in Little Rock, Arkansas. Bombings, fire bombings, and bomb threats continued throughout the 1960s.[20] White fear, however, was mostly attached to young "Negro gangs" armed with Molotov cocktails on the city streets. Officials dubiously speculated that "expertly made" firebombs created from "How to Make a Molotov Cocktail" represented a broad insurrectionary conspiracy.[21] High school students were seen as being corrupted by their older, radical brothers and sisters and inspired by their distribution of guerrilla warfare pamphlets and *The Anarchist Cookbook*. By 1976, Hoffman's *Steal This Book* had made an appearance at a congressional hearing on explosives when the director of the Bureau of Alcohol, Tobacco, and Firearms, Rex Davis, testified that New Jersey teenagers had used its bomb instructions in a gang war to blow up a liquor store, two cars, and a high school press box right after a game.[22]

In a 1973 hearing on a proposed safe schools act, a list of 229 school bombings, taking place in an eighteen-month period in 1970–1971, was entered into the record to demonstrate the need for federally funded security in public schools against an "atmosphere of terror."[23] Although no motive was provided for most of these incidents, the familiar firebomb suggested the terrorism waged against African Americans. The most sophisticated device in the report was a radio-controlled bomb, described "as a prank to celebrate the end of the school year."[24] In the same year, the FBI began publishing bomb data, giving the public a glimpse into bomb violence in schools, the fourth highest target of bomb violence after private residences, places of business, and automobiles. Of these 179 reported incidents, the FBI attributed almost all to "malicious destruction."[25] The second highest category was "anti-establishment" bombings, presented as if this were a transparently obvious motivation.

The developing rioter, gang member, white supremacist, and anarchistic vandal began to replace the young scientific genius as the popular image of the juvenile bomb maker, but this latter image persisted if the bomber was suburban and white. The police tended to give youthful suburban bombers the benefit of the doubt as having "a high level of curiosity" and "just out playing around."[26] Their scientific knowledge was usually mentioned in news reports, as when teens placed two time bombs in a Chicago suburban high school and were said to have learned how to make them in a science rocketry class.[27] Reporting on bombings that had destroyed three cars, an elementary school shed, and a number of mailboxes, a *Washington Post* journalist pondered why "bright kids" with an interest in math and science and from wealthy homes had a motivation to terrify their neighborhoods with explosives. They were substituting household chemical mixtures for licensed gunpowder, and as one police detective noted, "Once the right combinations are discovered, the formulas are quickly passed on to friends and 'spread like wildfire.'"[28] The myth of the genius suburban tinkerer later reached its apex with seventeen-year-old David Hahn, who, in 1994, built a breeder reactor in his backyard shed, and fourteen-year-old Taylor Wilson, who, in 2008, built a nuclear fusion reactor in his garage.[29] While "Radioactive Boy Scout" Hahn was portrayed as a troubled genius, Wilson was feted by Homeland Security, offered federal funding for his projects, and invited to give a TED talk.

The social construction of the suburban juvenile bomb maker, in which young bomb makers themselves participated, was of a bright, creative prankster, promising in science, perhaps contaminated by anarchistic political ideas in the degenerative aftermath of the 1960s. The more the government—local, state, and federal—cracked down on juvenile bomb makers, the more reason they had to frame their activities as a romanticized pure resistance to the state. Teenagers' own motivations for making bombs were murky, but this would change as they began discussing their activities on computer bulletin boards. They avidly embraced an idealized image of themselves as "social deviants," agents of "chaos," anarchists, and nihilists who disrupted an oppressive world of routine. A few of them sought technical processes that would give these imaginary identities a physical force—at least in theory—that would transform fantasies (especially revenge fantasies) into reality.

Pyrotechny, including bomb-making information, was a popular topic in a new communications technology with a concentration of adolescent male users. Bomb-making instructions began appearing on the Internet in the 1980s, especially when parents bought relatively inexpensive home computers—like the Atari and the Commodore—for their sons (and some daughters) to encourage technical and scientific exploration.[30] For bored teens, the computer provided social connection and the ability to play with anonymous identities in interactive environments. The world of networked computers was initially a libertarian space laden with heady utopian projections of freedom, decentralization, and the end of authority and property. In that world, many young people took attention-getting role-playing identities that creatively projected power and rebellion in the liminal space of the Internet.

With the exponential surge in their numbers in the 1980s, Internet bulletin boards (BBSs) had to compete for users, carving out niches of information. The topic of pyrotechnics got attention. It appealed to the combination of rebellion, edginess, and scientific curiosity that characterized these young users in the age of Angus MacGyver, the TV secret agent and former bomb technician who got himself out of scrapes by cobbling together explosive devices from innocuous items at hand. The early days of the networked computers—dominated by technicians and hobbyists—were about "hacking": at that time meaning borrowing and manipulating technology to one's own ends. As one "Angus Blitter" said about hacking, "The spirit to be able to take these components and put the technology that had been the domain of governments for so long and let the average person figure out how to use it—that's the promise of technology."[31] Information about weapons and explosives fell into that category. Just as the home hobbyist could hack computers to network, improve speed, circumvent pay systems, and get behind security walls, the young pyrotechnician could manipulate chemistry and bomb engineering in household and backyard laboratories, or, as was much more likely, merely talk about doing so. Open suburban spaces provided more opportunity for bomb experimentation.

When BBSs became a popular way of connecting, all kinds of potentially dangerous technical information were dumped into computer networks, tapped from many sources and time periods. The genre of the popular weapons manual—based on borrowing and collation—immediately found a niche, with few variations in its form and rebellious tenor. Older manuals were manually copied or, when the technology became available, scanned in their original form and passed through peer-to-peer file sharing. New collations of material appeared as computer users added real or imagined expertise. The chemistry of explosives, historical descriptions of bombs, and information about blasting can be found in the library, but paramilitary publishers had introduced a prolific inventiveness of explosive devices made from readily available materials found in households and workshops. The Internet expanded this inventiveness. The features of the Internet encouraged the mash-up, fostering a proliferation of experiments and recipes. Most of it was offered with a knowing Yippie wink that authorities couldn't recognize. With the freedom of anonymity, the pyrotechnicians took humorous names that mocked the professional worlds of their parents, names like "Gunzenbombs Pyro-Technologies," "Chaos Industries," "Omnipotent, Inc.," and "Dr. Badmind."

The Anarchist Cookbook was copied into the network very early on. It was written in short chunks of text that could be manually typed without very proficient typing skills and more easily transferred with the slow baud rate of the early modems. Many teenagers thought the book was banned (and perhaps it was by their school libraries), giving this activity the appeal of illicitness, danger, and resistance to authority. The anonymity of the Net in these early days encouraged the circulation of information without the usual fear of consequences, though rumors spread that the FBI was watching and could arrest those who disseminated information at any time. This fear was enhanced by news stories that featured Internet bomb-making instructions seized during arrests of teenagers.[32]

Pyrotechnics came to be called "Anarchy," in honor of *The Anarchist Cookbook*. The information was transferred from board to board, added to, and refined. New and improved versions—such as *The Jolly Roger Cookbook* and *The Big Book of Mischief*—appeared, collating the proliferation of related text files. Fragments of books from paramilitary and white supremacist publishers—like Kurt Saxon's *Poor Man's James Bond*—were copied. George Hayduke's books of revenge and dirty tricks were favorites, providing advice on how to annoy enemies with bad music or rig a lightbulb as a feces bomb. Taking their cue from these older books, BBSs like The Temple of the Screaming Electron (TOTSE) circulated illicit information on fraud, murder, drug smuggling, and bomb making. As the community transferred its knowledge to the graphical interface of the World Wide Web in the early 1990s, TOTSE's bomb making became a portion of its website called "Ka Fucking Boom." In many ways, the new technology made the older idea of the popular weapons manual, derived from a variety of sources, much easier as a self-publishing enterprise.

Since teenagers provided the information, it was generally considered unreliable, but the writers wrote with pride of their pyrotechnic household "art" that incorporated "some of the newer developments and state-of-the-art achievements in this religious pastime."[33] A primitive political idea of anarchism was present, but mostly to thwart perceived censorship and to justify mischief against authority figures and neighbors despised as polite society. Participants childishly defined "anarchy" as simply being bad. The writers often asserted their own violent authority by claiming to have special insider knowledge or to have risked life and limb in their experimentation. Shades of the paramilitary publishers still haunt the online instructions, with their worship of the private war and the self-gratifying mercenary and assassin, promotion of revenge and dirty tricks, fascination with massive firepower for its own sake, and the pretensions of the in-the-field rough guide with a tongue-in-cheek disclaimer, such as "For Educational Purposes Only." In that influence can be found the technological and psychological heritages of war and military training found in the Paladin manuals. The paramilitary publishers weaponized the adolescent fascination with explosives and dirty tricks. However, while they may have sometimes fantasized about acquiring weapons-grade plutonium and building a nuclear device, the new online pyrotechnics instructions incorporated the knowledge and emotional concerns of the disaffected suburban high school student. The imaginary targets for sardonic rage were the police, college students, jocks, neighbors who kick a dog, pets, the "sweet old bitch" next door, the "old man down the block who smokes," and "your mother when she bitches at you."[34] The scenes for these psychodramas were the hometown and the high school, both as targets and sources of supplies. Many of the props were the familiar artifacts of an American middle-class childhood, such as Elmer's glue, glue guns, firecrackers, Drano, pay phones, fingernail polish, razor blades, disk drives, Vaseline, medicine bottles, shotguns, balloons, aluminum foil, and heat radiators. A greater attention to precision such as metric measurements and weight ratios was borrowed from the science classroom, but the motivation of scientific curiosity had been replaced by an enraged tinkering that extended power and control over the everyday environment. In the end, the texts reveal the paucity of choices in identity, expression, and social belonging available to many creative young people, especially adolescent boys, in the late twentieth century.

In 1988, the son of a Brazilian embassy attaché and three other teenagers from Bethesda, Maryland, were killed constructing a pipe bomb in a garage. The press described them as the best chemistry students in their school, reporting that they had used explosives in filmmaking and bragged to a friend that they could make a better bomb than the one that brought down Pan Am Flight 103 in 1988 (the Lockerbie bombing).[35] A few months later, their deaths were connected to a seventeen-year-old, described as "an emotionally troubled young man of superior intelligence" who ran a computer bulletin board, Pyromaniac Production Systems, that provided information on car bombs, rockets, pipe bombs, and land mines to over one thousand subscribers, including the dead students.[36] A short while later, this youth was given a three-year sentence for his part in a pipe bomb explosion concocted by his gang, Damage Incorporated, as revenge against a former girlfriend. The judge explained that bomb-making information online was troubling and might be accessed by "some cowardly, yellow-bellied so-and-so."[37]

With this high-profile case so near Washington, DC, and carried to the nation by the AP wire, it would not be long before children's access to bomb-making instructions on the Internet would become the subject of a debate over federal censorship. Media coverage of mysterious young hackers with logic bombs and pipe bombs spoke to fears of a radically transforming technology still opaque to many people. Beginning with debates surrounding the Oklahoma City bombing, efforts at controlling information on the Internet would last for much of the 1990s, with controversial efforts to pass federal legislation. It would take a massacre by teenagers—the Columbine High School shooting in 1999—to break through a deep-seated reluctance to wade into arguments over the First and Second Amendments.

Eric Harris and Dylan Klebold's attack on the students and teachers of Columbine High School in 1999 presented the opportunity to push through the 842(p) statute against bomb-making instruction. Harris and Klebold murdered twelve students and a teacher and injured twenty-four more with sawed-off shotguns, a 9 mm semiautomatic handgun, and a carbine rifle. Like many other violent political radicals who thought that the right moment of explosion would overturn their social conditions, Klebold and Harris had imagined a far greater level of violence that would destroy their social microcosm and jumpstart a revolution of disaffected students against their perceived oppressors: institutional authorities and high school bullies. To that end, they placed two large, heavy propane bombs in the crowded school cafeteria. These bombs failed to detonate. The attackers also let off a number of "crickets" (bombs made from gunpowder tamped into CO_2 cartridges), Molotov cocktails, and pipe bombs. In all, they made ninety-nine bombs for their self-described "mission," though most were of faulty construction. The Columbine attack made the argument for censoring bomb making on the Internet seem like a prophecy, and the distinction between the terrorist and the juvenile experimenter now eroded completely as the two merged in the media-generated satanic figures of the black-clad, Doom-playing, Marilyn Manson fanboys: the Trenchcoat Mafia. While Harris's and Klebold's classmates described them as weird and psychotic (an analysis embraced by many psychological researchers fascinated by the case), they became symbolic representatives of the murky world of "dark teens" inhabiting "liminal, other, deviant, dark, hidden, secret and inaccessible" digital spaces.[38]

Much of the media attention fell on their involvement in playing violent video games like Doom, but Klebold and Harris were also participants in a little-understood youth subculture of "anarchy" on the Web with its displays of violent masculinity, enraged tinkering, vandalism, and aggressive anger at anything to do with the polite society of suburban environs. Sometimes embracing the self-descriptor "terrorist," the majority of youthful participants experienced "anarchy" as a psychic textual performance confined to a digital world that encouraged role-playing, experimentation, hyperbole, and sardonic humor, but they also valorized the willingness, daring, and rash bravery to turn thought into concrete action in the real world. This was one of several factors—none of them individually sufficient as cause—that influenced Klebold's and Harris's identities as murderers, willing to act on their verbal threats and plans. Ralph Larkin has observed that Klebold's and Harris's violence partly came from the paramilitary culture most strongly present in the Southwest—as embodied in Paladin Press—but the direct connection between a paramilitary identity and two teenage boys in the middle-class suburbs has not been explored.[39] A pathway exists between paramilitary manuals and the online spaces of angry, disaffected teens that Harris and Klebold inhabited.

Like many adolescents, Klebold and Harris were drawn to computers and spent much of their time tinkering with hardware, building custom machines, learning programming, playing video games, developing websites, dabbling in hacking, and participating in chat rooms.[40] They had several aliases, including Reb and Rebdoomer for Harris and VoDka for Klebold. Harris, especially, created an identity on the Web that skimmed the more violent edge of the hacker/anarchy discourse, attempting to impress his audience with tales of the revenge vandal "missions" of his "clan" and his superior, real-world knowledge of guns and bomb making. He disparaged not only those going about their "everyday routines," but those who engaged in empty talk about acquiring weapons and didn't know the proper terminology of bomb making: "Don' falkin' say anothuh falkin' WICK or I's gone to rip yer falkin' HAID off and YOU-rinate down you' falkin neck. ITS FUSE!"[41] The intended audience for these rants was other adolescents who were supposed to find them humorous, admirably daring, and expressive of their deep disaffection. Harris's online speech was an exaggerated version of texts like this by other participants in this digital subculture: "The reason I wanted to make this program is because I hate just about everyone on AOL. Yes, that probably means YOU. I'm sick of all the faggots, and I'm sick of all the God damn pedophiles."[42] Or, "Don't you hate Jews, Well, get some Twizers, A lighter and a quarter and hold the quarter in the twizers, and cook the thing with the lighter, Then just drop it on the ground when he walks past, The dick will pick it up and be a really Fuckhead."[43] Or, "[Beat] the crap out of wiggers, faggots, wimps and other popular assholes who think there cool and act like there gods in your school. They all make me want to hack up my spleen."[44] (Samir Khan's instructions for "mak[ing] a bomb in the kitchen of your mom," published in al-Qaeda's online recruitment magazine, make more sense within this context as an appeal to disaffected young men.)

It is probable that Harris and Klebold obtained information about bomb making from the Internet, although they also visited gun stores and gun shows where they might have encountered paramilitary manuals. Their interest in the most common devices found in online anarchy files points to their use of them. For example, they constructed CO_2 bombs, called crickets, for which online instructions, adapted from older gun show favorites like *The Poor Man's James Bond*, were quite popular in widely circulated and emulated files. Teens used them for small acts of vandalism like blowing up mailboxes, though as one online instructor explained, they could also be used "for crowd control or killing if shrapnel is added."[45] Pipe bombs, too, were widely discussed in competing online discussions. The origin of the killers' more complex propane bombs, using alarm clock firing devices, is murkier. The online *Terrorist's Handbook* suggested using propane canisters heated to explosion with a can of Sterno.[46] Propane canisters are ubiquitous in suburban neighborhoods and known to be dangerous, so it would be no surprise that they would be deployed in backlot experimentation. For all the terrible suffering at Columbine, Harris's and Klebold's inability to build sufficient bombs of any size—born of their faith in their fantasies—saved many lives. The easy-to-use guns were the murderous instruments.

Although the information from publishers like Paladin, Loompanics, and Angriff didn't cause this level of violence, the digital transfers of it became part of the warp of violent talk on the Internet that provided a vocabulary of rebellion for bullied, disaffected teens. In his exploration of cultural fears, Frank Furedi writes of the Columbine aftermath: "Children were not corrupted through exposure to bomb-making information. Rather, bomb-making information provided a template for channeling their already existing chaos and aggression. All children were treated as potential psychopaths, like Eric Harris, based on a statistically rare occurrence." The template was quite important, but it was larger than technical information, providing a social identity. Like teenagers for decades before him, Harris liked to blow things up. On his website, he bragged like Ragnar Benson about his "gut-wrenching brain-twiching ground-moving insanely cool" bomb experiments in a creek bed.[47] More than the explosive power, the paramilitary persona gave meaning to the guns and explosions: the covert operator carried the power of hard steel as a way of subverting a large, alienating institution. The outlaw identity, now highly armed, was especially embedded in the Southwest, the home of Paladin and *Soldier of Fortune*. It could inspire the rich, comic expressive work of an Edward Abbey, or the sardonic violence of the futile revolutionary. Harris's and Klebold's fantasies were like many before them, who, armed with dangerous information and action narratives, fantasized about blowing up the state, represented in its institutions, and inspiring others to do the same in a single revolutionary moment. The distributors of the dangerous instructional works that had been so influential on the anarchy sites stepped back and voluntarily removed offerings. After the shooting, Loompanics' Internet provider refused to sell books that influenced youth violence, and *Medicine Chest Explosives, Kill without Joy,* and Uncle Fester's *Silent Death* were dropped from the publisher's line.[48]

Mayhem Manuals and the Law

When homegrown terrorist Timothy McVeigh bombed the Oklahoma City Federal Building, the news included a sensational story claiming that for weeks before the incident, a recipe for a fertilizer and fuel oil bomb was "part of a surge in traffic" on white supremacist and paramilitary news boards. That surge, noted by the Simon Wiesenthal Center, was related to a purported crackdown on militia groups leading up to the anniversaries of the shooting at Ruby Ridge and the destruction of the Branch Davidian compound in Waco, Texas. The founder of the Center, Rabbi Marvin Hier, noted that bomb-making information, accompanying hate speech, was once difficult to track down but now was freely available. He focused on the peril to the nation's youth: "How many people out there, especially young people, are looking at this inflammatory stuff?"[49] The Oklahoma City bombing opened a discussion of bomb-making information on the Internet that gave the federal government the appearance of concrete action in the face of difficult, complicated struggles with armed dissenters and terrorists. Generating emergency legislation, this discussion was a hybrid of fears of terrorist attack, corruption of children, and a new, little understood technology.

Just a few weeks after the Oklahoma City bombing, the Senate Judiciary Committee's Subcommittee on Terrorism, Technology and Government Information held a hearing on "mayhem manuals," decontextualized from their sources and little understood. The shape of an ongoing debate about online bomb-making manuals was fashioned here. Pointing to the decision in *Brandenburg v. Ohio,* subcommittee chair Arlen Specter (D-Pa.) noted that "freedom of speech" and "public protection" were inevitably in conflict, a familiar argument that would later be enshrined as the "liberty versus security" debate over proposed antiterrorism legislation. Specter then suggestively presented a message from the Internet that offered to provide the technical details of Timothy McVeigh's truck bomb "solely for informative purposes." No one at the hearing mentioned that days after the bombing the *Washington Post,* too, had described how "absurdly easy" it was to make a fertilizer-fuel oil explosive.[50] Mainstream print news, under editorial control, was a protected province for sharing this information, while the Internet was an unknown, frightening domain full of potentially lethal anonymous actors. The information itself wasn't precisely the problem; it was the allegedly bad company in which it was found. Specter pointed to *The Big Book of Mischief*—a soon-to-be familiar literary Satan—which gave instructions on "how to make what they call an easy Molotov cocktail, which can be constructed by a 10-year-old, and how to manufacture book bombs."[51] Although the *New York Times Review of Books* had featured a Molotov cocktail on a 1967 cover and police officer Michael Schaack had provided diagrams of anarchist book bombs more than a hundred years before, the appearance of the information on the Internet provoked a moral panic—much of it centered on children. For Hier, who testified at the hearing, the danger was racist militias combining bomb-making information with hate speech and using that rhetoric to persuade young people to join them. Focusing on public safety, Senator Herbert Kohl (D-Wis.) warned of the "dark back alleys" of the information superhighway, using the example of a twelve-year-old boy who made "a crude napalm bomb" from instructions he found on the Internet "just days before the explosion in Oklahoma," as if these two events were related.[52] (The boy's father had turned him into the Missouri police.) The Department of Justice's counsel, Robert Litt, pointed to children who were "making bombs and, frequently, maiming or killing themselves."[53] The focus was specifically on the technical directions, seemingly sprung from nowhere, rather than their expressive contexts.

The senators who hoped to hear arguments in favor of censorship were disappointed. Senator Patrick Leahy (D-Vt.) strongly opposed the drumbeat for censorship, arguing that the government should not impose censorship, in violation of the First Amendment, on a new communications technology. Invoking the traditional corrective remedies of the marketplace of ideas, he argued that such a restriction would further estrange dissenters and "fuel their paranoia."[54] Robert Litt pointed to existing legislation that already covered conspiracy and the teaching of bomb making for use in a riot. He suggested that marking explosives with tagging agents and increasing investigative powers were better than censorship.

Compelling testimony came from Frank Tuerkheimer, who, when he was an assistant attorney general, successfully gained a prior restraint order against *The Progressive*, which planned to publish information about the hydrogen bomb. Now, with a change of heart, he argued against such measures. Taking a familiar tack, Tuerkheimer argued that bomb-making information is readily available in the *Encyclopedia Britannica* and the US Department of Agriculture's *Blaster's Handbook*. Technical information is content neutral, he suggested, and independent from any particular communications medium. Pointing to *Brandenburg v. Ohio*, he warned that any attempt to legislate bomb-making instruction has to focus on the intentions of the communicators and the immediate harms of the speech. As to the argument that children were especially susceptible to danger, he argued that parents should control such information just as they did the firearms in their homes. Specter retorted that low-value speech could be distinguished from high-value speech,[55] proposing that technical manuals were of low value and not of the loftier "articulation of ideas" protected by the First Amendment. As low-value speech, bomb-making manuals fell into a category of speech that might be subject to governmental censorship. Tuerkheimer countered: "I don't see how you can take the combination of thoughts as to how things are done, which are then put into writing or some other format that is published, and say Government can regulate it." To these arguments, an angry Dianne Feinstein (D-CA) responded, "We are teaching someone how to kill, and that is what these diagrams do. That is what the rhetoric behind them does. Not just to learn, but to kill. The language is incendiary; it is not academic. We are protecting this with the mantle of free speech." She then suggested "the doctrine of prior restraint is one that we really need to look to, frankly, examine our conscience as to whether this is how we want to raise our kids, learning how to build bombs, blow up other people."[56]

As with many discussions of popular weapons manuals, the majority of senators debated the issue showed little understanding of the speech they hoped to regulate, using instead broad characterizations and isolated sensational examples stripped of context. Examples like the lightbulb bomb, the phone bomb, the book bomb, and the baby food bomb were chosen for maximum symbolism.[57] As the most zealous supporter of Internet censorship, Feinstein frequently pointed to online instructions for the "baby food bomb," a device similar to a powerful firecracker made much more lethal by flying glass and attributed to an Internet denizen named "Warmaster." The "baby food bomb" conjured a world of endangered, contaminated children and ordinary objects made suddenly lethal, resonating with fears of everyday life transformed by terror. "Warmaster" had posted his baby food bomb on the online "Bullet 'N' Board" run by the National Rifle Association's legislative director and lobbyist, Tanya Metaksa, who had voiced her anger to Congress at another Feinstein-led legislative push to ban assault rifles.[58] Despite this suggestive subtext and the organization's ongoing battle with Democratic politicians over gun control, the National Rifle Association's role in promoting weapons making and obstructing the placement of taggants in explosives was not an issue in the hearing before a Republican-led Congress.

Later, as Feinstein argued for a prohibition against bomb-making instruction in the Comprehensive Terrorism Act (S. 735), cosponsor Joe Biden took up the "baby food bomb" again, reading Warmaster's complete instructions into the Congressional Record.[59] It did not seem to occur to him that he was disseminating the information, and he was visibly no Warmaster. Senators and their constituents were supposed to be the right hands, while the wrong hands were shadowy figures in cyberspace, on the outskirts of civilization, intent on corrupting children. Feinstein and Biden would have preferred that bomb-making instruction be censored entirely, with Feinstein urging prior restraint. However, they began to compromise on prohibiting bomb-making instruction that would knowingly enable a crime. Since, according to Feinstein, any such instruction has only criminal intent, any disseminator could be punished under the proposed law. In his argument to the Senate, Biden imagined a fourteen-year-old who has somehow become curious about a "baby food bomb": "Obviously if a 14-year-old kid comes to you and says, 'By the way, I want to learn how to make a baby food bomb that has the ability to blow up, has the power, like advertised here, that can bend the frame of a car,' you are telling me that you have to be able to prove conspiracy, If the guy says, 'I am happy to show you how to make that, just like I can show you how to make a rocket in the field for science class,' there is no distinction."[60] In this stretch of imagination, the child was both a "Dennis the Menace" with a computer and some dynamite, as Feinstein put it,[61] and the victim of some frightening anonymous adult on the Internet diabolically perverting "science class."

Little discussed was the 1993 World Trade Center bombing, where handwritten instructions, acquired through military training on the Afghanistan-Pakistan border, were central to the case against the conspirators. It was easier to focus on children reading bomb-making instructions on the Internet than on complexities of US citizens receiving military training abroad, networking with other conspirators, and achieving enough expertise to carry out a bombing back home. Timothy McVeigh's ability to devise and successfully deploy a massive truck bomb could not be explained by any alleged encounter with bomb-making instructions on the Internet. Indeed, in light of these horrific crimes, law enforcement agencies began to learn how ill prepared they were to detect and stop large-scale terrorist bombing plots, despite their record of spying on any groups they did not like. In the year that the Subcommittee on Terrorism, Technology and Government Information took up bomb-making information, it had also focused on bellicose, heavily armed militia groups that Specter proposed were a clear and present danger. Because of constitutional protections, these groups could not be punished on the basis of speech, and laws to ban paramilitary training in some states were under legal challenge.[62] Neither international terrorists nor domestic right-wing militias provided a convenient symbol upon which to hang a censorship argument. The apocryphal corrupted child, rather than the terrorist, was used to generate support for legislation to control bomb-making information on the Internet.

The Feinstein amendment was passed as part of the Comprehensive Terrorism Prevention Act of 1995, making it illegal to "teach or demonstrate the making of explosive materials" for use in a federal crime. This was a much narrower version that fell short of outlawing bomb-making materials on the Internet, and Feinstein continued to press for a more stringent federal law. Two attempts were made to add a similar amendment to two defense authorization bills, but these failed. Because of concerns about First Amendment issues and opposing testimony from explosives manufacturers, feelings in Congress were mixed.

The next iteration of terrorism prevention law, the Antiterrorism and Effective Death Penalty Act of 1996, removed the Feinstein amendment and, instead, ordered Attorney General Janet Reno to conduct a study of the constitutionality of restricting bomb-making information "in any media." The focus, however, was clearly on the Internet. Reno was in the midst of defending the controversial Communications Decency Act (Title V of the Telecommunications Act of 1996), which criminalized the digital transmission of indecent or obscene material to minors. This law received heavy criticism as an infringement of free speech and would eventually be struck down by the Supreme Court as overbroad. At the time, the Justice Department was keenly interested in criminalizing Internet activities such as hacking and pornography mostly under the argument that children needed safety on the Internet. Censorship of bomb-making information fell within this new purview.

The Justice Department's resultant report offered that "at least 50 publications" devoted to "fabrication of explosives, destructive devices and other weapons of mass destruction" could be found in print in the Library of Congress.[63] By now, this argument had been repeated ad nauseam. This time, it required a staffer or two to spend a few hours visiting the library catalog and conducting a quick search on the Internet for a list of titles. Some of these were books from Paladin Press, including *Guerrilla's Arsenal: Advanced Techniques for Making Explosives and Time-Delay Bombs* and *Ragnar's Guide to Home and Recreational Use of High Explosives*. The inclusion of a work by Ragnar Benson was cognizant of the recent Oklahoma City bombing. The soon-to-be infamous *The Poisoner's Handbook*—which would morph into the *Mujahideen Poisons Handbook*—was there. Books by the US Bureau of Mines and the Institute of Makers of Explosives were also mentioned, as were hobbyist Chuck Hansen's books on the design and manufacture of nuclear weapons. Acknowledging that even *Reader's Digest* contained detailed information about explosives in crime stories, the report then mentioned forty-eight "underground" publications, without ever defining what it meant by "underground." Many of the books it mentioned in this category were from Delta Press, the same kind of small distributor as Paladin Press. None of the texts were discussed in depth or contextualized. It mistakenly referred to the explosive that could be constructed from Ragnar Benson's *Homemade C-4* as a "military plastic explosive."

For the most part, the report presented its examples evenhandedly, using works from government agencies, paramilitary publishers, mainstream publishers, and Internet bulletin boards. It maintained that the government was concerned with publicly available "instructional information" rather than political advocacy. This qualification aimed to protect the government from accusations that it was quelling political dissent, but, as I have argued, the mere dissemination of information can in itself be a form of political dissent. The Justice Department's overt worry was that information on how to make and use explosives would fall into what the report called "the wrong hands," defined as both terrorists "intent on using explosives and other weapons of mass destruction for criminal purposes" and juveniles engaged in "youthful experimentation." Nevertheless, the Justice Department admitted that while the information was freely available, it had only "circumstantial evidence" that criminals and juveniles widely used the information it cited for making explosives and bombs. Of the few disparate criminal cases it listed, none required evidence in the form of bomb-making manuals. All the perpetrators were convicted under other statutes.

The Justice Department also claimed that bombing incidents had increased "four fold" between 1984 and 1994, but acknowledged that it had "no empirical data" that the increase was due to bomb-making information. Indeed, it may have been due to notorious insufficiencies and inconsistencies in police departments' voluntary reporting to two different federal agencies: the FBI and the ATF.[64] Supported by the Department of the Treasury to study the feasibility of tagging and marking explosives, a special committee of the National Research Council analyzed the FBI statistics for 1995. Complaining of the lack of statistically valid data, it nevertheless proposed that 45% of the 1,979 reported bombings were not aimed at causing significant injury, but were accidental detonations, explosions out in an open area, and vandalism against mailboxes and outbuildings with less than $100 damage per incident. Most of the known perpetrators were juveniles. The explosions involved gunpowder or simple chemical mixtures contained in pipe bombs.[65] Although one might intuit that teenagers were accessing instructions for those bombs on the Internet, the lack of any case studies or reliable statistical information—including statistics from pre-Internet days—made any conclusions tentative. Before the Internet came along, kids were setting off explosions, blowing up property, causing much aural disruption, and injuring themselves and their neighbors.

Despite the dubious causality, the Justice Department supported the idea of legislation like the Feinstein amendment to curb information that "may play a crucial role" for bomb makers. It acknowledged the potential First Amendment problems with censorship of truthful, lawfully obtained information, but compared bomb-making information to "conspiracy, facilitation, solicitation, bribery, coercion, blackmail, and aiding and abetting." It also asserted a distinction between advocacy of unlawful conduct, protected by the *Brandenburg* test, and "instructions" for conduct, which it argued was "brigaded with action" and was active participation in the illegal act. Manuals, it said, might be particularly culpable if they advertised an illegal purpose, but, if that was their only role, could only be used for a probative purpose against defendants in court. The many times Uncle Fester's *Secrets of Methamphetamine Manufacture* has been introduced as evidence, even if it can't be demonstrated that the user has read it, is an example of this now frequent probative use. Producers of bomb-making instructions could be punished, the report concluded, if they knew that a "particular person intends to use such teaching, demonstration or information for, or in furtherance of, an activity that constitutes a Federal criminal offense." This was the foundation for 842(p).

The proposed law languished for two more years until Eric Harris and Dylan Klebold went on their murderous mission at Columbine High School. Within a month, Feinstein and supporters successfully tacked an amendment to the Violent and Repeat Juvenile Offender Accountability and Rehabilitation Act of 1999. Senate discussion of the bill was filled with references to Columbine. Feinstein said, "The youngsters in Colorado who perpetrated the crime indicated they got the formula for the pipe bombs directly from the Internet."[66] The amendment was also included with the Kerr McGee private relief bill and signed by President Clinton, becoming 18 U.S.C. § 842(p). The reaction among longtime Internet shapers was hostility toward the new bill as a form of censorship aimed at the new media. An influential voice on the Web, Howard Reingold, wrote, "Any person who uses the Internet to actually bomb people ought to be prosecuted. Just knowing how to do it ought not be a crime."[67]

The history of the 842(p) statute reveals much about the US government's attempts to address fears of mass violence shaped by a new communications technology that made bomb-making information more accessible and adaptable through crowdsourcing. Old patterns of identifying scapegoats and enemies surfaced again, alongside a bewildered scramble to assert control over an anarchic space dotted with regions celebrating homemade weapons, antigovernment activism, and criminality. During the arguments for preliminary bills leading up to the 842(p) statute, the symbolic enemies became children—standing in for all US citizens—portrayed as aggressive and technologically destructive, and in need of a firm hand. They also stood as victims, justifying the state's protection in loco parentis. In the meantime, information about bombs, explosives, and other weapons surged on the Web, partly as a rebuke to these efforts at censorship and partly as an expression of technological skill through which small groups and individuals could fantasize acquiring military force. Section 842(p) began in a federal effort to censor bomb-making information on the Web and was perpetuated after 9/11 as a questionable means for prosecuting political enemies on the basis of speech. Unevenly applied in weak terrorism cases, Section 842(p) exacerbated the problem while providing a questionable law enforcement tool.

The first person prosecuted under the new law was nineteen-year-old Sherman Austin. In 2002, Austin was arrested on his way to a protest of the World Economic Forum in New York City. Austin was a suspected hacker and the webmaster of raisethefist.com, a host site for the writings of antiglobalization and antiwar activists. The month before, federal agents had searched Austin's house in Sherman Oaks, California, and seized his computers.[68] In New York, after demanding to know if he was a "terrorist," federal agents arrested Austin for distributing bomb-making information on the Internet. Austin struck a plea bargain and received a year in prison.

The evidence against Austin was *The Reclaim Guide*, a manual he claimed was written by another California teenager to encourage participants to disrupt meetings of the International Monetary Fund and the World Bank. Austin has said that he merely hosted it.[69] Promoted as "essential reading for anyone who is associated with groups that advocate and/or utilize sabotage, theft, arson and more militant tactics," *The Reclaim Guide* offered advice in avoiding surveillance and infiltration, choosing the right clothing for black bloc demonstrations, rescuing members from imminent arrest, forming barricades, and avoiding tear gas.[70] It also included a chapter that very briefly described the construction of Molotov cocktails, smoke bombs, pipe bombs, Drano bombs, soda bottle bombs, match head bombs, and a fuel-fertilizer bomb constructed of fertilizer wrapped in an oil-soaked rag. To any regular reader of bomb-making manuals, *The Reclaim Guide* is mundane in its dangers. The devices it offers—such as the Drano bomb—are already well known through word-of-mouth by many children with a taste for blowing things up. In protest of Austin's arrest, computer science professor David Touretzky mirrored *The Reclaim Guide* on his own web page to demonstrate that it wasn't so much the information as the venue. A respected computer science professor could host the information without fear of arrest, while an antiglobalization activist would be arrested and imprisoned for the same.

The advent of the Internet heightened the question as to whether bomb-making instructional speech—especially as disseminated in a new communications technology—should be an exemption to First Amendment protections. Increasingly used in terrorism cases, 842(p)'s evolution into law raised questions as to whether online popular weapons manuals are truly new and therefore require unprecedented regulation, whether such regulation is necessary and effective, and whether this form of online speech is distinct from other forms of technical speech. Although many have argued that the Internet is merely a carrier of information, it has distinctive features—like vastly expanded crowdsourcing, speed of dissemination, and global accessibility—that have changed the way popular weapons manuals are created and consumed. The borderless Internet is a library on steroids and partly driven by Id. Its massive scale has raised the stakes in the control of dangerous technical speech. Legal remedies have fallen into familiar tracks: sensationally identify and target a particular political group and argue that its access to information puts the public at unprecedented risk. Other Western democracies have imposed much harsher emergency regulations on this medium and have prosecuted perceived enemies of the state, including their own young people, for viewing such materials on their computers. Given the propensity of law enforcement agencies to target political groups when equipped with this kind of legal tool, the risks to expression and political freedom are simply too great.

7

Vast Libraries of Jihad and Revolution

After the 9/11 attacks, the FBI was given expanded powers to pursue terrorists in the United States. Its counterterrorism force grew exponentially. Over the next decade, the number of informants and agents in the field grew to ten times the number deployed during the COINTELPRO days, when the agency launched its now largely discredited program to investigate, disrupt, and destroy groups it saw as threatening to the nation.[1] These operatives have targeted the FBI's recent list of enemies of the state: al-Qaeda-inspired homegrown extremists, sovereign citizens groups, white supremacists, militias, anarchists, environmental and animal rights groups, Puerto Rican separatists, and lone wolves of any stripe. The FBI counterterrorism mission is to circumvent attacks before they occur, and so controversial sting operations have become a regular means to identify and arrest suspects seen as potentially violent. These operations rely on an FBI agent or highly paid informant soliciting conspiratorial and instructional speech from a suspect, and have led to suspicions that the FBI is engaging in unscrupulous methods. The informants offer themselves as technically adept trainers and explosives experts who talk suspects into bogus plots and engage them in speech that crosses the line into conspiracy and instruction. Under ordinary circumstances, many observers think, these suspects would have neither the means nor the will to carry out terrorist attacks. The statute 18 U.S.C. § 842(p), which bans the teaching or demonstration of a making or use of an explosive weapon, has provided a way of prosecuting suspects based on their conversations about weapons and their collections of popular weapons manuals and videos not linked to any specific act or plan. A provision of the USA PATRIOT Act, 18 U.S. Code § 2339, prohibits "providing material support to terrorists" and allows related forms of speech to be used against defendants in court. Since the laws act to catch persons on pretext, dangerous instructional texts have become key in demonstrating that persons are poised on the verge of action.

Stiff penalties now exist for speech that had been previously tolerated. For example, twenty-one-year-old Emerson Begolly was arrested for "soliciting others to engage in violent acts of terrorism" on the Ansar al-Mujahideen English

Forum, where members hold discussion on waging armed jihad. A new influential group of private terror experts see these kinds of forums as brainwashing spaces where "al-Qaeda supporters increasingly tuck their messages into more common rhetoric" and where "rhetorical terrorists" encourage others to "go operational."[2] Training with an arsenal of assault rifles on his father's Pennsylvania farm, the deeply troubled Begolly became a web administrator on the forum, urging attacks on police stations, synagogues, trains, daycare centers, and other public sites. Begolly called for "bombs, bullets and martyrdom operations."[3] A key piece of evidence against Begolly was his link to a bomb-making manual: *The Explosives Course* by "The Martyred Sheikh Professor, Abu Khabbab al Misri." The FBI decided to arrest Begolly after this posting. Compiled by the professor's students, *The Explosives Course* is a well-designed textbook that discusses laboratory procedures, safety precautions, and the basics of chemistry. Like Johann Most's *Revolutionäre Kriegswissenschaft*, it teaches students to make nitroglycerine and explains where to get ingredients from common sources. Professionalized with chemical nomenclature, well-drafted diagrams, and standard laboratory equipment, it is a compendium of more than one hundred years of DIY explosives and explosive devices, from Molotov cocktails to lightbulb detonators, from potassium chlorate to thermite, from nitroglycerine to hexamine peroxide. *The Explosives Course* offers a cool, more professional repackaging of old content. Like any textbook, it contains no inflammatory threats, just a note that it "is released as a reference to practical Shar'ee work of Mujahideen."[4] For posting this text with the admonition to use anonymizing software during a download, Begolly was charged under the 842(p) statute for providing bomb-making information with the intent that it be used in a federal crime of violence. This count was dropped during the plea bargain, when Begolly pleaded guilty to solicitation to commit a crime of violence and resisting arrest with a firearm. He received an 8½-year sentence. At the sentence announcement, US attorney Neil MacBride said, "Those, like Mr. Begolly, who solicit others to engage in acts of terrorism will be brought to justice and prosecuted to the fullest extent of the law."[5]

Begolly is an example of dozens of citizens who have been arrested and imprisoned in recent years for calls to armed jihad. The *Brandenburg* test, which demands that the speech incite an imminent lawless act, has been steadily eroded as the Department of Justice tries to shut down the discourse it believes is creating "homegrown violent extremists."[6] Popular weapons manuals and instructional speech are often featured in these cases as evidence of intent to "promote" acts of violence without any specific plans for action or targets.[7] This unevenly applied approach to speech has rapidly evolved and represents a new chapter in the state's use of popular weapons manuals to purge enemies of the state.

The Agent Provocateur

With the popular weapons manuals as a crucial prop, the FBI has created a theater of terrorism designed to expose a suspect's allegedly preexisting, culpable mental state—sometimes unconscious—to attack the United States. Many legal scholars have argued that predisposition is poorly theorized and ultimately meaningless, and yet efforts in court to refute predisposition, through notoriously difficult entrapment defenses, have routinely failed in recent terrorism cases.[8] For example, in a well-known case, a small-time drug dealer and Walmart nightshift shelf restocker, James Cromitie, described in court as "desperately poor," was approached in a mosque parking lot by an FBI informant, Shahed Hussain, posing as a wealthy Pakistani jihadist in the poor, largely African American community of Newburgh, New York. Both were inveterate liars and convicted criminals who had a history of inflating their identities with braggadocio. In an "Arabic accent," Cromitie introduced himself to Hussain as "Abdul Rehman" and lied that his father was from Afghanistan and that he himself had traveled there. In fact, Cromitie was born in Brooklyn, had no Afghan parentage, and held no passport. Although this conversation was not recorded, Hussain reported that Cromitie had threatened to "do something to America." Without the FBI verifying these details, it set off an investigation, called Operation Redeye for its use of secret video recording, during which Hussain spent months attempting to talk a very reluctant Cromitie into terrorist acts. For his part, Cromitie talked about his resentment of the government and Jews, which eventually, egged on by Hussain, turned into violent threats. But Cromitie wouldn't take the bait until he had lost his Walmart job, to which he longed to return. Hussain offered him a BMW, $250,000, a Caribbean vacation, and his own business, a barbershop.

With these incentives, Cromitie enlisted three others in a plot to bomb a Bronx synagogue and Jewish center and fire Stinger missiles at military cargo planes at Stewart Airport. Cromitie was not the mastermind; as the trial judge, Colleen McMahon would write, "I believe beyond a shadow of a doubt that there would have been no crime here except the government instigated it, planned it, and brought it to fruition."[9] With his FBI handler, Hussain directed the "Newburgh Four" to fulfill a religious imperative, provided the plan and the targets, drove them on reconnaissance missions (none had the means to own cars), and trained them in how to deploy Stinger missiles and cell phone–detonated bombs. The FBI provided the fake devices. On the way to the crime scene, the defendants were unable to connect the cell phones to the fake explosives, even with Hussain exhorting them with how easy it was. He ended up doing it himself. After putting a bomb in a car outside the synagogue, Cromitie exclaimed that he had forgotten to turn it on. The four were arrested at the scene and charged under several counts, including conspiracy to use weapons of mass destruction.[10]

Despite the defense's claim of entrapment and outrageous government conduct, a jury found them guilty. The judge argued vigorously against the government conduct in the case but gave the defendants the mandatory minimum sentence of twenty-five years. Although the judge believed the defendants capable of real violence, she hinted at the theatricality of "fantasy" terror operations: "Only the government could have made a 'terrorist' out of Mr. Cromitie, whose buffoonery is positively Shakespearean in its scope."[11] One of the defendants recalled, "We were following along, looking for the money—we was just playing the script."[12] A suspect in another investigation recognized Shahed Hussain as an informant, and wrote, "I had a feeling that I had just played out a part in some Hollywood movie where I had just been introduced to the leader of a 'terrorist' sleeper cell."[13] Many observers of the Cromitie case questioned whether the defendants had the predisposition and the will to become terrorists or were performing to the design of the informer.[14]

Rejecting the defendants' appeal, the appeals court parsed the word "design," as in whether Cromitie and the other defendants had a "design" already in mind to commit a bomb attack. Stating that "design" was "ambiguous" in discussions of predisposition, Judge Jon Newman argued for a special use of "design" in terrorism cases: "In view of the broad range of activities that can constitute terrorism, especially with respect to terrorist activities directed against the interests of the United States, the relevant prior design need be only a rather generalized idea or intent to inflict harm on such interests."[15] That sufficiently put the "design" in the minds of the defendants, rather than in the informant's operational invention and technical support (where an ordinary person might put a normative understanding of "design"). In a strongly worded dissenting opinion, Judge Dennis Jacobs wrote, "Wanting to 'die like a martyr' and 'do something to America' is not a formed design, and certainly not preparation."[16] Others have argued that in a fearful post-9/11 United States, the police, juries, and judges automatically consider any association with Islam to be a predisposition and design for terrorism, making an entrapment defense very difficult, if not impossible, to win.[17] (Entrapment defenses are difficult in any event.) Terror experts and government officials laud the Cromitie case as a successful intervention in "homegrown violent jihad,"[18] but questions remain as to government's fairness in its zeal to protect the public.

The courts must out of necessity to win jury convictions simplify the complex processes by which groups are formed and enter into mutual actions. Social theory understands that conversations may solidify groups and move them in certain directions; the introduction of ideas and technologies change behaviors. Technology isn't innocent in this situation. It doesn't simply provide a hollow conduit for preexisting impulses and intentions: it contributes to creating them. The old adage "Guns don't kill people. People kill people" lacks validity, since possession of a gun gives its owner a new capability and identity, a new relationship with the world.[19] The provision of technical instruction and plans, along with tools and devices to enact them, transforms actors. In the parlance of terror experts, it delivers "operational capacity" to culpable minds, but it also changes the very structure, identity, and action of the group: its design and its designs.

Dissenting groups with any historical knowledge understand the transforming influence of an agent provocateur. They would immediately suspect a person who approached them with expertise in weapons and pleasure in violent conversations. Such a person would immediately be known as dangerous, as a potential informer, and cast out. The tactic of sending in an unvetted stranger offering weapons instruction only works with the ignorant and naive. Gary Marx, who wrote a seminal work on the role of the informant in social movements, defined the agent provocateur as someone who "may go along with the illegal actions of the group, he may actually provoke such actions, or he may set up a situation in which the group appears to have taken or to be about to take illegal actions. This may be done to gain evidence for use in a trial, to encourage paranoia and internal dissension, and/or to damage the public image of a group."[20] Marx argued that the agent provocateur's role in encouragement and outright entrapment was "illusive," but wondered whether pursuers create their enemies through such influence and misdirect the group from harmless activities and conversations that might diminish violence. The infiltrating agent has the right hands to direct the plot while the suspect has the wrong hands of the emerging criminal, even though both are involved in the consequent action.

The Power Point of Terror

Spinning fantasies, infiltrating agents gain credibility by offering violent tools and teaching and, if successful, direct the suspect into action. In the Cromitie case, the government did the instructing, but in other cases, the suspects' possession of instructional texts has featured prominently. With expanding capacities to collect, store, and circulate multimedia texts, the digital libraries of terror suspects and their expert pursuers have become centerpieces of evidence. Courts have struggled with the admissibility of large bodies of texts and videos, some of them very unfamiliar to judges and juries. Government witnesses are often drawn from a pool of civilian terror experts, a tight network of university researchers (mostly in the social sciences), journalists, think tank employees and entrepreneurs. They are highly paid to participate in terror trials, and have what sociologists David Miller and Tom Mills call an "orthodox" view that favors "repressive policies at home."[21] In recent years, some independent, self-appointed terror experts have established consulting entities (Investigative Project on Terrorism, Counterterrorism Blog, Nine Eleven Finding Answers Foundation, Flashpoint) as repositories of digital texts they deem terroristic, selected through this ideological lens. Because so much of the government's pursuit of the terrorist threat is classified, these experts provide the public face of knowledge. However, they usually lack specialist or scholarly understandings of the groups they study beyond their prodigious collection of digital materials. Because their reputations and income are based on continually generating the threat, they have a stake in media-worthy convictions of terror defendants. The self-appointed terror experts pursue texts to what they believe are their origins, through degrees of separation, usually stopping at some association with al-Qaeda. Unable to comprehend the complexity of texts in highly mobile digital contexts, the experts pursue them always through their ideological lens. The technique is to gesture toward a vast library of information, some of it allegedly lurking in the "Dark Web," over which the expert has complete interpretive control, and then choose one or two texts alleged to be representative.

For example, *The Mujahideen Poisons Handbook* has been used in several cases in Europe and the United States to damn defendants.[22] It was initially announced as having been found on a "semi-official al-Qaeda" or a Hamas website, and described as a "jihadi training manual."[23] Another rumor alleged that it was "written by the veterans of the 1980s Afghan war."[24] Soon a terrorism consultant at the United States Military Academy, James J. F. Forest, included it, along with *The Anarchist Cookbook*, as a "prominent source of operational knowledge" in his book on terrorist training.[25] Neither of these books has ever been connected to a terrorist act. A further absurdity is that even a cursory knowledge of these manuals would show that the online text is a rewrite of Maxwell Hutchkinson's *The Poisoner's Handbook*, published by Loompanics, which carries a variety of folkloric recipes for eliminating "the barbarous and the cruel."[26] Written in the quaint language of "magick" herbals and illustrated with occult woodcuts, *The Poisoner's Handbook* caters to the 1980s' moral panics about teenage Satan worship. For example, it offers a recipe to convert "attractive scarlet and sable beans for rosary beads" into poisonous agents that will kill "the more religious target" who uses them. The author fantasizes about sending a weaponized rosary to the pope, though no FBI agent ever pursued Hutchkinson.[27] The book most notoriously offers a recipe for ricin using a blender, a coffee filter, a jar, some marbles, castor beans, acetone, and lye. In 2003, a group of young men in a London flat were arrested with twenty-two castor bean seeds and a few handwritten recipes derived from *The Poisoner's Handbook*. Tests for ricin in the apartment came up negative, but a misinformed staffer at the British Defense Science Technology Laboratory reported that the poison had been found, creating a public furor as various officials announced the finding of a "highly serious poison" that demonstrated a terrorist capacity for chemical and biological warfare. It took two years for the lab to admit its error. The same testing lab tried out the ricin recipe and found that at best, the product would have killed one person, but only if injected. If ingested, the ricin would have caused only abdominal distress.[28] This was hardly a weaponized substance.

The recipes in *The Mujahideen Poisons Handbook* were adapted from *The Poisoner's Handbook*, updating the types of household equipment to be used and alleging that the author, "Abdel Aziz," had applied a rudimentary scientific method, carrying out experiments on rabbits. The book offered "esoteric knowledge" from a mysterious "training course" led by one "Breather." The text mentions jihad and has some words in Arabic, but sounds like a juvenile hoax when the author warns, "Don't become an over paranoid James Bond figure, especially when you haven't done anything illegal even!" It is entirely possible that some prankster made up *The Mujahideen Poisons Handbook* by spicing the Hutchkinson manual with the most demonic forces of the day, Islamists, and a hint of real science. It is breathtaking that *The Mujahideen Poisons Handbook* has ever been used against a suspect, and demonstrates the ideological drive to fit any text containing certain buzzwords, such as "jihad" and "mujahideen," into a grand narrative of a relentless evil design.

Evan Kohlmann is a controversial expert who has testified in numerous terrorism cases and provides commentary on NBC News. Kohlmann has, he says, collected an "archive that is approximately three or four terabytes in size. . . . [It] contains records of virtually every single video recording issued by al Qa'ida or other Jihadi movements, every single magazine, every single communiqué, every single official statement."[29] Though he doesn't speak fluent Arabic or any other Middle Eastern language, he also claims a registered account on every online forum used by those he deems "violent extremists," a category in which—like an old Red baiter—he includes "sympathizers" and "fellow travelers."[30] Even in cases where prosecutors are not linking the defendants to al-Qaeda, Kohlmann inevitably mentions this most recognizable of terrorist organizations. Kohlmann has offered a troubling view that even prayers could be "material support" for terrorism.[31] Defense lawyers have condemned Kohlmann's typical testimony as unqualified, slanted, sensationalist, prejudicial, and based on nebulous, irrelevant associations. Federal prosecutors continue to hire him and judges to allow his evidence, usually within restricted parameters and despite vigorous protests from defense teams.[32] Asked to examine a volume of materials collected by terror suspects, Kohlmann focuses on one or two texts that are most egregious and representative of the terrorist threat. In an analysis of Kohlmann's testimony, law professor Maxine Goodman advises that he is "motivated by unfaltering devotion to one big idea" and a "single, central view of the world."[33] Kohlmann features a few "literary Satans" to simplify the message of an existential evil for the media and the courts.

Just before Christmas in 2004, *NBC Nightly News* ran an exclusive on a frightening twenty-six-minute video found in a "militant Islamic chat room." It was entitled "Explosive Belt for Martyrdom Operations." That night, NBC gave a description of its contents accompanied by suggestive clips, especially alarming since video has a greater emotive power and instructional efficacy then words. The video showed hands arranging ball bearing shrapnel in a suicide vest, which was then used to destroy a mannequin in an experimental blast. The story included a statement by Kohlmann, who explained that it was made for use in Iraq.[34] A month later, the video turned up in a terror investigation of three men in Toledo, Ohio—Mohammad Amawi, Marwan El-Hindi, and Wassim Mazloum. Amawi had gone to Jordan in 2003 to seek insurgency training, planning to fight in Iraq. Unable to find a group that would take him, he returned to Toledo and met an FBI informant, Darren Griffin, known as "the Trainer," who claimed to be a Special Forces veteran. Amawi solicited the other two men to join a cell, and Griffin offered them training in unconventional warfare, which they eagerly sought. He provided handgun instruction and often watched and discussed videos with them as they translated: one was the video on how to make a suicide vest. Griffin formed a plan to distribute training materials to insurgents in Iraq, and Amawi agreed. He tried to put the suicide vest video on a CD but it failed to transfer. For his part, El-Hindi showed Griffin where to obtain other online videos and photographs of bombs. Griffin flew with Amawi to Jordan, in the plan to distribute the video and other training information to insurgents, but the three suspects were arrested when Griffin's cover was blown. One of the charges against them was a violation of the material support provision. Amawi was charged under the 842(p) statute for "watching and discussing how to apply the techniques taught in [the suicide vest] video" and for providing Griffin with an electronic file with hundreds of documents, including one on how to manufacture explosives. The trial was slated for March 2008.

The prosecution chose Kohlmann to testify on the defendant's "voluminous" video, audio, and written materials, including the suicide vest video. He claimed that the suspects' digital library was second only to his own. In one of his initial reports, he also offered to discuss a document called *39 Ways to Serve and Participate in Jihad*. This text was already publicly reviled as dangerous at two congressional counterterrorism hearings in 2007, where testimony from terror experts built a view of al-Qaeda's infiltration and indoctrination. On two occasions, a US Military Academy terrorism expert argued that *39 Ways* is "similar to Marxism" and that mothers use it to "sociaize their children with a Jihadi mindset from an earlier age by reading them bedtime stories of the great Jihadi fighters."[35] Another Academy expert, Jarret Brachman, testified that al-Qaeda's online library of three thousand texts was the group's *Mein Kampf*. As an example, he used *39 Ways* to show how these texts inculcate hatred. He claimed that *39 Ways* contains passages urging mothers to show videos of beheadings, provide video games to teach children warcraft, and give them punching bags with the head of Ariel Sharon.[36] (This content doesn't appear in the at-Tibyan English translation discussed in a moment in the Tarek Mehanna case.)[37] Brachman argued that such texts should be translated and made more available to terror experts to fight al-Qaeda's messaging. Later, in 2009, Brachman again testified about *39 Ways*, implying that it single-handedly "expanded the ways that individuals could promote Al-Qaeda's ideology and capabilities."[38] Once a title is offered in congressional hearings, it has already been judged as damning evidence and will inevitably find its way into evidence lists.

The judge in the Toledo terror trial, James Carr, at first agreed with the defendants to exclude Kohlmann's testimony that the material originated with al-Qaeda, with which none of the group was associated. He disallowed the government from showing Kohlmann's prepared PowerPoint slides on his textual archive, which featured al-Qaeda but had little to do with the case. Carr wrote, "The risk of very unfair prejudice substantially outweighs any . . . probative value. Few terms have a greater inherent risk of prejudgment than terrorism, terrorist, jihad, and Al-Qaeda."[39] During the trial, he changed his mind and allowed Kohlmann to testify on an audio recording of the men watching the suicide vest video with a *nasheed* (chant) that allowed Kohlmann to link it to a jihadist website. As in many of these kinds of cases involving an FBI sting and a digital library of bad texts, the defendants received far short of the maximum sentence possible, life in prison, for terrorist convictions. Amawi received the longest sentence of twenty years.

39 Ways to Serve and Participate in Jihad

In 2013, in another case involving Kohlmann, Tarek Mehanna was accused of lying to the FBI; of traveling to Yemen where he tried, and failed, to join an al-Qaeda terrorist group; and of translating Arab-language materials and putting them on a website of the publisher, at-Tibyan. This website is sympathetic to al-Qaeda and a Salafi sect that advances a violent agenda based on strict fundamentalist readings of sacred texts. Mehanna refuted the accusation that he had sought terrorist training, claiming that he had gone to Yemen to pursue Islamic studies, but was unable to convince a jury or an appeals court of his story. It was the second accusation that drew vigorous public debate. Mehanna's many defenders claimed that the government could provide no proof that he had communicated with al-Qaeda or participated in a terrorist attack; he was being persecuted solely on the basis of his speech, on being a "keyboard jihadist."[40] Among the eight hundred government exhibits were forum and chat posts, dozens of "terrorist-related" texts, videos, and photographs, including images of Mehanna at the site of the Twin Towers, holding up an index finger and smiling, and of Mehanna's tidy desk, surrounded by antique leather-bound books with gilded titles.

Principal to the government's case was *39 Ways to Serve and Participate in Jihad,* which Mehanna had translated and posted to at-Tibyan. An FBI agent on the witness stand read excerpts from *39 Ways,* but on cross-examination acknowledged that he didn't know the author or that he was reading passages from sacred texts. The prosecutor, Aloke Chakravarty, described *39 Ways* as "essentially a training manual on how somebody can get ready to personally get into the fight."[41] He defined material support for the jury: "A way to provide material support is to provide your friends as personnel, or people who might read the translations, might read the propaganda that you put out on the Internet that you want to go fight."[42] Some outside observers noted that Mehanna might be compared to Axis Sally or Tokyo Rose, pseudonyms for several World War II propagandists, two of whom were famously tried and convicted of treason. (One of the Tokyo Roses, Iva Toguri D'Aquino, was pardoned after two state witnesses admitted that they had been coached by the FBI and perjured themselves.) Treason, however, requires that one "adhere to" and have a purpose to aid the enemy (like being paid by an enemy-owned radio station to spout propaganda), while the material support statute requires only that one know that one is aiding the enemy.[43] Chakravarty justified the inclusion of Mehanna's reading and viewing material—"a treasure trove . . . of information about Jihad"—as proof that he knew he was supporting al-Qaeda. The prosecutor told the court: "It's not illegal to watch something on television. It is illegal, however, to watch something in order to cultivate your desire, your ideology, your plots to kill American soldiers, or to help those, as in this case, who were."[44]

In truth, *39 Ways to Serve and Participate in Jihad* is not even "essentially" a training manual. It provides no information about tactics, maneuvers, supplies, combat techniques, targets, or weapons, as is ordinarily found in military and paramilitary training manuals. It has no drawings or photographs of weapons making and deployment, hand-to-hand combat, troop positions, and the other usual fare. It contains no directions in how to commit sabotage. Rather, it is a religious exhortation to battle and martyrdom, a warrior's code, and a call for others to fund, protect, and support the mujahideen, much of it taken from the Koran and Hadith. There are many other calls to arms in world literature, such as the collection of Japanese texts that explain the samurai way of the warrior, the Bushidō. In an amici curiae filed in Mehanna's appeal, forty-three academics and editors worried that the definition of material support could criminalize their own work of discussing, translating, and publishing so-called "pro-Jihadi" materials. The brief argued that the government had mischaracterized *39 Ways to Serve and Participate in Jihad*, "grossly overstating [its] significance . . . in advancing terrorist aims." The work, they argued, contained a standard argument about individual duty and religious obligation in "wars of self-defense": "To discuss the various ways an individual Muslim can contribute to a jihad of self-defense is not a sufficient feature of an Islamic religious text to say that it belongs to 'al Qa'ida's messaging' or 'propaganda for terrorism.' If it were, numerous standard texts would be so classified."[45] Marc Sageman, a formidable terrorism expert with field experience who was witness for the defense, told the court that *39 Ways* was "of course not" a training manual. As an example of a training manual, he pointed to the *Encyclopedia of Afghan Jihad*, an eleven-volume work based in part on US military manuals and found in al-Qaeda training camps. Ali Abdul Saoud Mohamed, once a sergeant in the Special Forces at Ft. Bragg, allegedly compiled it from US military manuals.[46] Sageman reported that al-Qaeda was not successful at recruiting through the Internet; in fact, its numbers had dwindled. In his scholarly discussion of terrorist recruitment, Sageman has maintained that formal religious instruction, such as encounters with religious texts, is not instrumental in creating terrorists. Rather, terrorists are made through social contacts and group dynamics.[47]

Kohlmann was brought in to testify that at-Tibyan was an organ of al-Qaeda and that Mehanna had translated *39 Ways* and provided English subtitles for an hour-long video, *The Expedition of Shayk Umar Hadid*, for al-Qaeda. Yet he could offer no concrete evidence that Mehanna's original document was from a direct al-Qaeda source. The evidence that Mehanna had been directed by al-Qaeda to disseminate *The Expedition of Shayk Umar Hadid* was also very weak, yet it gave the prosecution the opportunity to introduce video clips from a slick piece of al-Qaeda propaganda. *The Expedition of Shayk Umar Hadid* is a highly emotive call to martyrdom. It begins with images of bodies humiliated through torture and riven through war, features thoughtful and even cheerful future martyrs discussing their feelings and motivations, and presents them as media celebrities, heroes, and exalted beings in an afterlife.[48] The prosecution argued that Mehanna was involved in influencing others to jihad. Kohlmann testified that *39 Ways* is an al-Qaeda "instructional manual" for "individuals that are self-radicalizing."[49]

Within this framework, training means recruiting through a library, based on a theory of reading's irresistible emotional and spiritual appeal, a training of the mind toward a singular purpose through an inevitable interpretation. Contact with *39 Ways* is like catching a deadly virus: the appeals judge in the case compared terrorism to the "bubonic plague," as if it were an infectious agent. This view of reading sees it as directly injecting dangerous ideas into a blank, receptive mind. It is an instrumental view of texts that disregards cognitive processes and the way texts converse with other texts and discourses in the reader's environment. Reading a proscribed set of texts is not a predictable form of brainwashing. Mehanna described his own radicalization process as a contact with a variety of texts, including *Uncle Tom's Cabin, The Autobiography of Malcolm X,* and television news.[50] Without question, reading can be deeply affecting, shaping strong ideas and deep emotions, redirecting and transforming life journeys, creating spiritual and intellectual communities, and engaging the vast expanse of human experience in language. There is no evidence that merely reading a text creates a terrorist or that eliminating certain texts will diminish terrorism. If these texts created terrorists through mental contagion, terror experts with vast libraries would succumb.

In a rigorous cross-examination, the defense attorney argued that Kohlmann's activities are similar to Mehanna's: collecting, translating, and disseminating literature and videos. Kohlmann admitted that he had helped the Nine Eleven Finding Answers Foundation (a defunct terrorism consulting firm) post on its website translated statements by Osama bin Laden, videos of beheadings, and *The Expedition of Shayk Umar Hadid,* with English subtitles, under a "Propaganda" tab. As with previous experts who presented themselves as the right hands for dangerous instructional speech and policed its borders, the new independent terror experts are held above suspicion while being suspicious of most others.

Mehanna's case was poised as an interpretation of the material support statute that would determine whether political speech, specifically translation, constituted support for a terrorist organization. In a 2010 Supreme Court decision in *Holder v. Humanitarian Law Project,* the judges had ruled that material support statute forbade speech that "assisted" and was "coordinated" with a designated terrorist organization, with the exception of "individual advocacy." The question was whether Mehanna's translations constituted individual advocacy or had assisted al-Qaeda through a form of expertise: translation. The presentation of evidence had combined Mehanna's travel to Yemen and his translations to prove that he had given material support to al-Qaeda, and the jury had convicted him on every charge. He was sentenced to 17.5 years in prison, far short of the life sentence that might have been applied. Mehanna's supporters, including lawyers interested in civil liberties in terrorism cases, hoped that the appeals court would rule on whether translation constitutes material support and judge it protected. The appeals court declined the question, asserting that it would not override the jury. Yale law professor Noah Feldman called it "a classic maneuver of judicial avoidance," and many other lawyers wrote deeply divided opinions on the case variously supporting or condemning the outcome and discussing its relationship to *Holder.*[51]

A revised and expanded legal apparatus now exists to demonize texts: law enforcement agents collect titles they deem terroristic, federal prosecutors introduce them in court, highly paid government consultants and vigilante spies collect vast digital libraries of literature and serve as witnesses to their evil, juries are immersed in media stories informed by these experts that offer certain texts as the cause of violence, and judges are given opportunities to slap enhanced sentences on their readers, translators, and disseminators. These official entities and their satellites have a Manichean view of reading aimed at punishing those perceived as innately predisposed. Often shrouded in secrecy, they expect us to trust that they are the right hands to host texts, deciding what, when, and why we will read. Nevertheless, terrorism cases have not relied solely on literature and videos. Thus far, defendants have demonstrable deeds that make for convictions, like traveling to the Middle East for training or waving a firearm at FBI agents. The needless introduction in court of voluminous texts, videos, and photographs has a purpose far beyond conviction of the often-lowly defendant. It is an extravagant, oft-repeated spectacle of the state's condemnation not just of an enemy of the state, but The Enemy in all its textual and visual manifestations. "Training" and "instructional" manuals, however loosely defined, are intended to prove that The Enemy has concrete designs that ground ideology in action. Translation of an al-Qaeda "training" text may lead to prison, but producing one may lead to collateral death by drone attack, as in the case of Samir Khan, editor of al-Qaeda's online *Inspire* magazine.

The Charge of the Hutaree

The prosecution of terror cases stands in marked contrast to the outcome of the trial in 2010 of a small antigovernment group known as the Hutaree. Evidence included a collection of novels, political tracts, weapons manuals, and training videos and involved an informant who was a martial arts expert and an FBI agent who was a bomb technician and member of a US Army team that provides intelligence information on improvised explosive devices. The suspects were nine participants of the Hutaree militia, based in southeast Michigan, whose leader was a vocal radical, David Stone Sr. Stone collected a small group of relatives and friends and led them in training exercises for battle against a demonic enemy composed of the Antichrist, the New World Order, and its many agents, including the local police. The group was information-savvy, setting up a proselytizing and recruitment web page and collecting a store of reading materials, including works on theological, political, and social topics; guerrilla warfare; and weapons making. They also stockpiled survival supplies, guns, ammunition, tactical gear, helmets, and assault vests, and, according to the FBI agent, used them in field exercises that included gunfire and tripwires attached to homemade black powder bombs.

The FBI and the Michigan State Police investigated the Hutaree for two years, believing that the group intended to carry out violent acts. An informant and FBI agent Steven Haug were planted. The agent in charge claimed that having a man inside gave the FBI control over the group's "most dangerous asset: explosives."[52] This activity went beyond monitoring when Haug told Stone that he could obtain industrial-grade explosives from a friend's quarry. These would be more powerful than the easily available black powder used in Stone's pipe bomb demonstrations. In conversation with Haug, Stone's fantasy of power escalated as he imagined making an "explosively formed penetrator" (EFP), a shaped charge using plastic explosives to blast out a copper plate that can penetrate tanks and other armored vehicles. In a 2005 CNN report on Iraqi insurgent's use of these bombs, an excited Barbara Starr explained: "One end of a steel pipe is sealed with a plate. Then the detonation turns the plate into a lethal dart that travels at a rate of more than a mile per second."[53] It then showed an armored vehicle riddled with holes. The news media's interest in EFPs in Iraq leaked into other venues. A Discovery Channel video featuring shaped charges showed up on 9/11 conspiracy forums, where it was used as evidence that such devices made fake plane cutouts in the Twin Towers. EFPs are explained in Mike Vanderboegh's novel *Absolved,* which is a thinly disguised militia manual. The description of an EFP is narrated over the shoulder of "Mark 'Kraut' Mueller," an "ordnance officer" of the "Alabama Constitutional Militia" who has a hobby of creating "improvised munitions" from a bookshelf of Paladin Press manuals.[54] The reader is given a history lesson about the inventor of the shaped charge, chemist Charles Munroe, encountered earlier in this book for his participation in the government fight again anarchist bomb makers, a detail overlooked in *Absolved.* Fat, middle-aged, and suffering from congestive heart disease, Mueller studies Desert Publications' 1980 *Evaluation of Improvised Shaped Charges,* which shows how to make the devices from Coke cans, wine bottles, tin cans, and steel pipes. He constructs a rifle grenade and antitank weapon using shaped charges. Haug and Stone were not the only ones having ideas about EFPs and their potential for attacking symbols of government power.

The investigation came to a head when agents became concerned that the Hutaree was planning to kill a police officer and attack more police attending the funeral. The government claimed that the Hutaree intended this as the first shot in a revolution that would rally other violent militia groups. The defendants immediately framed the case as a violation of their constitutional rights under the First and Fourth Amendments. The question for the court was whether Hutaree's conversations were fantasies or concrete plans to create seditious "weapons of mass destruction," as federal law now defines all explosive devices.

To prove the predisposition of the Hutaree to act, the government produced texts as evidence that Judge Victoria Roberts divided between "conspiratorial and anti-government works" and technical handbooks.[55] The first set included three novels along with political tracts by Randy Weaver, an adherent of the Christian Identity faith whose wife and son were killed in a standoff with US marshals; Robert Depugh, the anti-communist zealot and founder of the long-defunct Minutemen; and Jack B. Otto, who perpetuated "forbidden knowledge" about conspiratorial Jewish cabals, organized as the Illuminati who run the New World Order. Masquerading as history but reading more like an anti-Semitic *Da Vinci Code*, Otto's work is difficult to distinguish from fiction. Also in the set were videos by radio host Alex Jones, proselytizer of the theory that a global elite is trying to control ordinary citizens through media spectacle, surveillance, and economic manipulation. The judge made an important distinction between these "conspiratorial and anti-government works" from Hutaree training videos and technical manuals found in their possession: *Ragnar's Homemade Detonators, Militia Field Manual, Sniper—Training and Employment, Improvised Munitions Handbook,* and two rifle manuals. The judge ruled that portions of the technical manuals were admissible but that the fictional works and political tracts, with two brief exceptions, were not. "Millions of Americans," she wrote, "read books by popular novelist Dan Brown, which are filled with conspiracy theory themes; it is impossible to say how many of them, if any, are inspired to action on account of the material they have read."

The texts collected to damn the Hutaree are typical of the conspiracist reading community. Teachers who speak with authority are welcome in a community of seekers with voracious appetite for information in an intensely emotional interpretive milieu obsessed with the mysterious workings of hegemony and power. Alienated from social and political institutions but with a real zest for study, anti-government conspiracists find meaning in collecting all sorts of eclectic information about history, law, politics, medicine, cooking, plants and animals, and weaponry. Many are very adept at citing legal chapter and verse in a defense of constitutional rights alongside explaining how to construct a silencer. The counterpart to frightful conspiratorial knowledge is technical knowledge about surviving outside of institutions and protecting the encampment. Whether canning a tomato, dressing a wound, organizing a patrol, or constructing a shaped charge, hands-on knowledge and practical skill alleviate anxiety over the sinister mysteries of the inchoate conspiracy and the looming disaster. Books with worst-case scenarios accompanied by practical know-how are often recommended as essential to surviving the end times. Old technologies and their lore are highly valued for their ease of use and detachment from complex, dependency-producing systems. Paladin Books, like Ragnar Benson's *Detonators,* fit well into this DIY survivalist craft ethos.

Ethnographer Richard G. Mitchell Jr. describes these antigovernment enclaves as critics of modernity with its "massive, monolithic, hyperrationalized, interdependent systems of production." They reject modernity to find meaning in "cultural crafting," seeking alternative sources of information and engaging in small-scale projects. Mitchell trained and drilled with an Oregon militia group and recounts an instructor discussing survivalism through Freud's *Civilization and Its Discontents* and Shakespeare's complete works.[56] This subculture has created a rich lore of alternative community, including a long-standing fascination with small guerrilla bands purifying a corrupt society with regenerative violence.[57]

The introduction of three distinctly different novels as evidence against the Hutaree was a failed attempt to demonstrate its worldview. The novels were *Hunter*, by William Pierce (aka Andrew McDonald); *Red Sky*, by Ron Rendelman; and *Patriots: Surviving the Coming Collapse*, by John Wesley Rawles. All three are political novels like Harriet Beecher Stowe's *Uncle Tom's Cabin*, Upton Sinclair's *The Jungle*, and Ayn Rand's *Atlas Shrugged*: Their fictional frameworks are delivery systems for ideas and hope to persuade the reader through strong emotional identifications. *Hunter* was well known to the FBI and had been introduced in the trial of Timothy McVeigh's associate, Terry Nichols. *Red Sky* was written by a self-described "prophet" and "leader" of the Jesus movement in Chicago. The book is a series of nonfiction political tracts from militia groups, conspiracy theorists, and survivalists glued together by a thin semiautobiographical plot involving a hapless, self-absorbed Chicago cabbie driver, "Scott White," who embarks on a pilgrim's progress. He is radicalized first by his encounters with Christian ideas, then by various conspiracy theories involving the usual machinations of the New World Order (represented in the United Nations), and finally by militia training and survivalist lore. A deeply pessimistic account, White's journey ends badly when the agents of the New World Order attack the militia compound where he has driven his Dodge Ramcharger to fight the forces of the Antichrist. His martyrdom is caught for the nightly news: "Scott's head blew apart, splattering the cross he held with his blood."[58] The plot is secondary to the long diatribes about the New World Order communicating by secret signs, implanting microchips in persons to make them docile, creating false flag operations, manipulating the economy to enslave the people, planning to use the sky as a huge brainwashing movie screen, and other familiar components of the vast conspiracy, with the homosexual conspiracy thrown in for good measure. At the end, tactical operations are described and practical advice given for survival during end times, such as stockpiling gasoline, hermetically sealed seeds, matches, fertilizer, toilet paper, and coffee (which "will be the rage in trade goods" after the coming collapse of order).[59] The book has a theory of reading: Scott White serves as an empty repository for knowledge that gains credibility through sheer accumulation, rather than any analysis and synthesis. This archetypal character is very susceptible to persuasion and control that ultimately leads to his gruesome annihilation. The reader is expected to be a similarly empty repository radicalized by the accumulation of information, although the outcome is filled with despair. Like *The Expedition of Shayk Umar Hadid*, it offers martyrdom as a spiritual solution to political struggle, but without the songs, cheerfulness, and earthly glory.

John Wesley Rawles's *Patriots* is a much more sophisticated work, though it, too, hybridizes fiction and nonfiction. Written by the author of SurvivorBlog, the book (the first of a series) is advertised as "a thrilling narrative depicting fictional characters using authentic survivalist techniques to endure the collapse of American civilization. Reading this compelling, fast-paced novel could one day mean the difference between life and death."[60] The main characters are middle-class professionals from Chicago who form a survivalist compound in Idaho and, after an economic collapse caused by hyperinflation, fight the minions of the United Nations who attempt to install a corrupt martial law and take away people's guns. The vision is of small bands of patriotic militia groups returning to a homesteading version of a more innocent colonial America. Much of the novel is given to instructing readers on fortifying the homestead against attack, choosing the right sort of gun, treating a wound, and other survivalist techniques. *Patriots* is like other survivalist novels that have elaborate discussions of making, handling, and stockpiling weapons and carrying out military maneuvers and attacks. They are hybrid forms: survival and paramilitary manuals encased in fanciful fictional scenarios of economic and social collapse and brotherly camaraderie in the face of a vague, sinister enemy. They owe their form, in part, to nuclear survival books like Dean Ing's *Pulling Through* (1983), which combined nonfiction plans for building a fallout shelter with a novella about a family using practical know-how to rebuild after an attack.

These novels are the creative outpourings of a heavily armed subculture in the United States, but difficult to connect to a plan of attack against police officers at a funeral. The prosecutors did not expect the jury to read or fully comprehend them. Instead, they told the judge that they planned to have an FBI agent "summarize the concepts" in the list of books and videos seized as evidence. The defendants filed a motion questioning the admissibility of this literature and the ability of an agent to summarize it. Judge Roberts delivered a ruling that illuminates many of the problems with the use of reading materials in court. She first agreed that a few pages from the nonfiction technical handbooks could be admissible, and had in prior cases been used to show the defendant's intent and motive, to demonstrate that co-conspirators were associated, to show that a defendant had adequate knowledge to carry out the plot, and to prove that a defendant was not engaging in empty rhetoric. Diagrams from *Ragnar's Homemade Detonators* showed how to make a crude trigger or pressure switch (looking quite prone to accidental detonation) from a clothespin.[61] The reissued army manual, *Improvised Munitions Handbook*, contained directions on making an armor-piercing shaped charge.

The judge cited *U.S. v. Parr*, in which *The Anarchist Cookbook* was introduced as evidence against a prison inmate who had threatened to blow up the federal building in Milwaukee because he wanted to be the next Timothy McVeigh. Though an appeals judge found the introduction of the entire *Anarchist Cookbook* to be an "abuse of discretion," he agreed that portions of it, which Parr had discussed with another inmate, "refuted his defense that he was merely engaged in hyperbole."[62] (*The Anarchist Cookbook* contains no discussion of blowing up federal buildings, but this ruling shows how these manuals, no matter how unrelated, can give an aura of seriousness by title alone.) Judge Roberts also cited the case of Elaine Brown (discussed in chapter 4), where books like *Guerrilla Warfare and Special Forces Operations* were used to show that the defendant had "knowledge of how to conduct armed resistance." The judge thus allowed that the texts were admissible, but only under the guiding rule that the "trial court must examine the complete contents of books and exclude portions that are not relevant or unduly prejudicial." In this case, the task might have proved a challenge, since the evidence list misspelled titles—like *Dragnar's* (properly *Ragnar's*) *Homemade Detonators*—and was hardly a demonstration that even the FBI investigators had bothered to read them. This sloppiness is routine in many such cases and suggests that agents hoover up books for a mere hint of subversion in the title.

To the defendants' complaint that an FBI agent couldn't be trusted to summarize the books or "testify to concepts in literature," Judge Roberts concurred, writing that FBI agents have no literary expertise and that "literary works simply are not the type of evidence susceptible to objective summation" as are business, tax, and phone records. The judge also acknowledged the subjectivity of reading, writing that if one hundred people were asked to write summaries of literature, they would write one hundred different summaries, of which each "would necessarily reflect the inherent assumptions of the person who composed it."[63] The judge insisted that the prosecution produce specific passages related to the charges.

The expert witness testimony of political scientist Michael Barkun, who has written extensively on conspiracy theories, was also denied and deemed irrelevant to the charges since he could not demonstrate that reading conspiracy theories predicted violent action. Barkun included the Hutaree as violent extremists in the second edition of his *Culture of Conspiracy*, arguing that the judge had failed "to come to grips with the Hutaree's worldview." He maintained that they were "the most conspicuous group whose conspiracist beliefs resulted in planned violence."[64] Yet Judge Roberts acquitted seven members of the Hutaree of the sedition charges. She ruled that the prosecution couldn't prove that the Hutaree had any specific plan or goal and had built its case on vague hate speech. Two of the Hutaree pleaded guilty to more minor charges of possessing .223-caliber rifles, but served no further jail time. Although US Attorney Barbara McQuade told the press that she was gratified that the Hutaree would "never be permitted to possess firearms again," many of their confiscated guns and more than 100,000 rounds of ammunition were ultimately returned to them.[65]

The state and federal prosecutors in the Hutaree case had initially trumpeted the arrests as a demonstration that not only Muslim communities were investigative targets. McQuade wrote, "Violent acts are not committed only by Muslims and Arabs. . . . We have a case against members of the Hutaree militia pending in our district, in which we have charged individuals with plotting to kill police officers."[66] When the Hutaree were exonerated of sedition, the flimsy evidence of balance collapsed, with commentators wondering whether Muslims were held to a different standard when it came to speech protections.[67] The Christian Hutaree had stockpiled a huge cache of weapons and spoken of their own holy war, but other than minor weapons charges, they had walked free. Damning literature was not used as spectacular evidence against them; the judge was very precise about the texts she would admit. No literary Satans, incendiary political speech, or abstract blueprints were allowed. Without all of this circumstantial textual evidence, the government's case collapsed. There was no sedition and no great Enemy. This is in marked contrast to the way literature is used against Muslim defendants accused of advocating armed jihad.

This grave contradiction can't be parsed by legal legerdemain. The unevenness with which similar texts are treated for different groups of defendants is glaringly obvious, especially within the historical context where surges of interest in dangerous instructional speech have been attached to public enemies. On a scale not seen since the McCarthy period, there is a concerted effort to feature dangerous reading through trial spectacles, where certain texts are presented through an ideological lens of preexisting guilt. The idea of terrorist instructional speech—already a dubious category—has expanded well beyond weapons manuals to encompass religious texts, novels, autobiographies, and other literary works: works that have traditionally been protected as creative expression. To show how uneven this is: Ayn Rand's *Atlas Shrugged* is a revolutionary novel that features rogue citizens carrying out pirate attacks and sending the nation into chaos and economic collapse. It presents a plan for destroying the nation and its institutions. Despite the frequent rallying cry of "Going Galt," no one has ever gone to trial with this book in evidence. If *Atlas Shrugged* became a literary Satan, a good portion of the current US Congress would be tried for sedition. Federal agencies, law enforcement operators, and informants, and a metastasizing realm of terror experts, select a few texts among many for their maximum symbolism as dangerous teachings, as if readers were golems of clay awaiting the animating instructional word to send them into monstrous action.

8

Weapons of Mass Destruction

With the rise of secretive large-scale weapons production, exemplified in the Manhattan Project, the ability of a small isolated group to steal technological power from the state became almost entirely impossible. From the days when anarchists threatened that they could use dynamite to level the field, the technology of the popular weapons manual fell far behind the military technologies of the state. After the Vietnam War, the manuals by the paramilitary publishers had a nostalgic feel, like veterans telling stories about their old war experiences, recycling older ideas about explosives, poisons, chemicals, bomb designs, and booby traps. Often relying on outdated textbooks and encyclopedias, the authors made obsolescence into a virtue, imagining postdisaster worlds when the high-tech production systems would fail and the old, accessible forms of knowledge would allow ordinary people to survive off the grid, live a more connected life, and defend the homestead. Weapons that could be made by hand, using simple processes, were a more satisfying, connected form of labor than the compartmentalized work of designing complex weaponry. By the 1980s, radical groups like Earth First! celebrated the simple wrench as a weapon that could break through complacency about environmental destruction. More recently, some authors of popular weapons manuals have aspired to a greater professionalism by adding the trappings of scientific concepts and procedures and multimedia descriptions that can be more easily imitated, but the weapons offered are simple in design and usability, not requiring complex manufacturing facilities and networks of technical expertise. The explosive devices that circulate could still have a devastatingly lethal effect and a great symbolic impact, but they pale in comparison to national military power to crush entire cities and destroy hundreds of thousands of lives with weapons of mass destruction, technologies that are too complex and difficult to emulate. The federal government's legal definition of "weapon of mass destruction" to mean any explosive device hides this imbalance.[1]

Designs for pipe bombs and claymore mines might be one thing, but designs for nuclear weapons in the hands of terrorists seem quite another. The truth is, however, that the basic designs have been out there for many decades, in the hands of ordinary citizens, for arguably very good reasons. The *Progressive* case of 1979 was an argument over whether a magazine should be allowed to publish the secret of the hydrogen bomb, which many interpreted as a frightening how-to guide to building one's own weapon of mass destruction. *The Progressive* revealed the ultimate weapons' secret to enhance democratic decision-making about the nuclear state.

The *Progressive* Case

In November 1979, *Progressive* magazine produced an issue called "The H-Bomb Secret: How We Got It and Why We're Telling It."[2] It included an article by antinuclear activist Howard Morland with illustrated details on the hydrogen bomb's mechanism. Morland summed up in a sentence, in ordinary language, the principle of the Teller-Ulam design for a two-stage thermonuclear detonation involving radiation reflectors. He claimed that he had collated the design from "employee recruitment brochures, environmental impact statements, books, articles, private interviews, and [his] own private speculation." Later, he would point to his high school physics textbook as providing important insight. Like many providers of popular weapons information in this period, Morland was a Vietnam veteran who'd had a falling out with the military. He drifted without a home and a steady job, but he possessed the technophile's obsession with organizing technical details and the atomic researcher's obsession with opening secrets. As Spencer Weart observed in his classic study of nuclear imagery, the early stories of atomic research commonly featured "a powerful authority who mastered the secret."[3] Morland's quest reflected this mythology surrounding nuclear weapons as he sought the political power of a public voice that would reveal the secret device hidden in a vast apparatus of resource extraction and technical production. His article would be a letter bomb that he hoped would blow open this system to public scrutiny. He traveled around the country by Greyhound bus or in a beat-up Volkswagen, staying with friends, telephoning nuclear scientists, and visiting the installations of the nuclear complex to tease out tiny bits of information and synthesize them. His public revelation of the "H-Bomb Secret" and the *Progressive*'s dare to the cult of secrecy provoked the Department of Energy, through the Department of Justice, to obtain a temporary restraining order on the publication, leading to a widely publicized six-month struggle over the legal limits of technical speech. The government finally dropped the case and the *Progressive* declared a win.

This oft-cited case has often been analyzed to critique the federal government's use of prior restraint and its voluminous classification of information. Historians, political scientists, free speech advocates, legal scholars, and journalists have mostly decried the government's actions in the case, arguing that more open public discourse—even of nuclear secrets—is needed for a healthy democracy and an innovative science. The *Progressive* case is often used as a textbook example of government overreach for attempting to cut off the freedom of the press and the free exchange of knowledge. From the beginning, when *Progressive* editor Erwin Knoll came out swinging against the unprecedented six-month prior restraint of the "H-Bomb Secret," discussions of the case have largely focused on the press and the First Amendment. Observers have shown little concern with the kind of speech, its historical roots, and its specific challenge to state control over weapons technology. Morland himself was angered by what he saw as the news media's erasure of his original intention: the exposure of scientific and technical information to undermine the secretive nuclear weapons complex. The existence of "The H-Bomb Secret" merely as a text, with only a conceptual discussion of a nuclear weapon, was enough to bring down the strong arm of the government in a contest over who was allowed to speak of nuclear weapons in technically detailed ways.

Morland's "H-Bomb Secret" has much in common with prior publications of dangerous instructional speech. It was positioned as a theft of violent technical knowledge from the state, offered in ordinary language to dissenters (the intended audience being antinuclear activists) for their technical education. Like Johann Most's critique of the mathematical jargon surrounding dynamite, Morland offered the secret as much simpler than the self-interested mystifications of the nuclear weapons complex. Morland used quotidian metaphors to describe weapons components—a soccer ball, a cantaloupe, cordwood, cookies, household garbage, carrots, and pencils—in an effort not only to offer a science education, but to make the hydrogen bomb real, to give it weight and heft in readers' minds. Morland had begun his antinuclear activity with agitprop, carting around in his car's trunk a model of a cruise missile made of galvanized steel and weighted with sand to make it "too real, too solid and heavy to be put aside."[4] Here again was the idea that weapons information provided a hard reality to a political cause, even if it remained in a textual, speculative realm with a Yippie edge of parody. The "H-Bomb Secret" emulated and mocked the nuclear complex's technophilic fascination with weapons, the paternalistic stance of many scientists, and the metaphors of strategic planners who have named high-tech weapons after not only the Greek pantheon, but common domestic tools: "cookie cutters," "Christmas trees," and "RVs."[5]

The opening line of "The H-Bomb Secret" was performative—"what you are about to learn is a secret"—suggesting that readers were about to enter a Twilight Zone where some alternative dimension existed beneath the everyday perceptions of ordinary people. The secret was understandable, Morland said, to "anyone familiar with elementary principles of college physics." He wrote that while not everyone was interested in technology, even in how radios worked, there were "millions of people in our highly technological society [who] are amateur experts on gadgets as varied as the electric doorbell and the nuclear power reactor."[6] Like other writers of popular manuals before him, Morland pointed to the native intelligence of many ordinary people as capable of grasping the science if presented plainly. Like these other writers, he claimed that the information could all be found in a library and translated into a popular vernacular. His readers were the children of what historian Thomas Hughes called the twentieth century's "gigantic tidal wave of human ingenuity" in systems building,[7] which spread out into the nooks and crannies of everyday life and thought and resurfaced as many technical enthusiasms. Reflecting these enthusiasms, Morland set out to prove that an ordinary person, even of low social status, who opposed the nuclear state could grasp the technology, including production, of a hydrogen bomb. He wrote, "The reason I wanted to tell the H-bomb secret was that it was a roadmap—you had to see the product that was being made in order to tell why they had factories in Oak Ridge, Tenn., and Denver, Col. So it tied all the factories together by showing this—like having a diagram of a car and saying the pistons are made over here and the engine block is made over there and that sort of thing."[8] Morland hoped that if citizens saw the way weapons were made across many facilities, they could enter debates over important policy questions, such as whether they should be paying for such a massive operation and whether production and testing were endangering health. Morland observed that the technical mystique surrounding nuclear weapons made citizens timid to enter into robust debates about them.

Like other popular weapons manuals, the "H-Bomb Secret" was dangerous because it provided information to ordinary people in accessible prose. Nuclear weapons were supposed to be preserved from all the many wrong hands by two protections: de jure, by the classification system and the prohibitions of the Atomic Energy Act, and de facto, by the immense complexity of building bombs with finely machined parts, highly processed and difficult to obtain materials, and intricate assemblies. The latter has been far more effective in preventing their manufacture by small groups of violent actors. Despite periodic alarms over "how to build a nuclear bomb" instructions on the Internet,[9] the knowledge of conventional explosive weapons—whether deployed by armies, nonstate small groups, or individual criminals—has been the source of far more trauma, murder, and mayhem. Instructions on how to build a bomb using a pressure cooker or a U-Haul truck as the containment vessel have been far more dangerous than conceptual diagrams of hydrogen bombs. By the mid-twentieth century, small groups and individuals could no longer aspire to the power of national armies with their vast research and development apparatuses and were much more likely to use time-tested, conventional explosive devices like the car bomb.[10] True innovation has been rare.[11] Risking self-destruction, delusional bombmakers frequently fail to create a successful explosion on the scale they imagine.

Morland's "H-Bomb Secret" defied the de jure protection of nuclear secrets; the de facto protections remained intact. Unlike prior forms of dangerous instructional speech, the essay avoided presenting information in the form of process and assembly, as in an instruction manual. Its aim was to expose the hidden apparatus of nuclear weapons manufacture, rather than arm the antinuclear movement with hydrogen bombs. "The H-Bomb Secret" was not a hydrogen bomb cookbook in the style of *Science of Revolutionary Warfare* or *The Anarchist Cookbook*, though it was, and continues to be, labeled as such. Morland and the *Progressive* staff vociferously denied that its intention was instructional, but its prepublication title, used by Judge Robert Warren who issued the injunction, was "How a Hydrogen Bomb Works," suggesting instructional content.[12] Its language and diagrams skirted a line with the federal government which saw the article as revealing how to make a weapon of mass destruction. Siding with the Department of Energy and the Department of Justice, Warren famously said that he did not want the secret to fall into the hands of the brutal Ugandan dictator Idi Amin, and called Morland's article "the recipe for a do-it-yourself hydrogen bomb."[13] Later, he acknowledged that Morland's article was "probably" not "a 'do-it-yourself' guide" for a hydrogen bomb to be built in a basement, but it "could possibly provide sufficient information to allow a medium-sized nation to move faster in developing a hydrogen weapon. It could provide a ticket to bypass blind alleys."[14]

Without much information, since discussions of the case were instantly classified, the news media repeated the provocative idea that the article explained how to build a hydrogen bomb in the basement or garage.[15] Blaming the government for the "bizarre misconception" that the magazine was allowing "*everyone* to construct a nuclear device," Erwin Knoll complained that he often met people who recognized him as the editor of the magazine that showed readers how to "build their own atomic bomb." Knoll would answer, "The *Progressive* isn't a hobbyists' magazine. We don't teach people how to build things. You must be thinking of *Popular Mechanics*."[16] The technical information was in the service of *dis*armament, not armament.

Scientists and Hobbyists against Secrecy

The context for the *Progressive* case was a social movement of both scientists and citizens to provide public information about nuclear weapons to enhance democratic decisions about them. Like the chemists of a prior generation who exercised a paternalistic control over dynamite, nuclear scientists were positioned between the containment culture of the atomic security state and the public. Nuclear scientists saw themselves as the right hands for the most destructive weapons ever invented, but not all of them supported the intense secrecy surrounding them. The nuclear security state saw all private citizens—scientists and nonscientists—as the wrong hands.

The idea of the Bomb falling into the wrong hands had been a worst-case scenario since the end of World War II. On August 6, 1945, President Harry Truman pointed to "Providence" as having delivered the bomb—the very power of the sun and the universe—to the United States and offered his gratitude that the Germans "did not get the atomic bomb at all."[17] Later, as the Cold War geared up, he declared, "In the hands of a nation bent on aggression, the atomic bomb could spell the end of civilization on this planet." He named these wrong hands as an "irresponsible government" or a "power-mad dictator," and thus the hands were attached to other nation-states because they had the substantial resources, including manufacturing facilities and technical networks, to build nuclear weapons.[18]

Beginning with the Manhattan Project, as is well known, a massive security apparatus and classification system was built up around nuclear weapons in an attempt to contain them and the thousands of scientists, engineers, technicians, and staff members who worked on them. Peter Galison has called this the "first act" of the security state, enshrined in two iterations of the Atomic Energy Act.[19] Everyone knew that dangerous technical secrets existed: so dangerous that even to "think about the unthinkable" might make Armageddon real. Most people outside the nuclear complex, even those who strongly opposed nuclear weapons, accepted an imperative that the principles and designs of such weapons had to be kept secret, even though the design of the atomic bomb had been publicized in the official Smyth Report days after the bombings in Japan.[20] The secrecy imperative was based on blind faith that secrets existed and could be kept within government offices, research laboratories, and manufacturing facilities that made up an extensive technological system over which the government presided.[21] Even openly thinking about a nuclear weapon, much less building one, outside these constraints was strictly forbidden. The classification system developed at this time, supported by corporate secrecy regarding intellectual property. All information about weapons design was bound by secrecy and seen as a potential form of instruction. With the growth of nuclear secrecy, in a narrowing of the right hands to a policymaking elite, all citizens outside the nuclear weapons complex were viewed as the wrong hands, while scientists, engineers, and technicians within the complex were viewed as potentially the wrong hands or conduits to the wrong hands, namely communist spies.

The Atomic Energy Act has been controversial among scientists since its inception for potentially precluding "the right of the people to information."[22] As the initial voices in a nascent antinuclear movement, some nuclear scientists spoke for civilian control over atomic power and urged public education in science. Using their prestige and authority, they weighed in on public policy, crossing into politics from the closed worlds of atomic research, with its tightly bound relationships to governmental institutions, funding, and goals. Early on Albert Einstein, as head of the Energy Committee of Atomic Scientists devoted to fundraising and community education, made public statements against atomic secrecy that would be often cited by critics of the nuclear arms buildup. While he did not advocate turning "the secret of the bomb loose on the world," he did suggest, "To the village square we must carry the facts of atomic energy."[23] Einstein promoted informing citizens about the new technology: "For there is no secret and there is no defense; there is no possibility of control except through the aroused understanding and insistence of the peoples of the world." Morland would often preface his discussions of the "H-Bomb secret" with this quotation.

As early as 1945, many scientists were resisting secrecy and questioning the entanglement of science with military projects.[24] Manhattan Project scientists, working in the Chicago Metallurgical Laboratory, founded the Federation of American Scientists to lobby for the prevention of nuclear war. To counter the government's assurances that the United States had a carefully guarded secret, inaccessible to the Soviet Union, the Federation took as its slogan "There is no secret."[25] The FAS founded the *Bulletin of the Atomic Scientists* to "educate the public to a full understanding of the scientific, technological and social problems arising from the release of nuclear energy."[26] Famous for its "doomsday clock," indicating the imminent possibility of nuclear war, the *Bulletin* delivered information on development in nuclear weaponry, proliferation, and policy. Known for providing scenarios for nuclear war and discussing its survivability, nuclear physicist Herman Kahn argued that citizens needed information to "rationally" assess the risks. Although much of Kahn's public commentary was devoted to explaining nuclear strategic planning, he wrote of the "constantly increasing problem of communication between the technologist and the layman, because of the specialization (one might almost say fragmentation) of knowledge." Kahn advised that some details about nuclear weapons had to remain "classified to some degree" but that technical details might be "of vital importance in resolving much broader social problems." Secrecy, he said, could be gotten around because "non-classified sources often give reasonable approximations of the data."[27] That some details had to be kept out of public minds and safely in the hands of scientists was mostly accepted, so that in 1946 when physicists and their students gave a controversial series of lectures on the hitherto unknown principles of the atomic bomb, they were speaking to other scientists. Nevertheless, they ran into censorship when they attempted to publish these open secrets in book form.[28]

With the growth of an antinuclear movement that questioned nuclear weapons development, testing, and stockpiling, the health questions from radiation effects were an important dimension of dissent. Citizens versed themselves in medicine and biology with the help of epidemiologists, physicians, and biologists like Ralph Lapp, E. B. Lewis, Linus Pauling, Helen Caldicott, and Barry Commoner. A proponent of educating citizens to engage in rational decision-making, Commoner and the mostly female members of the St. Louis Committee for Nuclear Information carried out a project in 1959 wherein citizens collected baby teeth and had them tested for Strontium-90.[29] Children who contributed received a card that read, "I gave my tooth to science."[30] Radiation's biological effects required scientific knowledge and provided a persuasive emotional connection to the perils of nuclear development. In 1969, another organization, Science for the People, promoted "science shaped by a citizen-created world" and called for the abolition of chemical, biological, and nuclear weapons.[31] The benefits of educating the population in the science of nuclear weapons had a firm foundation before Morland undertook his odyssey of information foraging. As Morland would find, the technical details of nuclear bombs were not as publicly persuasive as information about health effects, but they were important to a small group of atomic hobbyists who undermined the government's argument forbidding the revelation of the ultimate secret.

The Atomic Bomb Hobby

With the growth of security state came heretics, dissenters, and hobbyists who rejected the foundational secrecy that would classify even private thinking about nuclear weapons, codified in the "born secret" clauses of the 1946 Atomic Energy Act, which prohibited persons from revealing any information about the manufacture of nuclear weapons without permission, even if they had independently conceived the idea. These amateur technophiles produced documents that defied containment of nuclear weapons information within the small, protected sphere of a state-sanctioned elite. Like the old radicals who refused the claims of the professional chemists and military developers to a paternal control over dynamite, they refused the claims of scientists and military personnel to sole intellectual control over nuclear weapons. Laboring outside the state-legitimated knowledge domains, which they both admired and resented, they were fascinated by the power of the ultimate weapon. Some spent months, years, and even lifetimes collating pieces of knowledge from a vast array of unclassified documents, a mosaic of information that might be pieced together to uncover tantalizing technical secrets, always with the suggestion of other secrets in a deep well. The amateurs would help the *Progressive* win its case by arguing their right to pursue, collate, circulate, and read technical information about nuclear weapons. Some were motivated by the desire to freely pursue their intellectual interests; others, like Morland, by a horror of the government sheltering its supremely destructive weapons program from public scrutiny and criticism. The government tolerated the hobbyists, who eventually made significant contributions to the technological history of nuclear weapons, but attempted to suppress the political dissenters who openly discussed information that was supposed to be safely housed within the nuclear complex.

When the news that a court had slammed a prior restraint order on the "H-Bomb Secret" appeared, two hobbyists came forward with the claim that like Morland, they had put together the H-bomb secret and knew how to make the bomb. Both were incensed by the government's intervention in the intellectual pursuits of amateur nuclear woolgathering. One was Charles Hansen, a computer programmer who had been collecting information about the bomb for almost a decade. He wrote an eight-page letter and sent it to his senator and a small number of newspapers, including the *Chicago Tribune*. Accusing Department of Energy consultants of having leaked important information about thermonuclear weapons, he wrote, "Whether or not the DOE has . . . authority to arbitrarily classify and interfere with the thoughts and communications of private citizens is one of the many issues at stake in the PROGRESSIVE case." Further, he accused the DOE of suppressing data "in order to maintain a false illusion of secrecy, and to maintain a real monopoly over the dissemination of weapons-related information, and over the public discussion of American nuclear policies."[32] He then pointed to two encyclopedia articles by highly respected physicists Edward Teller and Hans Bethe that he claimed revealed much of the H-bomb secret. Hansen detailed the construction of a hydrogen bomb with concepts and technical descriptions he had gleaned from publicly available sources. As editors debated whether they should publish the damning letter, the *Madison Press Connection* stepped forward and printed it. Over time, Hansen would compile a huge resource on nuclear weapons published in *The Swords of Armageddon* and *U. S. Nuclear Weapons: The Secret History*, now used by historians as an authoritative account of US nuclear weapons programs.

The other hobbyist involved was Dimitri Rotow. An economics student at Harvard, Rotow had put together a number of nuclear weapons designs into a four-hundred-page document that he hoped to publish. Anticipating trouble, Rotow had alerted the DOE, which promptly confiscated and classified it. This made national news, and during the *Progressive* case, the ACLU employed Rotow to prove that Morland's H-bomb secret was already in the public domain. One "bright and early morning," as he would later tell a congressional hearing, he and his assistant strolled into the National Security and Resources Study Center at Los Alamos and ordered a report, "UCRL-4725: Weapons Development During June 1956." It contained (although the government later claimed that it was inadvertent) the H-bomb secret. Rotow made six copies that he mailed out to "very responsible people," alarming Senator John Glenn, who asked that he turn over the names right away.[33] The document proliferated, as the receivers of the copies further circulated and reproduced them. Nuclear activist Helen Caldicott, who was asked to review the article, carried a copy on a trip to Australia. The *Melbourne Sunday Observer* was planning to publish it when the US government stepped in to squelch any further dissemination. As Lawrence Lessig has observed, "When the cat is already out of the bag, preventing further publication does not return the cat to the bag."[34] Rotow had made copies of the document, Hansen had sent copies of his letter, and already reproduction was ensuring that technical secrets would be difficult to keep.

The government case against the *Progressive* collapsed when it was forced to admit that the H-bomb secret was already in the public domain. After the longest prior restraint order in US history, the "H-Bomb Secret" was published with neatly crafted diagrams showing the bomb's inner workings. A few months later, Hans Bethe, who had revealed part of the secret, suggested vaguely that building such a weapon "requires breadth of knowledge to understand just what these are and how to do them, and great care in doing them. Failing to do these things could result in a dud or in an accident fatal to some of the people concerned. For these reasons, I think it is totally unlikely that a terrorist group could make a bomb."[35] A staff member of Lawrence Livermore Laboratory, Hugh Dewitt, wrote, "Nowhere are there engineering details, equations, results of calculations or other serious technical information that a bomb design group would need for building a hydrogen bomb."[36] Thirty years later, it appears that these predictions were entirely correct.

Among the contenders in the *Progressive* case, an opposition was drawn between information and instruction. In this context, information is a discourse that engages its audience in deriving meaning, value, and judgment, while instruction is a discourse that gives its students skills to participate in material technical processes. The kinds of instructional speech that I've been discussing often carry the disclaimer that the author is merely providing information, as if information were not to be used for real-world making. This often seems a dissembling, its own cloaking in secrecy. In the *Progressive* case, a technical essay was providing information to inform the public, but was thoroughly confused with instruction. At the heart of this struggle is a gray area between potential uses of texts. To sequester scientific and technical information behind a cloak of secrecy has potentially dire consequences for democratic decision-making and for the evolution of human knowledge, as many observed during the *Progressive* case.[37] The "born secret" clause, which immediately classifies any thoughts expressed about the design of nuclear weapons, even by private citizens, is especially egregious.[38] At the same time, the instructional dimension carries a very real, if small, risk of mass violence. In 1979, it was possible for the federal government to weigh that risk and step down. But since the 9/11 attacks, the federal government has sequestered works in the public domain and placed controls on the publication and international exchange of scientific information. Fear of terrorism outweighs the sane weighing of the balance.

The Post-9/11 How to Make a Bomb

The post-9/11 political environment has tightened citizens' ability to obtain information about weapons production, even of very old, decaying weapons, in government facilities. Anthropologist Joseph Masco has discussed his attempt to obtain a photograph of a B-61 thermonuclear weapon that went into production in 1965. He had seen this photograph at a DOE hearing in Los Alamos, where it had been used to demonstrate the aging of weapons in the US arsenal. The photograph was in the public domain: it had been reproduced in a 1994 DOE publication called *Closing the Circle on the Splitting of the Atom*, which the agency billed as an effort to raise public awareness and to "hasten progress" in resolution of "existing environmental, safety, and health problems throughout the nuclear weapons complex."[39] The chapter entitled "Building Nuclear Weapons: The Process" features a human interest story on a historian at the now decommissioned Rocky Flats nuclear production facility near Denver, Colorado. Under the "new openness policies" of the early 1990s, the historian enjoyed educating visitors about the site, where warhead triggers had once been produced. He bemoaned the loss of workers and "the knowledge they've taken with them."[40] The photograph of the B-61 showed an intact bomb and an array of its component parts to illustrate the complexity of its former construction across many production facilities.[41] The reproduction of the image in a public government document put it within the domain of fair use. Masco was interested in reproducing the photograph for his research on the history of nuclear weapons production and policy, but the DOE refused his request, stating: "In regards to the B-61 picture, after September 11, 2001, a review was conducted of our visual library. As a result some images are not being released due to security concerns."[42] Masco concludes that the government's new "sensitive but unclassified" status regarding some conceivably dangerous texts and images is a shift in the "national security culture from a countercommunist to a counterterrorist state formation," centered in the nuclear bomb as a "cultural-political form."[43]

Although it may seem that the government has a compelling interest in withholding information about nuclear weapons—as confused as its self-censorship may be—the "sensitive but unclassified" status is in regards not so much to the sacred object as to the hands that might get any explosive weapons at all, no matter how primitive. I have had my own encounter with the post-9/11 "sensitive but unclassified" policy. In 2009, in the course of research for this book, I approached the National Archives and Records Administration (NARA) with a request for some radical pamphlets, including bomb-making pamphlets, entered into evidence long ago in a congressional hearing on riots and civil disorders. I already had a rough idea of the contents: they could have contained nothing more than directions for Molotov cocktails and primitive pipe bombs that could be found in countless other places. I never expected to encounter a problem with access, because I assumed that I could view the entire contents of a widely known congressional hearing. I was told, however, that NARA wouldn't provide them because of a Department of Justice directive that advised it not to give access "to materials that might support terrorist activity."[44] This seemed quite bizarre to me, since I couldn't imagine any conceivable situation in which an old pamphlet on Molotov cocktails would provide fuel for terrorism. The emphasis is not so much on the information object—like a nuclear bomb or a Molotov cocktail—as on the terroristic reader, now defined as anyone outside of the government's security orbit. Anyone at all might be a latent terrorist, even peaceful historians gleaning through old documents. Anyone at all might be contaminated with technical knowledge, even in its most basic form, and suspected of planning to launch an attack upon the government, its institutions, and its public displays. Before the twenty-first century, the government's domestic enemies were localized, well defined, and easily infiltrated and goaded into some kind of damning action. Now everyone who seeks knowledge is a terrorist in this corrosive view of the citizen.

The intensity of that view varies with the citizen-subject. Some suspects suffer much more severe consequences for viewing information about nuclear weapons, and the *Progressive* case had a dire fallout for Binyam Mohamed, a Guantánamo detainee from 2004 to 2009, when he was released by President Barack Obama. An Ethiopian citizen and temporary UK resident, Mohamed was trained in an al-Qaeda camp, suspected of involvement in a "dirty bomb" plot against the United States concocted with José Padilla, and arrested in Pakistan. Because the United States has classified most of the documents in the case—some observers believe to hide details of the extraordinary rendition and torture of suspects during the Bush administration—the facts are murky. Mohamed claimed that he was taken to CIA prisons in Pakistan, Morocco, and Afghanistan where he was brutally tortured. A summary of a small number of documents released by a UK court, in a civil suit filed to prove the collusion of MI5 and MI6 in the CIA interrogations, confirmed that Mohamed's treatment "could readily be contended to be at the very least cruel, inhuman and degrading treatment . . . by the United States authorities."[45] Mohamed was released from Guantánamo by

President Obama's order, all charges against him were dropped, and the British government offered him a substantial financial sum to drop his claim in the civil suit.

During his interrogation by US intelligence agents, Mohamed revealed that he had visited a website on how to build a hydrogen bomb. Later, a detainee threat assessment at Guantánamo carried the absurd claim that Mohamed had "learned of plans to use an 'H-bomb' from materials located on a computer at the house. Subject GZ-10016 [Abu Zubaydah] was intent on going forward with this attack."[46] (Much of the evidence against Mohamed had been gathered from Zubaydah, who had been waterboarded during his interrogation.) Mention of H-bomb plans provoked Mohamed's interrogators, he said, to more brutal treatment—sleep deprivation, death threats, and hanging by the wrists—to extract a confession that he was involved in an al-Qaeda plot to build an "A-bomb."

The text that Mohamed viewed, as he tried to tell his torturers, was a joke. According to news reports in Britain and Mohamed's lawyer, this text had been published over twenty years before in the alternative magazine *Seven Days*. Written by investigative journalist Barbara Ehrenreich, cultural critic Peter Biskind, and theoretical physicist Michio Kaku, "How to Make Your Own H-Bomb" was a comic response to government actions and media coverage in the *Progressive* case. It posed the question, "Was it really true that atomic and hydrogen bomb technology was so simple you could build an H-bomb in your own kitchen?" It then explained where to steal plutonium and find atomic bomb plans (the files of the Nuclear Regulatory Commission), how to enrich uranium, and how to hammer it into a sphere and create a chain reaction. In a gesture toward familiar anarchist cookbookery, they wrote that building a hydrogen bomb could be done in a kitchen with implements like bicycle pumps, ropes, buckets, vacuum cleaners, coffee cans, plastic milk containers, and stainless steel bowls. Once the H-bomb was in hand, a family could use it as a deterrent in neighborhood disputes and to ward off unwanted visitors: "A discrete sticker on the door or on the living room saying 'This Home Protected by H-bomb' will discourage IRS investigators, census takers and Jehovah's witnesses." This was all, of course, an obvious joke. It was republished in the *Washington Post*, where it advised that it had not been cleared by the Department of Energy. An admirer responded with a letter to the editor that concluded, "I am obsessed with owning my own bomb to balance the terror created by my neighbor, who already has one and who works for the Department of Defense."[47] With its technical content, amusing satire, and whiff of pyrotechnic anarchy, "How to Make Your Own H-Bomb" was appealing to early Internet denizens and typed into the old BBSs. It found a lasting place on the Web and was circulated all over the world, where some ignorant readers may have taken it seriously.[48] When Ehrenreich discovered the essay's role in the torture of Mohamed, she responded that, under the Bush administration, "post-9/11 America was an irony-free zone" and that "we had a government so vicious and impenetrably stupid that it managed to take my freedom of speech and turn it into someone else's living hell."[49] The CIA interrogators' willingness to believe that "How to Build Your Own H-Bomb," or even any threat that a few nonscientists could construct one from online information, demonstrates the potential damage to credibility and dangerous absurdity of using little-understood texts as evidence.

Many discussions of nuclear terror will point to the availability of directions online for making atomic bombs, hydrogen bombs, dirty bombs, and suitcase bombs. Although terror experts dismiss information as unimportant compared to the proliferation of fissile material and defecting technicians, they implicitly condemn that the information exists online, without exploring why it is online or what the potential purposes of that information might be. For example, in 1999, as legislation loomed to suppress weapons information on the Internet, the respected historian of terrorism Walter Laqueur wrote that popular magazines and online sources were providing information that led "the reader step by step through the process of becoming an atom bomb designer" and that "all these steps, though intricate, do not in theory present insurmountable difficulties for determined amateurs with a little knowledge of nuclear physics and access to the literature available in many public libraries."[50] Terror experts have claimed that a small nuclear weapon is the "Holy Grail for a terrorist organization such as al-Qaeda" and that "new technologies like the Internet now make the dissemination of information and knowledge [about them] infinitely easier."[51] In an earlier time, advocates of citizen science argued that citizens had a right and a responsibility to gather information and knowledge for democratic decision making. The recent alarmist claims represent a dramatic shift from an earlier discourse on the extreme difficulties of fully understanding and assembling nuclear weapons by those who have actually made them.

The *Progressive* case posed an important question as to whether citizens should have access to detailed information on the government's weapons of mass destruction, built to protect citizens at their expense. The fragile pact of secrecy demanded unquestioning trust, passive acceptance, and a tacit agreement not to independently pursue certain forms of knowledge for whatever reason. Since the nineteenth century, dissenters have refused to trust and accept the state's monopoly of force, realized, in part, in its control over weapons information and instruction. They have actively pursued knowledge, provoking governments to expose vulnerabilities, admit dangers, deflate claims, restore history, free technical information for public use, and often retaliate to reestablish control. Informative, rebellious, parodic, and flirting with grave dangers, the popular weapons manual has played a key role in this struggle.

Conclusion

Since the late nineteenth century's Second Industrial Revolution, a stream of court cases and congressional hearings have featured popular weapons manuals as a threat to the US government's idealized monopoly on violence, concretely realized in its control over a complex array of military technologies. The production of these manuals is a form of dissent that defies that control and upholds the sovereignty of the individual in the elevation of illicit military crafts made by ordinary hands. The compilers of popular weapons manuals determinedly provoke a powerful government—with vast technological resources for pulverizing enemies—to examine its leakages of information, its questionable covert wars, and its failures at perfect containment and public security. Despite their rare application, limited efficacy, and dated information, popular weapons manuals challenge the government's protective role and therefore its legitimacy. The discourse alone is enough to spur crackdowns and media panics over the latest public enemies with subversive knowledge and seemingly unprecedented access to dangerous information. In a nation where the right to own high-powered assault rifles is ardently defended, a mass shooter's ownership of *The Anarchist Cookbook* is treated as the most suspicious feature: the influence that leads to eruptions of murder and mayhem.

Those who produce popular weapons manuals are well aware of their unsettling effect. They know that even without a stated political intention, the circulation of dangerous information is, in itself, the provocation. They are usually not inventors or even users, but rather compilers and adapters who frame their literary work as unveiling esoteric information and delivering its power to the people. Technical information, they attempt to show, can't be effectively centralized, authorized, and contained, especially in the long run. On one hand, these texts are directed at readers who will revel in the fantasy of defying massive governmental power by learning its secrets, seeing through its elaborate shams, and demonstrating that handicrafts and popular mechanics can stand against it—fantasy because these works overstate their ability to deliver, and their directions are rough, amateurish, inexact, and extremely risky. Small groups have often fallen prey to the delusion that mastery of available technical information can give them an impossible power to rival armies or at least inspire general revolt. Popular weapons manuals foster the delusion that private citizens can concoct military technologies in their kitchens and backyard shed. On the other hand, these texts are directed at officials who have the means to crush dissenters if they should choose. Taking advantage of the democratic commitment to speech rights, producers of popular weapons manuals test the limits of the state's tolerance of speech that threatens its legitimacy. When the government tries, in various ways, to suppress popular weapons manuals, it reveals its vulnerability to demonization and overreaction. That is a desired response. The popular weapons manual can also serve as a form of blackmail, a threat that a group has the means to carry out an action if it doesn't get a desired response. What has evolved, then, is a contest over information in which the unequal contestants—one a slanted mirror of the other—play out a familiar set of moves, unable to leave a dangerous game.

The federal government, through congressional hearings and prosecutions of public enemies, has tried various strategies to suppress popular weapons manuals. The most severe form of control is direct censorship, which would impose similar penalties to the circulation of child pornography. The comparison to pornography aligns the control of popular weapons manuals with both public safety and moral concern and distaste. These censorship arguments have invoked endangered and endangering youths who are perceived as needing protection from dangerous, contaminating knowledge. Despite the surges of concern over popular weapons manuals, no substantial case has been made that censorship is justifiable or effective. One problem is that the technical information has circulated freely and has only caused concern when it is associated with public enemies and antigovernment rhetoric. Thus, the censoring impulse is not really directed at the dissemination of technical information but rather at radical political speech, protection of which has been long defended as the foundation of free speech. It might be argued that popular weapons manuals threaten the very existence of government by creating an alternative (albeit ramshackle) military power, and therefore must be eradicated in self-defense. But it is hard to imagine that directions for crickets and pipe bombs, or even cruise missiles, primitive anthrax, and hydrogen bombs, seriously threaten a nuclear state with weapons so highly manufactured that they can't possibly be made in a backyard. Because of its constitutional heritage, the United States has also fostered heavily armed militia groups, which view weapons training and instruction as forms of expressive political conduct. The allowance of massive private arsenals makes efforts to censor weapons manuals seem rather paltry.

Occasional federal legislative efforts to censor popular weapons manuals, most recently on the Internet, have failed against constitutional speech protections. However, that is no sign of tolerance. Popular weapons manuals aren't ignored. Rather, they are highly useful as evidence against public enemies, representing their seriousness of purpose and the technical means to carry it out. Since the late nineteenth century, the police have raided the libraries of enemies of the state and prosecutors have introduced bomb-making, sabotage, and tactical manuals against them, often by title alone, to dramatize their danger and malevolence. The courts have displayed an inconsistent treatment of this reading evidence, sometimes allowing it to prove a suspect's practical knowledge and conspiratorial design and sometimes forbidding it as irrelevant and prejudicial. The challenge has escalated with the vast circulation and storage capacities of digital technologies, so that police investigators and government consultants can confiscate and comb through hundreds of downloaded documents for the most damning associations. If this highly culled evidence is released, the news media contribute to the sensationalizing of isolated texts as evidence of alleged conspiracies by shadowy organizations to destroy social order.

The legal system has been unable to come to grips with the new digital terrain, and has been forced to rely on dubious experts to interpret these texts in a climate of fear. Given the ease of downloading texts and the hyperlinked navigations of the Internet, people's digital downloads are much less a coherent representation of identity, interest, and influence than a collection of print books. If the influence of reading was already difficult to prove, the scattered attention to and experimental consumption of digital texts are an even shakier foundation of evidence, given to highly questionable assumptions about the way readers read and derive meaning, ideas, pleasure, excitement, and usefulness from words. Government officials, agents, and consultants have demonstrated that they are bad readers, given to inattention, false representation, and limited ideological interpretation.

Although judges and politicians have, at various times, condemned popular weapons manuals, these texts have been quite useful in show trials and public hearings to characterize public enemies as more technically proficient and dangerous than they are. Through these spectacles, the government reasserts its necessity as public protector and sole proprietor of the dangerous information that it has disseminated through training, research, and development; private security and covert operations; and unclassified publication. There is a lasting tension between suppression and tolerance, both serving the purpose of naming enemies and purging dissent. Tolerance allows potential evidence to flourish in the form of weapons- and drug-making manuals produced and owned by those who believe that access to information is a right. That bookshelves and computer hard drives are now raided in investigations of political enemies shows how routine it is that reading materials can be used as evidence of design and intent.

Unquestionably, popular weapons manuals have been used by a small number of their readers to risk experimentation with homemade chemical concoctions and devices and, very rarely, to create effective lethal weapons deployed in crimes and terrorist attacks. Very few cases, however, have demonstrated any direct link between popular weapons instructions and the construction of a lethal device or design. The link is nearly always speculative as to how the work might have influenced or inspired the accused. Recently, the threat has escalated with the rise of digital media that allow, most importantly, the integration of photographs and videos. Visual instructions are more easily mimicked without the errors of textual misinterpretation. Because of limited access to expensive means of reproduction, the older manuals relied on textual explanation and crude drawings so that the novice would have difficulty carrying out the instructions. The new multimedia instructions are not only easier to follow but add a psychological identification with a set of hands working in simple steps. Videos add aural and visual excitement to the explosive spectacle. Multimedia instructions have raised the stakes in their easiness and appeal, and popular weapons manuals are now written with greater scientific exactness. However, advanced, highly technical weapons are still out of the hands of amateurs without access to considerable expertise, well-equipped laboratories, and manufacturing units. The horror that making an advanced weapon for mass slaughter might easily fall within the capabilities of nefarious hands haunts all public discussions of these manuals, but so far their information has not greatly evolved beyond formulas and designs available since the nineteenth century.

When Dzhokhar and Tamerlan Tsarnaev placed two pressure cooker bombs near the finish line of the Boston Marathon, killing three people and injuring hundreds of others, Internet forum contributors and journalists quickly made a link between images of the bomb remnants and the directions for a pressure cooker bomb in al-Qaeda's English-language online *Inspire* magazine. These easy step-by-step directions were conveyed through digital images. Since the pressure cooker bomb (a version of a pipe bomb using gunpowder) was not well known in the United States, the link between the Tsarnaevs' devices and the *Inspire* instructions seemed clear. The government indictment against the surviving brother, Dzhokhar, listed the *Inspire* article, downloaded onto Dzhokhar's computer, as key evidence against him. The courts have agreed that provable links between a weapon and the instructions used to make it—such as the link between a pressure cooker bomb and the *Inspire* instructional photos—allow those instructions to be used as evidence of technical know-how, despite historic protections of the right to read. But other works were listed in the indictment of Dzhokhar Tsarnaev: "The Slicing Sword, Against the One Who Forms Allegiances With the Disbelievers and Takes Them as Supporters Instead of Allah, His Messenger and The Believers," linked to Anwar al-Awlaki; "Defense of the

Muslim Lands, the First Obligation after Imam," by Abdullah Azzam; and "Jihad and the Effects of Intention upon It," published on the at-Tibyan web forum. Aligned with other much less significant terror cases that effectively used similar evidence, the Tsarnaev trial contributed to a much larger forum on an al-Qaeda contagion while punishing a heinous murderous attack.

To obtain the death penalty, the prosecution had an interest in proving the Tsarnaevs' link to al-Qaeda, even if only through what they'd read. But the incorporation of reading materials as evidence is troubling and reminiscent of historic cases, from the Haymarket trial on, in which nebulous associations cast a wide net over those who entertain dangerous ideas, implying that anyone who owns a selected constellation of texts is guilty of a terrorist design. Confiscated reading materials are tangential to physical evidence of, and eyewitness testimony to, the actual perpetration of a crime. They are incorporated to create an ideological forum in which the state can purge dangerous ideas and assert authority over who may entertain them. An extreme outcome to this evidentiary use of reading is the UK's Terrorism Act 2000, which criminalizes mere ownership of bomb-making guides and is selectively applied in arrests of suspected political radicals. The goal is a preemptive intervention in the suspected planning of terrorist attacks, but a great risk is that government, in a permanent emergency state, overreaches into the free exchange of ideas.

With their threat to arm a revolution, popular weapons manuals test the limits of political tolerance like no other form. It is a remarkable testament to US speech protections that a publisher like Paladin Press was allowed to profit for decades from really dangerous military manuals and only flinched when threatened with a civil suit. Those who publish or host this kind of information are most likely to back down because of liability, as in the *Hitman* case, rather than censorship efforts that raise the ire of civil libertarians and generate more interest in these texts. But the most effective force against circulation of popular weapons manuals has been time. Only a few historians know of *The Science of Revolutionary Warfare* that once provoked the hangman, even though the information about making DIY explosives and explosive devices was not so different than can be found in the manuals of our day. Changing social contexts, rather than direct efforts to suppress, have made *The Science of Revolutionary Warfare* irrelevant.

As a vast reservoir of multimedia texts across time and space, the Internet has now eased the difficulties of seeking out, using, and repackaging dangerous technical information, dashing any shaky illusion that it can be prevented from falling into the latest wrong hands. If libraries already contained everything one needed to know to blow up a building, the Internet has made it instantly available. Reading technical instructions, however, is no substitute for real hands-on experimentation and training at the core of technical expertise. Holding an easily obtained, semiautomatic weapon, with its instantaneous gratifications, is infinitely more dangerous than perusing crude, incomplete drawings of time bombs in *The Anarchist Cookbook*. The history of popular weapons manuals reveals that their danger may lie less in their informational content than in their provocation of the emergency state in its pursuit of public enemies and its vulnerable hold on its own means of violence. That the US government and its police forces have shown such lasting interest in these manuals testifies to their inevitable failures to achieve perfect security. Nevertheless, we citizens are still left with the problem of popular weapons instruction, now customary in the folkways of American violence.

NOTES

Introduction

1. The AQ Chef, "Make a Bomb in the Kitchen of Your Mom," *Inspire*, Summer 1431/2010, 31–40. Cryptome.
2. Peter Hoekstra, "Al Qaeda Goes Viral," *Wall Street Journal*, July 15, 2010. Proquest.
3. Mark Mazzetti, Charlie Savage, and Scott Shane, "How a U. S. Citizen Came to Be in America's Cross Hairs," *New York Times*, March 9, 2013; Charlie Savage, "Relatives Sue Officials over U. S. Citizens Killed in Drone Strikes in Yemen," *New York Times*, July 18, 2012.
4. *United States v. Dzhokhar A. Tsarnaev*, Indictment, Case 1:13-cr-10200-GAO, Doc. 57 (D. C. Mass., June 27, 2013), at US Department of Justice, http://www.justice.gov/usao/ma/news/marathon/.
5. US Department of Justice, "1997 Report on the Availability of Bombmaking Information," April 1997, available at http://www.justice.gov/criminal/cybercrime/bombmakinginfo.html.
6. Gabriel Wiemann, *Terror on the Internet: The New Arena, the New Challenges* (Washington, DC: United States Institute of Peace, 2006), 125–127.
7. Anne Stenersen, "The Internet: A Virtual Training Camp?" *Terrorism and Political Violence* 20(2008): 215–233; Michael Kenney, "Beyond the Internet: *Mētis, Techne*, and the Limits of Online Artifacts for Islamist Terrorists," *Terrorism and Political Violence* 22 (2010): 177–197.
8. Gil Ariely, "Knowledge Management, Terrorism, and Cyber Terrorism," in *Cyber Warfare and Cyber Terrorism*, ed. Lech Janczewski and Andrew M. Colarik (Hershey, PA: International Science Reference, 2008), 7–15.
9. UK law makes this possible under section 58 of the Terrorism Act. See Clive Walker, *Terrorism and the Law* (Oxford: Oxford University Press, 2011), 223.
10. "'Lyrical Terrorist' Found Guilty," *BBC News*, November 8, 2007, accessed March 13, 2008, http://news.bbc.co.uk/1/hi/uk/7084801.stm.
11. Sean O'Neill, "Teenager Had Bomb-Making Manual," *Times Online*, September 27, 2007, accessed March 5, 2008, www.timesonline.co.uk.
12. Lucia Zedner has discussed the rise of a "pre-crime logic of security" in criminal justice domains in "Pre-crime and Post-criminology," *Theoretical Criminology* 11 (2007): 261–262.
13. Ian Cram, *Terror and the War on Dissent: Freedom of Expression in the Age of Al Qaeda* (Berlin: Springer Verlag, 2009), 68.
14. Cass R. Sunstein, "Constitutional Caution," *Chicago Legal Forum* (1996): 372.
15. Clive Walker, *Terrorism and the Law* (Oxford: Oxford University Press, 2011), 18; Laura K. Donohue, *The Cost of Counterterrorism: Power, Politics, and Liberty* (Cambridge: Cambridge University Press, 2008), 306.
16. Donohue, *Cost of Counterterrorism*, 2.
17. A description of this short book, mostly known for its early reference to gunpowder, can be found in Lynn Thorndike, *History of Magic and Experimental Science*, vol. 4 (New York: Macmillan, 1923), 785–788 and in James Riddick Partington, *A History of Greek Fire and Gunpowder* (1960; Baltimore: Johns Hopkins University Press, 1999), 42–60.
18. Kenney, "Beyond the Internet," 178.

19. Historians and literary scholars have speculated that Morton's arrest on charges of selling arms was an excuse to punish him for his assault on Puritan proprietary, as represented in the phallic maypole ritual. The Puritans really feared the disintegration of their moral integrity and authority. See Richard Drinnon, *Facing West: The Metaphysics of Indian-Hating and Empire Building*, 3rd ed. (1980; Norman: University of Oklahoma Press, 1997), 9–13; Michael Zuckerman, *Almost Chosen People: Oblique Biographies in the American Grain* (Berkeley: University of California Press, 1993), 77–96. Others, most notably Alden T. Vaughan, maintain that the colonists were practicing self-defense. Small outlying communities of planters rightly feared a gun trade centered in community of "lawless, irresponsible, runaway" indentured servants. See his *New England Frontier: Puritans and Indians, 1620–1675*, 3rd ed. (1965; Norman: University of Oklahoma Press, 1995), 88–91.
20. William Bradford, *Bradford's History of Plymouth Plantation* (Boston: Wright & Potter, 1899), 287–288.
21. Slavoj Žižek, "Afterword: Lenin's Choice," in *Revolution at the Gates: A Selection of Writings from February to October 1917*, by Vladimir Ill'ich Lenin (New York: Verso, 2002), 300.
22. Hoffman mentioned Paladin Press and other paramilitary publishers as good sources for a "people's chemistry," though he did warn that they were of a "neofascist mentality." In *Steal This Book* (New York: Pirate Editions, 1971), 300. See also Alan Weitz, "Steal This Story," *Village Voice*, June 17, 1971, available online at blogs.villagevoice.com (accessed April 1, 2012).
23. Hoffman, *Steal This Book*, vi.
24. Abbie Hoffman, Letter, *Seed* 7.5 (1971): 4; SAC, New York, to Director, FBI, Letter, September 3, 1971, file on Abbie Hoffman, Part 11, available in the FBI Vault.
25. Robert C. Mardian, Assistant Attorney General, to Director, FBI, Letter, September 29, 1971.
26. Laura K. Donohue, "Terrorist Speech and the Future of Free Expression," *Cordozo Law Review* 27(2005): 271. See also Eugene Volokh, "Crime Facilitating Speech," *Stanford Law Review* 57(2005): 1095–1222.
27. The role of continuous legitimizing of power in state responses to terrorism is amply discussed in the criminology and critical security literature, especially in Foucauldian analyses of governmentalities and their intimate interventions in individual lives. See, for example, Andrew W. Neal, *Exceptionalism and the Politics of Counter-terrorism: Liberty, Security, and the War on Terror* (New York: Routledge, 2010); Miguel de Larrinaga and Marc G. Doucet, "Sovereign Power and the Biopolitics of Human Security," *Security Dialogue* 39 (2008): 517–537.
28. Bruce Hoffman, "Responding to Terrorism across the Technological Spectrum," in *In Athena's Camp: Preparing for Conflict in the Information Age*, ed. John Arquilla and David Ronfeldt (Santa Monica, CA: Rand, 1997), 347–351.
29. Peter Broks, *Understanding Popular Science* (Berkshire: Open University Press, 2006), 5–49; Ruth Oldenziel, *Making Technology Masculine: Men, Women and Modern Machines in America, 1870–1945* (Amsterdam: Amsterdam University Press, 1999), 54–90.
30. William Gurstelle, *Adventures in the Technology Underground: Catapults, Pulsejets, Rail Guns, Flamethrowers, Tesla Coils, Air Cannons and the Garage Warriors Who Love Them* (New York: Three Rivers, 2006), 10, 213.
31. "Kärnkraft i köket fick en hel värld att häpna," *Helsinborgs Dagblad*, August 14, 2011, accessed September 1, 2011.
32. I'm not implying that all anarchists are violent, but the term has been so often used to suggest violent resistance, especially alongside a fascination with technology, that I am adopting it here with that meaning in mind.

Chapter 1

1. *The Young Man's Book of Amusements* (Halifax: William Milner, 1850); James Cutbush, *System of Pyrotechny* (Philadelphia: Clara F. Cutbush, 1825). Cutbush's lengthy volume was written primarily for cadets at West Point, where he was employed as a chemist, and contained directions for making and deploying bombs as well as notes on poisons like curare. Pyrotechnics for young people included the making of quite dangerous substances and the

use of explosives for practical jokes. Chemistry journals, encyclopedias, and other scientific texts in this period had an eclectic mix of formulas for explosives and other dangerous mixtures.

2. Johann Most, *Revolutionäre Kriegswissenschaft* (New York: International Zeitungs Verein, 1885). References are to the English translation, *The Science of Revolutionary Warfare*, introduced as People's Exhibit 15 in *Illinois v. August Spies, et al.*, Criminal Court of Cook County, Illinois, 1886. It is available through the Chicago Historical Society.
3. "The Anarchist Most," reprinted from the *Springfield Register* (IL), *Chicago Tribune*, January 4, 1883.
4. "Herr Most," *Chicago Tribune*, December 25, 1882.
5. *Illinois v. Spies*, Trial Transcript, entered in *Spies, et al. v. People of the State of Illinois*, No. 1588 1 P.D. Error to the Criminal Court of Cook County, vol. 1, 479–480 (1886), Haymarket Affair Digital Collection, Chicago Historical Society.
6. Holgate was notorious for his self-promotion and was a confidence man who wildly inflated his technical abilities. He was known to the US Secret Service for his involvement in a plot to scam the British government by shipping nonworking clockwork bombs disguised in apple barrels, alleging them to have been purchased by Irish radicals and collecting money as an informant. "Infernal Machines," *Chicago Tribune*, February 23, 1885.
7. August Spies, "Address of August Spies," in *The Famous Speeches of the Eight Chicago Anarchists in Court*, 4th ed., ed. Lucy Parsons (1910; Chicago: Lucy Parsons, n.d.), 12–13.
8. Spies, "Address of August Spies," 15.
9. The phrase originated with French chemist Fernand Papillon. See Frank J. Sprague, "Nitro-Glycerine," in *Historical Sketch of the United States Naval Academy*, ed. James Russell Solely (Washington, DC: GPO, 1876), 293; George M. Mowbray, *Tri-Nitro-Glycerin: As Applied in the Hoosac Tunnel* (New York: Van Nostrand, 1874); Manuel Eissler, *The Modern High Explosives* (New York: John Wiley, 1884), 37.
10. Albert Parsons, "Address of Albert Parsons," in Parsons, *Famous Speeches*, 75.
11. Timothy Messer-Kruse argues that the evidence was sound and the judicial proceedings fair for the time: *Trial of the Haymarket Anarchists: Terrorism and Justice in the Gilded Age* (New York: Palgrave, 2011). Messer-Kruse uses forensic evidence found in bomb fragments, the trial transcript, and daily newspapers to suggest that the Haymarket defendants were guilty and damned themselves by making the trial into a forum for anarchist views. See also Robert A. Ferguson, *The Trial in American Life* (Chicago: University of Chicago Press, 2007), 191–232. For overviews of the Haymarket affair, see Paul Avrich, *The Haymarket Tragedy* (Princeton, NJ: Princeton University Press, 1986); James Green, *Death in the Haymarket: A Story of Chicago, the First Labor Movement and the Bombing That Divided Gilded Age America* (New York: Anchor, 2006); Carl Smith, *Urban Disorder and the Shape of Belief: The Great Chicago Fire, the Haymarket Bomb and the Model Town of Pullman* (Chicago: University of Chicago Press, 1995), 101–174.
12. See, for example, Avrich, *Haymarket*, 409; Kruse.
13. "Most's Manual of War, an Interview with the Arch-Heretic Concerning Its True Authorship," *Alarm*, December 17, 1887.
14. John P. Altgeld, *Gov. John P. Altgeld's Pardon of the Anarchists and His Masterly Review of the Haymarket Riot*, ed. Lucy Parsons (Chicago: Lucy E. Parsons, 1915), 301. Open Library.
15. Altgeld, *Pardon*, 301.
16. David Rabban, *Free Speech in Its Forgotten Years* (New York: Cambridge University Press, 1997), 65, 148.
17. Rabban, *Free Speech*, 44–56, 67.
18. "Anarchy," *Cincinnati Inquirer*, May 3, 1886.
19. George Hung and Julius S. Grinnell, *Brief on the Facts for the Defendants in Error, Spies, et al. v. Illinois, Supreme Court of Illinois* (Chicago: Barnard & Gunthorp, 1887), 63.
20. Hung and Grinnell, *Brief on the Facts*, 64.
21. This article was widely printed. See, for example, "The Anarchists: Sketch of Some of Their Machinery Found at Chicago," *Atchison Daily Globe*, May 31, 1886; "Worthy of the Devil," *Milwaukee Daily Journal*, May 17, 1886.
22. The police were later shown to have concocted evidence, and the chain of evidence was severely compromised, so the bombs produced in court may not have come from Lingg.

Timothy Messer-Kruse et al., "The Haymarket Bomb: Reassessing the Evidence," *Labor: Studies in Working-Class History of the Americas* 2.2 (2005): 39–52; Bryan Palmer, "CSI Labor History: Haymarket and the Forensics of Forgetting," *Labor: Studies in Working-Class History of the Americas* 3.1 (2006): 25–36.

23. The rhetoric of a people's chemistry began in Europe and the United States, but traveled to many places in the next two decades, including India, Argentina, and Tokyo. No comprehensive study of international radicalism yet exists that fully explores the connections.
24. Floyd Dell, "Socialism and Anarchism in Chicago," in *Chicago: Its History and Its Builders*, vol. 2, ed. J. Seymour Currey (Chicago: Clarke, 1912), 391.
25. "England's Resources of Civilization," *Irish World*, August 16, 1882.
26. "The Hostiles," *Irish World*, May 28, 1881; "The Skirmishing Fund," *Irish World*, April 16, 1881.
27. "A Sacred Trust," *Irish World*, December 30, 1876.
28. K. R. M. Short's *The Dynamite War: Irish-American Bombers in Victorian Britain* (New York: Gill and Macmillan, 1979) gives the most complete picture of the O'Donovan Rossa and Clan na Gael campaigns, but uses mostly sources from British law enforcement. Michael Burleigh sees the "Fenians" as the first modern terrorist group in *Blood and Rage: A Cultural History of Terrorism* (New York: Harper, 2009), 1–26. Firsthand accounts can be found in John Devoy, *Recollections of an Irish Rebel* (Shannon: Irish University Press, 1929); Devoy, *Devoy's Post Bag, 1871–1928*, ed. William O'Brien and Desmond Ryan, 2 vols. (Dublin: Fallon, 1953); Henry Le Caron, *Twenty-Five Years in the Secret Service: The Recollections of a Spy* (Yorkshire, England: EP, 1974); Robert Anderson, *Sidelights on the Home Rule Movement* (London: Murray, 1906).
29. William Lowell to James G. Blaine, June 25, 1881, Despatches from U.S. Ministers to Great Britain, 1791–1906, Micro. 30, Roll 138, National Archives and Records Administration (NARA); Frederick Frelinghuysen to James Lowell, November 25, 1884, Diplomatic Instructions of the Dept. of State, Micro. 77, Roll 86, NARA.
30. S2578, introduced and referred, 48th Congress, 2nd Sess., January 24, 1885. For an overview of the context for the bill, see M. J. Sewell, "Rebels or Revolutionaries? Irish-American Nationalism and American Diplomacy, 1865–1855," *Historical Journal* 29 (1986): 723–733.
31. Michigan, Public Acts No. 126; Wisconsin, chap. 342; Rhode Island, chap. 524; Delaware, chap. 625; Connecticut, chap. 114; Ohio, House Bill No. 824; Massachusetts, chap. 203. Details can be found in the State Sessions Laws, 1885. The argument that states address the problem can be found in Francis Wharton, "Dynamiting and Extra-territorial Crime," *Criminal Law Magazine*, March 1885, 155–181.
32. "To the Workingmen of America" [Pittsburgh Manifesto], *Alarm*, November 1, 1884.
33. "Manifesto of the International Working People's Association," in *Socialism in America: A Documentary History*, ed. Albert Fried (1970; New York: Columbia University Press, 1992), 209.
34. "The Military," *Alarm*, February 7, 1885; A. S., "Dynamite: Instructions Regarding Its Use and Operations," *Alarm*, June 27, 1885.
35. T. Lizius, "Dynamite," *Alarm*, February 21, 1885. Avrich identifies T. Lizius as Gerhard Lizius, secretary of the Indianapolis IWPA (*The Haymarket Tragedy*, 169).
36. Parsons, "Address of Albert Parsons," 82.
37. Avrich, *The Haymarket Tragedy*, 174.
38. Smith, *Urban Disorder*, 117.
39. "The Socialist," *Alarm*, October 25, 1885.
40. Charles Loudon Bloxam, *Chemistry: Inorganic and Organic*, 5th ed. (Philadelphia: Blakiston, 1883), 579.
41. Bloxam, *Chemistry*, v–vi.
42. M. Eissler, *A Handbook on Modern Explosives: A Practical Treatise* (London: Crosby, Lockwood, and Son, 1897), 56.
43. *L'Indicateur Anarchiste* (London: Imprimerie Internationale Anarchiste, 1885), Arxiu Històric de la Ciutat, Barcelona; Ernest Alfred Vizetelly, *The Anarchists: Their Faith & Their Record* (Edinburgh: Turnbull and Spears, 1911), 196–197.

44. Spies, "Address of August Spies," 23; W. C. Hart, *Confessions of an Anarchist* (London: E. Grant, 1906), 43.
45. Uri Eisenzweig, *Ficciones del Anarquismo*, trans. Isabel Vericat Núñez (2001; Mexico City: FCE, 2004), 72–73.
46. Emma Goldman, *Living My Life* (New York: Knopf, 1931), 89.
47. George Woodcock, *Anarchism: A History of Libertarian Ideas and Movements* (1962; Ontario: Broadview, 2004), 396.
48. Walter Laqueur, *A History of Terrorism* (New York: Little, Brown, 1997), 59–60; Gérard Chaliand and Arnaud Blin, "The 'Golden Age' of Terrorism," in *The History of Terrorism from Antiquity to Al Qaeda*, ed. Chaliand and Blin, trans. Edward Schneider, Kathryn Pulver, and Jesse Browner (Berkeley: University of California Press, 2007), 182; Leonard Weinberg and William L. Eubank, eds. *What Is Terrorism?* (New York: Chelsea, 2006), 36; Michael Burleigh, *Blood and Rage: A Cultural History of Terrorism* (New York: HarperCollins, 2010), 74–75; Benjamin Grob-Fitzgibbon, "From the Dagger to the Bomb: Karl Heinzen and the Evolution of Political Terror," *Terrorism and Political Violence* 16.1 (2004): 110–111.
49. Gabriel J. Rains, "Torpedoes," *Southern Historical Society Papers* 3 (May–June 1877): 257; Rains, "Torpedoes," Unpublished Notebook 93, Manuscripts and Archives Section, Museum of the Confederacy, Richmond, VA.
50. Sven Lindqvist discusses the erosion of ethics in British naval warfare in *A History of Bombing*, trans. Linda Haverty Rugg (New York: New Press, 2000), 18–19, 20.
51. Most, *Science of Revolutionary Warfare*.
52. Frédéric Trautmann, *The Voice of Terror: A Biography of Johann Most* (Westport, CT: Greenwood, 1980), 118–119.
53. "Most Spits His Venom," *Alarm*, December 24, 1884.
54. Trautmann, *The Voice of Terror*, 124.
55. "Dangerous Explosives: How to Manufacture Pyroxyline or Gun-Cotton, and also the Fulminates of Mercury and of Silver," trans. A. A., *Alarm*, May 16, 1885.
56. "Found Bombs in Trunk, West Side Police Make a Strange Discovery While Searching for a Criminal," *Chicago Daily News*, March 23, 1886.
57. Michael J. Schaack, *Anarchy and Anarchists: A History of the Red Terror and the Social Revolution in America and Europe* (Chicago: Schulte, 1889), 378.
58. Altgeld, *Altgeld's Pardon*, 305; Green, *Death in the Haymarket*, 283. Ebersold's revelations were included in Governor John Altgeld's reasons for pardoning the Haymarket survivors, Fielden, Neebe, and Schwab.
59. Frank Donner, *Protectors of Privilege: Red Squads and Police Repression in Urban America* (Berkeley, CA: University of California Press, 1990), 20.
60. Schaack, *Anarchy and Anarchists*,178.
61. Schaack, *Anarchy and Anarchists*, 40.
62. Henry James, *The Princess Casamassima* (New York: Macmillan, 1921), 44.
63. Schaack, *Anarchy and Anarchists*, 27.
64. A urea and nitric acid explosive is easier to make today since crystallized urea is available, and the enterprise would not depend on collecting a massive amount of urine. Nevertheless, the basic chemistry was available by the end of the nineteenth century. *Engineering* 68 (1899): 377; Charles Alexander MacMunn, *Outlines of the Clinical Chemistry of Urine* (London: Churchill, 1889), 164.
65. A sampling of advertisements featuring the chemists can be found in *Oshkosh Daily Northwestern*, February 5, 1895, col. 1; *Bismarck Weekly Tribune*, July 25, 1884; *Daily Interocean*, January 5, 1889; *Life* 15.369 (1890): 57.
66. Most Irish bombers arrested for possessing explosives were not tried under the Explosive Substances Act but under the Treason Felony Act of 1848. This act imposed longer sentences but made it easier for the prisoners to obtain eventual pardons. Sean McConveille, *Irish Political Prisoners, 1848–1922: Theatres of War* (New York: Routledge, 2003), 361–404.
67. Cliff Todd, Linda Jones, and Maurice Marshall, "Explosions," in *Crime Scene to Court: The Essentials of Forensic Science*, 3rd ed., ed. Peter White (Cambridge: Royal Society of Chemistry, 2010), 293.

68. Bernard Porter, *The Origins of the Vigilant State: The London Metropolitan Police Special Branch before the First World War* (Woodbridge: Boydell, 1987), 52.
69. The sulfuric acid detonator was common in bombs of this period. In this case, it was held in a glass bottle with a lead weight that was meant to shatter the glass when the device was thrown. The acid would detonate an explosive mixture—probably potassium perchlorate and sugar—and then dynamite in a three-stage process. The Irish bombers of this period were inventive, adapting large-scale military technologies to covert weapons. The sulfuric acid detonator was a military invention, called the Hertz Horn, used in mines in the 1870s.
70. "Parallel Cases," *Grip*, May 24, 1884, n.p.; "Crimes and Criminals," *Strand* 7 (June–July 1894): 127; "Colonel Sir Vivian Majendia," *Pearson's* 1 (January–June 1896): 560; "The Tail of a Kite," *Otago Witness*, June 4, 1896; "Daly's Deadly Bombs," *Fort Wayne Daily Gazette*, May 4, 1884; "The Dynamite Conspiracy," *Edinburgh Courant*, May 12, 1884.
71. Vivan Dering Majendie, "Nitroglycerine and Dynamite," *Choice* 1 (1883): 413.
72. "A Chat with Henry Rochefort: His Views on Anarchism," *To-Day* 2 (1894): 109.
73. "Dynamite: What It Is and How It's Made," *Irish World*, April 21, 1883.
74. Gary Bryan Magee and Andrew Stuart Thompson discuss the values of mobile professionals in transnational English-speaking networks in *Empire and Globalisation: Networks of People, Goods and Capital in the British World, c. 1850–1914* (Cambridge: Cambridge University Press, 2010), 137.
75. Charles E. Munroe, "The Effect of Explosives on Civilization," *Chautauquan* 9 (October–July 1888–1889): 205.
76. The mutual inspiration of radical bombers and military developers is beyond the scope of this study, but the commonality in their devices suggests an informal technical exchange. Some radicals encountered explosives as military recruits, and military researchers encountered amateur bombs through the popular press and through consultation on criminal cases.
77. Eissler, *Handbook on Modern Explosives*, viii, 1–2.
78. Eissler, *Handbook on Modern Explosives*, iii.
79. Thomas M. Chatard, *The Abuse of Explosives with Suggestions for Preventative Laws*, Annual Address of the President, Chemical Society of Washington, January 30, 1893 (Washington, DC: Gibson, 1893), 18.
80. Testimony of Thomas M. Chatard and Charles E. Munroe, Committee on Mines and Mining, Hearings, *Regulation of the Use of Explosives*, US House of Representatives (Washington, DC: GPO, 1917), 27–33; Charles E. Munroe, *Regulation of Explosives in the United States*, Bureau of Mines, Bulletin 198 (Washington, DC: GPO, 1921).
81. William J. Novak, *The People's Welfare: Law and Regulation in Nineteenth-Century America* (Chapel Hill: University of North Carolina Press, 1996), 55, 65.
82. J. West Roosevelt, "Rather Too Much Energy," *Scribner's* 19 (January–June 1896): 611–621.
83. Robert Barr, "The Chemistry of Anarchy," *Chemist & Druggist* 44 (1894): 117–121.
84. W. Winder, "Dynamite," *Frank Leslie's Popular Monthly* 14 (1885): 759.

Chapter 2

1. Arthur Woods, introduction to *Throttled! The Detection of the German and Anarchist Bomb Plotters*, by Thomas Joseph Tunney (Boston: Small, Maynard, 1919), x.
2. Richard Bach Jensen, *The Battle against Anarchist Terrorism: An International History, 1878–1934* (New York: Cambridge University Press, 2014).
3. *Cronaca Sovversiva*, March 9, 1918, quoted in Robert E. Park, *The Immigrant Press and Its Control* (New York: Harper & Brothers, 1922), 327.
4. For accounts of the Galleanisti and their connection to several bombings, see Paul Avrich, *Sacco and Vanzetti: The Anarchist Background* (Princeton, NJ: Princeton University Press, 1991), 45–57; John F. Neville, *Twentieth-Century Cause Célèbre: Sacco, Vanzetti, and the Press, 1920–1927* (Westport, CT: Praeger, 2004), 1–26; Nunzio Pernicone, "War among the Italian Anarchists: The Galleanisti's Campaign against Carlo Tresca," in *The Lost World of Italian Radicalism; Politics, Labor and Culture*, ed. Philip V. Cannistraro and Gerald Meyer (Westport, CT: Praeger, 2003), 77–98; Beverly Gage, *The Day Wall Street Exploded: A Story*

of America in Its First Age of Terror (Oxford: Oxford University Press, 2010); Charles H. McCormick, *Hopeless Cases: The Hunt for the Red Scare Terrorist Bombers* (Lanham, MD: University Press of America, 2005).

5. Louis Adamic, *Dynamite: The Story of Class Violence in America* (1934; Gloucester, MA: P. Smith, 1963), 193. See also Philip Sheldon Foner, *History of the Labor Movement in the United States*, vol. 5, *The AFL in the Progressive Era, 1910–1915* (New York: International, 1980), 8–31.
6. Alfred Horsley [Harry Orchard (pseud.)], "The Confession and Autobiography of Harry Orchard," *McClure's*, July 1907, 294–306; August 1907, 367–379; September 1907, 507–523; October 1907, 658–673; November 1907, 113–130.
7. Cleveland Moffett, *Careers of Danger and Daring* (New York: Century, 1903), 358.
8. E. I. du Pont de Nemours Powder Company, *The Farmer's Handbook: Instructions in the Use of Dynamite for Clearing Land, Planting and Cultivating Trees, Drainage, Ditching and Subsoiling* (Wilmington, DE: E.I. du Pont, 1912), 18.
9. For an account in English of the Conselice rebellion, see "Public Instruction and Starvation in Italy," *Nation*, June 26, 1890, 550. Context for the rebellions can be found in Jennifer Guglielmo, *Living the Revolution: Italian Women's Resistance in New York City, 1880–1945* (Chapel Hill: University of North Carolina Press, 2010), 32–40.
10. See, for example, William T. Brannt et al., *The Techno-Chemical Receipt Book* (Philadelphia: Baird, 1887), 27–28; Frederick Converse Beach, ed., *The Encyclopedia Americana*, vol. 11 (New York: Americana, 1904), n.p.; David Patrick and William Geddie, eds., *Chamber's Encyclopedia*, vol. 7 (Philadelphia; Lippincott, 1901), 510.
11. For accounts of the formation of Tunney's Bomb Squad, see Tunney, *Throttled!*; Richard Polenberg, *Fighting Faiths: The Abrams Case, the Supreme Court, and Free Speech* (1987; Ithaca, NY: Cornell University Press, 1999), 55–61.
12. Nunzio Pernicone, *Carlo Tresca: Portrait of a Rebel* (New York: Palgrave-Macmillan, 2005), 80–82.
13. For a sampling see "Inspector Egan Holding Bombs Placed in Cathedral," *Boston Globe*, March 3, 1915; "Police Foil Bomb Plot in St. Patrick's Cathedral," *Naugatuck Daily News*, March 3, 1915; "Bomb in Cathedral," *Washington Post*, March 3, 1915.
14. Pernicone, *Carlo Tresca*, 86; Avrich, *Sacco and Vanzetti*, 101.
15. Tunney, *Throttled!* 58.
16. "Assert Police Spy Made Their Bombs," *New York Times*, March 4, 1915.
17. Simon O. Pollock, *Simon O. Pollock in Defense of Frank Abarno and Carmine Carbone* (New York: Carlone, n.d.), 5.
18. Pollock, *Simon O. Pollock*, 5.
19. Pollock, *Simon O. Pollock*, 9, 13.
20. *Information Annual 1915* (New York: Bowker, 1916), 409.
21. "Two Hundred Infernal Machines in New York Every Year," *New York Times*, January 13, 1907. The *New York Times*' estimate of the yearly finds may have been exaggerated since the reporter appears to have included illegal fireworks as "infernal machines." Nevertheless, reports of bomb incidents were a regular occurrence in the *New York Times* and other newspapers across the country. In 1913, the arrest of a gang of extortionists (from the loose criminal affiliates popularly known as the "Black Hand") more than halved the number of bombings in New York, but dozens still occurred. See "New York Still Has Black Record of Bomb Outrages," *Syracuse Herald*, September 26, 1913; A. R. Parkhurst Jr., "How the Black Hand Began to Use the Bomb in America," *Washington Post*, July 26, 1914. For a history of the Black Hand, see Robert M. Lombardo, *The Black Hand: Terror by Letter in Chicago* (Urbana: University of Illinois Press, 2010).
22. Avrich, *Sacco and Vanzetti*, 154; "Activity in Washington," *New York Times*, June 4, 1919.
23. Gage, *Wall Street*, 325–326.
24. Avrich, *Sacco and Vanzetti*, 66, 104.
25. Avrich, *Sacco and Vanzetti*, 206.
26. Serious attention to *La Salute è in voi!* began with Robert D'Attilio's paper at the 1979 "Sacco-Vanzetti: Developments and Reconsiderations" conference at the Boston Public Library. D'Attilio discusses Tunney's and Hoover's interest in the book and put great emphasis on

it as revealing the political violence in Sacco's and Vanzetti's milieu. See the conference proceedings (Boston: Trustees of the Public Library of the City of Boston, 1982), 75–90.

27. Roy A. Giles, "Bombs and Bomb Plots," *Scientific American*, April 1923, 226–227; Polenberg, *Fighting Faiths*, 163.
28. See, for example, Charles W. Person, "Bombs!," *Technical World*, March 1914, 109–112, 146; "Imperiled Boston Public Studies Bombs," *Popular Mechanics*, July 1917, 31; "Unusual Activity Nowadays in Bomb Manufacture," *New York Times*, June 10, 1906, SM7; Fred W. Sandberg, "How Fashions Change in Bombs," *Chicago Daily Tribune*, April 30, 1911.
29. William J. Burns, quoted in Harvey J. O'Higgins, "The Dynamiters," *McClure's* 37 (1911): 352.
30. Russell Miller, *The Adventures of Arthur Conan Doyle* (New York: St. Martin's, 2008), 312–313.
31. William J. Burns, *The Masked War* (New York: Doran, 1913), 11.
32. Burns, *The Masked War*, 52.
33. Burns, *The Masked War*, 9.
34. The clockwork bomb had a long history, going back at least to bombs constructed from clockworks and gunpowder used during the American Revolutionary War. Alarm clocks were used in bombs deployed by Irish American radicals in the 1880s. These bombs nearly always failed. The cheap, portable dry cell battery was a new addition to improvised explosive devices but well known in industries like mining, where it was used to set off a detonating cap, as in McNamara's bomb.
35. Courtney Ryley Cooper was the ghostwriter for both the photoplay and the ensuing book. William J. Flynn, *The Eagle's Eye* (New York: McCann, 1919), 340.
36. William Nelson Taft, *On Secret Service: Detective-Mystery Stories Based on Real Cases Solved by Government Agents* (New York: Harper & Brothers, 1921), 52.
37. In the year that *Throttled!* was published, Tunney left the New York City police after a demotion from a rival who had ascended above him.
38. Tunney, *Throttled!* 53–57.
39. Tunney, *Throttled!* 68.
40. The sabotage manuals were also introduced as evidence at these hearings. *Bolshevik Propaganda*, before a Subcommittee of the Committee on the Judiciary, 65th Congress (1919), 6–10. Hathitrust.
41. Tunney, *Throttled!* 2.
42. Tunney, *Throttled!* 55.
43. Lee Horsley discusses the relationship between scientific investigation, early twentieth-century crime fiction, and the rise of the modern police state in *Twentieth-Century Crime Fiction* (Oxford: Oxford University Press, 2005), 22–23.
44. Joyce Kornbluh, ed. *Rebel Voices: An I. W. W Anthology* (Oakland, CA: PM Press, 2011), 61.
45. George Harrison, *The I. W. W. Trial: Story of the Greatest Trial in Labor's History by One of the Defendants* (Chicago: Industrial Workers of the World, 1918), 66.
46. Harrison, *I. W. W. Trial*, 74.
47. The text of California's criminal syndicalism law is reprinted in Haig Bosmajian, *Anita Whitney, Louis Brandeis, and the First Amendment* (Madison, WI: Farleigh Dickinson University Press, 2010), 157–158.
48. For a discussion of revolutionary syndicalism and the career and influence of Pouget, see Ralph Darlington, *Syndicalism and the Transition to Communism: An International Comparative Analysis* (Hampshire: Ashgate, 2008), 17–48; Howard G. Lay, "*Réflecs d'un gniaff*: On Emile Pouget and *Le Père Peinard*," in *Making the News: Modernity and the Mass Press in Nineteenth-Century France*, ed. Dean de la Motte and Jeannene M. Przyblyski (Amherst: University of Massachusetts Press, 1999), 82–138.
49. Emile Pouget, *Sabotage*, trans. and ed. Arturo M. Giovannitti (Chicago: Kerr, 1913), 37.
50. Pouget, *Sabotage*, 46.
51. Allen M. Ruff, "Socialist Publishing in Illinois: Charles H. Kerr & Company of Chicago, 1886–1928," *Illinois Historical Journal* 79.1 (1986): 24.
52. Some socialists drew a distinction between direct action (such as striking) and sabotage, but in common usage, direct action frequently included references to acts of sabotage. For

a flavor of this debate, see William E. Trautman, *Direct Action and Sabotage* (Pittsburgh: Socialist News Company, 1912); Samuel Gompers, editorial, *American Federationist*, January 1913, 533–537; Robert Hunter, "The General Strike VI: The Meaning of Sabotage," *Commercial Telegrapher's Journal*, January 1912, 206–208.

53. "Haywood's Cooper Union Speech," *International Socialist Review*, February 1912, 469–70.
54. Eugene V. Debs, "Sound Socialist Tactics," *International Socialist Review*, February 1912, 482; Nick Salvatore, *Eugene V. Debs: Citizen and Socialist* (Urbana: University of Illinois Press, 1982), 253–255.
55. Jeffrey A. Johnson, "Raising the Red Flag: Culture, Labor, and the Left, 1880–1920," in *Homer Simpson Marches on Washington: Dissent through American Popular Culture*, ed. Timothy M. Dale and Joseph J. Foy (Lexington: University Press of Kentucky, 2010), 191–202.
56. Most historians of the Wobblies assert that they were essentially nonviolent, though not consistently so, as a way of positioning themselves apart from violent anarchists. See Melvyn Dubofsky, *We Shall Be All: A History of the Industrial Workers of the World* (Chicago: Quadrangle, 1969), 156–165; Philip S. Foner, *History of the Labor Movement in the United States*, vol. 4, *The Industrial Workers of the World, 1905–1916* (1965; New York: International Publishers, 1997), 166–167. For a view of Wobbly protest culture, see Kornbluh, *Rebel Voices*.
57. Ralph Chaplin is recognized as the Wobbly who popularized the sabotage cat through stickering. His motivations are discussed in Mark W. Van Wienen, *Partisans and Poets: The Political Work of American Poetry in the Great War* (Cambridge: Cambridge University Press, 1997), 139.
58. *State v. Matt Moilen and Others*, 140 Minn. R. 112 (1918). Hathitrust.
59. *Attorney General A. Mitchell Palmer on Charges Made against Department of Justice by Louis F. Post and Others*, Part I, Hearing Before the Committee on Rules, 66th Congress (1920), 183.
60. Mike Davis, "The Stop Watch and the Wooden Shoe: Scientific Management and the IWW," *Radical America* 9 (January–February 1975): 69–95.
61. Walker C. Smith, *Sabotage: Its History, Philosophy and Function* in *Direct Action and Sabotage: Three Classic IWW Pamphlets from the 1910s*, ed. Salvatore Salerno (Chicago: Kerr, 1997), 10.
62. Elizabeth Gurley Flynn, *Sabotage*, in Smith, *Direct Action and Sabotage*, 10. See also Flynn, *The Rebel Girl: An Autobiography, My First Life* (1955; New York: International Publishers, 1973), 162–165.
63. Flynn, *Sabotage*, 5.
64. Flynn, *Sabotage*, 30.
65. Flynn, *Rebel Girl*, 164–165.
66. Melvyn Dubofsky, "The I. W. W. at One Hundred: The Return of the Haunted Hall?" *Working USA* 8 (2005): 535–543.
67. David M. Rabban, *Free Speech in Its Forgotten Years* (Cambridge: Cambridge University Press, 1997), 77–128; Rebecca N. Hill, *Men, Mobs, and Law: Anti-Lynching and Labor Defense in U.S. Radical History* (Durham, NC: Duke University Press, 2008), 139–141.
68. David M. Rabban, "The Emergence of First Amendment Doctrine," *Chicago Law Review* 50 (1983): 1213.
69. Stuart Marshall Jamieson, *Labor Unionism in American Agriculture* (Washington, DC: US Department of Labor, 1946; Arno, 1976), 65. The vast majority of historians of this period see it as a time of national hysteria, when government at all levels overstepped its bounds in pursuing radicals. For a recent discussion, see Geoffrey R. Stone, *Perilous Times: Free Speech in Wartime from the Sedition Act of 1798 to the War on Terrorism* (New York: Norton, 2004), 135–234.
70. William Preston Jr., *Aliens and Dissenters: Federal Suppression of Radicals, 1903–1933*, 2nd ed. (1963; Cambridge, MA: Harvard University Press, 1994), 146.
71. Robert Justin Goldstein, *Political Repression in Modern America from 1870 to 1976* (Urbana: University of Illinois Press, 2001), 125–129.
72. Ole Hanson, *Americanism vs. Bolshevism* (New York: Doubleday, Page, 1920), 224–229.
73. "Case of Charles Jackson," *I. W. W. Deportation Cases*, Hearings before the Subcommittee of the Committee on Immigration and Naturalization, 66th Congress (1920), 45.
74. A[nthony] Caminetti, Memorandum, March 14, 1919, in *I. W. W. Deportation Cases*, 28.

75. "What Has Been Proved at I.W.W. Trial," *New York Times*, August 4, 1918.
76. Chicago Commission on Race Relations, *The Negro in Chicago: A Study of Race Relations and a Race Riot* (Chicago: University of Chicago Press, 1922), 122–134.
77. *People v. Taylor*, 203 P. 85 (Cal. 1921).
78. Taylor's compatriot, John G. Weiler, also lost his appeal on the basis of the same argument and evidence. Hundreds of people were jailed under state syndicalism laws during this period. *People v. Weiler*, 204 P. 410 (Cal. 1922); Stephen M. Kohn, *American Political Prisoners: Prosecutions under the Espionage and Sedition Acts* (Westport, CT: Greenwood, 1994), 167, 168.
79. Ronald K. L. Collins and David M. Skover, "Curious Concurrence: Justice Brandeis's Vote in *Whitney v. California*," *Supreme Court Review* 1 (2005): 347.
80. Bosmajian, *Anita Whitney*, 108–109.
81. Qtd. in Woodrow C. Whitten, "Trial of Charlotte Anita Whitney," *Pacific Historical Review* 15 (1945): 293.
82. Al Richmond, *Native Daughter: The Story of Anita Whitney* (San Francisco: Anita Whitney 75th Anniversary Committee, 1942).
83. Vincent Blasi, "First Amendment and the Ideal of Civic Courage: The Brandeis Opinion in *Whitney v. California*," *William and Mary Law Review* 29 (1988): 653–698.
84. Holmes, Dissenting Opinion, *Gitlow v. People*, 268 U.S. 652, 673 (1925).
85. Louis D. Brandeis, Concurring Opinion, *Whitney v. California*, 274 U.S. 357, 377 (1927).
86. Richard Gid Powers, *Broken: The Troubled Past and Uncertain Future of the FBI* (New York: Free Press, 2004), 98. See also Athos G. Theoharis, *The FBI and American Democracy* (Lawrence: University Press of Kansas, 2004), 21–28.

Chapter 3

1. *People v. John Peter Archer*, B13074. 2000 Cal. App. LEXIS 641, ***25 (Cal. Ct. App. 2000).
2. Paul McLaughlin, *Anarchism and Authority: A Philosophical Introduction to Classical Anarchism* (Burlington, VT: Ashgate, 2007), 9.
3. Jeremy Varon, *Bringing the War Home: The Weather Underground, the Red Army Faction, and Revolutionary Violence in the Sixties and Seventies* (Berkeley: University of California Press, 2004), 171–187, 294–295.
4. William Ayers, *Fugitive Days* (Boston: Beacon, 2001), 18.
5. John Chamberlain, "More Bombs," King Features Syndicate, *Daily Kennebec Journal*, March 18, 1971, 31.
6. *Explosives Control*, Committee on the Judiciary, 91st Congress, 2nd Sess. (Testimony of Eugene T. Rossides), 84.
7. Quoted in "Nattering Nabobs," *New Yorker*, July 10–17, 2006.
8. William Powell, "Editorial Reviews: From the Author," *Anarchist Cookbook*, amazon.com, accessed September 6, 2008.
9. William Powell, qtd. in George Carvill, "'Anarchist's Cookbook' Offers No Apologies for Its Philosophy," *Bennington Banner*, March 31, 1971.
10. *Castro's Network in the United States*, Part 6, Hearing before the Committee on the Judiciary, 88th Congress (1963): 305, 354. For context, see Van Gosse, *Where the Boys Are: Cold War America and the Making of the New Left* (London: Verso, 1993), 244.
11. *Riots, Civil and Criminal Disorders*, Part 25, hearing before the Permanent Subcommittee on Investigations, Committee on Government Operations, 90th Congress, 1st Sess. (1970), 5314. Hereafter RCCD.
12. Kenneth O'Reilly, "The FBI and the Politics of the Riots," *Journal of American History* 75 (1988): 109–112.
13. RCCD 5343.
14. RCCD 5314.
15. RCCD 5315.
16. *Activities of Ku Klux Klan Organizations in the U.S.*, Part 2, Hearings before the House Committee on Un-American Activities, 89th Congress, 1st Sess. (1967): 2160, 2187, 2322. The transformation of the Ku Klux Klan from vigilantism to terrorism and the FBI surveillance

of white supremacist groups is discussed in John Drabble, "To Ensure Domestic Tranquility: The FBI, COINTELPRO-WHITE HATE and Political Discourse, 1964–1971," *Journal of American Studies* 38 (2004): 297–328.

17. Bill Shaw, "Tempo; Preaching a Gospel of Hate," *Chicago Tribune*, May 23, 1985.
18. J. Harry Jones Jr., *The Minutemen* (New York: Doubleday, 1968), 292–312.
19. *United States vs. Carlson, et al.*, Nos. 2337–341, 1970 U.S. App. LEXIS 10,931, *433 (1970).
20. Qtd. in Jones, *Minutemen*, 305.
21. Thomas C. Lynch, cover letter, *Para-Military Organizations in California*, Report, Bureau of Criminal Identification and Investigation, California Office of the Attorney General, California Department of Justice, 1965. Head of the Minutemen Robert Depugh later expressed anger that a so-called *Minuteman Manual* had been reprinted. There never was such a manual, he claimed, though he was never a particularly reliable witness. See his interview with Eric Beckemeier, in Beckemeier, *Traitors Beware: A History of Robert DePugh's Minutemen* (Hardin, MO: Beckemeier, 2007), 123.
22. Thomas Lynch, "A Career in Politics and the Attorney General's Office," interview by Amelia R. Fry, University of California, Berkeley, Regional Oral History Office, 1982, 233.
23. RCCD 5722.
24. RCCD 5722.
25. Alberto Bayo, *150 Questions for a Guerrilla*, ed. Robert K. Brown, trans. Hugo Hartenstein and Dennis Harber (Boulder, CO: Panther, 1963), vii.
26. Bayo, *150 Questions*, xvi, xviii.
27. Jesús Arboleya, *The Cuban Counterrevolution*, trans. Rafael Betancourt (1997; Columbus: Ohio State University Press, 2000), 126.
28. Robert K. Brown, *I Am Soldier of Fortune: Dancing With Devils* (Havertown, PA: Casemate, 2013. Kindle edition).
29. Barry M. Stentiford, *The American Home Guard: The State Militia in the Twentieth Century* (College Station: Texas A&M University Press, 2002), 165; James D. Munson, review of *"We Shall Fight in the Streets"* by S. J. Cuthbert and *Total Resistance* by Hans von Dach Bern, *Military Affairs* 30 (Summer 1966): 109–110.
30. Bayo, *150 Questions*, xiv.
31. RCCD 5652.
32. Richard Aoki, "The Greatest Opportunity of My Life," in *Samurai among the Panthers: Richard Aoki on Race, Resistance, and a Paradoxical Life*, ed. Diane C. Fujino (Minneapolis: University of Minnesota Press, 2012), 153.
33. "George Prosser, "An Introduction to Elementary Tactics," *Black Politics* 2.11–12 (1969): 26.
34. At the hearing, Brown denied supplying Sanders or any other leftist publications with any advertising copy.
35. Prosser, "Introduction to Elementary Tactics," 26.
36. Prosser, "Introduction to Elementary Tactics," 28.
37. *Sanders v. McLellan*, 463 F.2d 895 (1972): 1. Justia.com, accessed February 25, 2010.
38. *Sanders v. McLellan*, 46.
39. *Brandenburg v. Ohio*, 395 U.S. 444, 446 (1969).
40. Ohio Rev. Code Ann. § 2923.13 (1919).
41. *Hess v. Indiana*, 414 U.S. 105 (1973).
42. RCCD 5617.
43. U.S.C. 18, § 231 (a)(1) (2004); see also Philip B. Wright, "Effect of Federal Firearms Control on Civil Disorder," *Brooklyn Law Review* 35 (1968–1969): 435.
44. RCCD 5617.
45. Four cities were known to be involved: Milwaukee, Atlanta, Cleveland, and Richmond, California. In Cleveland, the probe was related to the bombing of a police station; in Richmond, the investigators were acting on a tip from an informant. Judith F. Krug and James A. Harvey, "Committee on Intellectual Freedom," *American Libraries* 1 (1970): 843–845.
46. Krug and Harvey, "Committee on Intellectual Freedom," 844.
47. *Stanley v. Georgia*, 394 U.S. 557, 564 (1969). Though cases in the lower courts, particularly regarding child pornography, have challenged the Court's ruling, it still stands as an important contribution to the interpretation of the First Amendment as protecting private reading.

48. *Stanley v. Georgia*, 565.
49. Judith F. Krug and James A. Harvey, "Intellectual Freedom," *American Libraries* 1 (1970): 751–752; "Memo to Members," *American Libraries* 1 (1970): 771.
50. Richard Spong, "Middle Brother Is Listening," *Raleigh Register*, July 22, 1970.
51. Art Buchwald, "Public Library Enemy #1," *Kingsport Times*, July 14, 1970.
52. George Lardner Jr., "Ervin Flays Reading Investigation," *Greeley Tribune*, July 10, 1970.
53. *Explosives Control* (Testimony of Eugene T. Rossides), 89–90.
54. "Head of Treasury Bars Book Search," *New York Times*, July 30, 1970, 25.
55. "ALA, IRS Representatives Agree on Snooping," *Library Journal* 95 (1970): 2859.
56. This surveillance program functioned from 1973 to 1976 and from 1985 until at least 1989. See Herbert N. Foerstel, *Surveillance in the Stacks: The FBI's Library Awareness Program* (New York: Greenwood, 1991).
57. "Librarians March on IRS Office," *Library Journal* 95 (1970), 837.
58. RCCD 5755.
59. William Hinkle III and Sidney Zion, introduction, *Scanlan's* 1 (January 1971): 12.
60. Paul L. Montgomery, "A Scanlan's Issue Delayed by Union," *New York Times*, October 3, 1970; "A.C.L.U. Plans Suit to Help Magazine," *New York Times*, October 23, 1970.
61. Edward Cowan, "Canadians to Release Scanlan's Monthly When Registration Is Submitted," *New York Times*, December 18, 1970; "Police in Montreal Seize a Monthly," *New York Times*, December 12, 1970; "Scanlan's Release Ordered in Canada," *New York Times*, December 25, 1970.
62. Sidney Zion, *Read All about It! The Collected Adventures of a Maverick Reporter* (New York: Summit, 1992), 121; David Armstrong, *A Trumpet to Arms* (Los Angeles: J. P. Tarcher, 1981), 148.
63. "U.S. Seizes and Then Releases 6,000 Copies of a Magazine on How to Make Bombs," *New York Times*, December 11, 1970.
64. Elia Katz, *Armed Love* (1971; Raleigh, NC: Boson Books, 2009), 115.
65. Frank A. Moyer, *U. S. Army Special Forces Foreign Weapons Handbook* (Boulder, CO: Panther Publications, 1970), v.
66. Joseph F. Stoffel, *Explosives and Homemade Bombs* (Springfield, IL: Charles C. Thomas, 1962), 35–42.
67. Bayo, *150 Questions*, 55, 57.
68. Howard Smith, "Scenes," *Village Voice*, February 25, 1971, 9.
69. "A Matter of Conscience," *Christian Science Monitor*, January 25, 1971; *Publishers Weekly*, February 1, 1971, 73.
70. Max Geltman, "Recipes for Destruction," *National Review*, July 27, 1971, 819.
71. Emile Capouya, review of *The Anarchist Cookbook*, by William Powell, *Commonweal*, March 12, 1971, 16–19. Anarchists have continued to reject the book as a misrepresentation of anarchism tied to old nihilist stereotypes, and some have suspected that the CIA concocted the book. See Crimethinc Workers' Collective, *Recipes for Disaster: An Anarchist Cookbook. A Moveable Feast* (Salem, OR: Crimethinc Workers' Collective, 2006); "Esperanza Godot," "Recipes for Nonsurvival," *Anarchist Library*, April 2002, http://flag.blackened.net/daver/anarchism/godot.html, accessed January 15, 2014.
72. File on *The Anarchist Cookbook*, Federal Bureau of Investigation, January 14, 1971–September 10, 1999. Obtain through a FOIA request by Government Attic, http://www.governmentattic.org/4docs/FBI-AnarchistsCookbook_1971–1999.pdf, accessed September 2, 2011.
73. Tom Bates, *Rads: The 1970 Bombing of the Army Math Research Center at the University of Wisconsin and Its Aftermath* (New York: HarperCollins, 1992), 371.
74. Harold A. Mathiak, *Pothole Blasting for Wildlife* (Madison: Wisconsin Conservation Dept., 1965); Bates, *Rads*, 31.
75. *New York v. Cruz*, 34 N.Y. 2d 362, 368 (1974): 368.
76. "Pistol May Link Patty to Bank Robbery," *Redland Daily Facts*, September 29, 1975, 2.
77. The first edition of *The Blaster's Handbook* was published by E. I. Du Pont Nemours in Wilmington, Delaware, in 1918 and was frequently updated. It was initially designed as

promotional material to sell DuPont products, especially to farmers who could use explosives to clear their fields.

78. Susan Stern, *With the Weathermen: The Personal Journal of a Revolutionary Woman* (New York: Doubleday, 1975), 238, 264.
79. Ayers, *Fugitive Days*, 147.
80. Thai Jones, *A Radical Line: From the Labor Movement to the Weather Underground: One Family's Century of Consciousness* (New York: Free Press, 2004), 230.
81. Stern, *With the Weathermen*, 238.
82. Cathy Wilkerson, *Flying Close to the Sun: My Life and Times as a Weatherman* (New York: Seven Stories, 2007), 327, 339.
83. "Aryan Nations Trial Focuses on Terrorist Items," *Spokesman-Review*, October 12, 1990; "Mail-Bomb Jurors Hear of FBI Raid," *Philadelphia Inquirer*, June 7, 1991.
84. Dudley Clendinen, "Abortion Clinic Bombings Have Caused Disruption for Many," *New York Times*, February 6, 1985.
85. Stuart A. Wright, "Explaining the Militarization at Waco: The Construction and Convergence of the War Narrative," in *Controversial New Religions*, ed. James R. Lewis and Jesper Aagaard Petersen (Oxford: Oxford University Press, 2005), 80.
86. For the classic on moral panics over youth, see Stanley Cohen, *Folk Devils and Moral Panics: The Creation of the Mods and the Rockers*, 3rd ed. (New York: Routledge, 2003).
87. Bill Montgomery, "Case against Teen 'Anarchist' Dismissed," *Atlanta Constitution*, February 12, 1997, B4.
88. Joan O'Brien, "Forum Finds You Can't Always Tell a Book. . .," *Salt Lake Tribune*, December 1, 1994.
89. *Bowling for Columbine*, DVD, dir. Michael Moore, MGM, 2003.
90. Ron Mott and Tracy Connor, "Colorado High School Shooter Read Bomb-Making Manual," *NBC News*, December 16, 2013; Tony Dokoupil, "After Latest Shooting, Murder Manual Author Calls for Book to Be Taken 'Immediately' Out of Print," *NBC News*, December 17, 2013.
91. Bruce Robinson II, "Public Bombings, Local Increase?" *Palm Beach Daily News*, August 19, 1971.
92. *United States v. Prevatte and Soy*, 66 F.3d (7th Cir. 1995), 841.
93. *United States v. Jones*, 863 F. Supp. (U.S. Dist. Ct. for the Northern District of Ohio, Eastern Division, 1994), 580.
94. *U.S. v. Sirica Bumpuss*, 27 Fed. Appx. (9th Cir. 2001): 470.
95. In 2002, the stolen files of a Portland police terrorism expert were turned over to a local newspaper, revealing the shocking extent of local surveillance operations from 1965 to 1980. Ben Jacklet, "The Secret Watchers," *Portland Tribune*, September 13, 2002, www.portlandtribune.com, accessed July 20, 2008. The surveillance activities of the FBI, particularly through its COINTELPRO operations, are already well known.
96. Frank Stearns Giese, obituary, *Oregonian*, August 15, 2006.
97. H. Bruce Franklin, *From the Movement Toward Revolution* (New York: Van Nostrand Reinhold, 1971), 166–167; *United States v. Giese*, 597 F.2d 1192 (9th Cir. 1979): 1192, available through LEXIS NEXIS Academic.
98. *United States v. Giese*, 1199.
99. Franklin, *Movement Toward Revolution*, 169; *United States v. Giese*, 1206.
100. *United States v. Giese*, 1206.
101. *United States v. Giese*, 1185. Both the majority and dissenting opinions referred to the prior case of Gregory Lee McCrea, who had been convicted of possession of an illegal firearm after the police found an automatic rifle, a machine gun, and a pipe bomb in his ex-wife's home. The police also confiscated several books: *The OSS Sabotage & Demolition Manual*, *Special Forces Demolition Techniques*, *Improvised Munitions Handbook*, and other books on explosives, guns, and counterinsurgency published by the US Army. Two of the books were used as evidence at McCrea's trial. Upon appeal, the higher court ruled that their admittance had been improper, but that the error was harmless because the prosecuting attorney hadn't featured the books in his arguments to the jury. In her dissent Judge Hufstedler maintained

that the admonition in McCrea against using books as evidence of motive and disposition was relevant in Giese's case. *U.S. v. McCrea,* 583 F.2d 1083 (9th Cir. 1978).

102. *United States v. Giese,* 1201.
103. *United States v. Giese,* 1207.
104. *United States v. Ellis,* 147 F.3d (9th Cir. 1998): 1134.
105. *United States v. Waters,* 627 F.3d (9th Cir. 2010): 359.
106. *United States v. Rogers,* 270 F.3d 1081 (7th Cir. 2001).
107. *United States v. Parr,* 545 F.3d (7th Cir. 2008): 493.
108. Michel de Certeau, *The Practice of Everyday Life,* trans. Steven Rendall (Berkeley: University of California Press, 1988).
109. Thomas I. Emerson, "Toward a General Theory of the First Amendment," *Yale Law Journal* 72 (1963): 879–880.
110. For an overview, see Chris Demaske, *Modern Power and Free Speech* (Lanham, MD: Rowman & Littlefield, 2011). For a discussion of the place of the "home" in discussions of privacy, see Jeffry M. Shaman, *Equality and Liberty in the Golden Age of Constitutional Law* (New York: Oxford University Press, 2008), 155–158.
111. For recent discussions of the child pornography cases, see David M. O'Brien, *Congress Shall Make No Law: The First Amendment, Unprotected Expression, and the U. S. Supreme Court* (Lanham, MD: Rowman & Littlefield, 2010), 15–36; Chalsea McLean, "The Uncertain Fate of Child Pornography Legislation," *Cornell Journal of Law and Public Policy* 17 (2007): 221–246; Yaman Akdeniz, *Internet Child Pornography and the Law: National and International Responses* (Burlington, VT: Ashgate, 2008), 93–140.

Chapter 4

1. Uncle Fester [Steven Preisler], *Silent Death,* 2nd ed. (Port Townsend, WA: Loompanics, 1997).
2. Uncle Fester [Steven Preisler], author web page, www.unclefesterbooks.com, accessed January 15, 2014.
3. Jonathan B. Tucker and Jason Pate, "The Minnesota Patriots Council," in *Toxic Terror: Assessing Terrorist Use of Chemical and Biological Weapons,* ed. Tucker (Cambridge, MA: MIT Press, 2000), 174.
4. Maynard Campbell, *Catalogue of Silent Tools of Justice* (Ashland, OR: Maynard Campbell, 1991), 50.
5. *U.S. v. Baker and Wheeler,* No. 95-2257, 1996 U.S. App. LEXIS 25,251, **14, 15 (8th Cir. 1996).
6. Kurt Saxon [Don Sisco], *The Poor Man's James Bond,* vol. 2 (El Dorado, AR: Desert, 1992), 3.
7. Investigator's report, Denver, CO, May 20, 1981, file on Paladin Press, Federal Bureau of Investigation, released to Government Attic under FOIA.
8. The reclassification occurred during the McClellan hearings, as discussed in chapter 3. Further details can be found in the FBI file on Paladin Press, January 9, 1973.
9. *Domestic Security (LEVI) Guidelines,* hearing before the Subcommittee on Security and Terrorism, 97th Congress, 2nd Sess. (June 24, 25; August 11, 12, 1982) (Testimony of Arleigh McCree).
10. "Paladin Press: A Brief History," Paladin Press website, http://www.paladin-press.com/company_history, accessed January 15, 2014.
11. Duncan Campbell, "Teaching Terror on the Right," *New Statesman,* June 16, 1978, 804.
12. Michael LaForgia and Adam Playford, "WikiLeaks Secret Cables Detail Local Firm's Role in Arms Trade," *Palm Beach Post,* September 11, 2011; "Sinn Fein Man's Son Jailed over Explosives," *Belfast Telegraph,* February 3, 2012; C. J. Chivers and David Rohde, "Turning Out Guerrillas and Terrorist to Wage a Holy War," *New York Times,* March 18, 2002; John Allison, "Terrorist Weapons and Technology," in *Combating Terrorism in Northern Ireland,* ed. James Dingley (New York: Routledge, 2009), 10.
13. C. J. Chivers, "Instruction and Methods from Al Qaeda Took Root in North Iraq with Islamic Fighters," *New York Times,* April 27, 2003.

14. John L. Russell III, *Involuntary Possession; or In the Steal of the Night* (Boulder, CO: Paladin 1976), 4.
15. According the Paladin's FBI file, the videotape, *Whispering Death,* was implicated in the murder of George Bromley in Merseyside, England, in 1997. Examples of cases involving Paladin's books on silencers: *Rodgers v. Florida,* No. SC01-185, 2006 Fla. LEXIS 1402 (Fla. 2006); *People v. Archer,* No. B130704, No. B135991, 2000 Cal. App. LEXIS 641 (2000); *United States v. Genova,* 92 Cr. 377 (SWK), 1992 U.S. Dist. LEXIS 16,552 (S.D.N.Y. 1992); *Wisconsin v. Stank,* No. 2004AP1162-CR, 2005 Wisc. App. LEXIS 939 (Wis. App. 2005); *New Jersey v. Pante,* No. A-296-97T4, 1999 N.J. Super. LEXIS 347 (N.J. Super. App. Div. 1999).
16. Richard Goldstein, "Rex Applegate, 84, Instructor of Deadly Skills," obituary, *New York Times,* July 27, 1998.
17. George Hayduke, *Mayhem!*
18. Al Jaffee, a contributor to the magazine, wrote his own book: *Mad Book of Magic and Other Dirty Tricks* (New York: New American Library, 1970).
19. CIA, *Freedom Fighter's Manual* (1983), Xeroxed copy, Radicalism Collection, Michigan State University Library. See also "Manual Instructs Sandinistas' Foes in Sabotage," *New York Times,* June 5, 1984.
20. Animal Liberation Front, "The ALF Primer: A Guide to Direct Action and the Animal Liberation Front," online version, http://www.animalliberationfront.com/ALFront/ALFPrime.htm.
21. *Eco-Terrorism Specifically Examining Stop Huntingdon Animal Cruelty ("SHAC"),* Hearing before the Committee on Environment and Public Works, 109th Congress, 1st Sess. (October 26, 2005) (Testimony of Skip Boruchin), 15. Stiff laws have been passed against what the government calls animal rights "ecoterrorism," namely the Animal Enterprise Protection Act of 1992.
22. *United States v. Fullmer, et al.,* 584 F.3d (3rd Cir. 2009).
23. Rod Smolla, *Deliberate Intent: A Lawyer Tells the True Story of Murder by the Book* (New York: Crown, 1999), 239; David Montgomery, "If Books Could Kill," *Washington Post,* July 26, 1998; Ragnar Benson [pseud.], *Mantrapping* (Boulder, CO: Paladin, 1981), 5.
24. Benson, *Mantrapping,* 83.
25. Ragnar Benson, *Ragnar's Big Book of Homemade Weapons* (Boulder, CO: Paladin, 1986), 3.
26. Benson, *Big Book,* 200.
27. Richard Bernstein, "Bombing Trial Defense Begins Its Case," *New York Times,* February 11, 1994.
28. Mattias Gardell, *Gods of the Blood: The Pagan Revival and White Separatism* (Durham, NC: Duke University Press, 2003), 194–195; Edward Wade Hawley and Olive Hawley Nadine Epstein, "White Supremacist Couple Pleads Guilty in Federal Court," *Christine Science Monitor,* February 5, 1987.
29. *Racially Motivated Violence,* Hearings before the Subcommittee on Criminal Justice of the Committee on the Judiciary, 97th Congress, 1st Sess. (March 4, June 3, and November 12, 1981) (Testimony of Charlene Mitchell), 46.
30. *Hate Crime on the Internet,* hearing before the Committee on the Judiciary, 106th Congress, 1st Sess. (September 14, 1999) (Testimony of Howard Berkowitz), 31. In an odd twist, *The Turner Diaries* publisher, the neo-Nazi National Alliance, eventually sold the rights to Lyle Stuart, who had published *The Anarchist Cookbook.*
31. Joseph Hartzler, opening statement, *United States v. McVeigh,* No. 96-CR-68 1997 WL 198,070 (D. Colo. April 24, 1997), Famous Trials website, by Douglas O. Linder (2014), http://law2.umkc.edu/faculty/projects/ftrials/mcveigh, accessed January 15, 2014. McVeigh had also sold another of Pierce's books, *Hunter,* used as evidence in his partner Terry Nichols trial, which had more specific details on how a bomb could be built using a Tovex primary detonator and sited next to a tall building with plate glass.
32. Stephen Jones, opening statement, *United States v. McVeigh,* April 24, 1997, Famous Trials.
33. Larry D. Macky, Closing Argument, *United States v. McVeigh,* May 29, 1997, Famous Trials.
34. *Homemade C-4: A Closer Look,* video, prod. Paladin Press, 1991.
35. Hartzler, opening statement, *United States v. McVeigh.*

36. *Rice, et al., v. Paladin Enter.*, No. 96-2412, 1997 U.S. App. LEXIS 30,889, **26–**38 (4th Cir. 1997).
37. Arguments against the court's decision in *Rice v. Paladin* are legion. See, for example, David Kopel, "The Day They Came to Sue the Book," *Reason* 31.4 (1999): 59–61; Cassandra M. Chin, "Holding the Publisher of a Murder Manual Liable for Aiding and Abetting Murder: A Travesty against Free Speech," *George Mason University Civil Rights Law Journal* 10 (1999–2000): 205–226; Elise M. Balkin, "Rice v. Paladin: The Fourth Circuit's Unnecessary Limiting of a Publisher's Freedom of Speech," *University of Baltimore Law Review* 29.2 (2000): 205–236; Amy K. Dilworth, "Murder in the Abstract: The First Amendment and the Misappropriation of Brandenburg," *William & Mary Bill of Rights Journal* 6 (1998): 565–592.
38. Avital T. Zer-Ilan, "The First Amendment and Murder Manuals," *Yale Law Journal* 106 (1997): 2700–2701.
39. Juliet Dee, "How-to Manuals for Hitmen: Paladin Press, a Triple Murder, and First Amendment Protection of Technical Information," *Communications and the Law* 23.2 (2001): 1–54.
40. Smolla, *Deliberate Intent*, 229–235.
41. Nancy Barr Mavity, *The Other Bullet* (Garden City, NY: Crime Club, 1930), 143.
42. Rex Feral [pseud.], *Hitman: A Technical Manual for Independent Contractors* (Boulder, CO: Paladin, 1983), 111.
43. Feral, *Hitman*, 10.
44. Feral, *Hitman*, 37.
45. Qtd. in Smolla, *Deliberate Intent*, 244.
46. Rex Feral [pseud.], *Hit Man On-Line: A Technical Manual for Independent Contractors* (1999).
47. Mark Del Franco, "Paladin Kills Off Part of Its Product Line," *Catalog Age*, April 2000, 14.
48. "Explosives Manual Teenager Jailed," *BBS News*, October 26, 2007.
49. Andrianna Kastanek, "From Hit Man to a Military Takeover of New York City: The Evolving Effects of *Rice v. Paladin Enterprises* on Internet Censorship," *Northwestern Law Review* 99 (2004): 383–436.
50. For example, a heavily armed Michael Edward Smith was arrested after stalking a synagogue. Taken from his bookshelf were *The Turner Diaries, Hunter, The Testing of Negro Intelligence, Chemistry of Powder and Explosives, and Advanced Anarchist Arsenal. United States v. Smith*, No. 04-5519, 2005 U.S. App. LEXIS 28,666, at **4 (2005).
51. Bob Black, preface, *The Right to Be Greedy*, by For Ourselves, Primitivism website, http://www.primitivism.com/greedy.htm, accessed January 15, 2014.
52. Scott Stossel, "Bound to Be Bad," *New Yorker*, October 12, 1998, 92.
53. Richard Seven, "Empowering? Illegal? Weird? Dangerous?" *Seattle Times*, November 7, 1999.
54. Uncle Fester [Steven Preisler], *Secrets of Methamphetamine Manufacture*, 7th ed. (Port Townsend, WA: Loompanics, 2005), ii. I include Preisler's books on methamphetamine because of a substantial crossover in "clandestine chemistry" and their use against defendants in legal cases involving weapons manuals. Preisler's work is important because it represents an enhanced attention to textbook chemistry.
55. Mick Farren, *Speed-Speed-Speedfreak: A Fast History of Amphetamine* (Port Townsend, WA: Feral House, 2010), 201.
56. *United States v. John Monroe Kime*, No. 95-2944, No. 95-3160, 1996 U.S. App. LEXIS 27,635, at **7 (8th Cir. 1996).
57. *United States v. Jeffrey Ford*, 22 F.3d 374, 381 (1st Cir. 1994).
58. There are a number of cases in the appeals records. See, for example, *United States v. Bobby Michael Chard*, 115 F.3d 631, 633 (8th Cir. 1997); *United States v. William D. Stockton*, 968 F.2d 715, 717 (8th Cir. 1992). One involves the digital copy of the book, *Ohio v. Jason Deibel*, Case No. 1-10-70, 2011-Ohio App. LEXIS 2984 (Oh. 2011).
59. *United States v. Autem*, 2006 U.S. Dist. LEXIS 3457, at **25 (D. Kan. 2006); *United States v. Clough*, 246 F. Supp. 2d 84, 88 (D. Me. 2003); *State of Washington v. Meckelson*, 2006 Wash. App. LEXIS 212, at **7 (WA Div. III 2006).
60. "Lemony Snicket Rallies Authors to Support the Tattered Cover," *Bookselling This Week*, December 14, 2001, American Booksellers Association, www.bookweb.org, accessed

December 19, 2013. Bridge Kinsella, "A Clean Well-Lighted Benefit for the Tattered Cover Raises $10K," *Publisher's Weekly*, January 28, 2002, 145. Proquest.

61. Eugene Volokh, "Crime Facilitating Speech," *Stanford Law Review* 57 (2005): 1095, 1105; Iam Cram, *Terror and the War on Dissent: Freedom of Expression in the Age of Al-Qaeda* (New York: Springer, 2009), 67–71.
62. *Tattered Cover, Inc. v. City of Thornton*, 44 P. 3d 1044, 1047, 1052, 1053 (Col. 2002). In *United States v. Rumely*, the Supreme Court overturned the conviction of the secretary of the Committee for Constitutional Government, which opposed the New Deal, for refusing to give Congress a list of book purchasers.
63. John Mutter, "Colorado High Court Backs Tattered Cover," *Publisher's Weekly*, April 15, 2002.
64. "Frequently Asked Questions," Paladin Press website, http://www.paladin-press.com/faqs.
65. Mark Frauenfelder, "Loompanics Going Out of Business," *Boing Boing*, January 23, 2006, http://boingboing.net/2006/01/23/loompanics-going-out.html.
66. Sean Gabb, "Loompanics: A Trip Down Memory Lane," Libertarian Alliance blog, September 2, 2012, http://libertarianalliance.wordpress.com/2012/09/02/loompanics-a-trip-down-memory-lane/, accessed January 15, 2014.
67. Scott Maccaulay, "Loompanics, RIP," Filmmaker blog, April 22, 2006, http://filmmakermagazine.com/2297-loompanics-rip/#.UucS9GQo6u4, accessed January 15, 2014.
68. Peder Lund, qtd. in J. Peder Zane, "You Too Can Be a Successful Criminal!" *New York Times*, July 24, 1994; "Mayhem Man," *New York Times*, August 18, 1996.
69. Erik Larson, *Lethal Passage: The Story of a Gun* (New York: Vintage, 1995), 169.
70. Paul Zielbauer, "A Nation Challenged: The How-to Book," *New York Times*, November 21, 2001.
71. Timothy Tobiason, *Scientific Principles of Improvised Warfare & Home Defense*, vol. 6-E, *Modified Bacteria Weapons* (Silver Creek, NE: Scientific and Technical Intelligence Press, n.d.), n.p. Tobiason's precursor was Larry Wayne Harris, a trained microbiologist and inveterate liar who wrote a manual, *Bacteriological Warfare*, on biological weapons, including anthrax. He was arrested after he had ordered and acquired bubonic plague virus. Jessica Eve Stern, "Larry Wayne Harris: The Talkative Terrorist," in Tucker, *Toxic Terror*, 227–246.

Chapter 5

1. Joyce Dierauer, email to author, January 20, 2012.
2. Don Liddick, *Eco-Terrorism: Radical Environmental and Animal Liberation Movements* (Westport, CT: Praeger, 2006), 18; Lawrence E. Likar, *Eco-Warriors, Nihilistic Terrorists, and the Environment* (Santa Barbara, CA: Praeger, 2011), 80.
3. See, for example, Harvey W. Kushner, *Encyclopedia of Terrorism* (Thousand Oaks, CA: Sage, 2003), 116; Walter Laqueur, *The New Terrorism: Fanaticism and the Arms of Mass Destruction* (New York: Oxford University Press, 1999), 202; Vincent Burns and Kate Dempsey Peterson, *Terrorism: A Documentary and Reference Guide* (Westport, CT: Greenwood, 2005), xxvii. An essay purporting that Abbey was instrumental in the rise of ecoterrorism misspells his name twice: Travis Morris and John P. Crank, "Toward a Phenomenology of Terrorism," *Crime, Law and Social Change* 56 (2011): 234.
4. For example, Steven Vanderheiden has argued for a clear distinction between a morally defensible "ecotage" and a morally indefensible "terrorism," largely based on the latter's embrace of killing noncombatants. Proponents of ecotage set moral limits and do not set out to overthrow an entire existing order. If caught, they take responsibility for their actions. Because of the unlawful destruction they propose, their actions can be seen as moving beyond civil disobedience, but do not constitute terrorism. See his "Eco-Terrorism or Justified Resistance? Radical Environmentalists and the 'War on Terror,'" *Politics and Society* 33 (2005): 425–446.
5. William E. Dyson, *Terrorism: An Investigator's Handbook*, 4th ed. (Waltham, MA: Anderson, 2011), 480.
6. George Michael, "Blueprints and Fantasies: A Review and Analysis of Extremist Fiction," *Studies in Conflict & Terrorism* 33.2 (2010): 153.

7. Edward Abbey, Letter to Eugene C. Hargrove, Editor of *Environmental Ethics*, November 3, 1982, reprinted in *Postcards from Ed*, ed. David Petersen (Minneapolis, MN: Milkweed, 2006), 128–129.
8. Enric Volante, "FBI Tracked Abbey for 20-Year Span," *Arizona Daily Star*, June 25, 1989, A1–A2. Edward Abbey's FBI file (March 8, 1947–October 29, 1952) is available online through the FBI Vault.
9. See Richard A. Posner's overview in *Law & Literature*, 3rd ed. (Cambridge, MA: Harvard University Press, 2009), 497–517. Cass Sunstein argues for the First Amendment protection of literature deemed to have political merit, but argues that the government can justify censoring literature that causes demonstrable harm, in *Democracy and the Problem of Free Speech* (New York: Simon and Schuster, 1995), 121–166.
10. *U.S. v. Curtin*, 489 F.3d 935, 959 (9th Cir. 2006).
11. Matthew Lyons, introduction, David Foreman and Bill Haywood, eds., *Ecodefense*, 3rd ed. (Chico, CA: Abbzug, 1993), 1.
12. David Foreman, editorial, *Earth First!* Ecostar Ritual Issue, March 20, 1982, 11.
13. William Burroughs, *The Soft Machine* (New York: Grove/Atlantic, 1966), 151.
14. Sam Love and David Obst, *Ecotage* (New York: Pocket, 1972), 20.
15. Love and Obst, *Ecotage*, 15.
16. Mike Royko, "Fox Gains Allies," Chicago Daily News Service, March 27, 1971.
17. Love and Obst, *Ecotage*, 179; Ray Fox [James Phillips], *Raising Kane: The Fox Chronicles* (Montgomery, IL: Kindred Spirits, 1999), 48.
18. Love and Obst, *Ecotage*, 177.
19. Mario Savio, Speech, University of California at Berkeley, December 2, 1964, "Mario Savio on the Operation of the Machine," video posted by cherumaz, August 9, 2010, YouTube, accessed January 24, 2012.
20. Renee Calderon, "Tucson's Eco Raiders Kill Another Billboard," *Tucson Daily Citizen*, April 28, 1973, 3–4. In an echo of the Fox, the Eco Raiders also dumped nonreturnable bottles at the bottling company, and then went on to inflict costly damage to housing development projects, destroying wiring and plumbing, spray painting slogans, and pouring gravel into fuel tanks of paving equipment. Tucson's sheriff thought the teen vandalism less worth pursuing than the murders in his town, and when the raiders were finally caught, they received light jail sentences, fines, and community service. Now, the terror experts have resurrected these long-forgotten teenagers as among the first "ecoterrorists." John Jennings, "Eco-Raiders Stay Ahead of the Law," *Tucson Daily Citizen*, July 19, 1973, 29; Brent L. Smith, Kelly R. Damphouse, and Paxton Roberts, *Pre-Incident Indicators of Terrorist Incidents: The Identification of Behavioral, Geographic, and Temporal Patterns of Preparatory Conduct*, Department of Justice, Doc. 214,217 (May 2006), 213; Dyson, *Terrorism*, 478.
21. "Berrien, Cass Billboards Fall," *News Palladium* (Benton Harbor, MI), April 15, 1971.
22. "Michigan Youths Fell Bill Boards," *New York Times*, April 25, 1971, 28.
23. Tom Miller, *Revenge of the Saguaro: Offbeat Travels through America's Southwest* (Washington, DC: National Geographic, 2000), 55.
24. Wallace Stegner, "Lake Powell," in *Marking the Sparrow's Fall: The Making of the American West*, ed. Page Stegner (New York: Henry Holt, 1998), 64.
25. Edward Abbey, *The Monkey Wrench Gang* (1975; New York: Harper, 2006), 6.
26. The *Monkey Wrench Gang*'s engagement with environmental issues is discussed in David N. Cassuto, *Dripping Dry: Literature, Politics, and Water in the Desert Southwest* (Ann Arbor: University of Michigan Press, 2001), 77–96.
27. Jim Harrison, review of *The Monkey Wrench Gang* by Edward Abbey, *New York Times*, November 14, 1976.
28. JRM, review of *The Monkey Wrench Gang* by Edward Abbey, *Albuquerque Tribune*, February 12, 1976. See also Roy Hudson, "Canyonlands Novel Setting," review of *The Monkey Wrench Gang* by Edward Abbey, *Salt Lake Tribune*, September 7, 1975.
29. Grace Lichtenstein, "Edward Abbey: Voice of the Southwest Wilds," *New York Times*, January 20, 1976.

30. Margot Hornblower, "A Clash of Values: Old and New at War amid Burnt Cliffs," *Washington Post*, December 31, 1979.
31. Miller, *Revenge of the Saguaro*, 46.
32. David Fenimore, "*The Monkey Wrench Gang* (1975)," in *Literature and the Environment*, ed. George Hart and Scott Slovic (Westport, CT: Greenwood, 2004), 101.
33. Abbey, *The Monkey Wrench Gang*, 319–320.
34. Abbey, *The Monkey Wrench Gang*, 325.
35. Edward Abbey, "The Remington Studio," in *One Life at a Time, Please* (New York: Holt, 1988), 195.
36. Abbey, *The Monkey Wrench Gang*, 79.
37. Abbey, *The Monkey Wrench Gang*, 89.
38. Edward Abbey, "Anarchism and the Morality of Violence," M. A. Thesis, University of Mexico, 1950, 44. For his description of the Haymarket bombing, Abbey relied on Louis Adamic's *Dynamite: The Story of Class Violence in America* (New York: Viking, 1934), a largely critical view of violence and violent talk in the labor movement. Abbey's thesis is an uninspired work, obviously written to please his thesis advisers, but he did carry with him some knowledge of anarchist history.
39. Richard G. Mitchell, *Dancing at Armageddon: Survivalism and Chaos in Modern Times* (Chicago: University of Chicago Press, 2002), 11.
40. Abbey, *The Monkey Wrench Gang*, 404.
41. Abbey, *The Monkey Wrench Gang*, vi. James M. Calahan discusses Abbey's exaggerations about his own life, including his romantic lie about his birthplace, in *Edward Abbey: A Life* (Tucson: University of Arizona Press, 2001), xi–xii.
42. Jay Davis, "Epilogue: A Twenty-First Century Terrorism Agenda for the United States," in *The Terrorism Threat and U S. Government Response: Operational and Organizational Factors*, ed. James M. Smith and William C. Thomas (USAF Academy, CO: USAF Institute for National Security Studies, 2001), 276.
43. Abbey's speech and the subsequent action are captured in video, *The Four Corners: A National Sacrifice Area?* Dir. Christopher McLeod, prod. McLeod, Glenn Switkes, and Randy Hayes, Bullfrog Films, 1983, 59 mins.
44. Martha F. Lee asserts that the Glen Canyon Dam caper provoked the FBI's interest in Earth First! as domestic terrorists. See *Earth First! Environmental Apocalypse* (Syracuse, NY: Syracuse University Press, 1995), 46.
45. Howie Wolke, "A Founder's Story," *Lowbagger*, April 6, 2006, http://lowbagger.org/foundersstory.html, accessed January 15, 2014.
46. Abbey, *Monkey Wrench Gang*, 144.
47. Scholarly studies of Earth First! have focused on its ideological moorings, especially its alleged apocalypticism and millenarianism. I see Earth First! as engaging in strategic rhetoric, with an aim toward developing an alternative libertarian community and preserving wilderness against encroaching technological systems. The apocalyptic rhetoric that sometimes appeared does not strike me as the group's purpose or motivation, and that interpretation lends itself to slippery-slope arguments. See Lee, *Earth First!*; Bron Taylor, "Diggers, Wolves, Ents, Elves and Expanding Universes: Bricolage, Religion, and Violence from Earth First! and the Earth Liberation Front to the Antiglobalization Resistance," in *Oppositional Subcultures in an Age of Globalization*, ed. Jeffrey Kaplan and Hélène Lööw (Walnut Creek, CA: Altamira, 2002), 26–74.
48. Dick Russell, "The Monkeywrenchers: Whatever Happened to Nice Little Old Ladies in Tennis Shoes?" *Amicus Journal* 9 (Fall 1987): 28.
49. B. N. Koehler, "For Ned Ludd," *The Earth First! Li'l Green Songbook*, 5th ed. (Chico, CA: Ned Ludd Books, 1986), 31.
50. Foreman, editorial, *Earth First!* March 20, 1982, 11.
51. A volume on deep ecology was originally planned, but went to another publisher. Ned Ludd Books later published a wilderness survey, a calendar of Crumb's illustrations *for The Monkey Wrench Gang*, and Howie Wolke's *Wilderness on the Rocks* (Tucson: Ned Ludd Books, 1991).
52. Foreman, editorial, March 20, 1982, 11.

53. Foreman, editorial, March 20, 1982, 11.
54. Foreman and Haywood, *Ecodefense*, 9.
55. Foreman and Haywood, *Ecodefense*, 10.
56. Foreman and Haywood, *Ecodefense*, 99.
57. Dave Foreman, *Confessions of an Eco Warrior* (New York: Harmony, 1991), 152.
58. E. H. "Christy" Thomas, "The 'Shop Committee' Cure for Industrial Unrest," *Labor Digest*, October 1920, reprinted in *American Review of Reviews* 62 (1920): 412.
59. Douglas Long, *Ecoterrorism* (New York: Facts on File, 2004), 34; Mike Roselle, *Tree Spiker: From Earth First! to Lowbagging. My Struggles in Radical Environmental Action* (New York: St. Martin's, 2009), 113–126.
60. 18 U.S.C. § 1864.
61. Sissela Bok, *Secrets: On the Ethics of Concealment and Revelation* (New York: Vintage, 1989), 25.
62. Linda A. Akers et al., "Expansion of Government's Notice to Offer Evidence Regarding 1986 Palo Verde Sabotage," *United States v. Davis, et al.*, 4, David Foreman Papers 233, Box 11.
63. In 1987, a lumber worker, George Alexander, was severely injured in a mill accident alleged to be caused by a tree spike. With no evidence, the lumber company blamed Earth First! and charged it with "environmental terrorism." It was not the first use of the phrase. See, for example, Eric Schwartz, "'Environmental Terrorism': Ecologists Escalate Fight over Nature," *Chicago Tribune*, May 30, 1981; Ken Slocum, "Radical Ecologists Pound Spikes in Trees to Scare Loggers and Hinder Lumbering," *Wall Street Journal*, November 14, 1985. Even unrolling a fake crack on a dam could bring the charge: see "Environmental Terrorism," *Los Angeles Times*, July 23, 1987.
64. *Nevada Wilderness Protection Act of 1989*, hearing before Subcommittee on Public Lands, National Parks, and Forests of the Committee on Energy and Natural Resources (Statement of Von Sorensen) 101st Congress (July 24, 1989), 122.
65. *Terrorism in the United States 1989*, report, Terrorist Research and Analytical Center (December 31, 1989), 4.
66. Defense Counsel Transcript, FBI Audio Surveillance, Frazier 001, Tape 1 of 1, Side A, February 5, 1988, David Foreman Papers 233, Box 14.
67. Fain 059R, Tape 1 of 2, Side A, May 5, 1989, transcript, David Foreman Papers 223, Box 12; Ilse Asplund, "Evan Mecham Eco Tea-Sippers: Another Perspective on the Arizona Bust International Conspiracy," Part 2, *Earth First!* 31.2 (2011): 18–22; Kimberly Dawn, "Let It Stay Forever Wild: An Interview with Peg Millett," *Earth First!* 21.1 (2000): 18.
68. Lee, *Earth First!* 132.
69. Frazier 089R, Tape 1 of 2, side A, August 24, 1988, transcript, David Foreman Papers 233, Box 14.
70. Fain 059R, Tape 1 of 2, Side A, May 5, 1989, transcript.
71. Arthur H. Rotstein, "Radical Environmental Group Has Uncompromising Philosophy," Associated Press, June 3, 1989, Lexis-Nexis.
72. Tom Fitzpatrick, "The Earth First! Bust," *Phoenix New Times*, June 7, 1989.
73. "Dismissal Sought for Earth First! Defendant," *Prescott Courier*, June 5, 1991.
74. See, for example, Christine Keyser, "Earth First! Trial Shows FBI Flair for Deception," *In These Times*, September 18, 1991, 7; Judi Bari, "FBI Lawsuit Lurches Forward," *Earth First! II*, January 31, 1997, 1.
75. David Foreman, "An Open Letter to My Friends," *Earth First!*, special edition, June 16, 1989, 3; qtd. in Patt Morrison, "Terrorists or Saviors?" *Los Angeles Times*, June 16, 1991.
76. Gerry L. Spence, "Motion to Dismiss Indictment for Prosecutorial Misconduct," *United States v. Davis, et al.* U.S. District Court, District of Arizona, David Foreman Papers 233, Box 11.
77. "New Indictment Hits Earth First! Defendants," *Phoenix Gazette*, December 15, 1990.
78. Phone interview with Ed Caldwell, June 21, 2012; *Kingman Daily Miner*, July 26, 1991, 5.
79. Foreman and Haywood, *Ecodefense*, 1.
80. Anonymous, "Dear Ned Ludd," column, *Earth First!* 29.7 (2009): 10.
81. T. V. Reed, *The Art of Protest: Culture and Activism from the Civil Rights Movement to the Streets of Seattle* (Minneapolis: University of Minnesota Press, 2005), 286–316.

Chapter 6

1. David L. Altheide, "Children and the Discourse of Fear," *Symbolic Interaction* 25(2002): 229–249; Joel Best, *Threatened Children: Rhetoric and Concern about Child-Victims* (Chicago: University of Chicago Press, 1990); Best, *Troubling Children: Studies of Children and Social Problems* (New York: Aldine de Gruyter, 1994); Geoffrey Pearson, *Hooligan: A History of Respectable Fears* (London: Macmillan, 1983).
2. Hofstadter argued that conspiracy theories and paranoia had become an acceptable, manipulative form of American political discourse. "The Paranoid Style in American Politics," in *The Paranoid Style in American Politics and Other Essays* (1952; Cambridge, MA: Harvard University Press, 1965), 3–40.
3. T. B. Aldrich, "The Story of a Bad Boy: Chapter VII," *Our Young Folks: An Illustrated Magazine for Boys and Girls*, April 1869, 205. ProQuest.
4. Tenney Lombard Davis, "Fireworks for Fun," *Technology Review* 42 (1940): 273.
5. Christopher Grotz, *The Art of Making Fireworks, Detonating Balls, &c.* (New York: King, 1821), 25.
6. Editorial, "Domestic Explosives," *New York Times*, June 23, 1876.
7. "Bomb Hoaxes Spread to Two More Schools," *Chicago Daily Tribune*, November 1, 1958.
8. "Missing Dynamite Caps Being Sought," *Eugene Register-Guard*, April 19, 1957; "Explosives Given Away by GI Kill 8-Year-Old Girl," *Beaver Valley Times*, May 13, 1953; "Still Hunting for Stolen Explosives," *Lewiston Evening Journal*, July 7, 1951; "Blasts Blamed on Teenagers," *Spokane Daily Chronicle*, October 24, 1958.
9. See, for example, "3 Juveniles Admit Thrill Bombings in Bethesda," *Washington Post*, June 9, 1954; "3 Boy Rocket Builders Admit 'Bombing' Test," *Los Angeles Times*, April 30, 1955.
10. "Young Edison Learning: Premature Explosion of a 'Bomb' Injures His Hand," *New York Times*, April 31, 1913: 1.
11. Oliver Sacks, *Uncle Tungsten: Memories of a Chemical Boyhood* (New York: Knopf, 2001), 77.
12. When Florida high school student Danielle Lee was charged with a felony for causing a minor explosion during an experiment, scientists took to Twitter to recount their own childhood experiments. See Andrew David, "On Stifling Scientific Curiosity, in the Most Egregious Way Possible," *Southern Fried Science*, May 1, 2013, http://www.southernfriedscience.com/?p=14,864, accessed August 30, 2013.
13. See, for example, "Boys Admit Letter Box 'Bomb' Blasts," *Washington Post*, October 11, 1953; "Four Juveniles Held in Theft of Explosives," *Los Angeles Times*, October 30, 1943; "Mystery Bomb Blasts Laid to Son of Doctor," *Chicago Daily Tribune*, April 5, 1946.
14. Bill Ayers, *Fugitive Days* (Boston: Beacon, 2001), 12–13.
15. "Juvenile Bomb Maker Is Made Ward of Court," *Chicago Daily Tribune*, April 12, 1951. Proquest.
16. "3 Juveniles Admit Thrill Bombings in Bethesda," *Washington Post and Times Herald*, January 9, 1954, 1. Proquest.
17. "Boy Warned in Cathedral Bomb Blast," *Washington Post and Times Herald*, August 11, 1956.
18. Michael W. Flamm, *Law and Order: Street Crime, Civil Unrest, and the Crisis of Liberalism in the 1960s* (New York: Columbia University Press, 2005), Kindle. Chapter 1; For an overview of the war on crime, see Jonathan Simon, *Governing Through Crime: How the War on Crime Transformed American Democracy and Created a Culture of Fear* (New York: Oxford University Press, 2007); Naomi Murakawa, "The Origins of the Carceral Crisis: Racial Order as 'Law and Order' in Postwar American Politics," in *Race and American Political Development*, ed. Joseph Lowndes, Julie Novkov, and Dorian T. Warren (New York: Routledge, 2008).
19. *RCCD*, Part 20, 4426.
20. Rollin J. Watson and Robert S. Watson, *The School as Safe Haven* (Westport, CT: Bergin & Garvey, 2002), 89–107. Ebrary.
21. Most famously, Los Angeles police chief William Parker displayed a Molotov cocktail to the city council after the Watts riots in 1965, claiming that it was "expertly made" and evidence of a conspiracy. James A. Geschwender, *The Black Revolt: The Civil Rights Movement, Ghetto Uprisings and Separatism* (Englewood Cliffs, NJ: Prentice-Hall, 1971), 266; RCCD, Part 8 (May 21–22, 27–28, 1968) (Testimony of Joseph Redden), 1705.

22. *Control of Explosives,* Hearing before the Subcommittee to Investigate the Administration of the Internal Security Act and Other Internal Security Laws of the Committee on the Judiciary, 94th Congress (April 8–9, 1976) (Testimony of Rex D. Davis), 8.
23. This list was compiled by the International Association of Chiefs of Police. *Safe Schools Act,* Hearing before the General Subcommittee on Education of the Committee on Education and Labor, 93rd Congress (February 26, 1973), 7–19.
24. *Safe Schools Act,* 15.
25. *Bomb Summary,* FBI Uniform Crime Reports, 1973, 5, 9.
26. Thompson S. Crockett (research director of the International Association of Chiefs of Police), qtd. in Harry F. Rosenthal, "Bombs: Bit of Americana," *St. Petersburg Times,* January 28, 1972; "3 Youths Held for Exploding 2 Homemade Bombs in Park," *Chicago Tribune,* March 7, 1977.
27. Henry Wood and John O'Brien, "5 Youths Questioned in School Bomb Plot," *Chicago Tribune,* January 30, 1976, 1.
28. Cynthia Gorney, "Montgomery County Youths Making Bombs for 'Fun,'" *Washington Post,* April 11, 1976, B1; Carlyle Murphy, "Pipe Bomb Damages Va. School," *Washington Post,* September 9, 1977; Darryl Enriquez, "Soda Bottle Explosives Are Blasting Mailboxes," *Milwaukee Journal,* December 6, 1990, WAU1.
29. Ken Silverstein, *The Radioactive Boy Scout: The Frightening True Story of a Whiz Kid and His Homemade Nuclear Reactor* (New York: Random House, 2004); Tom Clynes, "The Boy Who Played with Fusion," *Popular Science,* February 14, 2012, http://www.popsci.com/science/article/2012-02/boy-who-played-fusion?page=all, accessed August 30, 2013.
30. Phone interview with Jason Scott, October 12, 2011. My understanding of the BBS days of the Internet is indebted to Jason Scott, who has preserved many of the files from this early period. See his textiles.com site and his *BBS: The Documentary,* video recording, Bovine Ignitions Systems, 2005. I have also relied on the anarchy/pyrotechny files preserved by security expert Michael V. Scovetta at www.scovetta.com. Researching the world of the Internet in this period is particularly difficult because of the ephemerality and changeability of the files, which are usually undated and impossible to fully verify. However, there are usually common features and enough overlap and repetition to draw some conclusions.
31. Jason Scott, Part 1, "Baud," *BBS: The Documentary.*
32. Lynne Y. Edwards, "Victims, Villains, and Vixens," in *Girl Wide Web: Girls, the Internet, and the Negotiation of Identity,* ed. Sharon R. Mazzarella (New York: Lang, 2008), 18–19.
33. Anonymous, "The Anarchist's Home Companion," textfiles.com/anarchy/Incendiaries/ahc.txt, accessed July 5, 2012.
34. "How to Make Ammonium Nitrate," *Anarchy Today,* issue 2, article 7, Textfiles.com, accessed March 27, 2013; Anarchists-R-Us, "Terrorist Home Companion Part V," 1986, http://archives.scovetta.com/pub/textfiles/anarchy/incendiaries/anarhomc.ana, accessed October 1, 2013.
35. Alex Heard, "Browsing through the Bilge: Catalogues at the Fringes of the American Mind," *Washington Post,* June 16, 1991; "Police Look for Clues in Blast That Killed 4," *Washington Post,* January 2, 1989.
36. Paul Duggan, "Bomb Data Spread by Computer," *Washington Post,* April 28, 1989.
37. Paul Duggan, "Md. Man Gets Three Years in Bombing" *Washington Post,* January 6, 1990.
38. Sarah M. Pike, "Dark Teens and Born-Again Martyrs: Captivity Narratives after Columbine," *Journal of the American Academy of Religion* 77 (2009): 657.
39. Ralph Larkin has done the best job of surveying the social factors leading to the attack. He includes bullying in the social dynamics of high schools, the class hierarchies in the surrounding community, the national military posture, the desire for media celebrity, masculinity, the paramilitary postures of groups in the Southwest, and the growth of goth, punk, and white supremacist youth cultures as a resistance to corporate capitalism and class hierarchies. Larkin, *Comprehending Columbine* (Philadelphia, PA: Temple University Press, 2007); Larkin, "Legitimated Adolescent Violence: Lessons from Columbine," in *School Shootings,* ed. Nils Böckler et al. (New York: Springer, 2013), 159–178, Ebook. The prevailing popular and official view is that Klebold and Harris had abnormal psychologies: Klebold as a suicidal

depressive and Harris as a psychopath. See Dave Cullen, *Columbine* (New York: Twelve, 2009), chap. 40, Kindle.

40. Jeff Kass, *Columbine: A True Crime Story* (Golden, CO: Conundrum, 2009), chaps. 4, 7, 9, Kindle.
41. Columbine High School Shootings, Investigative Files, Jefferson County Sheriff's Department, released November 21, 2000, DVD: JC-001-010,426.
42. "Da Chronic," "Why I Wrote AOHell," http://textfiles.com/hacking/aohell.phk.
43. "Clarence Bodicker," "Anarchist of America," http://textfiles.com/anarchy/aofa-1.txt/.
44. "BeZeRKer," "Guide to Anarchy," http://textfiles.com/anarchy/anarchy.txt.
45. "Piro," Anarchist's Corner, July 15, 1989, http://archives.scovetta.com/pub/textfiles/anarchy/incendiaries/acorner.txt, accessed October 1, 2013.
46. Anonymous, "3.54 Bottled Gas Explosives," in *Terrorist's Handbook*, ed. Kloey Detect of Five 0, March 20, 1990, http://archives.scovetta.com/pub/textfiles/anarchy/incendiaries/terrhbk.txt.
47. *Columbine*, Investigative Files, 001-010,426.
48. Richard Seven, "Empowering? Illegal? Weird? Dangerous" *Seattle Times*, November 7, 1999.
49. Keith Schneider, "Talk on Bombs Surges on Computer Network," *New York Times*, April 27, 1995.
50. "Ammonium Nitrate Explosives Are Simple, Easily Made, Widely Used in Industry," *Washington Post*, April 21, 1995.
51. *The Availability of Bomb-Making Information on the Internet*, Hearing before the Subcommittee on Terrorism, Technology, and Government Information of the Committee on the Judiciary, 104th Congress, 1st Sess. (May 11, 1995), 2.
52. *Availability of Bomb-Making*, Hearing, 6.
53. *Availability of Bomb-Making*, Hearing, 14.
54. *Availability of Bomb-Making*, Hearing, 8.
55. In legal theory, a two-tier system exists to evaluate speech for protection. Some speech is graded into a "low value" category exempt from protection. Such speech acts include obscenity, libel, "fighting words," perjury, blackmail, and fraud. Hate speech is often argued to fall into this category. "High value" speech would include political debate, artistic expression, and scientific exchange. For an overview, see Wojciech Sadurki, *Freedom of Speech and Its Limits* (Dordrecht, Netherlands: Kluwer, 1999), 39–43, 370–374.
56. *Availability of Bomb Making*, Hearing, 51.
57. Dianne Feinstein, "Terrorism Prevention Act—Conference Report," Senate Session, 142nd Congress, *Congressional Record* (April 16, 1996): S3365–S3366.
58. Guy Gugliotta, "NRA, Backers Have Focused Ire on ITF," *Washington Post*, April 26, 1995, Lexis-Nexis Academic; Marie Cocco, "NRA: It's Not Just for Deer Hunters Anymore," *Newsday*, April 27, 1995.
59. Joseph Biden, "Terrorism Prevention Act—Conference Report," *Congressional Record* 142.49 (1996): S3454. A discussion of the legislative history can be found in Charles Doyle, *Bomb-Making Online: Explosives, Free Speech, Criminal Law and the Internet*, Report, Congressional Research Service, Library of Congress (September 8, 2003).
60. Biden, "Terrorism Prevention Act," S3449.
61. Dianne Feinstein, "Terrorism Prevention ACT—Conference Report," S3366.
62. John R. Moore, "Oregon's Paramilitary Activities Statute: A Sneak Attack on the First Amendment," *Willamette Law Review* 20(1984): 335–350; Joelle E. Polesky, "Rise of Private Militia: A First and Second Amendment Analysis of the Right to Organize and the Right to Train," *University of Pennsylvania Law Review* 144 (1996): 1593–1642; Ellen M. Bowden and Morris S. Dees, "Ounce of Prevention: The Constitutionality of State Anti-Militia Laws," *Gonzaga Law Review* 32 (1996–1997): 523–526; Nancy L. Rosenbaum, *Membership and Morals: The Personal Uses of Pluralism in America* (Princeton, NJ: Princeton University Press, 1998): 256–263.
63. *1997 Report on the Availability of Bombmaking Information*, Department of Justice, submitted to Congress (April 1977), available at http://cryptome.org/abi.htm, accessed January 16, 2014.

64. Committee on Smokeless and Black Powder, National Research Council, *Black and Smokeless Powders: Technologies for Finding Bombs and Bomb Makers* (Washington, DC: National Academy Press, 1998), 29–30.
65. Committee on Marking, Rendering Inert, and Licensing of Explosive Materials, National Research Council, *Containing the Threat from Illegal Bombings* (Washington, DC: National Academy of Sciences, 1998), 24–38.
66. Violent and Repeat Juvenile Offender Accountability and Rehabilitation Act of 1999, *Congressional Record* 145, part 7 (1999), http://www.gpo.gov/fdsys/pkg/CRECB-1999-pt7/html/CRECB-1999-pt7-Pg9874.htm, accessed January 16, 2014.
67. Howard Rheingold, "Why Cyberspace Should Not Be Censored," *The Well*, 1995, http://www.well.com/~hlr/tomorrow/terrorism.html, accessed July 9, 2012.
68. Sherman Austin, Search Warrant, Docket No. 01-0125M (C.D. Cal. January 16, 2002), at Cryptome, http://cryptome.org/usa-v-rtf-swa.htm, accessed September 7, 2012.
69. Joshua Frank and Merlin Chowkwanyun, "The Case of Sherman Austin: Muzzled Activist in an Age of Terror," *Counterpunch*, February 12–13, 2005, www.counterpunch.org/frank02122005.html, accessed July 10, 2009.
70. Although *The Reclaim Guide* was suppressed on raisethefist.com, a computer science professor at Carnegie Mellon University, David S. Touretzky, mirrored the site at http://forbiddenspeech.org/ReclaimGuide/reclaim.shtml, accessed July 10, 2009.

Chapter 7

1. Trevor Aaronson, *The Terror Factory: Inside the FBI's Manufactured War on Terrorism* (Brooklyn, NY: Ig, 2013); Michael German, "Manufacturing Terrorists," *Reason* 44 (2013): 6, 54–56.
2. Jarret Brachman, "Policing Al Qaeda's Army of Rhetorical Terrorists," *William Mitchell Law Review* 37 (2011): 5227.
3. *United States v. Emerson Winfield Begolly*, Indictment, No. 1:11cr326 (E.D. Va. July 2011).
4. Abu Khabbab al Misri, *The Explosives Course* (1432 H). At the time of this writing, the text could be found on numerous websites.
5. "Pennsylvania Man Sentenced for Terrorist Solicitation and Firearms Offense," press release, US Department of Justice, July 16, 2013.
6. Andrew V. Moshirnia, "Valuing Speech and Open Source Intelligence in the Face of Judicial Deference," *Harvard National Security Journal* 385 (2012–2013): 385–454.
7. A contributor to the DOJ's *Report on the Availability of Bombmaking Information*, Marty Lederman, questioned the use of words like "promote" and "solicit" in the Begolly case. "The Begolly Indictment and the First Amendment," *Balkinization* blog, July 15, 2011, http://balkin.blogspot.com/2011/07/begolly-indictment-and-first-amendment.html, accessed January 17, 2014. See also Robert Chesney, "Prosecuting Untargeted Online Advocacy of Terrorism and the Brandenburg Test," *Lawfare* blog, July 14, 2011, http://www.lawfareblog.com/2011/07/prosecuting-untargeted-online-advocacy-of-terrorism-and-the-brandenburg-test/#.UupxlnddX2E, accessed January 17, 2014.
8. For a history of entrapment doctrine, stemming from the positivist criminology initially espoused by Cesare Lombroso, see T. Ward Frampton, "Predisposition and Positivism: The Forgotten Foundations of the Entrapment Doctrine," *Journal of Criminal Law & Criminology* 103.1 (2013): 111–146. See also Dejan M. Gantar, "Criminalizing the Armchair Terrorist: Entrapment and the Domestic Terrorism Prosecution," *Hastings Constitutional Law Quarterly* 42 (2014): 135–160; Jessica A. Roth, "Anomaly of Entrapment," *Washington University Law Review* 91 (2014): 979–1034.
9. *United States v. James Cromitie, et al.*, Nos. 11-2763(L), 11-28824(con), 11-3785(con), 2013 U.S. App. LEXIS 17646, at **38 (2nd Cir., 2012).
10. For details of the case see *United States v. Cromitie*; David A. Lewis and Mark B. Gombiner, "Corrected Brief for the Defendant-Appellant Onta Williams," *United States v. James Cromitie*. The case was featured in an HBO documentary critical of the government's conduct: *The Newburgh Sting*, directed by Kate Davis and David Heilbroner (HBO, 2009).

11. Qtd. in Benjamin Weiser, "3 Men Draw 25-Year Terms in Synagogue Bomb Plot," *New York Times*, June 29, 2011.
12. Qtd. in Graham Rayman, "Were the Newburgh 4 Really Ready to Blow Up Synagogues?" *Village Voice*, March 2, 2011.
13. Kahlifa Ali al-Akili, qtd. in Karen Greenberg, "Documents, Blown Case Provide Rare Look into FBI Terror Stings," *Washington Post*, April 14, 2012.
14. For legal analyses, see Francesca Laguardia, "Terrorists, Informants and Buffoons: The Case for Downward Departure as a Defense for Entrapment," *Lewis and Clark Law Review* 17 (2013), 171–214; Wadie E. Said, "The Terrorist Informant," *Washington Law Review* 85(2010): 728–729.
15. *United States v. Cromitie*, at **205.
16. *United States v. Cromitie*, at **229.
17. David Smith, "Presumed Suspect: Post-9/11 Intelligence Gathering, Race, and the First Amendment," *UCLA Journal of Islamic and Near Eastern Law* 11 (2011–2012): 106; Laura Rovner and Jeanne Theoharis, "Preferring Order to Justice," *American University Law Review* 61(2012): 1331–1416.
18. Jerome P. Bjelopera, "American Jihadist Terrorism: Combating a Complex Threat," Congressional Research Service Report for Congress, 2013, 53–54.
19. Bruno Latour, *Pandora's Hope: Essays on the Reality of Science Studies* (Cambridge, MA: Harvard University Press, 1999), 193.
20. Gary T. Marx, "Thoughts on a Neglected Category of Social Movement Participant: The Agent Provocateur and the Informant," *American Journal of Sociology* 80(1974): 405.
21. David Miller and Tom Mills, "The Terror Experts and the Mainstream Media: The Expert Nexus and Its Dominance in the News Media," *Critical Studies in Terrorism* 2.3 (2009), Taylor and Francis Online.
22. The most famous was the UK case of the "Lyrical Terrorist," Samina Malik, who was initially convicted of collecting information useful for acts of terrorism, forbidden under the UK's Terrorism Act. She won an appeal. The book also featured in the case of Oussama Abdullah Kassir, of Bly, Oregon, convicted of running terrorist websites and setting up a training camp (*United States v. Kassir*, S2 04 Cr. 356 (JFK), 2008 U.S. Dist. LEXIS 51256 (S.D.N.Y. July 3, 2008)).
23. Mark Hosenball, "Al Qaeda's New Life," *Newsweek*, December 30, 2002–January 6, 2003, 46–47. Proquest; "Hamas Publishes Manual for Chemical Warfare," *Jerusalem Post*, January 3, 2003, A5.
24. "Scare Stories about Terrorist Threat Blown Away," *Irish Times*, April 15, 2005.
25. James F. L. Forest, *The Making of a Terrorist: Recruitment, Training, and Root Causes* (Westport, CT: Praeger Security, 2006), 89.
26. I immediately noticed the connection, as did blogger George Smith: "Documents Shown Here Can Get You Jailed," *Dick Destiny*, January 2, 2010, http://www.dickdestiny.com/blog/2010/01/documents-art-shown-here-can-get-you.html, accessed January 15, 2014.
27. Maxwell Hutchkinson, *The Poisoner's Handbook* (Port Townsend, WA: Loompanics, 1988), 8–9.
28. Milton Leitenberg, *Assessing the Biological Weapons and Bioterrorism Threat* (Carlisle Barracks, PA: Strategic Studies Institute, U.S. Army War College, 2005), 27–28; Lawrence Archer and Fiona Bawdon, *Ricin! The Inside Story of the Terror Plot That Never Was* (London: Pluto, 2010).
29. Evan Kohlmann, Testimony, *United States v. Tarek Mehanna*, Case 1:09-cr-10017-GAO, Dkt. 409, 26-99, US Dist. Ct., D. Mass., available at PlainSite.org, accessed March 14, 2015.
30. Evan Kohlmann, "The Real Online Terrorist Threat," *Foreign Affairs* 85 (2006): 115, 118.
31. Kohlmann, *United States v. Mehanna*, Dkt. 409, 26-137, US Dist. Ct., D. Mass.
32. Maxine D. Goodman, "Hedgehog on the Witness Stand—What's the Big Idea: The Challenges of Using *Daubert* to Assess Social Science and Nonscientific Testimony," *American University Law Review* 59 (2010): 635–684; Wadie E. Said, "Constructing the Threat and the Role of the Expert Witness: A Response to Aziz Rana's 'Who Decides on Security?'" *Connecticut Law Review* 44 (2012): 1552–1556; Rovner and Theoharis, "Preferring Order to Justice," 1394–1395.

33. Goodman, "Hedgehog," 638.
34. Lisa Myers and the NBC Investigative Unit, "Web Video Teaches Terrorists to Make Bomb Vest," *NBC Nightly News* video, December 22, 2004, http://www.nbcnews.com/id/6746756/#.UtnTNWQo6L0.
35. *Challenges for the Special Operations Command (SOCOM) Posed by the Global Terrorist Threat,* Hearing before the Terrorism, Unconventional Threats and Capabilities Subcommittee of the Committee on Armed Services, 110th Congress, 1st Sess. (February 14, 2007) (Statement of Joseph H. Felter), 117; *The Internet: A Portal to Violent Islamist Extremism,* Hearing before the Committee on Homeland Security and Governmental Affairs, 110th Congress, 1st Sess. (February 14, 2007) (Statement of Joseph H. Felter), 61.
36. *Challenges for the Special Operations Command (SOCOM)* (Statement of Jarret M. Brachman), 15.
37. Muhammad bin Ahmad as-Salim [Isa al-Awshin], *39 Ways to Serve and Participate in Jihad,* at-Tibyan, pdf. at Internet Archive, ia600405.us.archive.org, accessed December 30, 2014.
38. *Understanding Cyberspace as a Medium for Radicalization and Counter-Radicalization,* Hearing before the Subcommittee on Terrorism, Unconventional Threats and Capabilities of the House Armed Services Committee, 111th Congress, 1st Sess. (December 16, 2009) (Statement of Jarret M. Brachman), 36.
39. *United States v. Mohammed Zaki Amawi, et al.,* 541 F. Supp. 2d 945; 2008 U.S. Dist. Lexis 27632 (N.D. Ohio 2008).
40. Michael May, "Keyboard Jihadist?" *American Prospect* 23.5 (2012): 24–33.
41. Aloke Chakravarty, Opening Statement, *United States v. Tarek Mehanna,* Trial Transcript 3, at 32 (D. Mass., October 27, 2011).
42. Chakravarty, Opening Statement, 34.
43. Eugene Volokh, "Tarek Mehanna Conviction for Aiding al Qaeda Upheld," blog post, *The Volokh Conspiracy,* November 13, 2013; Benjamin Wittes, "Peter Margulies Responds to David Cole," *Lawfare* blog, April 21, 2012.
44. Chakravarty, Opening Statement, 38–39.
45. "Brief of Amici Curiae Scholars, Publishers, and Translators in the Fields of Islam and the Middle East in Support of Defendant-Appellant and Reversal," *United States v. Mehanna,* No. 12-1461, 2012, US Dist. 1st Cir., available at www.orick.com, accessed March 15, 2015, 18.
46. I haven't read this manual, and discussions of it—including its provenance and contents—lack credibility. It appears that Afghan fighters, like creators of these types of manuals before it, set up a self-publishing business (reportedly involving hand copying) to circulate military information from camp to camp. It seems likely that Paladin books ended up there since they have a global circulation, passed from hand to hand and then copied over the Internet. Michael Kenney has grouped "al-Qaeda" productions with the paramilitary publishers: *From Pablo to Osama: Trafficking and Terrorist Networks, Government Bureaucracies, and Competitive Adaptation* (University Park: Pennsylvania State University Press, 2007), 141–143.
47. Marc Sageman, *Understanding Terror Networks* (Philadelphia: University of Pennsylvania Press, 2004), 99–135, Ebook.
48. "The Expedition of Shaykh Umar Hadid," at-Tibyan, Al-Qaidah Network, uploaded by grand arbre, April 19, 2013.
49. Kohlmann, *United States v. Mehanna,* Dkt. 410, 46: 15-10, Us Dist. Ct., D. Mass.
50. A video and transcript of Mehanna's sentencing was posted on a website of his supporters and widely discussed and circulated. "Tarek's Sentencing Statement," Free Tarek website, http://www.freetarek.com/tareks-sentencing-statement/.
51. Noah Feldman, "Speech Isn't Free When Terrorism Is Involved," blog post, *Bloomberg Opinion,* November 14, 2013; Christopher Pochon, "Applying the Holder Standard to Speech That Provides Material Support to Terrorism in *United States v. Mehanna,*" *Harvard Journal of Law and Public Policy* 36 (2013): 375–390; Abel Nikolas, "United States v. Mehanna, The First Amendment, and Material Support in the War on Terror," *Boston College Law Review* 54 (2013): 711–750; Innokenty Pyetranker, "Sharing Translations or Supporting Terror: An Analysis of Tarek Mehanna in the Aftermath of *Holder v. Humanitarian Law Project,*" *National*

Security Law Brief 2 (2012): 21–42; Steven R. Morrison, "Conspiracy Law's Threat to Free Speech," *University of Pennsylvania Journal of Constitutional Law* 15 (2013): 865–920.

52. Dina Temple-Rason, "How the FBI Got Inside the Hutaree Militia," *All Things Considered*, NPR, April 12, 2010.
53. Transcript, *American Morning*, CNN, December 9, 2005, http://transcripts.cnn.com/TRANSCRIPTS/0512/09/ltm.01.html, accessed December 20, 2013.
54. Mike Vonderboegh, "Improvised Munitions Inc.," chapter of *Absolved*, Western Rifle Shooters Association blog, July 6, 2008, http://westernrifleshooters.blogspot.com/2008/07/vanderboegh-improvised-munitions-inc.html, accessed January 15, 2014.
55. *United States v. David Brian Stone, et al.*, No. 10-20123, 2012 U.S. Dist. LEXIS 16669 (E.D. Mich. February 10, 2012).
56. Richard G. Mitchell Jr., *Dancing at Armageddon: Survivalism and Chaos in Modern Times* (Chicago: University of Chicago, 2002), 9, 97. Mitchell's book is unusually sympathetic to militia groups, departing from the many works that depict militias as an existential threat to the nation. See James Coates, *Armed and Dangerous: The Rise of the Survivalist Right* (New York: Hill & Wang, 1995); JoEllen McNergney Vinyard, *Right in Michigan's Grassroots: From the KKK to the Michigan Militia* (Ann Arbor: University of Michigan Press, 2011).
57. See Macaba, *The Road Back*, 1973.
58. Ronald Rendleman, *Red Sky* (Sterling, IL: Sterling Productions, 1996), 161.
59. Rendleman, *Red Sky*, 130.
60. Advertising copy on Amazon, December 20, 2013.
61. "Ragnar Benson," *Ragnar's Homemade Detonators* (Boulder, CO: Paladin, 1993), 42, 45.
62. *U.S. v. Steven J. Parr*, 545 F.3d 491 (7th Cir. 2007), 502.
63. *United States v. Stone*, at **16.
64. Michael Barkun, *Culture of Conspiracy: Apocalyptic Visions in Contemporary America*, 2nd ed. (Berkeley: University of California Press, 2013), Kindle edition.
65. "Members of the Hutaree Militia Plead Guilty to Weapons Charges," press release, US Attorney's Office, Eastern District of Michigan, March 29, 2012; "60-Plus Guns Going Back to 3 Members of the Hutaree Militia," *Detroit Free Press*, May 16, 2012.
66. Barbara L. McQuade, "Searching for the Effective and Constitutional Responses to Homegrown Terrorists," *Wayne Law Review* 57 (2011): 256.
67. Nancy Murray, "It's Official. There Is a Muslim Exemption to the First Amendment," *On Liberty* blog, April 12, 2012, boston.com, accessed January 16, 2014; Matthew Harwood, "Why Violent Right-Wing Extremism Doesn't Scare Americans," *Mother Jones*, July 9, 2013.

Chapter 8

1. 18 U.S.C. § 2332(a) defining a weapon of mass destruction as a "destructive device," including explosive devices, was passed as part of the Violent Crime Control and Law Enforcement Act of 1994.
2. The *Progressive* (originally *La Follette's Magazine*) was founded in 1909 by Robert La Follette, a Wisconsin lawyer and politician who fought corporate influence and corruption in journalism and government and was devoted to the causes of nonviolence, free thought, and free speech. In his autobiography he wrote, "We are slow to realize that democracy is a life; and involves continual struggle." He was a strong supporter of academic freedom. Robert M. La Follette, *La Follette's Autobiography* (Madison, WI: Robert M. La Follette, 1913), x.
3. Spencer Weart, *Nuclear Fear: A History of Images* (Cambridge, MA: Harvard University Press, 1988), 55.
4. Howard Morland, *The Secret That Exploded* (New York: Random House, 1981), 50. The case was *United States v. Progressive, Inc.*, 467 F. Supp. 990 (W.D. Wis. 1979). See also A. De Volpi et al., *Born Secret: The H-Bomb, the Progressive Case and National Security* (New York: Pergamon, 1981); Bruce M. Swain, *The Progressive, the Bomb and the Papers* (Iowa City: Association for Education in Journalism, 1982).
5. Carol Cohn, "Sex and Death in the Rational World of Defense Intellectuals," *Signs* 12.4 (1987): 699.
6. Morland, "The H-Bomb Secret," *Progressive*, November, 1979, 6.

7. Thomas Hughes, *American Genesis: A Century of Invention and Technological Enthusiasm, 1870–1970* (Chicago: University of Chicago Press, 2004), 13.
8. Adam Malecik, interview with Howard Morland, "Controversial H-Bomb Article Raised Profile of Progressive Magazine," Channel 3000 (Madison), channel3000.com, accessed November 14, 2013.
9. President Clinton's secretary of defense, William S. Cohen, for example, warned during his confirmation hearing that weapons of mass destruction were "on the Internet, as to how to construct bombs," *Confirmation of William S. Cohen as Secretary of Defense*, Senate Armed Services Committee, January 22, 1997, www.fas.org.
10. For a history of this device, see Mike Davis, *Buda's Wagon: A History of the Car Bomb* (New York: Verso, 2007).
11. Adam Dolnik, *Understanding Terrorist Innovation: Technology, Tactics and Global Trends* (New York: Routledge, 2007).
12. De Volpi et al., *Born Secret*, 62.
13. Qtd. in Morland, *Secret*, 158.
14. *U.S. v. The Progressive, Inc.*, at 993.
15. Morland, *Secret*, 157–158.
16. Erwin Knoll, "The H-Bomb and the First Amendment," *William and Mary Bill of Rights Journal* 3(1994): 705.
17. Harry Truman, "Statement by the President Announcing the Use of the A-Bomb at Hiroshima," August 6, 1945, Harry S. Truman Library and Museum, http://www.trumanlibrary.org/calendar/viewpapers.php?pid=100, accessed December 1, 2013.
18. Harry Truman, "Atomic Energy," speech, delivered in Milwaukee, Wisconsin, October 14, 1948, in *The Truman Program: Addresses and Messages of President Harry S. Truman*, ed. M. B. Schnapper (Washington, DC: Public Affairs Press, 1949), 68.
19. Peter Galison, "Secrecy in Three Acts," *Social Research* 77 (2010): 941–947.
20. Alex Wellerstein, "Knowledge and the Bomb: Nuclear Secrecy in the United States, 1939–2008," PhD diss., Harvard University, 2010, 130–140.
21. Thomas Hughes discusses the Manhattan Project and subsequent weapons projects as a massive technological project, the first to employ "highly trained physicists and chemists, who interacted creatively with industrially experienced engineers, metallurgists, and skilled machinists." Government control over such a massive project was not unprecedented, but the Manhattan Project did provide a model "with its systematic linking of military funding, management, and contract letting, industrial, university, and government research laboratories, and numerous manufacturers." *American Genesis*, 385, 442.
22. Atomic energy commissioner W. W. Waymack, qtd. in "Waymack Fears New Effort to Impose Atomic Censorship," *Washington Post*, November 27, 1947, 13. Proquest.
23. Albert Einstein, interview with Michael Amrine, "The Real Problems Is in the Hearts of Men," *New York Times*, June 23, 1946, SM5, 6. Proquest.
24. Kelly Moore, *Disrupting Science: Social Movements, American Scientists and the Politics of the Military* (Princeton, NJ: Princeton University Press, 2008), 22–53.
25. Bernard Feld, qtd. in "The Bulletin and the Scientists' Movement," *Bulletin of the Atomic Scientists*, December 1985, 19.
26. "The Atomic Scientists of Chicago," *Bulletin of the Atomic Scientists of Chicago* 1.1 (1945): 1.
27. Herman Kahn, *Thinking about the Unthinkable* (New York: Discus, 1962), 39–40.
28. Alex Wellerstein, "A Tale of Openness and Secrecy: The Philadelphia Story," *Physics Today*, May 2012, 47–53.
29. Moore, *Disrupting Science*, 96–128; Michael Egan, *Barry Commoner and the Science of Survival: The Remaking of American Environmentalism* (Cambridge, MA: MIT Press, 2007), 15–78.
30. Egan, *Barry Commoner*, 68.
31. Moore, *Disrupting Science*, 158–189.
32. Charles Hansen, American Aviation Historical Society, to Senator Charles Percy, Letter, August 27, 1979, Federation of American Scientists website, https://www.fas.org/sgp/eprint/percy.pdf, accessed January 20, 2014.

33. *Erroneous Declassification of Nuclear Weapons Information*, Hearing before the Subcommittee on Energy, Nuclear Proliferation and Federal Services of the Committee on Governmental Affairs, 96th Congress, 1st Sess. (May 23, 1979) (Testimony of Dmitri Rotow), 10.
34. Lawrence Lessig, *Code: Version 2.0* (New York: Basic, 2006), 239.
35. Qtd. in Jeremy Bernstein, "Master of the Trade II," *New Yorker*, December 10, 1979, 79, 84.
36. Hugh E. DeWitt, "Has US Government Disclosed the Secret of the H-Bomb?" *Bulletin of the Atomic Scientists*, June 1979: 61.
37. See especially De Volpi et al., *Born Secret*. The authors of this book were scientists at Argonne National Laboratory who were deeply alarmed by the government's assertion of secrecy in the *Progressive* case.
38. Robert B. Laughlin, *The Crime of Reason and the Closing of the American Mind* (New York: Basic, 2008), 69–83.
39. *Closing the Circle on the Splitting of the Atom*, Report, Office of Environmental Management, US Department of Energy, 1994, back cover. Available at ndep.nv.gov.
40. DOE, *Closing the Circle*, 17.
41. DOE, *Closing the Circle*, 20.
42. Qtd. in Joseph Masco, "Sensitive but Unclassified: Secrecy and the Counter-Terrorist States," *Public Culture* 22(2010): 435.
43. Masco, "Sensitive but Unclassified," 438–439.
44. "Interim Guidance 1600-3, Access to Archival Materials in the Context of Concern about Terrorism," January 3, 2002.
45. "Binyam Mohamed: Read the Secret Torture Evidence," *Guardian*, February 10, 2010, theguardian.com.
46. Rear Admiral David Thomas, Memorandum, "Recommendation for Continued Detention under DoD Control (CD) for Guantánamo Detainee," December 26, 2008, 5, "The Guantánamo Files," *Guardian*, April 24, 2011.
47. "How to Make Your Own H-Bomb," *Washington Post*, April 29, 1979, B1; Peter Steinert, Letter to the Editor, *Washington Post*, May 8, 1979, A20.
48. "Basement H-Bomb Production," Textfiles, http://textfiles.com/anarchy/build_an_h_bomb.txt, December 15, 2013.
49. Barbara Ehrenreich, "My Role in the Torture of Binyam Mohamed," *Barbara's Blog*, February 23, 2009, http://ehrenreich.blogs.com/barbaras_blog/2009/02/my-role-in-the-torture-of-binyam-mohamed.html, accessed 15 April 2015.
50. Walter Laqueur, *The New Terrorism: Fanaticism and the Arms of Mass Destruction* (New York: Oxford University Press, 1999), 71.
51. David G. Coleman and Joseph M. Siracusa, *Real-World Nuclear Deterrence: The Making of International Strategy* (Westport, CT: Praeger Security International, 2006), 117.

SELECTED BIBLIOGRAPHY

The Manuals (Including Alleged)

A. A. "Dangerous Explosives: How to Manufacture Pyroxyline or Gun-Cotton, and also the Fulminates of Mercury and of Silver." *Alarm!* May 16, 1885, 3.

Abbey, Edward. *The Monkey Wrench Gang*. 1975; New York: Harper, 2006.

Adel-Aziz. *The Mujahideen Poisons Handbook*. N.p.: n.p., n.d.

Animal Liberation Front. "The Alf Primer: A Guide to Direct Action and the Animal Liberation Front." Online version. http://www.animalliberationfront.com/ALFront/ALFPrime.htm.

Anony. "The Anarchist's Home Companion." textfiles.com/anarchy/Incendiaries/ahc.txt. Accessed July 5, 2012.

Anon. *EOD: Improvised Explosives Manual*. Boulder, CO: Paladin, 1990.

as-Salim, Muhammad bin Ahmad [Isa al-Awshin]. *39 Ways to Serve and Participate in Jihad. N.p.*: At-Tibyan Publications, n.d.

The AQ Chef. "Make a Bomb in the Kitchen of Your Mom." *Inspire*, Summer 1431/2010, 31–40. Cryptome.

Bayo, Alberto. *150 Questions for the Guerrilla*. Ed. Robert K. Brown. Trans. Hugo Hartenstein and Dennis Harber. Boulder, CO: Panther, 1963.

______. *La guerra será de los guerrilleros*. Spain, 1937.

Benson, Ragnar. *Mantrapping*. Boulder, CO: Paladin, 1981.

______. [pseud.]. *Ragnar's Big Book of Homemade Weapons*. Boulder, CO: Paladin, 1986.

______. *Ragnar's Homemade Detonators*. Boulder, CO: Paladin, 1993.

Campbell, Maynard. *Catalogue of Silent Tools of Justice*. Ashland, OR: Maynard Campbell, 1991.

Central Intelligence Agency. *Freedom Fighter's Manual*. 1983. Xeroxed copy. Radicalism Collection. Michigan State University Library.

Cutbush, James. *System of Pyrotechny*. Philadelphia: Clara F. Cutbush, 1825.

Cuthbert, S. J. *"We Shall Fight in the Streets": Guide to Street Fighting. Ground, Defence, Attack, Use of Explosives, Arms and Equipment, Training, Exercises*. Boulder, CA, 1965.

Dach Bern, Hans von. *Total Resistance*. Ed. Robert K. Brown. Boulder, CO: Panther, 1965.

Du Pont de Nemours, E. I., and Company. *The Blaster's Handbook*. 1918, 1922, 1949, 1952, 1954; Wilmington, DE: Du Pont, 1966.

______. *The Farmer's Handbook: Instructions in the Use of Dynamite for Clearing Land, Planting and Cultivating Trees, Drainage, Ditching and Subsoiling*. Wilmington, DE: Du Pont, 1912.

"The Expedition of Shaykh Umar Hadid." At-Tibyan. Prod. Al-Qaidah Network. YouTube. Uploaded by grand arbre, April 19, 2013.

"Explosive Belt for Martyrdom Operations." Excerpted in "Web Video Teaches Terrorists to Make Bomb Vest." Lisa Myers and the NBC Investigative Unit / NBC Nightly News Video. December 22, 2004. http://www.nbcnews.com/id/6746756/#.UtnTNWQo6L0.

Flynn, Elizabeth Gurley. *Sabotage*. In *Direct Action and Sabotage: Three Classic IWW Pamphlets from the 1910s*, ed. Salvatore Salerno. Chicago: Kerr, 1997.
Foreman, Dave, and Bill Haywood. Ecodefense: A Field Guide to Monkeywrenching. Tuscon, AZ: N. Ludd, 1987.
Franklin, H. Bruce. *From the Movement Toward Revolution*. New York: Van Nostrand Reinhold, 1971.
Grotz, Christopher. *The Art of Making Fireworks, Detonating Balls, &c.* New York: King, 1821.
Guevara, Che. *Guerrilla Warfare*. New York: Monthly Review, 1961.
Harris, Larry Wayne. *Bacteriological Warfare: A Threat to North America*. Indianapolis, IN: Virtue International, 1995.
Hayduke, George. *Get Even: A Complete Guide to Dirty Tricks. Boulder*, CO: Paladin, 1979.
______. *Mayhem! More from the Master of Malice*. New York: Carol, 1988.
Hinkle, William, III, and Sidney Zion, eds. Special issue on Guerrilla Warfare. *Scanlan's* 1 (January 1971).
Hoffman, Abbie. *Steal This Book*. New York: Pirate, 1971.
Homemade C-4: A Closer Look. Video. Prod. Paladin Press, 1991.
"How to Make Ammonium Nitrate." *Anarchy Today*, issue 2, article 7. Textfiles.com. Accessed March 27, 2013.
Hutchkinson, Maxwell. *The Poisoner's Handbook*. Port Townsend, WA: Loompanics, 1988.
Anon. *L'Indicateur Anarchiste*. London: Imprimerie Internationale Anarchiste, 1885. Arxiu Històric de la Ciutat, Barcelona.
"Infernal Machines." *Chicago Tribune*, February 23, 1885.
Jolly Roger (pseud.). *Jolly Roger Cookbook*. November 9, 1990. www.textfiles.com.
Kloey Detect of Five 0, ed. *Terrorist's Handbook*. March 20, 1990. http://archives.scovetta.com/pub/textfiles/anarchy/incendiaries/terrhbk.txt.
Anon. *La Salute é in voi*. Available at the International Institute of Social History, Amsterdam.
Land Mine Warfare. Army Field Manual FM 20–32. 1959.
Love, Sam, and David Obst. *Ecotage*. New York: Pocket, 1972.
Macaba. *The Road Back*. N.p.: Macaba, 1973.
Marighella, Carlos. *Minimanual of the Guerrilla*. N.p.: New World Liberation Front, 1970.
Mathiak, Harold. *Pothole Blasting for Wildlife*. Madison: Wisconsin Conservation Dept., 1965.
McDonald, Andrew [William Pierce]. *The Turner Diaries*. Hillsboro, WV: National Vanguard Books, 1980; New York: Barricade Books, 1996. Online version.
Minutemen. "The Terrorist's Handbook of Explosives, Primers and Booby Traps." 1965.
Misri, Abu Khabbab al. *The Explosives Course*. 1432 H.
Morland, Howard. "The H-Bomb Secret." *Progressive*, November 1979, 6.
Most, Johann. *Revolutionäre Kriegswissenschaft*. New York: International Zeitungs Verein, 1885. Translated typescript. People's Exhibit 15, *Illinois v. August Spies, et al.*, Criminal Court of Cook County, Illinois, 1886. Chicago Historical Society. Also published as *Science of Revolutionary Warfare*. Combat Bookshelf Series. El Dorado, AR: Desert, 1978.
Moyer, Frank A. *U. S. Army Special Forces Foreign Weapons Handbook*. Boulder, CO: Panther Publications, 1970.
Necaev, Serge. *The Catechism of the Revolutionist*. 1869; n.p.: Kropotkin's Lighthouse, 1971.
Notes on Guerrilla Warfare. [Handbook for volunteers of the Irish Republican Army.] Boulder, CO: Panther, 1971.
Pouget, Emile. *Sabotage*. Trans. and ed. Arturo M. Giovannitti. Chicago: Kerr, 1913.
Powell, William. *The Anarchist's Cookbook*. Secaucus, NJ: L. Stuart, 1971.
Prosser, George. "An Introduction to Elementary Tactics." *Black Politics* 2.11–12 (1969): 26-28.
Rains, Gabriel. "Torpedoes." Notebook 93. Manuscripts and Archives Section. Museum of the Confederacy. Richmond, VA.
The Reclaim Guide. raisethefist.com. Mirrored by David S. Touretzky at http://forbiddenspeech.org/ReclaimGuide/reclaim.shtml. Accessed July 10, 2009.
Russell, John L., III. *Involuntary Possession; or In the Steal of the Night*. Boulder, CO: Paladin 1976.

Saxon, Kurt [Donald Sisco]. *The Poor Man's James Bond.* Vol. 1. Atlan Formularies, 1972; El Dorado, AK: Desert, 1991. Includes reprints of *Militants' Formulary* and *Explosives Like Granddad Used to Make.*

Smith, Walker C. *Sabotage: Its History, Philosophy and Function.* In *Direct Action and Sabotage: Three Classic IWW Pamphlets from the 1910s*, ed. Salvatore Salerno. Chicago: Kerr, 1997.

Special Forces Demolition Techniques. Extract from Army Field Manual FM 31-20. Boulder, CO: Paladin, 1965.

US Army, *Special Forces Handbook.* U.S. Army, ST131-180 (1965). Boulder, CO: Paladin, n.d.

Tobiason, Timothy. *Scientific Principles of Improvised Warfare & Home Defense.* Vols. 1–6. Silver Creek, NB: Scientific and Technical Intelligence Press, 1996–2001.

Trautman, William E. *Direct Action and Sabotage.* Pittsburgh: Socialist News Company, 1912.

Uncle Fester [Steven Preisler]. *Secrets of Methamphetamine Manufacture.* 7th ed. Port Townsend, WA: Loompanics, 2005.

______. *Silent Death.* 2nd ed. Port Townsend, WA: Loompanics, 1997.

US Army, *Explosives and Demolitions.* Army Field Manual FM 5–25. 1954; Boulder, CO: Paladin, 1967.

Boobytraps. US Army Field Manual, FM-531. 1965.

US Army, *Guidebook for Marines.* 11th ed. Washington, DC: Leatherneck Association, 1967.

Whispering Death. Video. Paladin Press. 36 mins.

Trial and Case Documents

Austin, Sherman. Search Warrant. Docket No. 01-0125M (C.D. Cal., January 16, 2002), on Cryptome. http://cryptome.org/usa-v-rtf-swa.htm. Accessed September 7, 2012.

Brandenburg v. Ohio, 395 U.S. 444 (1969).

"Case of Charles Jackson." *I. W. W. Deportation Cases.* Hearings before the Subcommittee of the Committee on Immigration and Naturalization, 66th Congress (1920), 45.

Gitlow v. People, 268 U.S. 652 (1925).

Hess v. Indiana, 414 U.S. 105 (1973).

Hung, George, and Julius S. Grinnell. *Brief on the Facts for the Defendants in Error. Spies, et al. v. Illinois. Supreme Court of Illinois.* Chicago: Barnard & Gunthorp, 1887.

Illinois v. Spies et al., Supreme Court, State of Illinois, November 26, 1887. Available through the Chicago Historical Society's Haymarket Affair Digital Collection.

New Jersey v. Pante, No. A-296-297T4, 1999 N.J. Super. LEXIS 347 (N.J. Super. App. Div. 1999).

New York v. Cruz, 34 N.Y. 2d 362 (1974).

Ohio v. Jason Deibel, Court of Appeals of Ohio, Third Appellate District, Allen County, 2011-Ohio-3520: P8.

People v. Archer, B13074. 2000 Cal. App. LEXI 641 (Cal. Ct. App 2000).

People v. Taylor, 203 P. 85 (Cal. 1921).

People v. Weiler, 204 P. 410 (Cal. 1922).

Pollock, Simon O. *Simon O. Pollock in Defense of Frank Abarno and Carmine Carbone.* New York: Carlone, n.d.

Vivian Rice, et al., v. Paladin Enter., No. 96–2412, 1997 U.S. App. LEXIS 30889 (4th Cir. 1997).

Rodgers v. Florida, No. SC01-185, 2006 Fla. LEXIS 1402 (Fla. 2006);

Sanders v. McLellan, 463 F.2d 895 (1972): 1. Justia.com.

Stanley v. Georgia, 394 U.S. 557 (1969).

State v. Moilen, et al., 140 Minn. R. 112 (1918). Hathitrust.

Tattered Cover, Inc. v. City of Thornton, 44 P.3d 1044 (Col. 2002).

United States v. Amawi, et al., 541 F. Supp. 2d 945; 2008 U.S. Dist. Lexis 27632 (N.D. Ohio 2008).

United States v. Autem, 2006 U.S. Dist. Lexis 3457 (D. Kan. 2006).

United States v. Baker and Wheeler, No. 95–2257, 1996 U.S. App. LEXIS 25251 (8th Cir. 1996).

United States v. Begolly, Indictment, No. 1:11cr326 (E.D. Va. July 2011).

United States v. Bumpuss, 27 Fed. Appx. (9th Cir. 2001).

United States vs. Carlson, et al., Nos. 2337–3341, 1970 U.S. App. LEXIS 10931 (1970).
United States v. Chard, 115 F.3d 631 (8th Cir. 1997).
United States v. Clough, 246 F. Supp. 2d 84, 88 (D. Me. 2003).
United States v. Cromitie, et al., Nos. 11-2763(L), 11-28824(con), 11-3785(con), 2013 U.S. App. LEXIS 17646 (2nd Cir. 2012).
United States v. Curtin, 489 F.3d 935 (9th Cir. October 3, 2006).
United States v. Davis, et al., No. 89-CR-192-PHX. (Ariz. 1989). Court Documents. David Foreman Papers. Denver Public Library.
United States v. Ellis, 147 F.3d (9th Cir. 1998): 1134.
United States v. Ford, 22 F.3d 374 (1st Cir. 1994).
United States v. Fullmer, et al., 584 F.3d (3rd Cir. 2009).
United States v. Genova, 92 Cr. 377 (SWK), 1992 U.S. Dist. LEXIS 16552 (S.D.N.Y. 1992);
United States v. Giese, 597 F.2d 1192 (9th Cir. 1979): 1192, available through Lexis Nexis Academic.
United States v. Jones, 863 F. Supp. (U.S. Dist. Ct. for the Northern District of Ohio, Eastern Division, 1994).
United States v. Kassir, S2 04 Cr. 356 (JFK), 2008 U.S. Dist. LEXIS 51256 (S.D.N.Y. July 3, 2008).
United States v. Kime, No. 95-2944, No. 95-3160, 1996 U.S. App. LEXIS 27635. (8th Cir. 1996).
United States v. McVeigh, No. 96-CR-68 1997 WL 198070 (D. Colo. April 24, 1997)
United States v. Parr, 545 F.3d (7th Cir. 2008): 493.
United States v. Prevatte and Soy, 66 F.3d (7th Cir. 1995).
United States v. Progressive, Inc., 467 F. Supp. 990 (W.D. Wis. 1979).
United States v. Rogers, 270 F.3d 1081 (7th Cir. 2001).
United States v. Rumely, 345 U.S. 41 (1953).
United States v. Smith, No. 04-5519, 2005 U.S. App. LEXIS 28666 (2005).
United States v. Stockton, 968 F.2d 715, 717 (8th Cir. 1992).
United States v. Stone, et al., No. 10-20123, 2012 U.S. Dist. LEXIS 16669 (E.D. Mich. February 10, 2012).
United States v. Dzhokhar A. Tsarnaev. Indictment. Case 1:13-cr-10200-GAO, Doc. 57 (D.C. Mass. June 27, 2013), at US Department of Justice, http://www.justice.gov/usao/ma/news/marathon/.
United States v. Waters, 627 F. 3d (9th Cir. 2010): 359.
Wisconsin v. Stank, No. 2004AP1162-CR, 2005 Wisc. App. LEXIS 939 (Wis. App. 2005);
Whitney v. California, 274 U.S. 357 (1927).

Government Documents

1997 Report on the Availability of Bombmaking Information. Department of Justice. (Submitted to Congress April 1977). Available at http://cryptome.org/abi.htm, accessed January 16, 2014.
Activities of Ku Klux Klan Organizations in the U. S. Part 2. Hearings before the House Committee on Un-American Activities. 89th Cong., 1st Sess. (1967).
The Anarchist Cookbook. Investigative File. Federal Bureau of Investigation. Released through FOIA to Government Attic, January 26, February 1, 2011.
Attorney General A. Mitchell Palmer on Charges Made Against Department of Justice by Louis F. Post and Others. Hearing before the Committee on Rules. 66th Cong., 2nd Sess. (1920).
The Availability of Bomb-Making Information on the Internet. Hearing before the Subcommittee on Terrorism, Technology, and Government Information of the Committee on the Judiciary. 104th Cong., 1st Sess. (May 11, 1995).
Bolshevik Propaganda. Hearing before a Subcommittee of the Committee on the Judiciary. 65th Cong. (1919). Hathitrust.
Bomb Summary. FBI Uniform Crime Reports, 1973.
Bureau of Criminal Identification and Investigation, California Office of the Attorney General. *Para-Military Organizations in California*. CA Department of Justice, 1965.
Castro's Network in the United States. Hearing before Committee on the Judiciary. 88th Cong. (1963).

Challenges for the Special Operations Command (SOCOM) Posed by the Global Terrorist Threat. Hearing before the Terrorism, Unconventional Threats and Capabilities Subcommittee of the Committee on Armed Services. 110th Cong., 1st Sess. (February 14, 2007).

Closing the Circle on the Splitting of the Atom. Report. Office of Environmental Management. US Department of Energy (1994). Available at ndep.nv.gov.

Columbine High School Shootings. Investigative Files. Jefferson County Sheriff's Department. Released November 21, 2000. DVD.

Confirmation of William S. Cohen as Secretary of Defense. Senate Armed Services Committee, January 22, 1997, www.fas.org.

Control of Explosives. Hearing before the Subcommittee to Investigate the Administration of the Internal Security Act and Other Internal Security Laws of the Committee on the Judiciary. 94th Cong. (April 8–9, 1976).

Davis, Jay. "Epilogue: A Twenty-First Century Terrorism Agenda for the United States." In *The Terrorism Threat and U.S. Government Response: Operational and Organizational Factors,* ed. James M. Smith and William C. Thomas, 269–278. USAF Academy, CO: USAF Institute for National Security Studies, 2001.

Despatches from U.S. Ministers to Great Britain. NARA, Micro. 30, Roll 138.

Diplomatic Instructions of the Dept. of State. NARA, Micro. 77, Roll 86.

Doyle, Charles. *Bomb-Making Online: Explosives, Free Speech, Criminal Law and the Internet.* Report, Congressional Research Service, Library of Congress, September 8, 2003.

Eco-Terrorism Specifically Examining Stop Huntingdon Animal Cruelty ("SHAC"). Hearing before the Committee on Environment and Public Works. 109th Cong., 1st Sess. (October 26, 2005).

Erroneous Declassification of Nuclear Weapons Information. Hearing before the Subcommittee on Energy, Nuclear Proliferation and Federal Services of the Committee on Governmental Affairs. 96th Cong., 1st Sess. (May 23, 1979) (Testimony of Dmitri Rotow).

Explosives Control. Hearing before Committee on the Judiciary. 91st Cong., 2nd Sess. (1970).

Hate Crime on the Internet. Hearing before the Committee on the Judiciary. 106th Cong., 1st Sess. (September 14, 1999).

Hoffman, Abbie. Investigative File. Federal Bureau of Investigation. FBI Vault.

"Interim Guidance 1600-3, Access to Archival Materials in the Context of Concern about Terrorism." January 3, 2002.

Nevada Wilderness Protection Act of 1989. Hearing before Subcommittee on Public Lands, National Parks, and Forests of the Committee on Energy and Natural Resources. 101st Cong. (July 24, 1989).

Paladin Press. Investigative File. Federal Bureau of Investigation. Released to Government Attic under FOIA.

"Pennsylvania Man Sentenced for Terrorist Solicitation and Firearms Offense." Press Release. US Department of Justice. July 16, 2013.

Racially Motivated Violence. Hearings before the Subcommittee on Criminal Justice of the Committee on the Judiciary. 97th Cong., 1st Sess. (March 4, June 3, and November 12, 1981).

Regulation of the Use of Explosives. Hearing before Committee on Mines and Mining. US House of Representatives. Washington, DC: GPO, 1917.

Riots, Civil and Criminal Disorders. Parts 24, 25. Hearings before the Permanent Subcommittee on Investigations, Committee on Government Operations, 90th Cong. 1st Sess. (1970).

Safe Schools Act. Hearing before the General Subcommittee on Education of the Committee on Education and Labor, 93rd Cong. (February 26, 1973).

State Sessions Laws, 1885. Library of Michigan.

Terrorism in the United States 1989. Report. Terrorist Research and Analytical Center (December 31, 1989).

Thomas, David, Rear Admiral. Memorandum, "Recommendation for Continued Detention Under DoD Control (CD) for Guantánamo Detainee." December 26, 2008. On the web at the Guantánamo Files, *Guardian,* April 24, 2011.

Understanding Cyberspace as a Medium for Radicalization and Counter-Radicalization. Hearing before the Subcommittee on Terrorism, Unconventional Threats and Capabilities of the House Armed Services Committee. 111th Cong., 1st Sess. (December 16, 2009).

Violent and Repeat Juvenile Offender Accountability and Rehabilitation Act of 1999. Congressional Record 145, part 7 (1999). http://www.gpo.gov/fdsys/pkg/CRECB-1999-pt7/html/CRECB-1999-pt7-Pg9874.htm. Accessed January 16, 2014.

Fiction

Aldrich, T. B. "The Story of a Bad Boy: Chapter VII." *Our Young Folks: An Illustrated Magazine for Boys and Girls*, April 1869, 205. ProQuest.

Barr, Robert. "The Chemistry of Anarchy." *Chemist & Druggist* 44 (1894): 117–121.

Burroughs, William. *The Soft Machine*. New York: Grove/Atlantic, 1966.

Mavity, Nancy Barr. *The Other Bullet*. Garden City, NY: Crime Club, 1930.

Rendleman, Ronald. *Red Sky*. Sterling, IL: Sterling Productions, 1996.

Roosevelt, J. West. "Rather Too Much Energy." *Scribner's* 19 (January–June 1896): 611–621.

Taft, William Nelson. *On Secret Service: Detective-Mystery Stories Based on Real Cases Solved by Government Agents*. New York: Harper & Brothers, 1921.

Vonderboegh, Mike. *Absolved*. Posted on Western Rifle Shooters Association Blog.

Winder, W. "Dynamite." *Frank Leslie's Popular Monthly* 14 (1885): 754–759.

Textbooks, Encyclopedias, and Almanacs

Bloxam, Charles Loudon. *Chemistry: Inorganic and Organic*. 5th ed. Philadelphia: Blakiston, 1883.

Brannt, William T., et al. *The Techno-Chemical Receipt Book*. Philadelphia: Baird, 1887.

Burns, Vincent, and Kate Dempsey Peterson. *Terrorism: A Documentary and Reference Guide*. Westport, CT: Greenwood, 2005.

Dyson, William E. *Terrorism: An Investigator's Handbook*. 4th ed. Waltham, MA: Anderson, 2011.

Eissler, M[anuel]. *A Handbook on Modern Explosives: A Practical Treatise*. London: Crosby, Lockwood, and Son, 1897.

______. *The Modern High Explosives*. New York: John Wiley, 1884.

Kushner, Harvey W. *Encyclopedia of Terrorism*. Thousand Oaks, CA: Sage, 2003.

MacMunn, Charles Alexander. *Outlines of the Clinical Chemistry of Urine*. London: Churchill, 1889.

Patrick, David, and William Geddie, eds. *Chamber's Encyclopedia*. Philadelphia; Lippincott, 1901.

Stoffel, Joseph F. *Explosives and Homemade Bombs*. Springfield, IL: Charles C. Thomas, 1962.

White, Peter. *Crime Scene to Court: The Essentials of Forensic Science*. 3rd ed. Cambridge: Royal Society of Chemistry, 2010.

Periodicals, News Organs, and Blogs

Alarm!
Albuquerque Tribune
All Things Considered
Arizona Daily Star
Atchison Daily Globe
Balkinization Blog
Barbara's Blog
BBC News
Beaver Valley Times
Belfast Telegraph
Bismarck Weekly Tribune
Bloomberg Opinion Blog
Boing Boing
Bookselling This Week

Boston Globe
Catalog Age
Channel 3000
Chicago Daily News
Chicago Tribune
Choice
Christian Science Monitor
Cronaca Sovversiva
Daily Interocean
Daily Kennebec Journal
Dick Destiny Blog
Earth First!
Edinburgh Courant
Eugene Register-Guard
Famous Trials Website
Filmmaker Blog
Fort Wayne Daily Gazette
Free Tarek Website
Greeley Tribune
Grip
Helsinborgs Dagblad
Inspire
In These Times
Irish Times
Irish World
Jerusalem Post
Kingsport Times
Lawfare Blog
Lewiston Evening Journal
Libertarian Alliance Blog
Life
Los Angeles Times
Lowbagger
McClure's
Milwaukee Daily Journal
Mother Jones
Nation
Naugatuck Daily News
NBC News
News Palladium
Newsweek
On Liberty Blog
Oshkosh Daily Northwestern
Otago Witness
Paladin Press Website
Palm Beach Post
Pearson's
Philadelphia Inquirer
Phoenix Gazette
Phoenix New Times
Popular Mechanics
Popular Science
Prescott Courier

Publisher's Weekly
Raleigh Register
Redland Daily Facts
Right to Be Greedy Website
Salt Lake Tribune
Seed
Southern Fried Science Blog
Spokane Daily Chronicle
Spokesman-Review
St. Petersburg Times
Strand
Technical World
Textfiles.com
Times Online
To-Day
Tucson Daily Citizen
Village Voice
Volokh Conspiracy
Wall Street Journal
Washington Post

Other Sources

Aaronson, Trevor. *The Terror Factory: Inside the FBI's Manufactured War on Terrorism*. Brooklyn, NY: Ig, 2013.

Abbey, Edward. "The Remington Studio." In *One Life at a Time, Please*. New York: Holt, 1988.

Adamic, Louis. *Dynamite: The Story of Class Violence in America*. 1934; Gloucester, MA: P. Smith, 1963.

Akdeniz, Yaman. *Internet Child Pornography and the Law: National and International Responses*. Burlington, VT: Ashgate, 2008.

"ALA, IRS Representatives Agree on Snooping." *Library Journal* 95 (1970): 2859.

Allison, John. "Terrorist Weapons and Technology." In *Combating Terrorism in Northern Ireland*, ed. James Dingley. New York: Routledge, 2009. 102–127.

Altgeld, John P. *Gov. John P. Altgeld's Pardon of the Anarchists and His Masterly Review of the Haymarket Riot*. Ed. Lucy Parsons. Chicago: Lucy E. Parsons, 1915. Open Library.

Altheide, David L. "Children and the Discourse of Fear." *Symbolic Interaction* 25 (2002): 229–249.

Anderson, Robert. *Sidelights on the Home Rule Movement*. London: Murray, 1906.

Aoki, Richard. *Samurai among the Panthers: Richard Aoki on Race, Resistance, and a Paradoxical Life*. Ed. Diane C. Fujino. Minneapolis: University of Minnesota Press, 2012.

Arboleya, Jesús. *The Cuban Counterrevolution*. Trans. Rafael Betancourt. 1997; Columbus: Ohio State University Press, 2000.

Archer, Lawrence, and Fiona Bawdon. *Ricin! The Inside Story of the Terror Plot That Never Was*. London: Pluto, 2010.

Ariely, Gil. "Knowledge Management, Terrorism, and Cyber Terrorism." In *Cyber Warfare and Cyber Terrorism*, ed. Lech Janczewski and Andrew M. Colarik. Hershey, PA: International Science Reference, 2008. 7–16.

Armstrong, David. *A Trumpet to Arms*. Los Angeles: J. P. Tarcher, 1981.

"The Atomic Scientists of Chicago." *Bulletin of the Atomic Scientists of Chicago* 1.1 (1945): 1.

Avrich, Paul. *The Haymarket Tragedy*. Princeton, NJ: Princeton University Press, 1986.

______. *Sacco and Vanzetti: The Anarchist Background*. Princeton, NJ: Princeton University Press, 1991.

Ayers, William. *Fugitive Days*. Boston: Beacon, 2001.

Balkin, Elise M. "Rice v. Paladin: The Fourth Circuit's Unnecessary Limiting of a Publisher's Freedom of Speech." *University of Baltimore Law Review* 29.2 (2000): 205–236.

Barkun, Michael. *Culture of Conspiracy: Apocalyptic Visions in Contemporary America*. 2nd ed. Berkeley: University of California Press, 2013.

Bates, Tom. *Rads: The 1970 Bombing of the Army Math Research Center at the University of Wisconsin and Its Aftermath*. New York: HarperCollins, 1992.

BBS: The Documentary. Video recording. Dir. Jason Scott. Bovine Ignitions Systems, 2005.

Beck, Ulrich. *The Risk Society: Towards a New Modernity*. London: Sage, 1992.

Beckemeier, Eric. *Traitors Beware: A History of Robert DePugh's Minutemen*. Hardin, MO: Beckemeier, 2007.

Bernstein, Jeremy. "Master of the Trade II." *New Yorker*, December 10, 1979, 52–108.

Best, Joel. *Threatened Children: Rhetoric and Concern about Child-Victims*. Chicago: University of Chicago Press, 1990.

———. *Troubling Children: Studies of Children and Social Problems*. New York: Aldine de Gruyter, 1994.

Bjelopera, Jerome P. "American Jihadist Terrorism: Combating a Complex Threat." Congressional Research Service Report for Congress, 2013.

Blasi, Vincent. "First Amendment and the Ideal of Civic Courage: The Brandeis Opinion in *Whitney v. California*." *William and Mary Law Review* 29 (1988): 653–698.

Bok, Sissela. *Secrets: On the Ethics of Concealment and Revelation*. New York: Vintage, 1989.

Bosmajian, Haig. *Anita Whitney, Louis Brandeis, and the First Amendment*. Madison, WI: Farleigh Dickinson University Press, 2010.

Bowden, Ellen M., and Morris S. Dees. "Ounce of Prevention: The Constitutionality of State Anti-militia Laws." *Gonzaga Law Review* 32 (1996–1997): 523–526.

Bowling for Columbine. DVD. Dir. Michael Moore. MGM, 2003.

Brachman, Jarret. "Policing Al Qaeda's Army of Rhetorical Terrorists." *William Mitchell Law Review* 37 (2011): 5225–5240.

Bradford, William. *Bradford's History of Plymouth Plantation*. Boston: Wright & Potter, 1899.

Broks, Peter. *Understanding Popular Science*. Berkshire: Open University Press, 2006.

Brown, Robert K. *I Am Soldier of Fortune: Dancing With Devils*. Havertown, PA: Casemate, 2013. Kindle edition.

Burleigh, Michael. *Blood and Rage: A Cultural History of Terrorism*. New York: Harper Collins, 2010.

Burns, William J. *The Masked War*. New York: Doran, 1913.

Calahan, James M. *Edward Abbey: A Life*. Tucson: University of Arizona Press, 2001.

Caminetti, A[nthony]. Memorandum. March 14, 1919. *I.W.W. Deportation Cases*. Washington, DC: GPO, 1920.

Cassuto, David N. *Dripping Dry: Literature, Politics, and Water in the Desert Southwest*. Ann Arbor: University of Michigan Press, 2001.

Certeau, Michel de. *The Practice of Everyday Life*. Trans. Steven Rendall. Berkeley: University of California Press, 1988.

Chaliand, Gérard, and Arnaud Blin, eds. *The History of Terrorism from Antiquity to Al Qaeda*. Trans. Edward Schneider, Kathryn Pulver, and Jesse Browner. Berkeley: University of California Press, 2007.

Chatard, Thomas M. *The Abuse of Explosives with Suggestions for Preventative Laws*. Annual Address of the President, Chemical Society of Washington. January 30, 1893. Washington, DC: Gibson, 1893.

Chicago Commission on Race Relations. *The Negro in Chicago: A Study of Race Relations and a Race Riot*. Chicago: University of Chicago Press, 1922.

Chin, Cassandra M. "Holding the Publisher of a Murder Manual Liable for Aiding and Abetting Murder: A Travesty against Free Speech." *George Mason University Civil Rights Law Journal* 10 (1999–2000): 205–226.

Coates, James. *Armed and Dangerous: The Rise of the Survivalist Right*. New York: Hill & Wang, 1995.

Cohen, Stanley. *Folk Devils and Moral Panics: The Creation of the Mods and the Rockers*. 3rd ed. New York: Routledge, 2003.

Cohn, Carol. "Sex and Death in the Rational World of Defense Intellectuals." *Signs* 12.4 (1987): 687–718.

Coleman, David G., and Joseph M. Siracusa. *Real-World Nuclear Deterrence: The Making of International Strategy*. Westport, CT: Praeger Security International, 2006.

Collins, Ronald K. L., and David M. Skover. "Curious Concurrence: Justice Brandeis's Vote in *Whitney v. California*." *Supreme Court Review* 1 (2005): 333–398.

Committee on Marking, Rendering Inert, and Licensing of Explosive Materials, National Research Council. *Containing the Threat from Illegal Bombings*. Washington, DC: National Academy of Sciences, 1998.

Committee on Smokeless and Black Powder. National Research Council. *Black and Smokeless Powders: Technologies for Finding Bombs and Bomb Makers*. Washington DC: National Academy Press, 1998.

Cram, Ian. *Terror and the War on Dissent: Freedom of Expression in the Age of Al Qaeda*. Berlin: Springer Verlag, 2009.

Crimethinc Workers' Collective. *Recipes for Disaster: An Anarchist Cookbook. A Moveable Feast.* Salem, OR: Crimethinc Workers' Collective, 2006.

Cullen, Dave. *Columbine*. New York: Twelve, 2009. Kindle.

Darlington, Ralph. *Syndicalism and the Transition to Communism: An International Comparative Analysis*. Hampshire: Ashgate, 2008.

D'Attilio, Robert. "*La Salute è in Voi!*: The Anarchist Dimensions." In *Sacco-Vanzetti: Developments and Reconsiderations*, 75–90. Boston: Trustees of the Public Library of the City of Boston, 1982.

Davis, Mike. *Buda's Wagon: A History of the Car Bomb*. New York: Verso, 2007.

———. "The Stop Watch and the Wooden Shoe: Scientific Management and the IWW." *Radical America* 9 (January–February 1975): 69–95.

Davis, Tenney Lombard. "Fireworks for Fun." *Technology Review* 42 (1940): 273–277.

Debs, Eugene V. "Sound Socialist Tactics." *International Socialist Review*, February 1912, 481–486.

Dee, Juliet. "How-To Manuals for Hitmen: Paladin Press, a Triple Murder, and First Amendment Protection of Technical Information." *Communications and the Law* 23.2 (2001): 1–54.

Dell, Floyd. "Socialism and Anarchism in Chicago." In *Chicago: Its History and Its Builders*, ed. J. Seymour Currey, vol. 2, 361–405. Chicago: Clarke, 1912.

Demaske, Chris. *Modern Power and Free Speech*. Lanham, MD: Rowman & Littlefield, 2011.

De Volpi, A., et al. *Born Secret: The H-Bomb, the Progressive Case and National Security*. New York: Pergamon, 1981.

Devoy, John. *Devoy's Post Bag, 1871–1928, ed. William O'Brien and Desmond Ryan*. 2 Vols. Dublin: Fallon, 1953.

———. *Recollections of an Irish Rebel*. Shannon: Irish University Press, 1929.

DeWitt, Hugh E. "Has US Government Disclosed the Secret of the H-Bomb?" *Bulletin of the Atomic Scientists*, June 1979, 60–63.

Dilworth, Amy K. "Murder in the Abstract: The First Amendment and the Misappropriation of Brandenburg." *William & Mary Bill of Rights Journal* 6 (1998): 565–592.

Dolnik, Adam. *Understanding Terrorist Innovation: Technology, Tactics and Global Trends*. New York: Routledge, 2007.

Donohue, Laura K. *The Cost of Counterterrorism: Power, Politics, and Liberty*. Cambridge: Cambridge University Press, 2008.

———. "Terrorist Speech and the Future of Free Expression." *Cardozo Law Review* 27 (2005): 233–242.

Drabble, John. "To Ensure Domestic Tranquility: The FBI, COINTELPRO-WHITE HATE and Political Discourse, 1964–1971." *Journal of American Studies* 38 (2004): 297–328.

Drinnon, Richard. *Facing West: The Metaphysics of Indian-Hating and Empire Building*. 3rd ed. 1980; Norman: University of Oklahoma Press, 1997.

Dubofsky, Melvyn. "The I. W. W. at One Hundred: The Return of the Haunted Hall?" *Working USA* 8 (2005): 535–543.

———. *We Shall Be All: A History of the Industrial Workers of the World*. Chicago: Quadrangle, 1969.

Edwards, Lynne Y. "Victims, Villains, and Vixens." In *Girl Wide Web: Girls, the Internet, and the Negotiation of Identity*, ed. Sharon R. Mazzarella, 13–30. New York: Lang, 2008.

Egan, Michael. *Barry Commoner and the Science of Survival: The Remaking of American Environmentalism*. Cambridge: MIT Press, 2007.

Eisenzweig, Uri. *Ficciones del Anarquismo*. Trans. Isabel Vericat Núñez. 2001; Mexico City: FCE, 2004.

Emerson, Thomas I. "Toward a General Theory of the First Amendment." *Yale Law Journal* 72 (1963): 879–880.

Farren, Mick. *Speed-Speed-Speedfreak: A Fast History of Amphetamine*. Port Townsend, WA: Feral House, 2010.

Fellman, Michael. *In the Name of God and Country: Reconsidering Terrorism in America*. New Haven, CT: Yale University Press, 2010.

Fenimore, David. "*The Monkey Wrench Gang* (1975)." In *Literature and the Environment*, ed. George Hart and Scott Slovic, 95–110. Westport, CT: Greenwood, 2004.

Ferguson, Robert A. *The Trial in American Life*. Chicago: University of Chicago Press, 2007.

Flamm, Michael W. *Law and Order: Street Crime, Civil Unrest, and the Crisis of Liberalism in the 1960s*. New York: Columbia University Press, 2005. Kindle.

Flynn, Elizabeth Gurley. *The Rebel Girl: An Autobiography, My First Life*. 1955; New York: International Publishers, 1973.

Flynn, William J. *The Eagle's Eye*. New York: McCann, 1919.

Foerstel, Herbert N. *Surveillance in the Stacks: The FBI's Library Awareness Program*. New York: Greenwood, 1991.

Foner, Philip Sheldon. *History of the Labor Movement in the United States*. Vol. 5, *The AFL in the Progressive Era, 1910–1915*. New York: International Publishers, 1980.

———. *History of the Labor Movement in the United States*. Vol. 4, *The Industrial Workers of the World, 1905–1916*. 1965; New York: International Publishers, 1997.

Foreman, Dave. *Confessions of an Eco Warrior*. New York: Harmony, 1991.

Forest, James F. L. *The Making of a Terrorist: Recruitment, Training, and Root Causes*. Westport, CT: Praeger Security, 2006.

Foucault, Michel. *Security, Territory, Population: Lectures at the Collège de France, 1977–1979*. Ed. Michael Senellart. Trans. Graham, Burchell. New York: Éditions du Seuil / Gallimard, 2004.

The Four Corners: A National Sacrifice Area? Dir. Christopher McLeod. Prod. McLeod, Glenn Switkes, and Randy Hayes. Bullfrog Films, 1983. 59 mins.

Frampton, T. Ward. "Predisposition and Positivism: The Forgotten Foundations of the Entrapment Doctrine." *Journal of Criminal Law & Criminology* 103.1 (2013): 111–146.

Frank, Joshua, and Merlin Chowkwanyun. "The Case of Sherman Austin: Muzzled Activist in an Age of Terror." *Counterpunch*, February 12–13, 2005, www.counterpunch.org/frank02122005.html. Accessed July 10, 2009.

Fried, Albert, ed. *Socialism in America: A Documentary History*. 1970; New York: Columbia University Press, 1992.

Gage, Beverly. *The Day Wall Street Exploded: A Story of America in Its First Age of Terror*. Oxford: Oxford University Press, 2010.

Galison, Peter. "Secrecy in Three Acts." *Social Research* 77 (2010): 941–947.

Gardell, Mattias. *Gods of the Blood: The Pagan Revival and White Separatism*. Durham, NC: Duke University Press, 2003.

Geltman, Max. "Recipes for Destruction." *National Review*, July 27, 1971, 819.

German, Michael. "Manufacturing Terrorists." *Reason* 44 (2013): 6, 54–56.

Geschwender, James A. *The Black Revolt: The Civil Rights Movement, Ghetto Uprisings and Separatism*. Englewood Cliffs, NJ: Prentice-Hall, 1971.

Giles, Roy A. "Bombs and Bomb Plots." *Scientific American* 128 (April 1923), 226–227.

"Godot, Esperanza." "Recipes for Nonsurvival." *Anarchist Library*. April 2002. http://flag.blackened.net/daver/anarchism/godot.html. Accessed January 15, 2014.

Goldman, Emma. *Living My Life*. New York: Knopf, 1931.

Goldstein, Robert Justin. *Political Repression in Modern America from 1870 to 1976*. Urbana: University of Illinois Press, 2001.

Goodman, Maxine D. "Hedgehog on the Witness Stand—What's the Big Idea: The Challenges of Using *Daubert* to Assess Social Science and Nonscientific Testimony." *American University Law Review* 59 (2010): 635–684.

Gosse, Van. *Where the Boys Are: Cold War America and the Making of the New Left*. London: Verso, 1993.

Green, James. *Death in the Haymarket: A Story of Chicago, the First Labor Movement and the Bombing That Divided Gilded Age America*. New York: Anchor, 2006.

Grob-Fitzgibbon, Benjamin. "From the Dagger to the Bomb: Karl Heinzen and the Evolution of Political Terror." *Terrorism and Political Violence* 16.1 (2004): 97–115.

Guglielmo, Jennifer. *Living the Revolution: Italian Women's Resistance in New York City, 1880–1945*. Chapel Hill: University of North Carolina Press, 2010.

Gurstelle, William. *Adventures in the Technology Underground: Catapults, Pulsejets, Rail Guns, Flamethrowers, Tesla Coils, Air Cannons and the Garage Warriors Who Love Them*. New York: Three Rivers, 2006.

Hansen, Charles. American Aviation Historical Society, to Senator Charles Percy. Letter. August 27, 1979. Federation of American Scientists website, https://www.fas.org/sgp/eprint/percy.pdf. Accessed January 20, 2014.

Hanson, Ole. *Americanism vs. Bolshevism*. New York: Doubleday, Page, 1920.

Harrison, George. *The I. W. W. Trial: Story of the Greatest Trial in Labor's History by One of the Defendants*. Chicago: Industrial Workers of the World, 1919.

Hart, W. C. *Confessions of an Anarchist*. London: E. Grant, 1906.

Haywood, Bill. "Haywood's Cooper Union Speech." *International Socialist Review*, February 1912, 469–470.

Hill, Rebecca N. *Men, Mobs, and Law: Anti-Lynching and Labor Defense in U.S. Radical History*. Durham, NC: Duke University Press, 2008.

Hoffman, Bruce. "Responding to Terrorism across the Technological Spectrum." In *In Athena's Camp: Preparing for Conflict in the Information Age*, ed. John Arquilla and David Ronfeldt, 366–390. Santa Monica, CA: Rand, 1997.

Hofstadter, Richard. "The Paranoid Style in American Politics." In *The Paranoid Style in American Politics and Other Essays*, 3–40. 1952; Cambridge, MA: Harvard University Press, 1965.

Holland, H. Brian. "Inherently Dangerous: The Potential for an Internet-Specific Standard Restricting Speech That Performs a Teaching Function." *University of San Francisco Law Review*, Winter 2005, 353–412.

Horsley, Lee. *Twentieth-Century Crime Fiction*. Oxford: Oxford University Press, 2005.

Hughes, Thomas. *American Genesis: A Century of Invention and Technological Enthusiasm, 1870–1970*. Chicago: University of Chicago Press, 2004.

Hunter, Robert. "The General Strike VI: The Meaning of Sabotage." *Commercial Telegrapher's Journal*, January 1912, 206–208.

Jamieson, Stuart Marshall. *Labor Unionism in American Agriculture*. Washington, DC: US Department of Labor, 1946; New York: Arno, 1976.

Jensen, Richard Bach. *The Battle against Anarchist Terrorism: An International History, 1878–1934*. New York: Cambridge University Press, 2014.

Johnson, Jeffrey A. "Raising the Red Flag: Culture, Labor, and the Left, 1880–1920." In *Homer Simpson Marches on Washington: Dissent through American Popular Culture*, ed. Timothy M. Dale and Joseph J. Foy, 191–202. Lexington: University Press of Kentucky, 2010.

Jones, J. Harry, Jr. *The Minutemen*. New York: Doubleday, 1968.

Jones, Thai. *A Radical Line: From the Labor Movement to the Weather Underground: One Family's Century of Consciousness*. New York: Free Press, 2004.

Kahn, Herman. *Thinking about the Unthinkable*. New York: Discus, 1962.

Kass, Jeff. *Columbine: A True Crime Story*. Golden, CO: Conundrum, 2009. Kindle.

Kastanek, Andrianna D. "From Hit Man to Military Takeover of New York City: The Evolving Effects of *Rice v. Paladin Enterprises* on Internet Censorship." *Northwestern Law Review* 99 (2004): 383–436.

Katz, Elia. *Armed Love*. 1971; Raleigh, NC: Boson Books, 2009.

Kenney, Michael. "Beyond the Internet: *Mētis*, *Techne*, and the Limits of Online Artifacts for Islamist Terrorists." *Terrorism and Political Violence* 22 (2010): 177–197.

———. *From Pablo to Osama: Trafficking and Terrorist Networks, Government Bureaucracies, and Competitive Adaptation*. University Park: Pennsylvania State University Press, 2007.

Knoll, Erwin. "The H-Bomb and the First Amendment." *William and Mary Bill of Rights Journal* 3 (1994): 705–714.

Kohlmann, Evan. "The Real Online Terrorist Threat." *Foreign Affairs* 85 (2006). www.foreignaffairs.com, accessed March 19, 2015.

Kohn, Stephen M. *American Political Prisoners: Prosecutions under the Espionage and Sedition Acts*. Westport, CT: Greenwood, 1994.

Kopel, David. "The Day They Came to Sue the Book." *Reason* 31.4 (1999): 59–61.

Kornbluh, Joyce L., ed. *Rebel Voices: An I. W. W. Anthology*. Oakland, CA: PM Press, 2011.

Krug, Judith F., and James A. Harvey. Committee on Intellectual Freedom. *American Libraries* 1 (1970): 751–752, 771, 843–845.

La Follette, Robert M. *La Follette's Autobiography*. Madison, WI: Robert M. La Follette, 1913.

Laguardia, Francesca. "Terrorists, Informants and Buffoons: The Case for Downward Departure as a Defense for Entrapment." *Lewis and Clark Law Review* 17 (2013): 171–214.

Laqueur, Walter. *A History of Terrorism*. New York: Little, Brown, 1997.

———. *The New Terrorism: Fanaticism and the Arms of Mass Destruction*. New York: Oxford University Press, 1999.

Larkin, Ralph. *Comprehending Columbine*. Philadelphia, PA: Temple University Press, 2007.

———. "Legitimated Adolescent Violence: Lessons from Columbine." In *School Shootings*, ed. Nils Böckler et al., 159–178. New York: Springer, 2013. Ebook.

Larrinaga, Miguel de, and Marc G. Doucet. "Sovereign Power and the Biopolitics of Human Security." *Security Dialogue* 39 (2008): 517–537.

Larson, Erik. *Lethal Passage: The Story of a Gun*. New York: Vintage, 1995.

Latour, Bruno. *Pandora's Hope: Essays on the Reality of Science Studies*. Cambridge, MA: Harvard University Press, 1999.

Laughlin, Robert B. *The Crime of Reason and the Closing of the American Mind*. New York: Basic, 2008.

Lay, Howard G. "*Réflecs d'un gniaff*: On Emile Pouget and *Le Père Peinard*." In *Making the News: Modernity & the Mass Press in Nineteenth-Century France*, ed. Dean de la Motte and Jeannene M. Przyblyski, 82–138. Amherst: University of Massachusetts Press, 1999.

Le Caron, Henry. *Twenty-Five Years in the Secret Service: The Recollections of a Spy*. Yorkshire, England: EP, 1974.

Lee, Martha F. *Earth First! Environmental Apocalypse*. Syracuse, NY: Syracuse University Press, 1995.

Leitenberg, Milton. *Assessing the Biological Weapons and Bioterrorism Threat*. Carlisle Barracks, PA: Strategic Studies Institute, US Army War College, 2005.

Lessig, Lawrence. *Code: Version 2.0*. New York: Basic, 2006.

Liddick, Don. *Eco-Terrorism: Radical Environmental and Animal Liberation Movements*. Westport, CT: Praeger, 2006.

Likar, Lawrence E. *Eco-Warriors, Nihilistic Terrorists, and the Environment*. Santa Barbara, CA: Praeger, 2011.

Lindqvist, Sven. *A History of Bombing*. Trans. Linda Haverty Rugg. New York: New Press, 2000.

Lombardo, Robert M. *The Black Hand: Terror by Letter in Chicago*. Urbana: University of Illinois Press, 2010.

Long, Douglas. *Ecoterrorism*. New York: Facts on File, 2004.

Lynch, Thomas. "A Career in Politics and the Attorney General's Office." Interview by Amelia R. Fry. University of California, Berkeley, Regional Oral History Office, 1982.

Magee, Gary Bryan, and Andrew Stuart Thompson. *Empire and Globalisation: Networks of People, Goods and Capital in the British World, c. 1850–1914*. Cambridge: Cambridge University Press, 2010.

Majendie, Vivian Dering. "Nitroglycerine and Dynamite." *Choice* 1 (1883): 409–413.

Masco, Joseph. "Sensitive but Unclassified: Secrecy and the Counter-Terrorist States." *Public Culture* 22 (2010): 433–463.

May, Michael. "Keyboard Jihadist?" *American Prospect* 23.5 (2012): 24–33.

McConveille, Sean. *Irish Political Prisoners, 1848–1922: Theatres of War*. New York: Routledge, 2003.

McCormick, Charles, H. *Hopeless Cases: The Hunt for the Red Scare Terrorist Bombers*. Lanham, MD: University Press of America, 2005.

McLauglin, Paul. *Anarchism and Authority: A Philosophical Introduction to Classical Anarchism*. Burlington, VT: Ashgate, 2007.

McLean, Chelsea. "The Uncertain Fate of Child Pornography Legislation." *Cornell Journal of Law and Public Policy* 17 (2007): 221–246.

McQuade, Barbara L. "Searching for the Effective and Constitutional Responses to Homegrown Terrorists." *Wayne Law Review* 57 (2011): 255–260.

Messer-Kruse, Timothy. *Trial of the Haymarket Anarchists: Terrorism and Justice in the Gilded Age*. New York: Palgrave, 2011.

Messer-Kruse, Timothy, et al. "The Haymarket Bomb: Reassessing the Evidence." *Labor: Studies in Working-Class History of the Americas* 2.2 (2005): 39–52.

Michael, George. "Blueprints and Fantasies: A Review and Analysis of Extremist Fiction." *Studies in Conflict & Terrorism* 33.2 (2010): 149–170.

Miller, David, and Tom Mills. "The Terror Experts and the Mainstream Media: The Expert Nexus and Its Dominance in the News Media." *Critical Studies in Terrorism* 2.3 (2009), Taylor and Francis Online.

Miller, Martin. "Ordinary Terrorism in Historical Perspective." *Journal for the Study of Radicalism* 2 (2008): 125–154.

Miller, Russell. *The Adventures of Arthur Conan Doyle*. New York: St. Martin's, 2008.

Miller, Tom. *Revenge of the Saguaro: Offbeat Travels through America's Southwest*. Washington, DC: National Geographic, 2000.

Mitchell, Richard G. *Dancing at Armageddon: Survivalism and Chaos in Modern Times*. Chicago: University of Chicago Press, 2002.

Moffett, Cleveland. *Careers of Danger and Daring*. New York: Century, 1903.

Moore, John R. "Oregon's Paramilitary Activities Statute: A Sneak Attack on the First Amendment." *Willamette Law Review* 20 (1984): 335–350.

Morland, Howard. *The Secret That Exploded*. New York: Random House, 1981.

Morris, Travis, and John P. Crank. "Toward a Phenomenology of Terrorism." *Crime, Law and Social Change* 56 (2011): 219–242.

Morrison, Steven R. "Conspiracy Law's Threat to Free Speech." *University of Pennsylvania Journal of Constitutional Law* 15 (2013): 865–920.

Mowbray, George M. *Tri-Nitro-Glycerin: As Applied in the Hoosac Tunnel*. New York: Van Nostrand, 1874.

Munroe, Charles E. "The Effect of Explosives on Civilization." *Chautauquan* 9 (October–July 1888–1889): 203–205.

———. "Regulation of Explosives in the United States." Bureau of Mines, Bulletin 198. Washington, DC: GPO, 1921.

Munson, James D. Review of *We Shall Fight in the Streets* by S. J. Cuthbert and *Total Resistance* by Hans von Dach Bern. *Military Affairs* 30 (Summer 1966): 109–110.

Murakawa, Naomi. "The Origins of the Carceral Crisis: Racial Order a 'Law and Order' in Postwar American Politics." In *Race and American Political Development*, ed. Joseph Lowndes, Julie Novkov, and Dorian T. Warren. New York: Routledge, 2008. 234–255.

Neal, Andrew W. *Exceptionalism and the Politics of Counter-Terrorism: Liberty, Security, and the War on Terror*. New York: Routledge, 2010.

Neville, John F. *Twentieth-Century Cause Cèlébre: Sacco, Vanzetti, and the Press, 1920–1927*. Westport, CT: Praeger, 2004.

Nikolas, Abel. "United States v. Mehanna, The First Amendment, and Material Support in the War on Terror." *Boston College Law Review* 54 (2013): 711–750.

Novak, William J. *The People's Welfare: Law and Regulation in Nineteenth-Century America*. Chapel Hill: University of North Carolina Press, 1996.

O'Brien, David M. *Congress Shall Make No Law: The First Amendment, Unprotected Expression, and the U.S. Supreme Court*. Lanham, MD: Rowman & Littlefield, 2010.

Oldenziel, Ruth. *Making Technology Masculine: Men, Women and Modern Machines in America, 1870–1945*. Amsterdam: Amsterdam University Press, 1999.

O'Reilly, Kenneth. "The FBI and the Politics of the Riots." *Journal of American History* 75 (1988): 109–112.

Palmer, Bryan. "CSI Labor History: Haymarket and the Forensics of Forgetting." *Labor: Studies in Working-Class History of the Americas* 3.1 (2006): 25–36.

Park, Robert E. *The Immigrant Press and Its Control*. New York: Harper & Brothers, 1922.

Parsons, Lucy, ed. *The Famous Speeches of the Eight Chicago Anarchists in Court*. 4th ed. 1910; Chicago: Lucy Parsons, n.d.

Partington, James Riddick. *A History of Greek Fire and Gunpowder*. 1960; Baltimore: Johns Hopkins University Press, 1999.

Pearson, Geoffrey. *Hooligan: A History of Respectable Fears*. London: Macmillan, 1983.

Pernicone, Nunzio. *Carlo Tresca: Portrait of a Rebel*. New York: Palgrave-Macmillan, 2005.

———. "War among the Italian Anarchists: The Galleanisti's Campaign against Carlo Tresca." In *The Lost World of Italian Radicalism; Politics, Labor and Culture*, ed. Philip V. Cannistraro and Gerald Meyer, 77–98. Westport, CT: Praeger, 2003.

Petersen, David, ed. *Postcards from Ed*. Minneapolis, MN: Milkweed, 2006.

Pike, Sarah M. "Dark Teens and Born-Again Martyrs: Captivity Narratives after Columbine." *Journal of the American Academy of Religion* 77 (2009): 647–679.

Pochon, Christopher. "Applying the Holder Standard to Speech That Provides Material Support to Terrorism in *United States v. Mehanna*." *Harvard Journal of Law & Public Policy* 36 (2013): 375–390.

Polenberg, Richard. *Fighting Faiths: The Abrams Case, the Supreme Court, and Free Speech*. 1987; Ithaca, NY: Cornell University Press, 1999.

Polesky, Joelle E. "Rise of Private Militia: A First and Second Amendment Analysis of the Right to Organize and the Right to Train." *University of Pennsylvania Law Review* 144 (1996): 1593–1642.

Porter, Bernard. *The Origins of the Vigilant State: The London Metropolitan Police Special Branch before the First World War*. Woodbridge: Boydell, 1987.

Posner, Richard A. *Law & Literature*. 3rd ed. Cambridge, MA: Harvard University Press, 2009.

Powers, Richard Gid. *Broken: The Troubled Past and Uncertain Future of the FBI*. New York: Free Press, 2004.

Preston, William, Jr. *Aliens and Dissenters: Federal Suppression of Radicals, 1903–1933*. 2nd ed. 1963; Cambridge, MA: Harvard University Press, 1994.

Pyetranker, Innokenty. "Sharing Translations or Supporting Terror: An Analysis of Tarek Mehanna in the Aftermath of *Holder v. Humanitarian Law Project*." *National Security Law Brief* 2 (2012): 21–42.

Rabban, David. "The Emergence of First Amendment Doctrine." *Chicago Law Review* 50 (1983): 1205–1355.

———. *Free Speech in Its Forgotten Years*. New York: Cambridge University Press, 1997.

Rains, Gabriel J. "Torpedoes." *Southern Historical Society Papers* 3 (May–June 1877): 255–260.

Reed, T. V. *The Art of Protest: Culture and Activism from the Civil Rights Movement to the Streets of Seattle*. Minneapolis: University of Minnesota Press, 2005.

Rheingold, Howard. "Why Cyberspace Should Not Be Censored." *The Well*, 1995. http://www.well.com/~hlr/tomorrow/terrorism.html. Accessed July 9, 2012.

Richmond, Al. *Native Daughter: The Story of Anita Whitney*. San Francisco: Anita Whitney 75th Anniversary Committee, 1942.

Roselle, Mike. *Tree Spiker: From Earth First! to Lowbagging. My Struggles in Radical Environmental Action*. New York: St. Martin's, 20096.

Rosenbaum, Nancy L. *Membership and Morals: The Personal Uses of Pluralism in America*. Princeton, NJ: Princeton University Press, 1998.

Rovner, Laura, and Jeanne Theoharis. "Preferring Order to Justice." *American University Law Review* 61 (2012): 1331–1416.

Ruff, Allen M. "Socialist Publishing in Illinois: Charles H. Kerr & Company of Chicago, 1886–1928." *Illinois Historical Journal* 79.1 (1986): 19–32.

Russell, Dick. "The Monkeywrenchers: Whatever Happened to Nice Little Old Ladies in Tennis Shoes?" *Amicus Journal* 9 (Fall 1987): 28–42.

Sacks, Oliver. *Uncle Tungsten: Memories of a Chemical Boyhood*. New York: Knopf, 2001.

Sagebrush, Johnny, *The Earth First! Li'l Green Songbook*. 5th ed. Chico, CA: Ned Ludd Books, 1986.

Said, Wadie E. "Constructing the Threat and the Role of the Expert Witness: A Response to Aziz Rana's 'Who Decides on Security?'" *Connecticut Law Review* 44 (2012): 1545–1562.

———. "The Terrorist Informant." *Washington Law Review* 85 (2010): 687–738.

Salvatore, Nick. *Eugene V. Debs: Citizen and Socialist*. Urbana: University of Illinois Press, 1982.

Schaack, Michael J. *Anarchy and Anarchists: A History of the Red Terror and the Social Revolution in America and Europe*. Chicago: Schulte, 1889.

Schnapper, M. B., ed. *The Truman Program: Addresses and Messages of President Harry S. Truman*. Washington, DC: Public Affairs Press, 1949.

Sewell. M. J. "Rebels or Revolutionaries? Irish-American Nationalism and American Diplomacy, 1865–1855." *Historical Journal* 9 (1986): 723–733.

Shaman, Jeffry M. *Equality and Liberty in the Golden Age of Constitutional Law*. New York: Oxford University Press, 2008.

Short, K. R. M. *The Dynamite War: Irish-American Bombers in Victorian Britain*. New York: Gill and Macmillan, 1979.

Silverstein, Ken. *The Radioactive Boy Scout: The Frightening True Story of a Whiz Kid and His Homemade Nuclear Reactor*. New York: Random House, 2004.

Simon, Jonathan. *Governing through Crime: How the War on Crime Transformed American Democracy and Created a Culture of Fear*. New York: Oxford University Press, 2007.

Smith, Brent L., Kelly R. Damphousse, and Paxton Robers. *Pre-Incident Indicators of Terrorist Incidents: The Identification of Behavioral, Geographic, and Temporal Patterns of Preparatory Conduct*. Department of Justice. Doc. 214217 (May 2006).

Smith, Carl. *Urban Disorder and the Shape of Belief: The Great Chicago Fire, the Haymarket Bomb and the Model Town of Pullman*. Chicago: University of Chicago Press, 1995.

Smith, David. "Presumed Suspect: Post-9/11 Intelligence Gathering, Race, and the First Amendment." *UCLA Journal of Islamic and Near Eastern Law* 11 (2011–2012): 85–154.

Smolla, Rod. *Deliberate Intent: A Lawyer Tells the True Story of Murder by the Book*. New York: Crown, 1999.

Sprague, Frank. "Nitro-Glycerine." *Historical Sketch of the United States Naval Academy*. Ed. James Russell Solely. Washington, DC: GPO, 1876.

Stegner, Wallace. *Marking the Sparrow's Fall: The Making of the American West*. Ed. Page Stegner. New York: Henry Holt, 1998.

Stenersen, Anne. "The Internet: A Virtual Training Camp?" *Terrorism and Political Violence* 20 (2008): 215–233.

Stentiford, Barry M. *The American Home Guard: The State Militia in the Twentieth Century*. College Station: Texas A&M University Press, 2002.

Stern, Susan. *With the Weathermen: The Personal Journal of a Revolutionary Woman*. New York: Doubleday, 1975.

Stone, Geoffrey R. *Perilous Times: Free Speech in Wartime from the Sedition Act of 1798 to the War on Terrorism*. New York: Norton, 2004.

Sunstein, Cass R. "Constitutional Caution." *Chicago Legal Forum* (1996): 372.

———. *Democracy and the Problem of Free Speech*. New York: Simon & Schuster, 1995.

Swain, Bruce M. *The Progressive, the Bomb and the Papers*. Iowa City: Association for Education in Journalism, 1982.

Taylor, Bron. "Diggers, Wolves, Ents, Elves and Expanding Universes: Bricolage, Religion, and Violence from Earth First! and the Earth Liberation Front to the Antiglobalization Resistance." In *Oppositional Subcultures in an Age of Globalization*, ed. Jeffrey Kaplan and Hélène Lööw, 26–74. Walnut Creek, CA: Altamira, 2002.

"Terrorism Prevention ACT—Conference Report." Senate Session, 142nd Congress, *Congressional Record*, April 16, 1996: S3365–S3366.

Theoharis, Athos G. *The FBI & American Democracy*. Lawrence: University Press of Kansas, 2004.

Thomas, E. H. [Christy]. "The 'Shop Committee' Cure for Industrial Unrest." *Labor Digest*, October 1920. Reprinted in *American Review of Reviews* 62 (1920): 412–415.

Thorndike, Lynn. *History of Magic and Experimental Science*. Vol. 4. New York: Macmillan, 1923.

Trautmann, Frédéric. *The Voice of Terror: A Biography of Johann Most*. Westport, CT: Greenwood, 1980.

Tucker, Jonathan B., and Jason Pate. "The Minnesota Patriots Council." In *Toxic Terror: Assessing Terrorist Use of Chemical and Biological Weapons*, 159–183. Cambridge, MA: MIT Press, 2000.

Tunney, Thomas J. *Throttled!: The Detection of the German and Anarchist Bomb Plotters*. Boston: Small, Maynard, 1919.

Vanderheiden, Steven. "Eco-Terrorism or Justified Resistance? Radical Environmentalists and the 'War on Terror.'" *Politics and Society* 33 (2005): 425–446.

Varon, Jeremy. *Bringing the War Home: The Weather Underground, the Red Army Faction, and Revolutionary Violence in the Sixties and Seventies*. Berkeley: University of California Press, 2004.

Vaughan, Alden T. *New England Frontier: Puritans and Indians, 1620–1675*. 3rd ed. 1965; Norman: University of Oklahoma Press, 1995.

Vinyard, JoEllen McNergney. *Right in Michigan's Grassroots: From the KKK to the Michigan Militia*. Ann Arbor: University of Michigan Press, 2011.

Vizetelly, Ernest Alfred. *The Anarchists: Their Faith & Their Record*. Edinburgh: Turnbull and Spears, 1911.

Volokh, Eugene. "Crime Facilitating Speech." *Stanford Law Review* 57 (2005): 1095–1222.

Walker, Clive. *Terrorism and the Law*. Oxford: Oxford University Press, 2011.

Watson, Rollin J., and Robert S. Watson. *The School as Safe Haven*. Westport, CT: Bergin & Garvey, 2002. Ebrary.

Weart, Spencer. *Nuclear Fear: A History of Images*. Cambridge, MA: Harvard University Press, 1988.

Weinberg, Leonard, and William L. Eubank, eds. *What Is Terrorism?* New York: Chelsea, 2006.

Wellerstein, Alex. "Knowledge and the Bomb: Nuclear Secrecy in the United States, 1939–2008." PhD diss. Harvard University, 2010.

———. "A Tale of Openness and Secrecy: The Philadelphia Story." *Physics Today*, May 2012, 47–53.

Wharton, Francis. "Dynamiting and Extra-territorial Crime." *Criminal Law*, March 1885, 155–181.

Whitten, Woodrow C. "Trial of Charlotte Anita Whitney." *Pacific Historical Review* 15 (1945): 293.

Wiemann, Gabriel. *Terror on the Internet: The New Arena, the New Challenges* Washington, DC: United States Institute of Peace, 2006.

Wienen, Mark W. *Partisans and Poets: The Political Work of American Poetry in the Great War*. Cambridge: Cambridge University Press, 1997.

Wilkerson, Cathy. *Flying Close to the Sun: My Life and Times as a Weatherman*. New York: Seven Stories, 2007.

Wolff, Robert Paul, Barrington Moore Jr., and Herbert Marcuse. *A Critique of Pure Tolerance*. Boston: Beacon Press, 1969.

Woodcock, George. *Anarchism: A History of Libertarian Ideas and Movements*. 1962; Ontario: Broadview, 2004.

Wright, Philip B. "Effect of Federal Firearms Control on Civil Disorder." *Brooklyn Law Review* 35 (1968–1969): 433–457.

Wright, Stuart A. "Explaining the Militarization at Waco: The Construction and Convergence of the War Narrative." In *Controversial New Religions*, ed. James R. Lewis and Jesper Aagaard Petersen. Oxford: Oxford University Press, 2005. 75–97.

Zakin, Susan. *Coyotes and Town Dogs: Earth First! and the Environmental Movement*. New York: Viking, 1993.

Zedner, Lucia. "Pre-Crime and Post-Criminology." *Theoretical Criminology* 11 (2007): 261–262.

Zer-Ilan, Avital T. "The First Amendment and Murder Manuals." *Yale Law Journal* 106 (1997): 2697–2702.

Zion, Sidney. *Read All about It! The Collected Adventures of a Maverick Reporter*. New York: Summit, 1992.

Žižek, Slavoj. "Afterword: Lenin's Choice." In *Revolution at the Gates: A Selection of Writings from February to October 1917*. By Vladimir Ill'ich Lenin. New York: Verso, 2002.

Zuckerman, Michael. *Almost Chosen People: Oblique Biographies in the American Grain*. Berkeley: University of California Press, 1993.

INDEX

Note: The letter 'n' following locators refers to notes